Foxfire 8

edited by
ELIOT WIGGINTON
and **MARGIE BENNETT**
with an introduction by
Eliot Wigginton

Anchor Press/Doubleday
Garden City, New York
1984

This book is dedicated to the Aunt Aries, the Terry and Mack Dickersons, the Rufus Morgans, the Etta and Charlie Ross Hartleys, the Kenny Runions, the Margaret and Richard Nortons, the Leonard Webbs, and the Pearl and Oscar Martins of the mountains. They and scores of others like them have contributed unselfishly and joyously to the contents of this series of books; now that they are gone, the value of the contributions they made becomes daily more evident. Through these books, thanks to the energy they gave, they live on as touchstones for all of us.

Eliot Wigginton, who started the Foxfire project with his ninth- and tenth-grade students in Rabun County, Georgia, in 1966, still teaches English there today at the new consolidated Rabun County High School. Students in Wig's English classes, as a part of their language arts curriculum, continue to produce *Foxfire* magazine and the Foxfire book series. Royalties from the sale of the books are directed back into the educational program to pay salaries and expenses involved in offering at the high school some sixteen additional experiential community-based classes ranging from television and record production to photography, folklore, and environmental studies.

Margie Bennett has worked as Eliot Wigginton's associate at the high school for the last ten years. As a member of Foxfire's board of directors, she, with her students, is directly responsible for a substantial portion of the contents of this book. She and Wig and the rest of the Foxfire staff strive daily not only to do whatever they can to help make the Rabun County High School one of the best public high schools in Georgia, but also to join forces nationally with a growing number of advocates who believe that America's public school system can be a powerfully positive and affirmative force in the lives of our nation's youth.

Foxfire 8, like its predecessors, contains articles first published in *Foxfire* magazine. This Anchor Press edition is the first publication of *Foxfire 8* in book form. It is published simultaneously in hard and paper covers.

Library of Congress Cataloging in Publication Data
Main entry under title:
FOXFIRE 8.
1. Appalachian Region, Southern—Social life and customs. 2. Country life—Appalachian Region, Southern. 3. Handicraft—Appalachian Region, Southern. 4. Folklore—Appalachian Region, Southern. I. Wigginton, Eliot. II. Bennett, Margie. III. Foxfire. IV. Title: Foxfire 8.
F217.A65F693   1984   306'.0974   82-45573
ISBN 0-385-17740-2
ISBN 0-385-17741-0 (pbk.)

Foxfire 8

CONTENTS

INTRODUCTION

I like small towns. I have yet to encounter one that is not endlessly fascinating. I like to look at the architecture and the use of trees and plantings and open spaces. I like to look at the physical relationships between public buildings and businesses and neighborhoods. I like to read the local newspaper, listen to the local radio station and talk with the residents to see how they feel about their town: what features cause a feeling of pride to well up within them, and what aspects they would change if they could. I like to see how decisions are made that affect the community and its citizens. I like to examine the interactions between locals, tourists and outsiders, and part-time residents. I like trying to find out what qualities individuals or businesses or organizations can have that cause them to be regarded as assets or liabilities. I like to see how the residents of a town deal with its growth, with its decline, or with its death.

My favorite small towns do not have an architectural theme newly imposed upon all the buildings, complete with fake fronts and dishonest airs—the result of some convulsion of the chamber of commerce. Rather, in my favorite towns the buildings that have been erected over time have been reasonably well preserved over time, giving a satisfying, honest mix of architectural styles—mistakes and all—to interest the eye. A courthouse square, with oaks and benches and a few assorted monuments, helps, I think; especially if it squats where the two main streets cross right in the middle of things, resulting in one of those confusing, round-the-block-with-exits-at-each-compass-point highway tangles that slows one down at the same time it states, "Despite the confusion and the inconvenience, the courthouse square stays, thank you." Railroad tracks help too, especially if they run right through town and still carry trains several times a day. So do water towers, several unpaved streets, sidewalks wide enough for kids with bicycles and mothers with strollers, cafés where the owner himself or herself serves a daily dinner of a meat and two or three edible vegetables and french fries don't appear on the menu (which is written each day in chalk on a blackboard over the counter), and grocery stores where it takes an hour or more to purchase a few simple items because one knows most of the people in the aisles and each wants to visit. Well, I could go on indefinitely but this is getting us nowhere. Suffice it to say that the best of such towns, in my opinion, have a stable year-round population that is reasonably compatible, a healthy, well-diversified economic life not dominated by one single industry, abundant recreational opportunities ranging from a decent library and movie theater to softball fields and a public pool, a community school in which parents and grandparents take a more than passing interest, a diversity of religions from which to select, and some mechanism by which the people at large can come together regularly for political and planning purposes. Towns with a positive collective consciousness. Towns with sidewalk sales and a Christmas parade. Towns whose residents close protectively in around members who are sick or injured or in distress.

In our county, there is a host of small towns ranging in size from Clayton, the county seat with a population of just over two thousand, to Rabun Gap, which is actually just a post office and the Rabun Gap-Nacoochee School. Each of the towns is completely different in character, despite the geographical proximity which has most of them strung out like beads along the state highway that bisects our county. This somewhat unfortunate physical arrangement guarantees that without the proper kind of cooperative planning, as this part of the country grows, the city limits and the individual character of each city will become completely irrelevant as development turns the length of the highway into one long commercial strip.

Mountain City is one of the beads on the string. It is of particular interest to us at Foxfire because on the mountainside immediately behind the town we have been reconstructing the old log buildings that make up our staff housing, office, and storage complex—all functions, in other words, for which there is no space at the Rabun County High School where most of us teach.

Mountain City used to be quite a town, if what I have understood from the residents who lived here then is accurate. In the early 1900s, when the present state highway was just a muddy stripe down the county's back, life was centered around the railroad tracks that ran parallel to it. There was a depot that, if one considers a town a living organism, was its heart. By the 1930s, products manufactured in the city limits by a large sawmill and a factory that produced dogwood shuttles for the textile industry were shipped out by rail,

PLATE A Mountain City's railroad depot and associated industries, circa 1928.

as were the apples that were grown locally and sorted and boxed at a packing house near the depot. Cars loaded by local loggers with tanbark and hand-hewn crossties were also shipped out, as were boxes and bags of produce and medicinal herbs, bundles of animal hides, and crates of live chickens. Goods that farm families and merchants had ordered arrived at the depot. Mail came and went daily. The arrival of the train was one constant—always an event—and before the train arrived, and long after it departed, groups of people would be gathered on the platform or around their horses and wagons visiting and exchanging news and opinions.

Across the road, opposite the depot, Mountain City had a business district of sorts complete with several grocery stores, a barbershop, a gristmill, a tavern, a café, churches, a school, and most of the other amenities of small-town life. It even had a baseball team that played the teams in surrounding towns. Two large three-story wooden hotels with grand thirty-foot-wide porches and family-style meals dominated the landscape. Built to accommodate the tourists that began visiting this area before the turn of the century, they were hubs of summer activity. Guests with their trunks and parcels arrived by train, adding to the confusion at the depot, and they were met by horse-drawn buggies that carried them to their accommodations. Regular square dances and social events on the hotels' porches were attended by local residents and tourists alike, and people still talk of the music that used to drift out over the town on those evenings.

And there was a gazebo, oddly enough, with a stone water fountain in front that ran twenty-four hours a day and formed yet another casual gathering place for the residents.

Today the town of Mountain City consists of two small grocery stores—one with gas pumps—three gas stations, a mobile home sales lot, a summer gift shop, a post office, a pants factory, several churches, and a square dance hall run on Saturday nights by the American Legion. Not bad for a town of 450, but some very funda-mental elements are missing. The community's school, for example, is gone, a casualty of consolidation. So is the railroad. The depot, the tracks, the trestles, the platforms, and the associated businesses are gone. Products and services and mail and visitors still flow smoothly in and out of our county and the town, and no one is particularly inconvenienced by the loss of the train, but these goods flow from and to hundreds of different locations over a twenty-four-hour span of time with the ease and flexibility only paved highways and vehicles can bring, and what is missing is the best contribution the railroad made: it shoved all these activities into a funnel, forced them to come together simultaneously in the same location twice a day, and consequently forced the attention of the town's residents and businessmen and visitors upon themselves as a distinct collection of individuals living together and dependent upon one another at one self-contained location on the globe. Because of the railroad, they saw themselves whole and complete once in the morning as the train went north and once in the afternoon as the same train headed back south, every day; and the fact that the train stopped at all simply reinforced the subconscious but vital psychological no-tion that they, as a group, were important enough to stop *for.*

Contrast this with the fact that even as I write, the state highway that bisects Mountain City is being widened to four lanes in a move that issues a totally different psychological message: you as a town are no longer important. Consequently we must shove you back from the edges of our road, widen it, and move the vehicles using it through (not to) your town without stopping. The message, once perceived, is disastrous to a town's collective psyche.

That, to say nothing of the fact that the homes which face the highway and once had a wide buffer of trees and lawn have had to sacrifice much of that buffer to the construction and now sit that much closer to the road's edge; or the fact that another victim of the project is the town fountain, which was located on the road's right of way; or the fact that elderly residents who don't drive, kids on roller skates, and all the other residents who live across the road from the only two grocery stores and used to cross on foot to make their purchases are going to have to think long and hard about setting out across four busy lanes of asphalt with no traffic lights to aid them.

Finally, both hotels are gone. One burned to the ground years

PLATE B Mountain City's business district today, facing the state highway in the process of being widened.

ago, creating a glow in the sky that people who are old enough to remember claim could be seen for twenty miles. The other was abandoned and torn down more recently. Its last official role was to serve as the boardinghouse in which some of the final scenes of *Deliverance* were filmed. In its place is a trailer park.

In September of 1977, our organization purchased the site of the hotel that burned. Over the intervening years, an ambitious plan has evolved for its use through asking the following questions:

—What do the older residents most miss about the town as it was?

—What do the town's residents see as the most pressing needs of the present and future?

—How can our organization wed the answers to these questions to its own educational philosophy and goals and, through the marriage, serve both?

As a first step in answering these questions, one of my staff members, Sherrod Reynolds, and I organized a special experimental class at the high school composed of five students, two of whom lived in Mountain City. Described on pages 20 and 21 of the introduction to *Foxfire 6*, the end result of the course was a series of community meetings, a town beautification committee, and a shopping list of community needs.

The following year we were approached by Alan Levy, a graduate student in the school of landscape architecture at North Carolina State at Raleigh, about the possibility of working with us at no charge on a project related to his field, the data from which could be the subject of his final thesis. We put him to work in Mountain City. Using the priorities lists from the previous town meetings, he began

PLATE C Sherrod Reynolds with Kenneth Law and Jimmy Free in our experimental Mountain City class.

PLATE D Mountain City's first town meeting. The mayor, Gordon Cathey, is at the far right of the front group. Wig and Sherrod are beside him. The high school students who were in the class are at the left.

to visit other residents individually both to ask essentially the same questions asked at the meetings, to double-check and revise the priorities list, and to gather opinions as to how the residents saw Foxfire's property as being used to the greatest benefit to the town at large. He repeated the same procedure at our school with several groups of students who lived in the town, and then again with small groups of six to eight adult residents, including a meeting of the town's newly formed local development corporation. Tape-recording everything, he drew up a new consensus. The broader, more general items on the consensus included such desires, almost universally applauded, as a cleaner community in general and an organized attempt at town beautification; more jobs and more recreational opportunities for the community—especially for the teenagers; and a new town water system and a town sewer system. More specific desires included such things as the request from one person that the mayor do something about the noise from youngsters' motorcycles on his street, and that the city provide better road maintenance. Beyond those, there were a number of suggestions as to very specific things that people would like Foxfire to do with the hotel property. One family, for example, asked that we leave the large trees and not clear the land completely. Several asked that the metal water tower that once served the hotel and had become a community landmark be saved. Several students asked that we put in a video arcade. Others requested a swimming pool and ball field.

Armed with his lists, Alan came to meetings of both our staff and our Community Advisory Board to explore ways that our organization's capacities and goals and the community's desires might fit, and to explore compromises. Requests like those for a video arcade, for example, were not only completely inconsistent with our philosophy but also beyond our limited resources. In other areas we were a good deal closer. The process was like walking through a minefield, however. Consider the following:

We knew that we had created some hard feelings both in the county itself and among tourists passing through because the mountainside property to which we had moved a number of log buildings and our collection of artifacts had not been opened as a tourist attraction. What we wanted on that mountainside was a working base of operations that included office and storage spaces and staff housing—open, of course, to students and their families, our contacts and other community residents, but closed to the general traveling public. There was no way at all that we could deal with a crush of tourist traffic, given the relative inaccessibility of the property, the lack of enough flat acreage for parking, the absence of a museum in which they could occupy their time on self-guided tours, and our desire for some calm and quiet so we could get some work done. An original overriding reason for purchasing the Mountain City property, which fronted on the main state highway, had been our belief that someday, if the money became available, we might build some sort of restoration there that would satisfy tourists' desires to see, and perhaps purchase, something of Foxfire and something authentically Southern Appalachian, and that would quiet the criticism of those local motel owners and merchants who had had to bear the brunt of the tourists' complaints concerning us.

The residents of Mountain City, however, were nearly unanimous in their wish *not* to have something built specifically to draw tourists to their town, thus increasing the flow of traffic, the congestion, and the noise, and resulting in the accompanying parasite development of fast food joints and gift shops.

All well and good. How then to deal with the accompanying contradictions? In the absence of a tourist draw and adjacent outlets, how could products be marketed effectively enough to create and preserve those jobs the community wanted? Residents were almost unanimously opposed to town zoning or an overall plan for ordered and controlled growth. Their idea of a solution to parasite development was the vague hope that nothing would ever happen to stimulate it, and, in the worst case, that they could politely and successfully ask the developer of a proposed restaurant to go away. What if the owner of the proposed restaurant was one of their own children who had graduated from business school and returned home with plans for making a decent living? What then?

Luckily, as an organization we were under no pressure to make any immediate moves. From the time we purchased the land to the fall of 1982, we did not touch it. We simply continued, intermittently, the process of gathering opinions, wrestling with contradictions, refining our organizational goals, and groping, with Alan's help and the help of a series of consultants and a succession of board meetings, toward an overall plan for what came to be known, rather unglamorously, as the Mountain City Project.

Finally, in 1982, a working master plan having been approved by our staff, our community board, the Mountain City Development Commission, and the mayor, among others, we cleared one corner of the property and built the first building. Now, organizations like ours that are basically break-even propositions have extremely limited financial resources and a fear that amounts almost to a paranoia about being in debt. Thus it has always been necessary for us to make every project we undertake serve as many purposes simultaneously as possible—and be paid for in advance. The first project is a good case in point. For years I had believed we could start a regional publishing house that could be successful enough financially not only to create jobs for several local people but also to allow us to expand on the educational options we could offer our students. The problem was that we had never had enough money to be able to test the idea properly. Finally, through the Georgia Council for the Arts we were able to secure a grant that allowed us not only to hire a person for one year to coordinate the development of several manuscripts, but also to print one book which would double as an issue of *Foxfire* magazine and be sent to all our subscribers to test their response. The person hired was Linda Page who, as one of my former tenth-graders, had helped put out the very first issue of *Foxfire* and then had worked with the magazine as an editor through her senior year. During the period covered by the grant, *The Foxfire Book of Wood Stove Cookery*, written entirely by Kim Hamilton and Dana Holcomb, two of our seniors, was published and distributed as an issue of the magazine to a warm and generous response. In addition, Linda began working to flesh out the manuscript for a book solely devoted to Aunt Arie Carpenter, perhaps the most popular informant ever featured in this series of books. On the promise of those two projects, we negotiated a major advance from the E. P. Dutton Company. The contract allowed them to print and distribute Foxfire Press products to bookstores nationally while giving us the right to purchase those products at cost for our own direct-mail distribution. Using the advance, three more local people were hired, word-processing equipment was purchased and installed, and that first building (constructed to house the new publishing operation) was built on the hotel property. Consistent with our determination to make all projects do double duty, that first building was designed for us by Paul Muldawer, an Atlanta architect, as an energy-efficient, low-cost passive solar home. Built by Claude Rickman, a former student who now has his own construction firm in the county, the building serves not only as the Press offices, but also as a model home comparable in price to the mobile homes so many local residents purchase in the mistaken belief that they have no other options. Those who prefer the solar option simply acquire a set of plans from the architect at a nominal fee and hire their favorite contractor to build it—a contractor who presumably employs local people. If Foxfire Press survives (and *Aunt Arie: A*

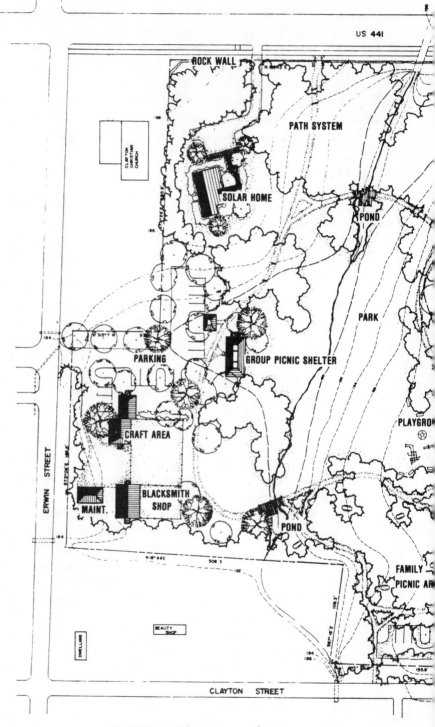

PLATE E   The master plan.

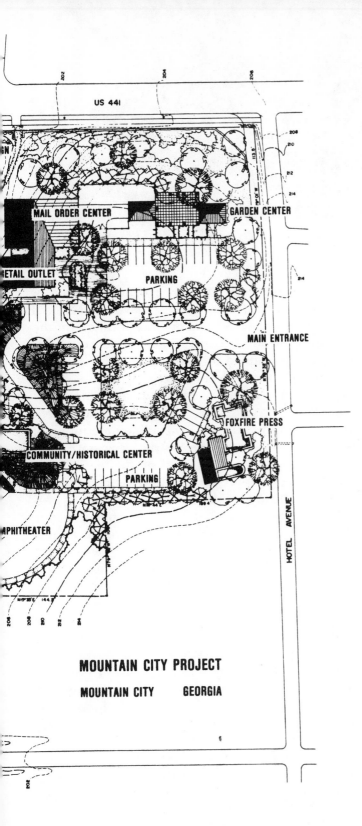

US 441

MAIL ORDER CENTER   GARDEN CENTER

RETAIL OUTLET   PARKING

MAIN ENTRANCE

FOXFIRE PRESS

COMMUNITY/HISTORICAL CENTER

PARKING

AMPHITHEATER

HOTEL AVENUE

MOUNTAIN CITY PROJECT
MOUNTAIN CITY   GEORGIA

PLATE F The solar house, serving as offices for Foxfire Press.

Foxfire Portrait, a 1984 calendar, and a greatly expanded version of that cookbook, the first products from the Press, have all been well received), a larger building will be built at another location on the property and the solar house will become a staff residence. Meanwhile a new activity has been added to the town that fits squarely within the expressed wishes of the local residents.

During the summer of 1983 we discovered and were able to acquire the most magnificent two-story log home I have ever seen. As it was abandoned and on the verge of irreparable deterioration, we decided to dismantle, move it, and reconstruct it at once on a part of the Mountain City property designated on the master plan as the site for a two-building complex devoted to a county historical and genealogical archive. The log building, when completed, is projected to be the offices, meeting areas, and base of operations for the Rabun County Historical Society. The archive building, for which we hope to be able to raise the funds in the future, will be adjacent to the log structure and will house, in a fireproof, humidity- and temperature-controlled environment, our entire collection of tape recordings, videotapes, negatives, old photographs, maps, and our growing library of Appalachian materials. With the addition of the county historical society's archives and genealogical materials and a full-time archivist, a whole range of services can be provided for local people, including public meetings and programs of historical interest, the copying of historical documents and photographs, and the duplication of tape recordings and videotapes and photographs for family members whose parents and grandparents were interviewed by our students, or by members of the society.

While the bulldozers were on the property preparing the site for the log house, we had them also grade out the necessary parking areas, the site for the future Press building, and, along the stream that bisects the property, do the grading and shaping for a large memorial park and open-air amphitheater. Over the years the property was deserted and neglected, an almost impenetrable tangle of privet and blackberries and honeysuckle had grown up under the scattered canopy of larger tulip poplars, maples, oaks, and locusts. Leaving nearly all the large trees, even in the areas set aside for parking, we had the tangle of undergrowth removed and the ground dressed and seeded, creating a truly beautiful oasis of both greenery and shade, with open grassy spaces, in the middle of town. With the proposed addition of a fountain and gazebo to replace the former ones, and the creation of a lovely landscaped area set aside, with appropriate markers, as a memorial to the deceased individuals of the residents whose patient input and instruction make up the contents of our books, the park will become an area which will replace the depot platform and hotel porches as a place to gather to visit, have family picnics and reunions, relax, and enjoy regular concerts and public events of all descriptions.

Two tracts of land on the property will remain untouched for now, awaiting not only funding but also cleared signals from both the community and our organization as to their best use. Proposed is a direct-mail operation that would distribute products from Foxfire and other Appalachian organizations which, like us, are finding that

PLATE G   The log house being moved to Mountain City.

marketing and distribution is the Achilles heel of all our endeavors. Thanks to a grant from the Public Welfare Foundation, we are now exploring that operation's feasibility. A retail outlet that could be housed in a separate section of the mail-order facility would be an entirely appropriate addition. For the second tract, we are studying the feasibility of some traditional crafts activities that would involve local people. For several summers, for example, we have experimented with a blacksmithing program that employs a professional blacksmith and two high school students engaged in the production of a line of items, such as fireplace tools, that we market by mail to our magazine subscribers. Though the program is not profitable at the moment, a portion of the expenses involved in running it is being offset, and it may grow to the point where it can at least pay for itself.

And so we find ourselves in the midst of yet another experiment, I think one of the most intriguing we have yet attempted. Though it does not fill all the desires of the community, and though it cannot replace much of what was best about Mountain City when it was a thriving town, it has the potential of becoming a magnet to which local people from both Mountain City and the surrounding county will be drawn for recreation, for public meetings, for historical, cultural, and preservation activities, and for work. And though visitors passing through the county will be welcome to stop in and explore the facility, a major shift in its purpose, through local input, has caused it to emerge as a center of activity for community people of all ages rather than a highway tourist attraction.

And it remains entirely and emphatically consistent with our educational philosophy, opening a whole new world of learning options for our students. Already, for example, thirteen-to-seventeen-year-olds have been deeply involved in the overall planning process, town meetings, the production of manuscripts for Foxfire Press, marketing surveys, and the dismantling and reconstruction of a historic building (as well as the complete photographic documentation of that entire process and the gathering of the history of the structure through a study of courthouse records and a series of tape-recorded interviews, all for publication as an entire issue of our magazine, which will be created by still more students). Already over a dozen have had full-time summer jobs directly related to the work on that site. In the future, if all goes well, those numbers will increase exponentially as new options are added. In fact, there should not be a single activity taking place there, from work at the archives through operating a direct-mail center and retail outlet, that will *not* involve our students. Moreover, plans are now being made for a range of activities so comprehensive that a student suspended from school could report to the Mountain City site daily, continue his or her education uninterrupted through solid experiential, community-based alternatives, and reenter the high school at an appropriate time still on grade level and not having lost any ground academically at all.

It may not happen, of course. The costs for such an undertaking may be prohibitively high. I know that it cannot happen through the royalties generated by the Foxfire books, as those funds are totally committed to the existing core program and the mountainside facility. That fact means that the Mountain City project can be realized only through money raised from other sources. That money may not be forthcoming. Our board may decide that the project is too ambitious. Foxfire Press may fail. The sky may fall.

Chicken Little notwithstanding, it is projects like the one in Mountain City that intrigue me. It is somewhat frustrating to know that for less than the cost of two lanes of a mile of Interstate highway we could accomplish the entire project and run it for years. But that aside, it is endlessly fascinating to watch such a project evolve, one step at a time, and to watch our organization's relationship to our community and our school growing in different directions and being refined and redefined as new options for involvement present themselves. And it is rewarding, to say the least, to be part of an organization that, rather than continually plowing only in the same furrows, looks at the same time to new ground.

BEW

BLACKS IN APPALACHIA

The following section features five mountain people from our area who are different from many others we have interviewed only in the fact that they happen to be black and thus happen to represent a distinct minority in our part of the country. Though we have featured members of this community before [Beulah Perry, for example, in *The Foxfire Book*, page 119; *Foxfire 2*, page 394; *Foxfire 3*, page 398; *Foxfire 7*, page 100; Carrie Stewart in *Foxfire 5*, page 495; Selma Mosley, *Foxfire 7*, page 88], this is the first time we have made a conscientious attempt to give them the amount of space they deserve.

For this section, I interviewed Bruce Mosley, Harley Penland, and Anna Tutt. Connie Wheeler, Pat Marcellino, and Ricky Foster interviewed Carrie Stewart, to record some additional information beyond what was included in *Foxfire 5*, and Carrie's next-door neighbor, Viola Lenoir, whom we had not met previously.

Some of the black people in our community were hesitant to allow me to write about them. I value their friendship no less and I was so pleased just to get to know all of them and to be able to introduce some of them to you.

When I first started this venture to find out how black people came to live here, I had not thought that there could possibly have been many slaves in this area, because it was secluded. Also, I did not think economic conditions on a mountain farm would have fostered the southern plantation idea. I expected that of the few black people here, most had moved in after the Civil War and I wanted to find out what reasons brought them here. I was wrong! Many white people here owned at least two or three slaves, and several black people told me stories their parents or grandparents had told them about "slave times." There was even a slave market in Franklin where Mrs. Stewart's father had been sold on the block as a small boy. There are some people, like Beulah Perry and Anna Tutt's grandmother, who came here in the 1920s and 1930s with people they were working for in south Georgia and Florida and decided to stay.

This was not an easy project. It took some false starts and I ran into some dead ends—people who just didn't want to talk about things they felt might offend me, such as problems between blacks and whites, and often it seemed the younger people were more hesitant about their parents' talking with me than the older people themselves. A hundred-year-old woman who had a lot of really valuable things to say about her past and present simply did not want to be recorded. Often people said they thought what they had to say was not worth writing down.

Then there's the fact that I am a young white woman and at first some people didn't feel they could be candid with me.

What they did share with us, however, is wonderful material, and I am more grateful to them for their time than they can know. Perhaps this section will begin to give them some of the representation they so richly deserve.

LYNN BUTLER

ANNA TUTT

Anna Tutt's enthusiasm is contagious! When I first met her, I was surprised and excited by her energy and her openness with me. We met at a senior citizens' dinner sponsored by the Georgia Mountain Planning Commission in Clarkesville, Georgia. Mrs. Jo Bennett and Mrs. Norma Allen, two ladies who work hard to make a lot of older people feel their lives are still very worthwhile, invited us. They wanted us to meet some of these folks who had wonderful stories to tell about things that had happened in their lives. I could just never feel, though, that Anna was old enough to be a "senior citizen." She's so young in appearance and actions.

PLATE 1   Anna Tutt.

She lives in a small white frame house in Cornelia, on the same street with her brother and sister. She lives simply, caring for her nieces and nephews from time to time, looking after her house and her cats, and going to town, where she knows so many of the people because she has lived and worked here most of her life.

Anna is a very independent person who has never married. Her friendliness and concern for people win her friends everywhere. She seems to open people up to the good in themselves and to make them feel happy and at ease. Her life has not been an easy one, I learned as she told me about herself, but she wastes no time feeling sorry for herself. Therefore people get real pleasure being with her. I'm glad I'm one of Anna's friends.

LYNN BUTLER

We lived on a large farm in Columbia County, Georgia, when I was small. My father was a tenant farmer and we lived in a house there on the land.

We children had chores to do. One of them was getting the cows to and from the pasture—that was fun! We'd have a row of cows going down the road toward the pasture, and sometimes they'd get on the other side of the creek that ran through the pasture when it had been raining, and the water would get up and they couldn't get back across until the water subsided.

Each cow had a different bell and we knew which cow was which by the sound of its bell. We'd call the different cow when we went to let the bars down across the pasture gate. All of them would usually come, but sometimes when one didn't we'd say, "Uh-oh, a snake must've got her." [The old belief was that a blacksnake] would go between the cow's knees and tie her up some way so she couldn't move, and it'd be there getting the milk itself just like someone milking the cow. We'd go get our daddy to go and kill the snake—get it off with a stick or something—and then bring the cow home. Our grandmother lived nearby and she would always tell us that the milk was poisoned and not to drink any [from that cow] for a few days. It would be muddy-looking, you know—not clear and white.

They grew corn, cotton, peanuts, wheat, oats, and cane on the farm. We children worked in the field, but I tried to get out of it as much as I could. I always had to go to the spring to get water or do something to keep from working. We children had to keep up with our parents on our row, picking cotton or whatever. I'd see my daddy had his row out and he'd start on mine and come back and meet me. I'd think, "Oh, Pa loves me. He's going to help me." But sometimes he had a switch in his hand and he'd meet me about halfway and say, "Young lady, I told you to bring that row on up here." I don't think he ever whipped me but once or twice, though.

He whipped me one time when he'd sent me to the spring for water. He was plowing and it was about a mile to the spring. I went by the garden on the way and oh, how I loved cucumbers. Instead of getting a cucumber and going along to the spring, I went to the spring first and got the water and came back and then got a cucumber and sat down in the shade to eat it. I forgot about my pa and just set the bucket down. I was eating my cucumber when I heard him call me, "Anna, oh, Anna."

So I buried the cucumber and picked up the bucket and started

PLATE 2 Lynn Butler with
Anna and one of her cats.

to run to him with the water. He took one swallow and said, "This
water is hot!"

He had a switch and you'da thought it was an Indian dance down
there. Dust was flying! I was dancing and he was whipping! Whenever
I see a cucumber, I think of that time. I never will forget it.

I remember my mother whipping me one time. Sometimes she'd
have two or three cows milking at one time and we'd get lots of
good thick milk. I'd stay with the babies when everyone else went
out to work. One time I got this little pan and got some of the
clabbered milk with the rich cream. I went behind the smokehouse
to drink the milk. I don't know why I was hiding—they were all
out in the field. I had a little old pet pig and I had to give him
some, too. When my mother came home she said, "Who broke
the cream on this milk?"

I said, "I don't know, ma'am."

She said, "Well, if you tell me the truth, I won't whip you." So
I said I did and she just told me not to do it anymore.

Well, I got hungry for the milk again and I did it again. When she came home, she wanted to know who had done it and I told her. So she carried me to the buggy house and whipped me. That was another Indian dance out there in the buggy shed! I never did go in the milk after that. She said if you broke the cream, you wouldn't get much butter and that's what we lived on then—butter, hot biscuits, and jam and jellies—stuff like that.

I've got to tell you this about our boss man during the boll weevil time. You know what boll weevils are? Well, they were eating the cotton crop up, so Mr. Gross sent us some black molasses in a barrel and some arsenic. He told my daddy to mix the molasses and arsenic together and to make a mop out of some rags tied on a stick. Then dip the mop in a bucket of that molasses and arsenic mixture and go down the row swabbing it on the cotton. Well, we didn't mix the arsenic with the molasses. We got hungry for the molasses and ate the molasses up and the boll weevils ate the cotton up.

I recall one time when a man was hanged. I was about seven or eight years old. We children woke up and heard our father walking about the house in the dark. We said, "Pa, what's the matter?"

He said, "They're hanging someone over there." It was about a mile there, I guess, across a creek. And it seems like it was a white-looking oak tree. I think they used to say a hanging tree never had any leaves on it.

He said, "Y'all be quiet because if they come and ask me to help take him down, I'll have to go." Naturally we were frightened but that was all that was said. He felt he was compelled to go if they came and asked him to help take the body down.

We children never said anything. I don't know whether our father kept it from us or what it was. I never heard what they were hanging the man for. I don't even know whether it was legal or not.

Families used to be close when I was young. Jobs in these mills and plants have separated a lot of families. The father is coming in as the mother goes out, and the children are left practically alone to rear themselves and don't know what to do. Children need their parents. When we lived in the country, and came in from school in the afternoons, my mother was always there in a rocking chair by the big fireplace and if it was wintertime, my father was out hunting or cutting wood. They'd always have something cooked up. We'd go to the stove and look in the warmer and get something to eat. Then we'd do our chores, bringing in wood chips or firewood, or going to the spring getting water for the night.

Nowdays when the children come home, Mama's nowhere to be seen and Papa either because they're on a job. I say the "wants," the material things of the world, have got it like this now. That's why the children are like they are. We just came in automatically looking for our mama to be there, and if we didn't find her at home we wondered what the matter was. We'd go hunting for her.

And people don't make the children go to church or school like they used to. Now sometimes when we're going to church, the road is full of little children playing ball. If you don't train them when they're little, which way are they going when they grow up? I blame the parents for that. They could send the children to church now, and when they get grown and want to change, that would be their business.

Our father passed when I was about nine years old. We children lived around with different relatives for a while. That wasn't a hardship then. If you were in the family, they would take you in. Then our mother married again and we went to live with her in Grovetown. She died when I was about fifteen. My grandmother had moved up here to Cornelia with some white people she had worked for in Appling. She said she had a dream that our father came and placed all of us with her, so she came and took us back with her and that's the way we came up here.

We didn't farm up here [except for a little garden]. I was in my early teens and my sisters and brothers were too small to work. My grandmother used to wash and iron for a living. They wore those white celluloid collars at that time and I can recall she'd have those collars ironed up just as pretty. She hooked them together and had a row of them on a clean cloth down in front of the fireplace drying out. She used that celluloid starch on them and she could do them up so pretty. She washed "on the lots" they called it. She'd go to people's homes and wash their clothes the old-fashioned way— in a black pot. She'd wash and hang the clothes on the line and then go to the next house and wash for them. She sent us to school that way. She sacrificed for us.

We don't have winters here like we used to have. When we came up here in March of 1927, there was snow on those mountains right over there, just like a white cap, and the ground was frozen hard. That's the way it stayed for a long time. We used to have severe winters here.

PLATE 3

Now where we had come from, if we *saw* snow, just a fourth of an inch, if it covered the ground, we wrote all our friends up north and told them we had *snow*. Then we came up here and snow would be laying on Yonah Mountain for four weeks at a time and that wind came sweeping down off of there! It was cold! We lived in a house worse than this one. It wasn't even sealed or anything and we could feel that air coming in on our backs. We just had a little fireplace and we were glad to see somebody go to bed because we'd move a little closer in to the fire.

We lived over near the railroad cut then. People there worked on the railroad a lot and took out the old crossties for fuel. The head man was nice enough to let us use those little old things you ride on. We'd all load the discarded crossties and carry them off to use for fuel.

I don't know what would have become of us if it hadn't been for the nice white people here and around in Habersham County. They would give my grandmother clothes for us. I remember the Tatums, especially, who gave clothes to the boys. The people that had gardens and hogs and cows would give us things, too. We didn't have the best there is, but we were happy.

In the wintertime we used to have collard greens, baked sweet potatoes, or sweet potato pie, and my grandmother sometimes had a hog out in the pen, so along about this time of year it was fresh meat and cornbread. She had a cow for buttermilk and butter. We had chickens in the yard and she'd always pen one or two up about two or three days before she wanted to kill them and she'd feed them good. She wouldn't just go to the yard and get one. She sure knew how to cull out the hens if they were past the laying stage. She'd make dumplings out of them or something like that. Chicken tasted more like chicken then. It had a flavor to it. Only way you know you're eating chicken now is that it says so on the label. We had plenty to eat. It wasn't the finest, but we had plenty.

My grandmother loved to can. She'd take the apple peelings and make jelly out of them and make apple butter or preserves out of the apples. Now that's good—apple preserves are! She was thrifty and canned everything out of the garden there was. I wish you could have known her. To me she was beautiful.

She made a home for us. She didn't go out much [at night]. She always had a little sewing basket. They don't make them like that now—it was a strong basket with a little handle to it and it was woven like these big cotton pickers' baskets. She had it filled with quilt scraps or her crocheting and her scissors and her thread. She'd always be sitting by the fire making a quilt or sewing on something. I wish I could live the kind of life she lived. Now you take me—I go, go, go all the time. She said, "Stay at home sometimes. People get tired of seeing you." She was so different from me. She could sit and be contented. She was a very quiet person and seemed to have foresight. Indians are noted for that, you know, and she was part Mohawk Indian. She was dark with wavy black hair.

I remember her when she was still a young woman. She never was a gadabout person, always a home person. And she always took interest in us. [When my parents were still alive and we were small], if we decided we wanted to go and stay with our grandmother, we just went—then she just lived down the road. We could go down to her home looking for something to eat in the stove. If we wanted to stay overnight, it was all right. She had these old high wooden beds, and we always felt welcome.

When I was young, they used to have what they called "frolics," and I always wanted to follow the older crowd. My mother would say, "You're too young. If I was you, I wouldn't go. That's a rough crowd." But my grandmother would just say, "No, stay at home." And we stayed, too. That was just the difference in the two.

Our grandmother never whipped us a day in our lives but when she got through telling us that we would be liars or murderers or something we wouldn't want to be, that was punishment enough. Just let us do something wrong and she would start her sermon.

She told us to pay our honest bill even if we had to eat cornbread and water. She believed in honesty, no matter what. She told us never to lie. She didn't like lying and she didn't allow us to have rough friends.

Our grandmother was very strict with us. We had to be in before dark, and when we were dating, a boy didn't just pop up at our home. He had to ask for a date. Sunday afternoons and, I think, probably about the middle of the week, Wednesday night, were date times. I'd always ask my grandmother if a certain boy could come over. She'd say yes, and we'd sit in the sitting room there. We didn't have a parlor or a company room—we did our courting right there. We played "Mississippi" or checkers, something like that. Or else my boyfriend would tell me a story out of the Bible. If I got a kiss, we had to sneak it as he was going out the front door.

As I got older, if we went anyplace, when we came back and were standing there in the yard talking, my grandmother wouldn't embarrass us. She'd wait until my date was gone and then she'd say, "You do your talking before you get here and when you get to this door, you come in the house." She didn't allow loitering around or anything like that.

But the older children who lived on the hill went on out and we wanted to go too. Sometimes there were social suppers, as we called them, and our step-grandfather (our grandmother was married at that time) would go with us if he wasn't too tired. When he was ready to come back home, he'd always say, "Well, I'm ready to go," and some of the others would say, "You all got to go already?" We'd say yes and we didn't talk back. We got our coats and went. We knew we had to get up in the morning.

My grandmother was a licensed midwife but I can't remember much about it. She served the white and black alike and was highly thought of by both. She'd stay in [white people's] homes and they respected her, treated her nice and paid her well. They would come and get her. She delivered babies in Demorest and Baldwin, all around. She enjoyed it. She loved helping people.

She always had those hospital gowns and a white cap. She carried a satchel with towels and Lysol, scissors, cotton, and gauze—different things like that. Nobody bothered that satchel. She attended meetings for midwives at the health department. They would get briefings of what to do and what to have in their little satchels. I imagine her satchel's still in that trunk there, because we left all her things like they were when she passed.

Back when we children were small and lived in the country, she used to give us horehound and rabbit tobacco tea. They called it "life everlasting." And for a high fever, she'd pour boiling water over an herb called fevergrass. Mostly she gave us horehound or castor oil. She'd give us that old castor oil and a piece of peppermint candy, and when we burped it up we'd keep tasting that castor oil. That castor oil bottle was about two inches wide and flat and cost just about a dime. We used to hate to cough because we'd know we would get castor oil even for that.

But my grandmother wasn't a harsh person and we hardly ever took any medicine unless we had a cold or a headache. She would tell us to smell of a little camphor or put some camphor on our foreheads. Sometimes she'd put a little on a spoon of sugar and have us taste it for a sore throat. She wasn't much of a medicine-taker herself, so we didn't take much either.

On Sundays we automatically got up, going to Sunday school and church. My grandmother didn't have to ask us, "Are you all going to Sunday school?"—we just got up and got ready. We didn't stay out like the children do now, either. We went back home after church. Sometimes we'd go to B.Y.P.U., and if we went to church at night our neighbors chaperoned us.

Every Sunday our grandmother gave us all a nickel apiece and we didn't spend it for candy or anything else. We didn't dare do anything like that. We put that nickel in the Sunday school plate like we thought maybe she could see through us and know what we did.

I believe that children were a little more afraid of their parents or the rules were more strict for us then. Children were more obedient. You give a child a nickel now and he doesn't want it. He wants *money*, he says, and holds out for a quarter. And we didn't have cafés or stores to go spend it at either.

They used to have camp meetings and we'd go to them together, too. When I first came up here I didn't know the differences between the denominations. As a child we went to the church where they were having services. I don't know if we did it religiously or because there was nowhere else to go.

We'd go to our church over here when we had services and then [when the other church had services], I'd ask, "Aren't you all going to the other church?" And some of the older ones would say, "No, they don't come to our church, so we don't go out there."

I thought that was such a shame. We weren't taught that. We went to church wherever it was and took part in the services. So I think I broke that [barrier] down. Now the Baptists go to the Methodist church on their preaching Sunday and so on. Whenever there's a program at the Methodist church now, everybody goes.

As a rule, the colored people used to feel like it wasn't church if they didn't have shouting and hallelujah stuff. Now that's the way we were brought up. That used to be the difference in the white and colored services, but I think the whites are turning more to this Church of God stuff now. When we used to have revival meetings, the minister would preach hell and damnation, and "it might be your last time." We little children were just crying and going on. It would scare us to death nearly. I joined the church fifty-seven times, I guess, when I was a little girl and probably the next day we little children would get to quarreling and I'd say, "You told a story."

And they'd say, "Oh, we're going to tell Mama you said 'story' and you won't get baptized." That would knock me out of getting baptized every time.

I did finally get baptized when I was about nine. My father, my oldest brother, and I were all baptized at the same time. My father was in his thirties, I guess, and at that time they had what they called testimonials or experiences, where people told about the experience they had on up until they got saved. I don't think I was [at church] the night our father gave his testimony, but we heard about how he had joined the church and we were glad. We were all baptized along in October out in a place called Mount Carmel Church. I really didn't know what it was all about, but I was following in my father's footsteps.

I haven't been baptized again but I did have what I called a second conversion, or really the first one because when I first joined, I didn't really know what was going on. I think as you grow, you learn by experience. Then you look back and see how the Lord has taken care of you and you just grow into faith.

We used to go to school through pine thickets and broom sage, because it was a bit of a ways there. If we had fried rabbit in our lunch pail, we'd sit so everybody could see it. That was a big treat. But if we had peas and cornbread or something like that, we'd always turn our backs and sit on a log to eat it, because that wasn't very special.

School was fun then, really. We'd sit on benches and there was a big old stove in the center of the room to keep us warm. It took me the longest time to learn my ABC's. I could say them by heart but I didn't know what they looked like. And I used to read by

PLATE 4

the pictures. If I saw a picture of a bird or a kite in the primer,
I'd just say "bird" or "kite" when the teacher asked me. I couldn't
spell either. If they told me to spell cake, I'd spell it k-a-k-e and
get it wrong.

We could look out the windows at school and see men digging
ditches for waterlines and our teacher said, "You see those men
out there? It takes ten or fifteen men two or three weeks to dig

that ditch now, but one day they'll have a machine that will dig it in so many minutes with one man operating the machine."

We said, "Oh, he doesn't know what he's talking about." We couldn't see it back then, but it's here now. Everything's push-button.

In our class here in Cornelia, there were about twenty people that graduated. They came from Lavonia, Banks County, and other places to go here. The other [colored] schools didn't carry the higher grades and they would send their children into Cornelia. So my sister, brother, and I all finished high school. Not many people got to do that down in the country. Fourth grade was all that they had there. When we lived on the farm, we only had three months of school a year because we had to stop and knock cotton stalks and cornstalks and clean up the fields, things like that. We'd go from sometime in December to about February or March, but if there was something to pick, something we had to do on the farm, we'd have to miss time from school. In Cornelia we went to school full time and I was glad of that.

At our graduation, when we had to say our orations I was so scared. I couldn't wait for my turn to come. I wanted to hurry up and get it over with.

After I got grown, there used to be dances [in the summertime] up at Lakemont at a pavilion. It was large and wide and wasn't screened in. There were places built up so far where you could sit and just watch. It wasn't integrated, but on Monday and Thursday nights the colored people went to dance. Many white people came and watched us dance. They came from different places and brought their help with them. We could hardly wait for those nights. Some of the white people we worked for would come and root for different ones of us that worked for them when we'd have these little contests with balloons and things. We were so proud for them to be there and see us dance that we'd show out sure enough.

I went up there one time with a dramatic club that some young white girls belonged to. There were about twenty-five or thirty of them and we stayed at Dr. Jargen's cabin. Now that was fun! I was to cook breakfast and dinner for them while we stayed there. We just had a good time. I think we were there about a week. The cabin wasn't sealed well and some of them would climb up on the top of the partition and ask me to hand them up a piece of toast or bacon, and I would. Why, they just had the time of their life there. I enjoyed those girls so much. Some of them gave me some of the prettiest clothes and some gave me money. It was a pleasure to me to go up there.

It used to be the tradition that people from New York and Florida would come up in the mountains in the summer. They had nice houses up here and they had servants' homes and some of them would bring their chauffeurs, butlers, and maids with them. Some of the colored people around here would go up to the mountains, working all summer long and making enough money to last through the winter months.

I used to love to clean house when I worked in people's homes. They never had to tell me to take the curtains down or wash the windows. If I thought it needed to be done, I did it. At that time, organdy curtains were popular and I just enjoyed taking those curtains down and starching them and then ironing them. I would wash the windows, wash the floors and everything. I never did like to cook much, though.

During the time that Dillinger and his bunch was going around doing the kidnapping and all, I was working for some people here in Cornelia. If they were out of town for something, I would stay there with the children, and honestly, I would have died for those children. I loved them so. They would be asleep, so I wouldn't sleep myself. I'd stay awake all night until the folks came in, because I thought, "Now if somebody comes in and tries to bother these children, they will have to get me first." I didn't have any gun or anything. I guess I was going to fight them [with my hands] or something.

That was the kind of relationship that existed between the whites and the blacks at that time. The blacks were very grateful for jobs because jobs were scarce. I was lucky to work in some prominent homes and I can say that I love every one of those people I worked for. The ministers and lawyers were the ones that usually hired help. Not everyone could afford to. Our family has worked in the Kimsey family ever since we've been up here. Of course, I've worked around in different homes and in offices, too, over the years.

I've been to church with some of the people I've worked for. I worked for Mr. Stewart, the president of the telephone company here. He invited me to be a witness at his grandson's christening. I had never seen a christening before. As maids in the prominent homes, we would help with wedding receptions or whatever. We'd all dress up in our pretty white uniforms and our hair all done up and look nice so we wouldn't embarrass the people we worked for. We felt highly honored to be invited to their daughters' weddings.

I guess I never married because I was busy helping my grandmother with the younger children. I had proposals and I thought

I loved the ones that asked me, but I'd always think back to my family and my grandmother. I thought it was so beautiful and good of her to go out in the cold weather to hang up clothes for other people when they would freeze up in her hands, all to give us an education. I was afraid that if I married, they'd suffer. I'd share my pay. If I made $2.50, I'd give my grandmother $1.50 and keep the other dollar. We were always a close family. I'm very fond of my sister's children and her grandchildren. I feel like they are mine too, in a way. I've always loved children, although I don't have too much patience with them anymore.

A lot of people look back [on the segregation and hard life] with hurt but I don't want to do that. I think the blacks have more now than they used to. When we first came to Cornelia, very few blacks owned their own homes. That was just the way people lived then. They lived as was customary then. I can't phrase it like I want to but we were in a different stage of life then than now.

BRUCE MOSLEY

I have had such a good time doing this article with Bruce Mosley that it shouldn't be called work. We'd just sit down and start talking about anything and everything, and before either of us realized it, we would have two hours of taped conversation. I was always ready to go back for more. Bruce is a wonderful storyteller and I enjoyed just being there listening. He told me stories that had been told to him by his grandmother when he was a little boy walking through the woods with her, looking for pine knots for a good fire, and later, sitting by that fire. He said she always told him he was "the worst one for asking questions."

Bruce was born and raised in Clayton and has lived here off and on most of his life although he has spent some time in California, New York, and North Carolina, where he met his wife, Selma. Often when I went to the Mosleys', she would play and sometimes sing some of the beautiful religious songs she has written for the piano. She directs the choir at their church and plays the piano for other churches as well. It seems she and Bruce know almost everyone in Rabun County and they know them. They are two people I'll always remember and I hope they'll always welcome me into their home as they have this year.

Bruce heard many of the stories he tells from his grandmother, Polly Mosley. I think it was important to Polly that Bruce know some of the things she told him over and over again, and he loves to tell people about them now.

PLATE 5   Bruce Mosley.

Bruce still enjoys horseback riding and likes to keep a horse. He works with the livestock at the Dillard House Farms, and it is there that we made some of these portraits of him.

LYNN BUTLER

You wouldn't believe it if I was to even tell you how old I am. I've come up with the old-timers. I was born in nineteen and eight. Lots of older people knows me up at Dillard and Rabun Gap and Warwoman and Persimmon and Lakemont—all over Rabun County. Lots of the youngsters don't know me much now. They see me riding my horse and doing this and that and they don't believe I'm that old.

So the old folks say, "Well, he ain't a-joking. He's just that old." And those youngsters say, "How do you know?"

And they say, "Well, I've known him from a day old, a baby." But some of these people's dead now that knowed me from when they were a day old even.

I never have seen my father but there's older people here—Harley Penland, who lives out here—he knowed my father. He come from Charleston, South Carolina, into this part. He was Spanish, I think

PLATE 6

they said. There's two kinds of Spanish people, dark Spanish and a white Spanish. Well, my father was a dark Spanish. His name was Charlie Griggs. Mrs. Em Walls brought my father into this country from Charleston when he was just a boy, back before the Civil War. This was back in slavery times.

My grandmother taught me about the old times. She came from Murphy, North Carolina, and she was three-quarters Cherokee. Her name was Polly and I called her Mama because she raised me from a day old. My mother had inflammatory rheumatism and they had to turn her in a bed sheet, her skin was so tender. My grandmother took me and raised me on a bottle. [My mother's] dead now. I was kind of shy around her, but I felt like Polly was my mama.

My grandfather was Pank Mosley. I was three months old when he died. They said I looked just like him. Pank was a slave. When the Yankees came down and was freeing the colored people, he was just a lad of a boy and they said that he took up with the Yankee soldiers so they put him to work. He didn't do much. Said he just went with them and they gave him cigars to smoke and he said he was scared to smoke. Said he'd see a white person and run. They asked him what he was running for now that he was free, and he couldn't believe it for years because they'd been done so bad. They was whipped and not allowed to pray. The Yankees would leave these [black] children with different ones that they'd captured and say, "Now, these children's free and you've got to leave them alone." The Yankees wanted them to take care of the children and not to put them under bondage again.

Polly had also been a slave and she was seven years old when the Yankees came in. Her daddy was John Southard. She was in Murphy when the Yankees came down and freed the colored. Their name was Southard from the family who owned them.

I can remember every bit of what my grandmother told me. She used to carry me up on Screamer Mountain on Sundays and take one of these tow sacks and an ax and knock these rich pine knots off of logs and we'd build fires out of them in the woods when we were 'coon hunting and campin' out. Then a lot of times on weekdays when the sun would be pretty and warm, she'd tell me to get my ax and we'd go down to the woods and get pine knots. She'd say, "I just want to get out of this house awhile." She was always wanting me to go with her. She'd say, "Let's set down here on this log and rest awhile."

It would come about she'd say, "I've toted many a sack of pine knots for my mother for her to split up pine with and my daddy to start a fire in the cookstove."

I'd go to asking questions. Then she'd go to talking about these high mountains way on back to Tallulah Gorge and how she and my grandfather Pank had walked from Murphy across to Hiawassee and through Towns County on through Blairsville and Young Harris. That was just a panther trail, a hog trail, through there. They'd go back and forth to visit her folks.

She'd also tell me some about her mother and grandmother, and about when the Yankees came through where her grandmother was working for those white people that had her under bondage.

My grandmother saw those Yankees when she was seven years old. She said they came in riding on the prettiest big horses and had their boots all shined up, and they were just marching like soldiers. When the people saw them coming they were all scared to death, not knowing what it was all about. She said her mama was working in the kitchen and she said she like to have fainted.

Their owner said, "What in the world are we going to do? What are they up to?" He was afraid they were going to burn down the house.

The people [who owned Bruce's mother and grandmother] had these big old geese that would blow at you and bite you. Mama said one of the Yankee soldiers had his old long sword, and he took it and whacked off one of those goose's heads when it blew at him. This white woman came out yelling, "Don't you kill my geese!" And he says, "Be quiet there, lady." And you know, she never had took orders from anyone before because she was white. Grandma Polly told me her husband was wanting to go get his gun to shoot one of them, so they had to wrestle him down to the ground. He wanted to fight but they just slapped him down. She said the Yankees told them they were coming to free the colored people and the owner said they weren't either. The soldiers shoved him against the wall and he called his wife to go get his gun. She just cried that the Yankees were come to take their darkies away. Some of the soldiers heard her and said they hadn't come to take them away, but the darkies were going to go in peace if [the Yankee soldiers] had to take them back with them.

My grandmother said the young white boys from the house came in and said it was a revolution and warned all the people to do like the Yankees told them if they didn't want to get in trouble.

One of the captains there made one of the white boys go get his ax. They were standing by one of those big old cribs (bigger than this house) full of this pretty white corn. That soldier busted that lock off, and the door flew open. The crib was so full of corn it just came running out on the ground—just poured out. One of the other soldiers got up in the crib and was pushing it out with his feet for all the people to get to it. Mama said she was seeing this, said she was peeping out of an old wooden smokehouse and it was right next to the crib. They came in there next. See, they kept locks on these doors to keep the colored people from going in and stealing food. She said it was a lot of times her mama and daddy would have to go in and steal something just to get enough to eat that was half good because the white people allowanced the meat out to the [colored people] a little piece by piece, and if there was any left over they'd give it to the dogs first.

[But, you know] these white people thought there was nothing on earth like my grandmother's father, John Southard. They let him do all kinds of things. He was their top black man there on the farm, and if he told one of those white boys what to do about

PLATE 7   Bruce at the Dillard House Farm.

their work, they would listen to him, or their daddy would want to know why they didn't. My grandmama said they were under one of the best crews of white people that there was, back through that country. She said that there were so many [slaves] that were treated really brutally and she said that [their owners] kind of stuck their neck out for them, being good to them like that. Still, they were slaves and all the good treatment didn't make *that* any different.

Now those Yankees I was talking about got one of the biggest hams that [there was in the smokehouse]. It was getting around noontime and they were wanting lunch, so they knocked out the doorway and brought out this old long table that the white people used to eat on and they set it out in the yard for all them soldiers to eat on. They had my grandmother's mother cutting up ham for them to eat and some of those Yankee boys knew how to cook so they got a big fire started in the old wood stove and cooked their dinner right there like they owned the place. They told my grandmother's mama to sit down and they wouldn't let her do any of the work. They were fixing dinner. They told her to take her rest, and when they put the dinner on the table, they told her to eat. But she couldn't. She was so scared, she couldn't swallow a thing. She just sat there and watched those Yankees eat all that food. The people had some of these old-fashioned teacups in the house, and one of the Yankees told one of the white boys to go and get them. When my mama's grandmother started to get up, they wouldn't let her. [She was to sit down and eat.] They said they'd find anything they wanted in the house and if there was any money, they'd find that too. She said then the old man started to cry, and those Yankees told him they didn't want to steal his money, but they meant to take it and give it to the colored people. They said they were doing this by law. They stayed there that night and she said that the [colored] people wanted to go away but the Yankees wouldn't let them go. They said they should stay right there and the soldiers would put a guard over them in the night to make sure nobody bothered them, and that's what they did.

Then the next morning when the rest of their company came along to join up with them, they read off a paper from Washington telling [the white people] how they had to be good to the colored people and not hold them under bondage any more. She said they told the plantation owner that there was another division coming up after them to make sure they were doing right so they had better do like they were told. She said after the Yankees left, all the [white] people were afraid to do any different.

You ought to have heard my grandmother tell it. She'd go to crying and I'd tell her to stop talking. She said she wanted me to know how it used to be and how it was changed for her people and changing even more for me in my time. She said that this segregation coming down was for a reason—for the races to get to know one another better and get to love one another and get along together.

Now I'm telling you how bad it used to be for them then. You've got a heart and I do, and it makes you feel pretty sad to hear how folks was treated. It's good to see how far God has brought us along to change things.

The colored race is growed. We've grown strong since we were freed. There was a time when we didn't have a chance. The Lord fixed it. We were pushed back or knocked back and dared not say anything. We'd have to go to the back door and knock. If [the white people] wanted to let us in, they'd say, "What do you want?" They'd recognize that dog before they would me.

Now, I've worked in some places around in Florida and some parts of the North, and it ain't been too long ago in these places I'm a'talking about that there was some pretty bad discrimination. When they got to putting the white children and the colored children in the schools together, they fought for a long time and they're still fighting in Boston and some of them places. The children didn't understand what it was all about. They don't understand that they need to go to school together and learn one another and get to find out that I'm as good as you and you're as good as me.

I've been to school here in Rabun County and over near Canton. I didn't ever go any further than the eighth grade and I didn't learn then. I didn't want to go. I didn't like the teacher. He whipped me when I got through school one day. I thought my grandmother was the only one should whip me. I quit when I was about to go up to the next grade.

How long has it been that the colored race has been freed? Over a hundred and ten years since then and you know, since then the race has gone way on up in the world and they're still growing now. There's colored lawyers and mayors now, and it's coming when it will be even better for everybody. But you know why? We have had help from the younger generation of people coming up now. You all won't stand for this stuff [racial discrimination and mistreatment because of color] like they used to have.

You take Martin Luther King and his people—he fixed it so that the white and black people just had to live more peaceful with one

another. You see how far things have changed? And it's going to
get better. It's going to come sooner than any of us think. I don't
know but that we'll have a colored President someday. I may not
see it. You may not see it. But things will be better on this earth.
I hope I *will* see it. I really do.

HARLEY PENLAND

*Harley Penland is a soft-spoken black man who is now eighty-three years
old. Except that he moves around slowly and cannot see very well anymore,
I would have thought him many years younger.*

*His family used to live on Black Branch in the Rabun Gap community.
At one time many black families lived there, but they have moved out for
various reasons, until now, to the best of my knowledge, there are no black
people living north of Clayton in Rabun County. Instead, most of them live
in a neighborhood in Clayton.*

*Mr. Penland owned quite a bit of land at one time and farmed some of it
and kept horses and other livestock. As his health failed, he sold off some of
it and only has a small garden now. He did purchase a horse recently "for
his boys," Lewis and Jesse—sons from his second marriage, to Sydney, in
1948.*

*It was during the cold winter of early 1977 that I visited Mr. Penland to
learn about his background and how his family came to live there in the
mountains. We would sit talking in his snug living room, the doors to the
rest of the house closed off to save heat, his pretty little five-year-old grand-
daughter playing quietly in a big chair. Time would fly by as I listened to
his stories of early times in Rabun County, his various jobs as laborer, soldier
in World War I, and finally as a trucker driving over much of the Southeast.
He has had some bad experiences just being a black person living in our
mountains. Because of the prejudice against anyone not white that used to
exist, not many black people stayed, although for many this is the only home
they've ever known; their families were brought in more than 150 years ago.*

LYNN BUTLER

My father and his mother came from Danielsville, Georgia. The
Penlands [in Franklin, North Carolina] bought them when my daddy
was young. His father was a slave and my daddy was [born into
slavery and] freed a little while after he was born.

My mother's name was Georgia Scruggs. She was from here. The

PLATE 8   Harley Penland.

Scruggses had bought my grandma [and so my mama carried their name].

We moved from out on Black Branch near Rabun Gap to Clayton (a little further out this road) into a little two-room log house. We built a kitchen down the side. We had a stove in there and a long table we all ate on. There was a long bench against the side of the wall and we pulled it up when we'd all get to the table. That house has been tore down. It was wore out. My daddy built two houses after that out there. Those little wood houses didn't last much over fifty years back then. They can now 'cause they put a bottom under them before they build them. Then they just had rocks on each end and a chimney in front and a door on each side.

We had school only about three months in a year. That's all they gave the colored folks. I think the white folks had six and up to nine months later on. Our school would get up to fifth grade, or maybe eighth—I don't remember. My daddy made me work all the time. Some people got up to the eighth grade but I never could.

Then there's some that's smarter than others. I was one of the slug-gish ones, I think. Or at least my daddy wouldn't let me go to school. He'd make us pile rocks here and around there. He was one of the old heads—didn't believe in colored folks havin' no educa-tion. My mother wasn't that way but my daddy was. He thought when you got where you could write your name, that was education enough. Lots of old folks had that in their head—from slavery, you know.

There was eight of us children altogether. Two died very young and then a sister who was older than I—she's dead now and one of the boys who lived in Sylva over in North Carolina and he's buried at Waynesville. There was four of us brothers.

More [colored] people lived back up there on Black Branch [when I was young] than there are [in all Rabun County] now. Back then, people farmed all those bottoms. It wasn't in hay. Most of the farmers would have four to six head of mules. They'd hire a bunch of coloreds to come and work one day or two or three days at a time and that's the way [the colored folks] got along. All of them raised a garden for something to eat. Back then you didn't have to have fertilizer like you do now. You could put some cornfield beans in and pick beans from now on. Everybody had a cow for milk and butter—sometimes two or three cows to a family. It was big families then—eight and nine to a family. They wanted 'em on the farm so they could raise lots of stuff cheaper.

Then [the colored] folks started moving [from Black Branch]. First one family and then another. It was foggy up in there back then. My aunt Lou Johnson had a large family and they claimed that that fog was against them. She lost a bunch of boys to TB. The colored folks were subject to TB, but there wasn't hundreds of them killed by it [as it's been told].

The Gibsons used to be up there at Black Branch. Mr. Gibson owned a big portion of that mountain land up there. They were the last colored people to move from Black Branch. He went to work for Georgia Power and then he built a house out here [at Clayton]. There used to be plenty of [colored] families out there—the Conleys and lots of Gibsons. They moved to Waynesville, North Carolina, or moved north. It's hard to find any of them now.

After I moved to Clayton, I had a job at a lumberyard. The lumber-yard was there in Mountain City. I had to walk all the way there and back besides working at home. There was some white families that lived out here below Mountain City in log houses, and they'd stand out on the road threatening-like. They just wanted to see you run. I never was really bothered by none of them, but I have a brother older than I am and they got after him once and broke out his windshield. The law wouldn't do nothin' about it. That's the way the biggest of it was done. Didn't have no protection, and just at the last they got to killin'. Two or three people was killed before it was all over with.

This place used to be tough country, you know. The whites was bad on the coloreds. It was almost as bad as the way they treated the Indians. I don't know which was the worst—they kept the coloreds to do the work and run the Indians onto the reservation, so I just don't know which was treated the worst.

I think they tried to take some land from some [colored] people up here but they missed it on Elam Gibson. He had some up in the valley. [The surveyors] run the line and they got an outside fellow to come in. Old man Elam had lots more land than he thought he had and they was tryin' to take that from him. They did that over here in the courthouse. One of the lawyers in Clayton got up and rared around and said this was a white man's country and always would be.

The sheriff came to some houses back over here one time. He come to get a fellow and he had a little trouble getting him. The jury found the fellow guilty of the crime and [recommended that he] be put in the chain gang. The judge said, "I oughtn't to do that but because he's a nigger I'm going to give him some time." That's the reason I tell you this place used to be bad.

It got so we couldn't get jobs at all and then some scattered to Atlanta and up to New York, around to different places. They just left out for one thing and another. They could get work then by going north.

We went across the water in 1914 to fight in World War I. I heard that they treated all the men [white and colored] the same. I just didn't believe it, see. I was raised here. I was single when I was in the Army, stayed in there three years. I was drafted. I never volunteered to go—no, siree! I didn't believe we were ever going to find no land. We stayed on the water seventeen days and nights. We had to go around by where the Germans had that ocean planted in mines and we was tryin' to dodge 'em and that's what took us so long. The ship was named *President Grant* and it got blowed up before I got back to the States.

We were in British France. That was close to the foreign line,

PLATE 9

and boy, they had the soldiers there! Every week or two they moved more in, they was killing 'em so fast. They'd load 'em up and carry the train up to the front and that was the last we'd see of them.

At first I wasn't expecting to get back, so I sent nine hundred dollars back to my sister. When I seen we was going to get away, I went to spending some but I wasn't expecting to get back. It didn't worry me then. Don't worry me much more now than it did then. Nothin' you could do about it.

Some of the boys stayed over there [after the war was over]. I had my bags packed, ready to come home. I came home and stayed here awhile before I went to Pennsylvania. I worked up there in a rug factory awhile. Then I worked in a rock quarry. Stayed a year or two up there and wanted to come back to Clayton.

When I first got back, I used to haul tanbark to Sylva, North Carolina. And I'd take truckloads of apples and cabbages to Hartwell and Elberton and all out through the country. I could sell more stuff out in the country than I could in town. Lots of folks out in the country were working so hard they didn't have time to plant a big garden and I could sell lots of cabbage and apples and potatoes, anything I raised. We could make up around a hundred dollars by November and that would do us till spring. Hundred dollars won't do you a week now—what about it!

I also worked up at the Rabun Gap school one summer, helping to make cement when they were building [some of those school buildings]. There was several of us working there. We were paid $1.25 for a day—ten hours a day. I put in about eleven hours because

I'd be there covering up my mortar but I'd come home every night. I had some boys I was hauling back and forth that was workin' up there too, and they would pay me twenty-five cents a day to carry them there and back. I made good at it at that time. The labor was all paid the same. They had colored folks to come and do the plastering but there wasn't no colored brickmasons there. I couldn't lay brick. I've laid a few rock in my time, but anybody that's laid rock would claim they'd rather lay rock as brick.

I built part of this house before I was married the first time. Then I've been adding to it ever since. I was about thirty-two or thirty-three years old. I bought the lumber as I could—let it lay stacked up for about two years. I went to a rock quarry and got the rock and built the porch. A rock mason built the chimney.

I [had] bought this place in the early 1940s after my daddy put it in a loan—had forty acres more or less. He lost it to the loan company and I redeemed it, took up the payments and paid the loan off. Didn't have to pay but about three dollars and something to the loan company. When he bought the place, he only gave two hundred dollars for it. That was way back then. In the 1970s I sold seventeen acres off of it, or give it away really—never got but four thousand dollars for it. I held on to it as long as I could. I got disabled and couldn't make a garden. I get so tired. I want to do, but I can't. I haven't done nothing to amount to anything in two year. I've been in the hospital a couple of times and I've been taking pills for sugar [diabetes] for 'bout fifteen years.

I think maybe the living is better for the colored people now, if they do right—don't bother nobody else's business and just do right.

CARRIE STEWART

While working for Foxfire last July, I received a call from another Foxfire student, Mary Hardman, telling me of two ladies from Franklin, North Carolina, that she thought we would be interested in interviewing. The ladies were Carrie Stewart and Viola Lenoir, Carrie's next-door neighbor. On the scheduled day, Pat Marcellino, Ricky Foster, Mary Hardman and I set off with a tape recorder, tapes, cameras, and many questions stewing in our heads. When we arrived, Carrie was sitting on her front porch flipping through a newspaper. We called a greeting that went unheeded. Carrie's great-granddaughter came onto the porch, greeted us, and explained that Carrie's hearing wasn't too good.

We moved into the living room and began the interview. Everything went smoothly despite Carrie's hearing impairment. And despite the fact I had read about her in Foxfire 5 *before meeting her, I was not prepared for the kind of person she is—the warmest, most* alive *person I've ever met. And some of the work she had done—well, it's gorgeous! She has pieced beautiful quilts and hooked some of the prettiest rugs out of mere strips of discarded cloth. She seems to have never had an unhappy day in her life, and I fell totally in love with her.*

When the interview was completed, we invited Carrie to come next door with us while we interviewed Viola. She accepted and we all walked next door. Viola greeted us with a smile and warmly invited us into her home. Although she had never been interviewed before, she didn't show a single sign of being a beginner. Viola, with all her warmth and friendliness, led us through the interview expertly and also taught us many new things.

That one day in July, with the help of two lovely ladies, we all sat and focused our minds back to a century ago when things were so very different, but seemed like present reality to us.

CONNIE WHEELER

Law, there's so many old-timey ways. I know a lot of young folks say, "Why, law, was you living when so-'n'-so happened?" I say, "Yes, I was living then."

[My grandmother] had a loom that had shuttles. She'd throw that shuttle through there and pull it—*bam!,* and she'd put it through there—*bam!* Sometimes she'd miss, you know, and drop the shuttle and we'd have to go and pick it up for her. She used to weave cloth, wool thread and cotton thread, and I remember she made us petticoats out of that cloth. My daddy wore undershirts made of wool in the wintertime. It looked like they'd scratch him to death, but they didn't, I reckon.

Yeah, she used to weave all the time. She had a spinning wheel where you would twist the thread. I took many a round on that making thread. And she had another thing called a reel that you would use to make hanks of thread, then you'd fasten them, then wash 'em. We'd knit our stockings after we got things ready. Now, 'round 'bout now we'd be knitting—getting ready for our winter stockings. I've 'bout forgot how to turn a heel. I saved one sock and I was gonna rip it up and see how to turn a heel.

We'd try to have two pairs of stockings apiece for all of us children. Then on Saturday night we'd wash our stockings and hang them up. That made me think of Santa Claus. I remember when we used to hang our stockings up Christmas Eve night and a friend of mine—he's dead now—put a switch in my stocking. Lord, I just cried!

PLATE 10 Connie Wheeler (right) with Carrie Stewart looking through an old family scrapbook.

Way back there we didn't have oranges like they do now, so we wouldn't each get one in our stocking. There was three or four of us children and Grandmother would cut up one orange and give me a piece and her a piece and her a piece. One child didn't get a whole orange. Oranges were high.

My daddy's sister's husband made shoes. Way back there you could go to town and buy a great long strip of leather. Then they didn't have brass tacks to nail the soles on, so they'd go out in the woods and get this maple wood and the old man would make little pegs by hand. They had a sewing awl—a thing to pierce holes with—and a pegging awl. The pegging awl would punch holes and you'd put in these little wooden sticks, and the sewing awl would sew up the shoes with thread—I think they said it was flax thread. They had a piece in the side of the shoe and a little brass tip around the toe and they could get 'em for fifty cents a pair.

I was just thinking, wouldn't it be terrible if children thought they had to wear shoes now like they wore then? Pegs and soles and all those little tacks in there? They had some kind of iron file that could be pushed in and out in the shoe and smooth those tacks off so they couldn't be felt. The shoes didn't hurt our feet because since we went barefoot all the time in summer, our feet were tough.

People who could afford it would have a pair of shoes for the larger girls to wear to church on Sunday. The rest of the little ones would go barefooted. Before we'd get up to the church—the road was so muddy then, you know—children would wash their feet and get 'em all cleaned up, then put their clean shoes on and go on in the church.

I remember when this road here was nothing but solid mud. People'd go to town and wear some old shoes till they got to what they call the foot of town hill. Then they'd change and put on the

PLATE 11 Carrie Stewart.

good shoes and put the others in the bag and carry 'em up town. The road was all that muddy! All along the road, people had meadows where they cut their grass for winter feed and sometimes people got over the fence and walked in the field out of the mud. Oh, it was terrible!

[Talking about going to town], one time my sister-in-law and I were going to town and she didn't have on any garters. She was short and stepped quick and she was just flying. Hadn't noticed her stocking down, you know, and she met some white boys and they were just killing themselves laughing. So she turned around and looked and said, "Wonder what they's laughing [about]?"

I said, "Look at your stocking." She liked to of had a fit!

We all had to work when we was growing up, too. My mother would have us helping and doing everything. Laundry work and all like that. My grandmother—after I got good size—would take in people's washing. I got a many a swarp with a wet towel or something 'cause I washed something and it wasn't clean. I had to put it back and do it over again, remembering that all around the shirt collars I had to be very careful. We didn't *half* do things; you had to do it right.

Most everybody wore aprons then. Even now I'm not fixed if I don't have my apron put on; I gotta have an apron with a pocket on it.

And I remember when we girls started using snuff. Well, I reckon everyone thought they ought to try it, too. The first snuff I tried to use made me so drunk! I had to go to bed and I was so sick! I thought I'd never want any more.

[Back then's when I learned how to quilt, too.] I started quilting when I was a little girl. Old man John A. Deal—he's been dead for years—and Miss Sally Stalkup—she's dead and her parents are all dead—had sewing school every Thursday. We would go to sewing school and sew four little squares together, two dark and two light. That started me in the quilt business.

A friend of mine's daughter lives in Texas. Well, her daughter's husband's father wore bow ties all the time and he wanted a quilt made out of bow ties, so I made him one with nothing but bow ties. It took me a long time, but I enjoyed it. I like to piece quilts anyway. When I finished with it, I sent it to him. He's dead now but he said he wanted that passed on down in his generation. His son, his grandson, and on down.

When I used to be quilting, this girl wanted to learn to quilt and she didn't know how to put her hand in the right place and quilt. She'd stick her needle down and then she'd reach under and pull it back up. She'd try then she'd put it down, then she'd turn the quilt over and she'd look and she'd pull the needle back. She laughs now 'bout how she used to try to quilt like I quilted. I always like to make all my corners neat, and if it doesn't do to suit me, I'd rip it out and cut it down to fit.

I still have my quilting frames. They're over a hundred years old. My grandmother owned 'em in her lifetime. And one of 'em got the end broke off, and she got a piece of tin and wrapped it around [the frame]. That tin's around there yet and she's been dead for years.

One lady wanted to know if I wanted to sell my quilting frames. She said she'd like to have 'em. I said, "No!"

[The next thing we asked Carrie to talk about was some of her experiences in school.]

What we call blouses now were called waists. I only had one teacher. One time he said, "Isn't there a button on that waist?"

"No, sir."

"Well, when you go home ask your mother for a needle and get

PLATE 12 Carrie with a quilt she made.

a button and sew a button on that waist 'fore you come back." He was very strict.

Some of the kids hadn't thought about their hair being combed, so he said, "Don't you all have a comb at your home?"

"Yes."

"Well, you didn't comb your hair before you came. Well," he said, "I'm gonna bring a comb and all the kids that come with their hair not combed, I'm gonna have their hair combed." You ought to have saw 'em gettin' their hair straightened out. He taught from the bottom up. He didn't spare nothing.

There was one girl in our class that couldn't catch on somehow. I could make it better'n she could in addition and subtraction and she wanted me to show her. But he didn't allow that. If you wanted to know something, ask him. He caught up with this girl askin' others to help her and he took her out of the first class and put her back where she started from. People's not strict now like they were then. As far as I remember I think about all my schoolmates that I remember are dead.

Way back then, instead of having pens and things they had feathers. They called 'em quills. I had one daughter who was very apt in spelling things and there was a feather we wrote with, and it was spelled q-u-i-l-l—quill, but she said, "Q-u-i-l-l—feather." Her brother teased her so about it that I had to whip him. But that'd just tickle him to death for her to spell "q-u-i-l-l—feather." She argued and she said, "Well, the feather was there."

He said, "Well, q-u-i-l-l doesn't spell feather."

Well, she wanted to know why they would put it there, "quill" and then say "feather."

They kept up pretty good. I tried to rear my children like that teacher taught me and I done pretty good at it, I reckon, 'cause I reared seven children. I had twin babies, a little girl and a little boy. The little girl didn't live long. The boy died not long ago. He lived to be seventy-seven years old. And if I live to see the twenty-eighth of November I'll be one hundred and three years old. And I have children, grandchildren, great-grandchildren, and great-great-grandchildren, I reckon.

My children and grandchildren respect me; they all do. They know I'd hit 'em in a minute. I have one granddaughter, and I forget what she did now, but I was quilting, I think, and she was sitting down on the floor and she said something—I don't know what it was, but I had something in my hand and I got up. She said, "Let me get outa here, Granny's gonna cut me in two with that stick!"

PLATE 13

My children's scattered all over everywhere. I have a grand-daughter in Germany. It's been years since they came to a reunion.

People had big families [back] then. My parents had ten children, seven girls and three boys. Let's see, there's Carrie, Emma, Lizzie, Maggie, Virginia, Harris, Dramp, and Charles. There was a crowd of us. They had a long dining table with a bench at the back of it. We'd all get lined up there and have dinner. We had breakfast in the morning and dinner at twelve o'clock and at night we didn't have any vegetables, we just had milk and bread. You didn't eat a whole lot of vegetables. You ate a light supper.

We had grits and bacon for breakfast when I was a little girl. In fact, it wasn't bacon that you buy in the store, it was your own homemade bacon. Great long slab of meat, you know, that we sliced and fried. And I always did like plenty of grease—it suited me.

Way back then not many people had flour to make biscuit bread. We'd have cornbread mostly and sometimes we'd have a little biscuit bread. I've forgotten now what a five-pound bag of flour used to cost, but flour was high. Why, I've eat as much cornbread for break-fast as I have biscuit bread. My grandmother used to make light bread. She'd put it up somehow and let it rise, then she'd make loaves and put it up where it was warm to let it rise [again], and bake it. I never did like it.

[I raised my children to respect Sundays, too.] I wonder sometimes if people really think about living for God like they did back then. They just do anything during the week and then when Sunday comes, why, they have to be good.

On Sunday you used to read your little cloth books and played around. You didn't do things on Sunday that you did weekdays.

Now they play ball and do everything else on Sunday—anything you want to do on Sunday is all right. But I still don't think it's right. If it was so allotted to give sacrifice for one day, I think you ought to do it. But they don't do it now. There was a little saying: "He on Sunday that cuts his corn will always wish he was never born." You didn't trim your toenails or your fingernails and things like that on Sunday. It may be a pretty good idea.

People taught the children so different then. You could take a crowd of children to the church if you wanted to, but you didn't hear no whooping an' hollering. Uh-uh. They'd go in there and would sit quiet. But now people leave their children at home and go to church and leave them there to cut up. I don't know, it's so different to what it once was. There's so many things that children don't know anything about now. Well, I guess everything is changed.

I was just thinking that in the church, the women would sit on one side and the men would sit on the other side. The women and men didn't all sit on the same side. I wondered why that was.

I bet a million times I sat on a church bench with my little ones strowed along there—you know, my children sitting up on the bench. I would always take a little half-gallon bucket of water and a little tin cup. We had pint cups and half-pint cups back then. I'd take that little bucket of water and a little half-pint cup and I'd set all my little ones on the bench and my oldest daughter, Ella, would slide off the bench and give the little children a drink of water if they wanted one. I never allowed my children to run in and out of the church.

I had one son, he was very comical. There was a preacher that

PLATE 14

liked him because he was kind of comical. Like, you know, he loved to do things? So one Sunday he asked the preacher could he sit up there in the pulpit with him? The preacher said, "Yes! You can sit up here."

My boy said, "Well, can I sing?"

The preacher said, "Yeah, you can sing if you want to." And you know, I had to keep punching him to keep him from singing too loud!

Way back then they had outside toilets, you know, and these children would go there to this toilet and spread paper over the holes and they'd have prayer meetings there. I was just thinking about how funny it was. They'd have prayer meetings, you know, and they'd pray and they'd shout. Well, they wasn't makin' like children, they was makin' it real. And they'd have what they call the mourners' bench. They'd say, "Well, he wants to be converted. Wants to turn to Christian." And he'd go to mourners' bench. Well, some of the older ones'd go to talk to him, you know, and tell him how to pray and all like that. And after a while one would jump up, you know, and just shout and holler. But they don't have times like that now; children don't play like that.

[We learned from her interview in *Foxfire 5* that she was a midwife, and we asked her more about it.]

I really don't know how long I was a midwife; I think my first lesson was when I was seventy-four. I had all my belongings: my cap, my apron, fingernail file. I had all the things that belong to a midwife. And I had a bandage for the patient. You know, at that time when girls' monthlies came around they were prepared for it. They had belts and a little concern to wear. The midwives had all that, too. Every month we had to carry all these things to class. The lady inspector, Mrs. Gaines, inspected all of 'em. Everything had to be washed, ironed, and folded a certain way. If it wasn't you had to take it back and do it over. We had to be very, very careful. Talk about sanitation now—they were more sanitary then than they are now 'cause they were careful about things like that. But there's no need in being so sanitary.

When I was a licensed midwife, there was a crowd of us. One lady's health wasn't very good and so the teacher advised her not to try to do it because she wasn't very well. Her kidneys operated so often until she couldn't take care of herself. The lady said, "I don't see why, I don't wait on nobody but my own folks, my own children."

The teacher told her it didn't make any difference. She said, "You don't wanna kill some of them or injure their health." So the teacher had her to stop.

It was years after that they had a—I don't know what they called it: a union meeting or something—and all these—as many as was living—midwives met. We got some kind of prize or something for following all the rules and regulations. I think there were about three that got those prizes. I was just tickled to death 'cause I got one while I was in it! Anything I was in I liked to carry it out according to the rules and I'd do it, too. But after my husband died I quit because you go all times of night and I couldn't keep up with it. That's been years and years ago.

[At the end of our interview, we asked Carrie if she'd ever taken any vacations.]

I liked Florida fine. I just felt like I was in the middle of the world! I thought it was a beautiful place. And sand! I told 'em, I said, "At home when you get out, you get red clay in your shoes and when you go out here you get sand in your shoes." But I enjoyed it down there all except it was so hot that you couldn't sleep at night hardly. I like it up here best. I told 'em this suited me better.

VIOLA LENOIR

[*Carrie was invited to go with us on our next interview, with Viola Lenoir— they've been next-door neighbors and friends for years—and she helped us by opening this interview*]:

I know when Viola was born. Her mother and I were schoolmates. I nearly broke my neck to go see Callie's baby!

[Viola smiles, shakes her head then begins]:

I can't remember from a baby. But I can remember the year I was born and what month. I don't think a kid could remember three years old, though. Not at my age.

[We asked her to tell us some history about her family.]

My grandmother on my daddy's side was full-blood African. The white people separated her and her husband. They brought her to the United States and left him in Africa. Her first child was born over here in the United States. She wasn't quite as tall as I am, but she was twice as big. That's the fattest woman you ever seen! She could work, but she couldn't read or write. She did common labor. I mean common labor like cut wood, saw wood, mind babies, cook and work in the cornfield. I call that common labor. Now that's what Mama 'n' them said—I don't know.

I don't know what tribe of Indians my mother's mother came from and I don't know where she came from. She came from Georgia to here. Her and her husband. But her husband died and left her with four children, two boys and two girls. They were practically Indians. You see, my race is mixed up—Africans and Indians.

Anyway, I just can't give no account of her, but I do know she couldn't read and she couldn't write and my daddy's mother couldn't either. I used to read to her on Sunday evenin's after Sunday school and I did the same thing for my mother's mother. They were just tickled to death when I got to where I could read.

[During her grandmother's time, there weren't any schools. Later, the Episcopal church conducted church and school in the same building, and finally a school building was erected.]

My daddy couldn't read. He wouldn't go to school because he didn't like it. If he went to school, he'd have to be quiet and couldn't run rabbits or fish! Neither one of my uncles could read and write because they wouldn't go to school either. They'd work good, though. They stuck with their parents in a farming business.

My mother could cook and she was a practical nurse. She got her nurse's training just by going on calls with doctors. She had an eighth-grade [education]. She was one of the first bunch of colored people that got religion and education.

I don't reckon she was a slave. If she was, [the white people] just let her go. We didn't talk about slavery. We just talked about how good people was to us. As I was big enough to go into the third grade, this white woman come and took me away. My mother let me go on account of this stomach. We were practically on starva-

PLATE 15   Viola Lenoir.

PLATE 16 Miss Elizabeth
Kelly, the lady Viola lived with
as a small child.

tion! This woman, Miss Kelly, offered to take me to stay with her.
She also fed my daddy and mama and brother.

So I was with Miss Elizabeth Kelly the beginning of my young
life. She was a schoolteacher. She taught me up to the seventh grade.
That's all the education Viola has, but I'm just as proud of it as if
I'd went to a thousand colleges.

Miss Kelly taught me in her bedroom. I slept in that bedroom
and I dressed in that bedroom. She scared me half to death the
first time she put me in a tub of water. I hadn't been used to a
bathtub; I didn't know nothing about water and lights. We had kerosene lamps, but she had electric lights, you know. Lord, I thought
I was somebody in that place.

She wouldn't let me wear colored dresses; I had to wear white
ones. You see, I was colored, so she wanted me to have white.
She said it made me look better. I stayed with her till I was twenty-
three years old.

Miss Kelly was a good friend that I could trust. If I got messed
up with my figures, I'd take 'em to her and she would work 'em
out for me. And I trusted her and I loved her just like I did my
mother; she felt just like Mama to me. Yeah, I had two homes,
one with Miss Kelly and one with my parents.

PLATE 17   PLATE 18

And talk about holding something against the white people? Some folks may can—I can't! They *saved my life,* my parents and my brother. We would have starved to death if it wasn't for her. I tell you I just can't give white people no bad name. I swear I can't.

I always thought that the white people couldn't be bad. Anybody can be bad if they want to, but I didn't think they could because Miss Kelly and her family were so good to me. I just thought all white people were like that. And, of course, all the friends I've met that were white would treat me just like she did. I could go downtown and drink juice in the drugstore [just like the white people]. So I just don't think about the mixing or fighting between the whites and the colored. When it came to touching you and beating you up and cussing you out, I just don't know nothing about that kinda stuff. I have seen some colored people come from Murphy and a little ol' place called Canton and they'd have scars on 'em. On their faces and all like that.

They hung two or three Negroes here for going with white women. They hung 'em where the town bridge is. That was the hanging place. Nobody didn't see the men that were hung except the ones that did it. When they hung the last one, I was married. You see, the black men would slip and do these things and the women would slip around and have these men. But you didn't know about it until you saw it in the paper. They didn't do anything to the white women. But the hangings really scared everybody. I figured it'd start a war, but it didn't.

I think Macon County's colored have gotten sorta straightened out and could see—as this old man said—"between the trees." I don't think they've ever fought. The only thing that I know of is how the Indians once owned Macon County. I don't know whether

PLATE 19

Macon County fought 'em out or bought 'em out. It happened, you see, before I was old enough and had enough education to keep up with it. Take a little sixth-grade student and they don't know too much about law and stuff. I didn't pay much attention 'cause that's not cooking a pot of peas.

Everywhere I worked they treated me just like I was a baby, and some of them called me "Kid Vile," you know; all kind of funny nicknames. I honest-to-goodness can't give Macon County, where I've been born and raised, a bad name for being against colored people.

When I was fifteen years old I could go into a kitchen and cook like a grown woman. I guess that's what led me to working in hotels. The first one I cooked in was what they call the Willis House.

I reckon you all know what these hotels are like. See, I just cooked. I didn't know about nothing they was doing inside. I was in the kitchen all the time. I worked for two hotels in the summer and one in the wintertime. They had these companies to come from the North and the South and stay six weeks or three months. They was good to you, too.

[I also worked in people's homes] nursing children. In fact, I got a seven-hour-a-day job and I'd go work with somebody that had children.

[At this point we asked her if she'd ever been married. She grinned shyly and informed us that she had been married not once, but twice. We asked her to tell us about both of her husbands.]

My first husband and I got along pretty good about the first four or five years. He was a blacksmith who came from Georgia and, of course, he liked his drink. Him and my daddy was good friends 'cause my daddy loved his drink, too. But that didn't suit me.

Mama liked it. She'd sing songs and cut up and carry on with them, but she didn't drink. She put up with my daddy's drinking, but I wouldn't put up with my first husband's drinking. He washed my face with my daddy's drinking. I told him it didn't make no difference to me, but he had to get outa my house. He said it wasn't my house, it was his. I said, "Well, it's ours, but you are getting out!" So we kept fussing till—I'll just say I run him off. Anyway, that passed.

He left me, went off, and came back and we got back together again. And I happened up with this little girl. And that didn't suit me at all 'cause I didn't want no children, period! And, of course, I wouldn't take nothing for her now. But I did not want any children then!

But anyways, I stayed on with him and he got to saying that he was gonna build the house bigger, you know, and fix it up nice so I could raise his children. I said, "Who's gonna have 'em?"

He said, "You, of course."

I said, "You're joking. I ain't gonna have no more. I've had all I'm gonna have." So we separated again. There was a law that gives the girl child to the man and gives the boy children to the woman, so I had a time trying to keep that youngun. I looked at the judge, I said, "Judge, I had that baby, and if I have to go to the road, I'm taking it with me."

The judge just looked at me and said, "Young lady, keep your mouth shut." He was gonna give her to me anyhow because I had the home.

My daughter is the reason I married the second time. She came home and said that she wanted me to buy her a daddy. That "everybody has a daddy in school but me." She was almost in tears. And that just like to've killed me [so I remarried].

The second one did pretty good. He didn't drink too much before we got married. He'd slip and drink after we were married and sometimes he'd get too much. I was just about to put him out and he decided he'd come out of his church and come into my church. Well, I couldn't afford to kick him out of the house then. We'd sit down, knees together, and hold right hands in church. And I don't know whether y'all can remember the chapter—I can't remember, but I think it's in St. Matthew—where it says don't have but one husband and they's one love. It's there somewheres. I can't remember just how it goes, but anyhow we held hands and went to church. After he came into the St. Cyprian's Episcopal Church [originally a black Episcopal church], the bishop made him superintendent and made me assistant superintendent.

He passed away in 1964. I was satisfied he wasn't gonna live 'cause he had heart trouble and paralysis. He got to where you couldn't tell him nothing.

I caused myself to be a good Christian. There was some alcoholic people who lived down the road here below me and they had some children. I was worried about the children, but I didn't know how I was supposed to get to the children without running into the parents. And I also thought I was too good for them, you know. But one Sunday—I don't know whether God told him to or what happened—Father Coble came to me with his text and said, "Be ye doers of the word and not hearers only."

I was holding too much against those drunken people. I wasn't treating them with a Christian attitude at all. I just thought I was too good to even speak to them, let alone try to help 'em. I wasn't doing that, period, and—honest—I tried it. I was scared to death afraid to go down there. I didn't know whether I ought to take a pistol to shoot 'em off of me or what. They'd drink something terrible, and especially along the last of the week.

Well, I read [to them] every night and I prayed hard and I went on and taught them enough so that I had their four children for baptism on Saturday before Easter. Then I told Father Coble how I was scared to death at first to bother with them folks. I said, "When I used the word 'love' I got in just as nice as pie." And there was still one of those children who came up here and washed my windows for me this Easter past. And before that, one of 'em went with me to town. I hate to go to town by myself 'cause I can't see too good. I can see better this year than I did last, but I still can't see too good. She went with me and helped me buy stuff. All before that, why, they were practically scared to pass the house, let alone come in. They thought I was just too good.

But I prayed to God to take those feelings away from me, so I wouldn't give anybody a bad feeling. I hope He's answered my prayers.

You folks don't know how proud I am that I can grab your hand. You don't know what it is to go in a church with only five or six people there. You just think you've been so dirty to God that He ain't gonna give you any blessings. We need all these people that move in here—white and black. We need 'em to join with us to help us. I told the bishop that the church wasn't built for colored. It was built for people. I said, *"It was not built for colored!"*

I asked two or three of these elderly white men what they thought of mixing with us—I just came right out and asked 'em! I said, "What do y'all think about mixing with us, joining us?" And each one said it was all right, that he couldn't see any difference, just differences in color. I said, "Well, I'm about the blackest one in here and I won't rub off on you."

The church was built because the people here didn't have any religion of any kind and they didn't know one hand from the other hardly. They put the church up to help take people to God. And it has stood. It'll be a hundred years old next year. That same old house'll be a hundred years old!

Now the church is real pretty since we worked and fixed it up. And I don't know why Father Coble says he doesn't want two hundred members here. I think we ought to make the church bigger. We ought to build an education house where we can have our Sunday school and different things for young folks now.

We used to have a big time here—all the different churches would come together up there. Everybody'd have his own table. We'd sing and pray and then each one would go around and buy something off the other feller's table. I got to thinking about it and we haven't had it here for years. I said, "I'm not gonna sit here and look out that window at those trees where we used to have such a good time there." You came when you got ready and you'd go when you got ready. Some of us would bring record players and we'd have such fun! We'd sing gospel songs and all that sorta stuff.

I was the third baby that was born into St. Cyprian's Church. I'm still here and, as you see, I'm having to live by myself, but I don't care 'cause I know God loves me. That church is what I call *my home.* Both ways. Heavenly and Earthly.

I haven't missed a convention in fifteen years. As long as I can walk and see a wink, they're not keeping me from going places 'cause I'm going and doing everything I can. Everybody [at the conventions] claims that I haven't changed. I said, "Well, I'm bound to be changed some 'cause I can't see good and I can't walk good and I can't remember." They all say, "Oh, you remember enough." I thought to myself, "I must've been a terrible mess then, when my mind was good." They certainly were [glad to see me at the convention this year]. They [had nice things to say]. They treated me just as nice—why, I've never been treated any nicer in my life.

I have to go back one more time. I've got to go either in September or October when the women have their fall convention. I want Father Coble to see how many he can take. This year after they saw who I was, I didn't even have to have a food card. All I had to do was just show up and I got what you was supposed to have cards for.

And this Mr. Moore—he's one of the funniest men we have down at our congregation—he told me, "You know," he says, "I believe you'd be a pretty good woman if you didn't talk so much. What makes you talk so much?"

I says, "Because I got a tongue." His wife, it just tickled her to death. But they are the sweetest couple.

Oh, I had a good time, though, workin' in the church and I'm still stickin' with it. I'll tell you something—you all may not know this—the book of Psalms will help you live a sure enough life. Read that book of Psalms! Every time I would just about get ready to quit, I'd read my night lesson in Psalms and I'd find something to bring me up. That's the truth. But boys, I just wouldn't take nothing for the book of Psalms. I love it.

I feel good at my age when I think what I had to come through. I'm sure you just don't know. I had some rough days and some rough weeks, but I've had a lot of good ones too.

SOUTHERN FOLK POTTERY

AN APPRECIATION

By John A. Burrison

You are about to meet many of the practicing folk potters remaining in the United States. As folk potters, they participate in a ceramic tradition passed on from one generation to the next. Such traditions are conservative and thus resistant to change, providing the potters with a body of tried and true designs and handcrafting production methods that fit comfortably into their agrarian way of life. In this respect folk potters differ from the academically trained studio potters and the assembly-line tableware and flowerpot factories that produce the bulk of clay products with which the reader would be familiar.

Among the ceramists of the industrialized world, folk potters are now very much in the minority, quaint survivals, to some, representing a throwback to an earlier era. In order to gain some perspective on the kind of society and approach to craftsmanship these contemporary folk potters represent, it might be useful to exercise our historic imaginations and reconstruct something of the fabric of life they once fully participated in and contributed to. We do not have to travel too far back in the past for this, as the changes which made them anachronisms took place, in the South, in this century. Let us set our time machines, then, to 1900, selecting for our visit a fairly typical farming community in the foothills of northeast Georgia.

It is the fall of the year. The day is bright and crisp, and the brilliant gold and red of the trees add visual emphasis to the distinctive smells of seasonal activities. Folk pottery is in use everywhere. Across from the campground where revivals are held in the summer, the Dorseys are putting up their garden produce. Beans, corn, beets, and cabbage are being pickled in pottery churns and cylindrical "kraut" jars, while apple and pumpkin butters cook before being sealed in smaller fruit jars. The Dorseys will eat well through winter and spring. Up the road, the Pitchfords have been making sorghum syrup; the stripped cane stalks are being fed into the creaking mule-drawn mill and the resulting juice is transferred to the oblong evaporator where the pungent odor of boiling molasses candies the air. From the collecting barrel the finished brown sweetening is funneled into stately syrup jugs which will be stoppered with corncobs and stored in the smokehouse until needed in the kitchen. In the cove on the other side of Long Mountain, a family of "blockaders" fills two dozen smaller jugs with the product of its labors, a clear but potent liquid that will make some who taste it feel good but put others in a fighting mood. Not far from the Methodist church, the Davidsons have been butchering a fattened hog and bull-calf; some of the meat will be smoked, some is being packed in brine in pottery jars, while the rendered lard is poured into smaller jars to be used in cooking. Back on the main road (which will not be paved for another thirty years), Mrs. Meaders is placing the morning's milk in cream risers to cool in the springhouse. The skimmed cream will be added to clabbered cream in the stoneware churn and converted, by a half hour's pumping of the dasher, into butter and tangy buttermilk, the latter to be served from a large pitcher at dinner, with the leftover butter returned to the springhouse in a covered crock.

While these activities would have been characteristic of just about any agricultural settlement in the turn-of-the-century South, some readers may have recognized by the family names that in one respect the place we have visited is special. This is the Mossy Creek District of southern White County, and all the families mentioned were involved in the potter's craft. Most of the wares they were using then would have been made by their own hands, with the bulk of their production sold at ten cents a gallon to their neighbors or wagoned to general and hardware stores to be marked up for resale. Since the 1820s over seventy folk potters have worked at Mossy Creek, the largest of Georgia's pottery centers; brothers Lanier and Edwin Meaders are still operating there. On that same autumn day in 1900, the men in these families would have been turning out ware in the jug shops or "burning" it in their kilns, the dark columns of woodsmoke signaling that fresh loads of vessels soon would be available.

One popular misconception about southern folk pottery is that it is a mountain craft. While it is true that the Appalachians have been a stronghold for much folklore, relatively few potters operated there, or for that matter in the lower Coastal Plain. In the Carolinas and Georgia, pottery-making was focused instead in the rolling Piedmont heartland, where the largest deposits of stoneware clay occur and where the population has been concentrated. In other words, the pioneer potters settled where their suspicions of good clay could be confirmed and where they had access to a steady market, and their success attracted other potters. In Georgia all eight centers, where most of the state's 400 folk potters have worked, were located in the Piedmont Plateau or on the fall line (the transitional zone separating the lower Piedmont from the upper Coastal Plain). Mossy Creek is the most northerly, and it is on the upper fringe of the Piedmont. There were just a few isolated mountain potteries, including one operated in the 1880s at Rabun Gap near the present Foxfire headquarters. The same distribution pattern applies to North Carolina, although there was a small pottery center in mountainous Buncombe County (one of that state's three "Jugtowns"). In most cases the jugs, jars, and churns used in the Highlands were wagoned there from the Piedmont.

Another common fallacy about the region's folk potters is that the craft was for them largely a creative and recreational pursuit, as it is for many of today's studio potters and ceramics hobbyists. The fact is that pottery making was a business, most often a part-time one to supplement farming income. The folk potters did not think of themselves as artists, but as artisans serving the utilitarian needs of the community.

The craft was kept alive mainly by the institution of the family, rather than by the more urban system of formal apprenticeship. The pottery centers often were dominated by "clay clans" like the Browns, twenty-five members of whom have potted in eight southern states over at least eight generations. Dynastic ties were consolidated through intermarriage, so that in many centers most of the potters were related to one another. Each center developed its own distinctive ceramic traits—vessel types and shape variations, glazes, approaches to marking, handle and rim detailing—by which typical examples can be identified.

Pottery traditions were spread westward through the South during the initial inland migration period. For example, the alkaline stoneware glazes known only in the Deep South and consisting of slaked wood ashes or lime mixed with clay, sand, and water, which appear to have originated in South Carolina at the beginning of the nineteenth century, had been carried as far as Texas by the 1830s. Following the initial migration, some potters stayed put, while others had itchy feet. Itinerant potters like William J. Hewell of Gillsville, who is said to have introduced the concept of the face jug to Mossy Creek where he preferred to work, could be important disseminators of ceramic ideas. An even more mobile twentieth-century Georgia potter was Atlanta-based E. Javan Brown, who potted in North Carolina, Florida, and Alabama besides many Georgia locations (he built the Wilson Pottery kiln in Banks County).

These potters shared in a regional ceramic tradition, certain features of which are limited to or concentrated in the South. There is much to be learned about how and why these traits emerged; some may be extensions of Old World models introduced by immigrant potters, while others most likely are responses to environmental, economic, and social conditions peculiar to the region. Still very much a mystery, the alkaline glazes represent one of the most significant of these "southernisms." They are virtually identical to the high-firing ash- and lime-based glazes used for two thousand years in the Far East, the only other area of the world where they are well known. It has been theorized that an educated potter like Abner Landrum of the Edgefield district in South Carolina came across a description of Chinese alkaline glazes first published in the eighteenth century and recognized them as a cheap and more consistently available substitute for the salt that otherwise would have been used to glaze stoneware. In this light, it is intriguing that the Meaderses refer to their ash glaze as "Shanghai" glaze, as if to suggest initial awareness of an Oriental inspiration.

Certain pottery forms also are concentrated in the area. One is the large, two-handled syrup jug, bulbous or ovoid during the antebellum period but later becoming more straight-sided. The prevalence of this form is linked to the importance of molasses in the region, but it may be derived from the quite similar English earthenware wine jar of the eighteenth and nineteenth centuries. Another regional pottery type is the ceramic grave marker, intended as a tombstone or planter and varying widely in design. The dates on inscribed examples found in some pottery centers from the Shenandoah Valley to Texas suggest that they were produced as inexpensive alternatives to stone markers during the hard times following the Civil War. A final example is the face jug, still being made by several southern potters. Now sold as folk-art novelties, at one time they were the potter's occasional joke to relieve the monotony of routine production, and before that, as the interview with Charlie Brown indicates, they may have served a more serious magico-religious purpose associated with death and burial. Vessels with grotesque or stylized faces are attributed to South Carolina slave potters, and one scholar believes the tradition to have grown out of West African funerary sculpture, perhaps reinforced by the English Toby jug.

Some of the folk potter's equipment is exclusive to the region, as well. Most important here is the rectangular kiln, very different from the round northern kilns and possibly derived, via colonial Virginia, from Germany, France, or England, where similar kilns are known. When these kilns were enveloped in earth to improve insulation and inhibit expansion, they were known as "groundhog" kilns; unenclosed ones were more often called "tunnel" or "hog-back" kilns. Another piece of equipment that seems to be unique to this part of the country is the ball-opener lever attached to the rear crib wall of the potter's wheel and used to gauge a uniform bottom for larger wares.

A final regional characteristic is the very endurance of the tradition. A handful of old-fashioned potters still operate in the Deep South, whereas their counterparts in the industrialized, change-oriented North became extinct many years ago. These southern folk potters maintain an essentially nineteenth-century approach to pottery making, and in so doing provide a window into the past. Still, they have not been entirely uninfluenced by technological advancements around them. Trained in a core tradition that included mule-drawn wooden clay mills, foot-powered treadle wheels, alkaline glazes ground by hand in a stone mill, the wood-burning rectangular kiln, and a repertoire of functional wares related to food and drink, each has made certain concessions which allow him or her to function more efficiently in the absence of younger helpers.

Of the folk potters presented here, North Carolina's Burlon Craig is perhaps the most traditional, in that he has departed least from that core of old-fashioned traits. Even he, however, has mechanized his clay mill, added commercial chemicals to his glazes, and increased the proportion of decorative wares geared to customers from outside the community. Lanier and Edwin Meaders could be viewed as slightly less traditional, as they have adopted electric-powered (although homemade) metal clay mixers, retired the stone glaze mill by using preprocessed ingredients (while still producing alkaline glazes which, in basic composition, are the same as the hand-ground ones), and, like Burlon, have come to emphasize more ornamental wares (Lanier's face jugs, Edwin's roosters) to meet outside demand. Then there is Alabama's Norman Smith, the last to work in a log shop and use a wooden (if tractor-driven) clay mill, but who has electrified his wheel and limited his glazing to Albany slip, a smooth, brown, natural clay glaze from the Hudson Valley of New York which some southern potters began to embrace for its ease of preparation when it became available after the Civil War. Despite these deviations from the core, all four potters still fire their wares in wood-burning rectangular kilns and otherwise work in a preindustrial way.

A larger group of southern folk potters could be described as transitional; while rooted in the older tradition, they were less reluctant to change as events in the twentieth century made the old-fashioned handcrafting of food-related vessels less practical. The first of these events was Prohibition, which in Georgia began in 1907 and continued into the national Prohibition of 1920. This dramatically lowered the demand for whiskey jugs, which for many potters had been their chief stock-in-trade. The growing availability of glass and metal containers for storing food and drink, modern refrigeration methods, the rise of commercial dairies, and a general shift from rural self-sufficiency to dependence on a cash-based economy also affected the folk potters. Few who managed to survive these changes could weather the Great Depression without making major alterations in their approach, as cash to purchase their wares was harder to come by.

One solution to declining demand for folk pottery was to switch to the making of "dirt cheap" unglazed garden pottery. In so doing, the Hewells of Gillsville chose a path which continued to emphasize hand-craftsmanship, while the Merritts of Crawford County in middle Georgia took the more radical road of machine-molded flowerpots. The hand-thrown planters of the Hewells became a later tradition, as successive generations and spin-offs such as the Wilson Pottery kept producing them. Davis Brown, after moving to Arden, North Carolina, from Atlanta, arrived at another solution: the manufacture of tablewares and French-style cookware mostly formed by jiggering machines. The potter's wheel was not abandoned, however, and Davis's grandsons, Charles and Robert, occasionally use it for face jugs. The Hewell, Wilson, and Brown shops are included here to illustrate some of the directions southern folk potters in this century were forced to take as the only alternative to abandoning the craft altogether. Contrasting them with the more traditional operations makes it clearer just how separate the old-fashioned potters are from modern ways of making clay products.

The Craig, Meaders, and Smith potteries probably will not survive beyond the present generation, for younger members of the families have not taken up the profession. The Foxfire pottery feature thus does a great service by documenting both the technological and human dimensions of the craft while it still exists as a living tradition.

Where to See Southern Folk Pottery

Nancy Sweezy (former co-owner of North Carolina's Jugtown Pottery), working through the Smithsonian's Office of Folklife Programs, has assembled a group of wares by and photographs of contemporary southern folk potters that your local museum may choose to rent from the Smithsonian Institution's Traveling Exhibit Service (SITES). It includes works by all those potters treated in the Foxfire feature. A similar exhibit, but planned to include historic as well as contemporary traditional wares, is being organized by University of South Carolina art historian Randy Mack and will open at the university's McKissick Museums (in Columbia) in the spring of 1986 before traveling elsewhere in the South. In the summer of 1983 Alabama State Folklorist Hank Willett and the Montgomery Museum of Fine Arts launched a show, "Traditional Pottery of Alabama," which includes work by Norman Smith as well as historic pieces, and will visit various museums in Alabama and elsewhere in the South through the spring of 1984.

Two small private museums are devoted to local historic folk pottery: Dorothy and Walter Auman's museum at their Seagrove Pottery in Randolph County, North Carolina, features wares from that section of the state (including the transitional period), while Carlee and Ralph McClendon's Pottersville Museum near Edgefield, South Carolina, spotlights the stoneware of antebellum Edgefield district. Public museums such as the Smithsonian's National Museum of American History in Washington, the Mint Museum of History in Charlotte, North Carolina, the Museum of Early Southern Decorative Arts at Winston-Salem, North Carolina, the University of North Carolina's Ackland Art Museum at Chapel Hill, the Charleston Museum, and the Florida State Museum at Gainesville have been building southern folk pottery holdings, but many of their pieces are in storage. As yet there is no sizable permanent display available to the public, but the Atlanta Historical Society is seeking funds for a planned Georgia Folklife Center which would exhibit a large body of wares as part of my collection of Georgian and other southern folk artifacts, presently in storage. Finally, the Smithsonian's documentary film "The Meaders Family: North Georgia Potters," is available for rental or purchase from Audio Visual Services, Pennsylvania State University, University Park, PA 16802.

Selected Bibliography

The following publications treat the living pottery tradition in the South or are key background studies of the historic period. Those designated as exhibit catalogs may no longer be available for sale.

Auman, Dorothy Cole, and Zug, Charles G., III. "Nine Generations of [North Carolina] Potters: The Cole Family." In *Long Journey Home: Folklife in the South*, edited by Allen Tullos, pp. 166–74. Chapel Hill, N.C.: Southern Exposure, 1977.

Barka, Norman F., and Sheridan, Chris. "The Yorktown Pottery Industry, Yorktown, Virginia." *Northeast Historical Archaeology* 6 (1977): 21–32.

Bivins, John, Jr. *The Moravian Potters in North Carolina.* Chapel Hill: University of North Carolina Press for Old Salem, Inc., 1972.

Bridges, Daisy Wade, ed. *Potters of the Catawba Valley, North Carolina* [exhibit catalog]. Ceramic Circle of *Charlotte Journal of Studies*, 4. Charlotte, N.C.: Mint Museum of History, 1980.

Burrison, John A. "Alkaline-Glazed Stoneware: A Deep-South Pottery Tradition." *Southern Folklore Quarterly* 39 (1975): 377–403.

————. *Brothers in Clay: The Story of Georgia Folk Pottery.* Athens: University of Georgia Press, 1983.

————. "Clay Clans: Georgia's Pottery Dynasties." *Family Heritage* 2 (1979): 70–77.

————. "Folk Pottery of Georgia." In *Missing Pieces: Georgia Folk Art 1770– 1976* [exhibit catalog, no longer available], edited by Anna Wadsworth, pp. 24–29, 86–103. Atlanta: Georgia Council for the Arts and Humanities, 1976.

————. "The Living Tradition: A Comparison of Three Southern Folk Potters." *Northeast Historical Archaeology* 7–9 (1978–80): 33–38.

————. *The Meaders Family of Mossy Creek: Eighty Years of North Georgia Folk Pottery* [exhibit catalog, no longer available]. Atlanta: Georgia State University, 1976.

Byrd, Joan Falconer. "Lanier Meaders—Georgia Folk Potter." *Ceramics Monthly* 24, no. 8 (1976): 24–29.

Chappell, Edward A. "Morgan Jones and Dennis White: Country Potters in Seventeenth-Century Virginia." *Virginia Cavalcade* 24 (1975): 148–55.

Counts, Charles, and Haddox, Bill. *Common Clay.* Atlanta: Droke House/ Hallux, 1971.

Coyne, John. "The Meaderses of Mossy Creek: A Dynasty of Folk Potters." *Americana* 8, no. 1 (1980): 40–45.

Crawford, Jean. *Jugtown Pottery* [North Carolina]: *History and Design.* Winston-Salem, N.C.: John F. Blair, 1964.

DuPuy, Edward L., and Weaver, Emma. *Artisans of the Appalachians: A Folio of Southern Mountain Craftsmen.* Asheville, N.C.: Miller Printing Co., 1967.

Eaton, Allen H. *Handicrafts of the Southern Highlands.* New York: Dover Publications, 1973 (reprint of 1937 edition).

Ferrell, Stephen T., and Ferrell, T. M. *Early Decorated Stoneware of the Edgefield District, South Carolina* [exhibit catalog]. Greenville, S.C.: Greenville County Museum of Art, 1976.

Greer, Georgeanna H. "Alkaline Glazes and Groundhog Kilns: Southern Pottery Traditions." *The Magazine Antiques* 111 (1977): 768–73.

————. *American Stonewares: The Art and Craft of Utilitarian Potters.* Exton, Pa.: Schiffer Publishing, 1981.

————. "The Folk Pottery of Mississippi." In *Made by Hand: Mississippi Folk Art* [exhibit catalog], edited by Patti Carr Black, pp. 45–54, 66, 83–85. Jackson: Mississippi Department of Archives and History, 1980.

————. "Groundhog Kilns—Rectangular American Kilns of the Nineteenth and Early Twentieth Centuries." *Northeast Historical Archaeology* 6 (1977): 42–54.

————. "The Wilson Potteries [Texas]." *Ceramics Monthly* 29, no. 6 (1981): 44–46.

Rice, A. H., and Stoudt, John Baer. *The Shenandoah Pottery.* Berryville, Va.: Virginia Book Co., 1974 (reprint of 1929 edition).

Rinzler, Ralph, and Sayers, Robert. *The Meaders Family: North Georgia Potters.* Smithsonian Folklife Studies, no. 1. Washington, D.C.: Smithsonian Institution Press, 1980.

Sayers, Robert. "Potters in a Changing South." In *The Not So Solid South: Anthropological Studies in a Regional Subculture,* edited by J. Kenneth Morland. Southern Anthropological Society Proceedings, no. 4, pp. 93–107. Athens: University of Georgia Press, 1971.

Schwartz, Stuart C., comp. *North Carolina Pottery: A Bibliography.* Charlotte, N.C.: Mint Museum of History, 1978.

Smith, Samuel D., and Rogers, Stephen T. *A Survey of Historic Pottery Making in Tennessee.* Division of Archaeology Research Series, no. 3. Nashville: Tennessee Department of Conservation, 1979.

Vlach, John Michael. *The Afro-American Tradition in Decorative Arts* [exhibit catalog]. Cleveland, Ohio: Cleveland Museum of Art, 1978.

————. "Slave Potters." *Ceramics Monthly* 26, no. 7 (1978): 66–69.

Willett, E. Henry, and Brackner, E. Joe. *Traditional Pottery of Alabama* [exhibit catalog]. Montgomery, Ala.: Montgomery Museum of Fine Arts, 1983.

Wiltshire, William E., III. *Folk Pottery of the Shenandoah Valley.* New York: E. P. Dutton, 1975.

Zug, Charles G., III. "The Alkaline-Glazed Stoneware of North Carolina." *Northeast Historical Archaeology* 7–9 (1978–80): 15–20.

———. "Jugtown Reborn: The North Carolina Folk Potter in Transition."
Pioneer America Society Transactions 3 (1980): 1–24.

———. "Pursuing Pots: On Writing a History of North Carolina Folk Pottery." *North Carolina Folklore Journal* 27 (1979): 34–55.

———. *The Traditional Pottery of North Carolina* [exhibit catalog]. Chapel
Hill: Ackland Art Museum, University of North Carolina, 1981.

THE MEADERS POTTERY

Let me begin with a brief digression:

In my opinion, one of the most inspired activities the Smithsonian Institution has ever sponsored is the annual Festival of American Folklife, held every summer on the Mall in Washington, D.C. To that festival, at the invitation of the Smithsonian, come scores of traditional craftspeople and musicians who spend days demonstrating their talents before the thousands who pass by to visit and stare in fascination. Ferreted out by regional field workers who send in stacks of recommendations, those finally invited are brought to Washington, fed, housed, and paid an honorarium by the Institution. Theoretically, they represent the most authentic and traditional aspects of their own cultures—whatever those cultures happen to be.

The first festival, held under the auspices of the Smithsonian's Division of Performing Arts, was during the week of the Fourth of July in the summer of 1967. It was a genuine success (and it and the ones that followed were directly responsible for many of the local and regional festivals that communities around the nation now sponsor to celebrate their own cultures in their home environment—both to the delight of those practitioners who thought people had stopped caring, and to the gratitude of spectators who became reacquainted with cultures and traditions on which they had turned their backs).

The director of that Smithsonian festival was Ralph Rinzler. I was introduced to Ralph in Washington by mutual acquaintances when I happened to be in town on a matter unrelated to the festival: the survival of a little magazine I cared deeply about called *Foxfire*. Ralph became one of our earliest supporters, sending copies to people like Pete and Toshi Seeger (who began to donate 35mm film and printing paper to us) and Bruce Jackson (who shepherded a request for a $500 donation to *Foxfire* through the Newport Folk Foundation), and writing warm letters of encouragement. In one, for example, dated January 26, 1968, he wrote:

"I am deeply impressed with the breadth of scope and concern for detail in your articles on folklife subjects. They bring a fresh approach to this type of documentation by coupling the accurate presentation of a body of fact with a warm rendering of the spirit of a people. Let's hope that *Foxfire* will make its way into enough libraries to influence the scholar's approach to the same subject matter.

"Rather than see the publication struggle against odds, I would encourage its publication in a less expensive way even resorting, if need be, to mimeographing to keep it alive. While I can't help but admire the feeling for layout and design, I would rather read *Foxfire* in mimeographed form than not at all."

Further on in that same letter he said, "I am enclosing transcripts of some interviews with Cheever Meaders. They will give you a feeling for another guy's approach to interview technique and the type of material he seeks. If you would like to go down to Cleveland with some students and talk with Cheever's wife and son who are still making pottery there and then do an article, perhaps using some of the enclosed in combination with what you yourself get, let me know and perhaps we can work on an article together." [The quotations from Cheever and Quillian used in the following chapter are from those transcriptions.]

Through Ralph, who subsequently served for years on the Board of the Foxfire Fund, Inc., I began to realize the existence of that vast network of people out there who care about folk culture and its survival, and I began to understand the fact that our hopelessly unprofessional activities in Rabun Gap had an importance and a dimension that I had never before suspected. The Smithsonian, for example, through Ralph, had already filmed Cheever Meaders at work before his death on November 26, 1967, and gathered the material for a book [see Bibliography]. In addition, Lanier and Arie and other members of the family had been taped. Pieces of the family's work were in the Smithsonian's collection. All this activity had been taking place in an adjacent county, and yet we had never heard of the Meaders family at all. After Ralph, as it were, we began to get serious.

An article in the Washington *Post* by Sarah Booth Conroy, published on June 30, 1968, to preview highlights of the second annual Folklife Festival, mentions the Meaders family. It says, in part, "Rinzler first heard about the Meaderses from Ben Shahn, the contemporary artist. Shahn had seen the face jugs that the Meaders family makes.

"For the festival, Rinzler bought 288 face jugs—not a one with the same face—to sell for $7.50.

"To get the jugs up to Washington in one piece was a neat trick. Rinzler couldn't get them packed and shipped. So he found a college student who, without pay, drove a truck to the hills, packed them, and brought them back.''

Well, not quite, unless Ralph contracted for a second shipment of pottery to be hauled up there that I was unaware of. What actually happened was that Ralph called and asked if I would be willing to load up that pottery and bring it to Washington, all expenses paid. Summer vacation had just started, I agreed, and one of my students, Tommy Wilson, and I rented a U-Haul trailer from Curly Pennington, who owns the Gulf station in Dillard. We hooked it to the back of my Bronco and gathered up not only the shipment Lanier had prepared but also several crates of the pottery of W. J. Gordy of Cartersville.

That event really initiated Foxfire's long friendship with the Meaders family.

[On rereading this, I find it sounds vaguely like an obituary for Ralph. Nothing could be less appropriate. Ralph is alive and well and still doing great things at the Smithsonian. And in case you haven't been to one of those festivals yet, they're still held every year on the Mall.]

ATE 20 The front of the p, and Lanier. The pot- s wheel is to the left just de the front door.

PLATE 21 Canisters formed part of the Smithsonian shipment. Lanier turned the canisters and lids and Arie, his mother, decorated them with grapes and leaves.

PLATE 22 Lanier wraps and packs one of the canisters as Tommy Wilson looks on.

PLATE 23 Another portion of the shipment. There were two types of face jugs: the one-gallon variety shown here . . .

PLATE 24 . . . and several two-gallon types, Lanier's first.

PLATE 25 Also included were small bean pots, some with lids . . .

PLATE 26 . . . and small jugs.

PLATE 27   The trailer, with
our crude sign attached.

PLATE 28   With the trailer left behind in the basement of one
of the Smithsonian buildings, we were free to become tourists.

The first member of the Meaders family to settle in what is now White County was apparently Christopher Columbus Meaders, a son of John Meaders, who had moved to Franklin County, Georgia, from Virginia to accept homestead land awarded to him for his service in the American Revolution. Christopher acquired his 260-acre farm in 1848, lost several of his sons in the Civil War, and passed most of his estate on to his eighth and youngest child, John Milton Meaders. John supported his family through farming, blacksmithing, and hauling and swapping produce and local pottery in wagons to surrounding towns.

By 1892, undoubtedly influenced by the fact that neighboring potters were making a living with their churns, pickling jars, pitchers, and whiskey and syrup jugs, he had decided to start his own operation across the road from their house. He and his sons built a log shop, railroad tunnel kiln [out of bricks they made and fired themselves in a scove kiln], glaze mill and a mud mill, and since none of them could make pottery themselves, he hired a local potter named Williams Dorsey (whose father, Tarp Dorsey, also owned a shop), and later Marion Davidson to turn for them for two cents a gallon (ten cents for each five-gallon churn).

John had eight children. All are dead now. The six sons (Wiley, Caulder, Cleater, Casey, Quillian, and Cheever) all learned to turn. As Cheever, the youngest (born in 1887), said in the interview with Ralph Rinzler, "[Williams and some others] would take time out to come and make enough for burning what we call a kilnful, and then [my older brothers] was a-practicing with them all the time. They just went to work with these other fellows that'd come in. And my oldest brother [Wiley], it wasn't long till he was a-making pottery. There's never been a better potter in this country than he was. He'd make the smoothest churns. One time a fellow by the name of Powers come down and told him that he wanted him to make him twenty one-gallon jugs. Said, 'I'm gonna fill 'em fulla whiskey. Now,' he says, 'I want 'em to hold it.' And he made them jugs for him and [Rugus Powers] took them on, filled 'em up, and hid 'em in the woods in an old stump hole. Well, he broke down and took sick with typhoid fever. And they stayed there six weeks or a month just like he'd put 'em there. He said that when he went back to get 'em, they hadn't seeped one bit. Said they held just like a bottle. That was Rufus Powers.

"[So] when I was a boy Wiley done all the turning. Course, I would keep that clay fixed for him and do some other work around. I didn't turn any then. I just let him do the turning."

As they grew older and married, the sons either started their own operations nearby or moved away. Casey, for example, moved to Catawba County, North Carolina, where Burlon Craig now works [see the following chapter], to set up a pottery shop. Ultimately only Cheever remained at his father's shop, and he eventually took it over about 1920.

Inevitably the work of the Meaderses became intertwined with members of other families in the area who also knew how to turn, and whose descendants we also interviewed for this book. Cleater, for instance, after five years as a railroad section foreman, started a pottery shop during World War I and hired Maryland (Bud) Hewell of Gillsville to help him. Several members of the Brown family also worked with the Meaderses. Members of both families were interviewed for this book.

Several years after Cheever married Arie in 1914, he was running his father's operation. He and Arie had eight children—four sons and four daughters. All the children were active around the pottery shop, helping as they could, but the four sons (Lanier, John, Reggie, and Edwin) were the most directly involved. All learned to turn, but in the final analysis credit must be given to Lanier for being the son most responsible for the survival of the pottery shop to date. When his brothers drifted away to pursue other occupations, Lanier—despite occasional breaks from the operation himself to take intermittent jobs in a textile mill or welding frames for mobile homes in Gainesville—stayed.

Cheever faced several difficult times keeping his business alive. The first came with the advent of glass canning jars and refrigerators, which caused the need for churns and pickling jars and jugs to wane. The inclusion of his work in Allen H. Eaton's *Handicrafts of the Southern Highlands* (Russell Sage Foundation, 1937), the paving of the highway past his shop, and articles about Cheever in various magazines brought tourists by the carload and enough business to make it worth keeping the shop open. The influx of tourists, however, with the inevitable irritations that dealing with them caused, was one of the factors contributing to his announcement, near age seventy, that he was quitting.

And then an amazing thing happened. Arie, who had stayed away from the shop to raise their family, decided to try her hand at turning, and the combination of her unquestionable artistic flair and the attention she began to receive lured Cheever back for a fruitful period that lasted, according to Edwin, more than ten years. Though he continued to spend most of his energy turning traditional ware,

PLATE 29   Arie Meaders, foreground, weighing clay, with
Cheever behind her, turning.
Their granddaughter Kathy is
watching. The scales over
Cheever's head are still hanging
in the same place in the shop.
This photo, from a 1958 issue
of *Georgia Magazine,* accompa-
nied an article by Maryanne
Kidd, a person partly responsible for the revival of interest in
the Meaderses' pottery.

he would also turn new shapes that Arie drew out for him, or turn
jars and vases that she would then decorate with applied clay grapes
and leaves or morning glory or dogwood blossoms. She, of course,
turned her own ware on the wheel he set up for her in the back
room of the shop, and decorated it with experimental glazes. It
was a collaboration that continued until shortly before his death
on November 26, 1967.

Ten years after Cheever's death, Arie retired to their home to
begin crocheting and making pillows with rural scenes or flowers
or butterflies cut out of colored cloth stitched to one side. Lanier,
meanwhile, had gradually moved closer and closer to the point of
carrying on the work of the pottery himself. When we first met
him, for example, he and Arie together had filled the Smithsonian

order, but shortly thereafter he was back at work welding in Gainesville. A heart attack there brought him home again, and back to the shop where he has basically remained ever since.

Any discussion of the future of the Meaders operation ends with a question mark. As I write this, I am four days away from taking this chapter to Doubleday in New York. Two of my students—Bert Davis and Richard Trusty—and I just visited Lanier again. Arie is in the hospital in Gainesville, having just had part of one leg removed, at age eighty-six, because of diabetes. Lanier is trying to decide whether or not to go to Washington in two weeks to accept one of 1983's sixteen National Heritage Fellowships awarded by the National Endowment for the Arts. Bedeviled and distracted, as always, by well-meaning customers and curiosity seekers making demands on his time and energy, he is talking again, as always, of quitting. But several weeks ago he, with his cousin, Cleater Meaders, Jr., built a new kiln that is a gem. Edwin "Nub" Meaders, the youngest brother, who began making pottery again three years ago, seems to be enjoying the work and the attention, but for how long no one can say. Cleater is in the process of building a kiln of his own near Lanier, but the extent to which he will use it is the subject of some family speculation. As I said, it always seems to end with a question mark.

But what is unquestionable is the impact Lanier and his family have had on our lives. He and Arie and Edwin probably don't know it, but they are very, very highly regarded by a whole gang of Rabun County people who have met them over the years and think they are some of the most special, most appealing people on this earth.

BEW

[Editor's note: This chapter begins with a major interview with Arie in which we encouraged her to talk about her childhood and her life with Cheever in depth in an attempt to put her career as a potter in its proper perspective as a piece in the fabric of a long life, well lived. It is followed by a section that deals with the more technical aspects of pottery making, which is interspersed with explanations from Cheever and Lanier. The chapter ends with our recent interview with Edwin, who showed us the complete process for making one of his pottery roosters, the single most popular item he makes. It's a full, rich chapter, one of the most complex we've ever attempted, and we hope it works. For an even more detailed treatment, however, refer to either John Burrison's book, *Brothers in Clay*, or that by Ralph Rinzler and Robert Sayers, both of which are listed in the bibliography following John Burrison's introduction.]

Arie Meaders

I was born in Macon County, North Carolina, in 1897 near the Union Methodist Church. We lived on Skeener. I knew Aunt Arie Carpenter [see *The Foxfire Book,* pages 17–30], that you all interviewed. Her church would come over there t' Union Church for revivals. People'd take off and *have* revivals back then, but they don't now. They have something they *call* revival, but it's not like what we had.

And Jake Waldroop [see *Foxfire 6,* pages 25–53], he's my daddy's first cousin! My daddy was a Waldroop [the name is spelled, alternatively, Waldrop]—Eli Rufus Waldroop—and I suppose all of them Waldroops over there is kin to him because that's where Granddaddy first settled. My granddaddy was Joab Moore Waldroop, and Jake's daddy was Bill Waldroop. They called him "Black Bill." [laughing] He was dark-complected.

Now, my grandfather's father came from Ireland. He was named Ned. Him and his brother come over here together. I don't know where they settled at first—I think one went to Tennessee—but Joab Moore Waldroop then come into Macon County and raised his family in Franklin. That's just about all I know of the background. I do wish I had a' got more of it while my last aunt that had it was alive. I intended t' go back and get some more information, but she died before I could have nerve enough t' go!

My daddy went to Tennessee when he was a young man to work for one of these Waldroops who was an uncle. I think he was running a government still. And he was helping him there. Well, he worked out some money there with him and he sent it back to my granddaddy, Joab, and Joab bought him sixty-five acres of land joining his land for about two or three hundred dollars. That was a lot of money back then. Then my daddy married there in Tennessee and brought Momma back to North Carolina, and that sixty-five acres of land is where I was born and raised. He married Lydia Francis Holder. She came from Harriman, Tennessee. I think there were ten or eleven of them. And that was my mother. She had worked before she married, and she had bought her a stove and a sewing machine and a rocking chair—They said, "You need everything in the world BUT a rocking chair!"—that's what she brought to North Carolina with her. She never did use the stove very much. She was

PLATE 30   Arie Meaders talking with Wig.

used t' cooking on the fireplace where she was raised up, and she didn't enjoy cooking on the stove, seemed like, until she'd go t' baking a cake or something like that. Otherwise she used the fireplace in our log house.

Our original log house had two rooms downstairs and then there was an old attic—had ladder steps that went up. It didn't have stair steps. You'd go up through a cathole like. Had a [trapdoor] with leather hinges t' turn down over it when cold weather come. Then we opened it up in the summertime. First thing Daddy did was build a kitchen out a' boards and framing t' th' main house, and a chimney. That's where the cooking was done. That was the first thing he done. I don't remember anything about him building that [because I wasn't born] only he said he built it, and Momma said he did.

For cooking, she had a large Dutch oven, and I've got the oven here yet if none of 'ems not carried it off. It's got three legs, but it don't have any handle. She used pot hooks to go in the two eyes that was on the side of the oven, you know. She'd set the oven on the fire and get it hot. Then she'd pull some coals out on the hearth and set the oven on those and put her bread in there. She always made three pones that went around in that big oven. Then she'd put the lid in the fireplace and get it good and hot and put it on top of the oven and put coals on top of it to cook that bread.

And when she went to make a pie, it was the same way. If she was gonna make a tart pie, she had little tart piepans that she used to make fresh green apple pies. She'd get 'em ready and set the piepans in that big Dutch oven to cook, and when they was done, she'd have more made up and take them out and put another one in. She cooked a lot of them that way, too. I wouldn't get but just one or two cooked!

Then she had a big pot to cook beans in, or boil backbones and spareribs in, or anything you was gonna have like that—or turnips. You cooked all that in the pot. Then we had a great big old open frypan with a great big long handle on it, and that's what she fried her meat in. Pull the coals out on the hearth and just set that pan right on it, and the meat would just cook, and it would be good, too.

Our uncle had a fireplace with a crane to hang pots from, but we didn't have anything like that. Everything went out on the hearth. The beans would sit right in front of the fire and just cook on one side. That was soup beans or green beans, either one. She put coals around it to try to keep it cooking all around, but she'd have to turn the pot around every once in a while and let the other side cook. And she'd pull the coals out and put her coffeepot on there. She'd always have a kettle, now, that she het her water in— or she heated her water in. People laugh at me for saying "het" [laughing]. And she'd have her water hot and pour it in there on her ground coffee, and it wadn't but a few minutes till the coffee would boil, being as the water was already hot, you know, and the coals was under it. Didn't take but a few minutes.

Now when she went to make her cobbler pies, she'd use her wood stove because she couldn't get her cobbler pan in the Dutch oven, but she could get it in the wood stove. But otherwise she used the fireplace. She was just raised to [cooking that way], and she'd manage it pretty good! But you had to stay right there with it! [laughing]

And law, I remember them blackberry pies she used to make. When we'd make a blackberry pie, they'd be so many flies they'd nearly eat you up! Took two to mind the flies off the pies so the rest could eat. Had no screens nor nothing like that. Oh, we *had* flies then. My, my. It was terrible. We'd use a brush from the shade tree a lot of times to keep them off the table; and then we had a cane that we got off the creek bank, and we'd roll so many layers of paper on part of it and then split it with the scissors [so strips of paper would hang down from it] and that made a pretty good fly brush. Us biggest children was always the ones that [stood over the table keeping flies away while the others ate]. They had to do it. It had to be done or they'd eat a fly! I don't see how in the

PLATE 31

world people lived. Wadn't no wonder they had lots of typhoid fever back then.

Put the leftovers in the little cupboard that Poppa had made. By five o'clock in the evening they was gone and had to cook some more!

The main log house was a little longer than this room [about twenty-four feet]. I believe they said Eli Ledford built it. He was a cousin of my daddy's but I don't know how in the world come him a kin to them. But they claim kin, and I guess they are because my daddy was kin t' lots of people up in there. Eli would visit when he was a old man. He worked up yonder at Chattanooga in the roundhouse up there on the trains.

But in this house, they was a partition went down the middle, and the front room just had room over in that corner for a bed, and then there was a great big fireplace here in the middle, and then a door [in the partition] that went in to a back bedroom. It took sticks a' wood about three feet long for that fireplace! Then the back bedroom had three beds in it, and it was *just* big enough for three beds! And that was it. There wasn't a living room or anything like that. We all had the measles and then the chicken pox and then the mumps one winter—one right after the other—and they moved two more beds into that front room with the fireplace for us. And one bed was right up against the front door! If you *got* in [at all] you had t' go in at the back! [laughing]

And we always had the thrash [see *The Foxfire Book*, pages 347–59] when we was babies, you know. I reckon it's caused from nastiness. I don't know what else. Well, anyhow, we always had it. And there was an old man by the name of Ty Setser that lived up above us there, and everybody that had a baby that had the thrash took that baby up there to him, and he'd take that baby off out where they couldn't see it, and he'd doctor it, and they didn't know what he done. I'd a' been afraid he was gonna kill it! [laughing] I guess his family knew what he was using, but they wouldn't tell. But it got out somehow or another that it was garden sage he used—rubbed their mouths with it or made some tea or something. I guess he kept a supply on hand because they was always going to him.

For any other kind of sickness, about all the remedies we had was castor oil and turpentine and kerosene oil and lard! [laughing] You'd mix kerosene oil with lard and rub it on your chest if you had a chest cold.

Now my mother never did make any yellowroot tea until her latter days before she died, but she cured herself of ulcers with it. Made it her own self. Went and dug it and made it herself. And she used mayapple for liver medicine. She took the roots and made it up into a tea. It's dangerous, though. It is. She like to got killed one time. She took too much. After we come to Georgia, it was plentiful, and she just got plenty of it! She took an overdose, and if we hadn't a' got the doctor there when we did, I guess she'd a' died. Law, she swelled up like . . . Now, the doctor told her it was all right in a moderate dose. "But," he said, "you just took too much!"

Then she had a thing they called "comfey" [comfrey] that made a poultice, and she would also make poultices for her headaches out of horseradish leaves. She'd take the horseradish leaves and lay them down on the hearth where she had cooked dinner and wilt them? Then she'd rub them together and lay them on a rag and lay them to the back of her neck. She didn't put it up here on her forehead. She always put it to the back of her neck, and that drawed the pain back that way, see? Got it out of her head.

And we always had plenty of mutton tallow. My granddaddy had sheep, and grandmother had a recipe that she made, and she used mutton tallow and English resin and pine resin—just like you get out of the trees here—and a little turpentine, and hog lard, and she'd melt that all up together. It was good for everything: sores and cuts and bruises and burns. She also had a recipe for soap. She couldn't use this homemade soap like we used, so she made her soap out of lard and sal soda. That soda was store-bought, and it's strong as ashes. It made a white soap, and I always thought it was the best-smelling soap. She always had sores on her hands from gettin'em gouged or anything, and she'd wash her hands in that soap and it'd just cure them up.

Now they was eleven of us children when we lived in North Carolina and one was born a couple of years after we moved to Georgia. I was the third from the top. The two oldest ones are both dead. There's only just five of us left—two brothers and two sisters and me. And after three or four of us girls got up big enough that we didn't want t' sleep downstairs with the little ones, why, we went upstairs. Grandma give us an old bedstead and we took that up there and put it up and made us a tick and filled it full a' straw. That's what we used t' sleep on! That used t' be a mattress! [laughing] We'd empty them mattresses out every spring when them thrashers'd come along. They'd thrash fresh wheat straw, you know, and we'd get fresh straw every year and fill them up. We done some good sleeping!

We didn't have any locks on our [house] doors like we have nowadays. We just had a wooden latch and a leather string run through a hole, and at night we'd pull the string in so nobody couldn't get in. [laughing] I reckon that's what they done it for! And get up of a morning and stick the string back through that hole.

Had two windows, one on each side of the door. And they had glass in 'em. Then in the kitchen we had one with glass in it and one shutter. The shutter was where we throwed the dishwater out and the waste wash water, you know. We had t' carry that water from a spring, and I thought that was an *awful* job! I'd a' lots rather stopped at the branch and a' got it, but I had t' go on t' th' spring and get it. [laughing] Yeah. We had t' carry water t' do everything we done. When we mopped, we could carry water from the branch then—it was between the house and the spring—but we had t' get it at the spring for everything else. Carry it in a tin bucket. I guess it held about three gallon. And I used t' think it was an *awful* long ways t' that spring, but I went back up there several times since and I found out it was just at the edge of the yard!

Ha! And you oughta seen the scrub mop we had! We had a shuck mop. It was a big block of wood with big auger holes bored in it, and we'd stuff shucks in that [see *Foxfire 3*, page 451], and then we'd get sand and we'd have some hot water and lye soap, and we'd scatter the sand over the floor and we'd go t' work. Then sweep the sand out the best we could and then get some renching [rinsing] water and rench it. Just rench it t' where it would run out the easiest. And the inside of the house had poplar boards [ten and twelve inches] wide. It was sealed with 'em. We didn't [paper the walls with newspapers like some families did]. Every spring we'd clean them walls with some of that lye soap and water mixed. Scrub 'em.

We also had an old scrub broom that a man would make out of a hickory limb [see *Foxfire 3*, pages 449–50]. You had to use 'em a good bit before they'd work good, though. They'd finally get soft and they'd get to where they'd hold the sand and then you could push the sand on the floor pretty good. Move everything out and just scrub them floors and walls good with sand and water and lye soap.

Then we had a barrel just sawed in two t' make two big wooden tubs, and had a washpot, and that's how we washed clothes. We filled that iron washpot full a' water and built a fire under it t' get that water hot, and then put some of that hot water in one of the tubs, and put some more water in the iron pot [to replace it]. So then that first tub contained the warm water to scrub the clothes in before we put them in the pot to boil. We always got them as clean as we could before we boiled 'em. Had soap and warm water and had these old rub boards that come around. We done it with our *hands* before the rub boards come—my mother did—but when the rub boards come, she got a rub board and it was a lotta help, too.

Then we took 'em out of there and put 'em into the iron pot of clean water and fresh soap. We boiled 'em there until they was clean. Then we took 'em out, and we had cold fresh water in the second tub. That was the first renching water. Then we emptied out the dirty water in the first tub and put fresh clean water in the first tub for the second renching. We always renched 'em twice in cold water from the branch just a few steps away from where we was washing. Then we wrung 'em out with our hands just like you do a washrag and hung 'em on the garden gate and the garden fence, and bushes and anything we could find.

Did all that with lye soap. We had a lye [ash] hopper [see *The Foxfire Book*, page 156], and we'd save our ashes out of the big fireplace, and we'd carry water from the branch and pour on them ashes and had two boards fixed in a trough at the bottom, and the lye'd run down that trough into a one-gallon pitcher. And every time that one-gallon pitcher'd get full, we'd empty it up into a bigger jar—maybe a four-gallon churn—and then take it and pour it in that same iron pot we boiled the clothes in, and get it a-boiling and keep adding more to it and keep it boiling. I don't know how many jarfuls of that it took t' boil down to get enough lye strong

enough t' eat the meat scraps up, but finally she'd throw in a meat
skin, and if that lye began t' eat on it, she knew it was ready t'
pile the meat skins and scraps and all the rest of it in. So then
she would put them meat scraps in there and, pshaw, you could
just see it a-going. Go t' stirring it and oh, that lye'd just tear that
all t' pieces. Just vanishing! Then you'd test it [for its strength].
Just dip your paddle in there and [put your finger on it and touch
it to your tongue]. Taste it! And if it was too strong, it'd burn the
hide off! Yeah. But you just dab it to your tongue and you can
tell how strong it's getting! Then if it's too strong, just add more
meat scraps and skins and just any kinda grease we had. I've heard
of some people adding sassafras for scent, and I did that one time
myself. It does make it pretty good. It makes it slick. Seems like it
don't get hardened the way it does when it's made the other way,
you know. It'll get dried out if you make too much at one time
and it would get hard if you spread it out on a board and let it
dry out, but we kept it in jars to where it wouldn't dry out. It was
kinda like a jell. It was too hard t' use when it was dried out. We
had t' wet it up again t' use it.

We even washed with that lye soap. My head has been washed
a-many a time with lye soap. I remember one time that they was a
family that lived pretty close to us, and their little boy had lice on
his head. Well, it has been said that that family carried lice all the
time. And he come there one day with his mother, and he had
him a little straw hat. You've seen these stiff straw hats—brim about
that wide? He had one of them, and my oldest brother wanted t'
wear that hat, and the other little boy wanted t' wear his cap, so
they exchanged headpieces. Oh, law, Momma had a time after that.
She took that lye soap and just *lathered* our hair good with it and
then tied it up in a rag and made us *sleep* that way! Well, I don't
know whether that killed 'em or not. And she combed and she
combed. I thought she was a-gonna kill me a-combing with a fine
comb! [laughing] But she finally got shed of 'em.

And baths—they's been wrassles over that! [laughing] Sometimes
in summertime we'd have a tub of water t' take a bath in, and we'd
all take it in the same tub! It was hard in the wintertime, I'll tell
you. Course, we had two fireplaces, and always when one'd go in
the kitchen t' take a bath, the others'd stay in the other room; and
then another'n 'd go in—swap about that way—and get his pan of
hot water. Had two water kettles, you know, and had t' keep water
going on the stove the whole time.

We sure had t' work. Oh my goodness, yes! We raised corn and we raised sorghum cane and we raised pumpkins and we raised sweet potatoes and Irish potatoes and anything that'd grow in a garden. Had to! They was such a crowd of us. Pickled beans and kraut and [sorghum] syrup. That's what I was raised on. That's the reason I can't hardly get away from it now! I really liked that. Oh my goodness, I reckon I did! Another man in the community had the syrup mill. That syrup took the place of sugar. We didn't have no sugar for a long time. I remember when we got our first sugar. Anyway, they would bring their cane there and make it themselves, or he would make it up for 'em for so much of the syrup. But now that man could *make* syrup. He was a good syrup maker.

Momma used some of that syrup t' pickle with. She cooked her beets and peeled 'em and put 'em in a churn jar, and she took boiling water and melted as much sorghum syrup as she wanted t' go in that. It was more water than syrup—just sweetened water. And she'd get that water up over them beets, and if she didn't have some already made, she'd go to our neighbor's and get some of that what you call "mother." It's a thick thing like a jell, and she'd put some of that in there and that would make it work and that sweetened water would make like vinegar, you know, and that would make pickles.

But for kraut, I always just worked salt up in my chopped kraut and then packed it down in a jar and put a good clean rock on top with a rag wrapped around it. And the water would come up over it, you see. Otherwise that kraut would just keep rising and it'd just come up out of the churn as it worked! [laughing] And beans and cucumbers the same way.

Now we didn't have any glass cans t' put any food in till just a few years before we moved from up there. I remember my mother bought the first glass cans in that community that had been bought, and everybody told her that she was a-gonna *kill* her *family!* "Don't you know that glass'll *break* and get in that food and *kill* 'em?"

"No," Momma says, "I ain't afraid of it." She wadn't afraid t' try *anything.* So she canned a lot in them, and the neighbors got t' coming, you know. They didn't know how t' can with 'em, and they got t' coming and bringing their vegetables and they'd get her t' help can 'em and show 'em how. They was afraid of it. And after they seen she was a-having such good luck with 'em, why, the stores went t' selling 'em pretty much, then.

Before that, we had some little [stoneware] jars about [10 inches] high, and they had a little round shoulder on 'em, and they were kinda the color of that chair [brownish red]. I don't know where

PLATE 32

they came from. And they was pretty slick, too. But from what I
have seen from now on since then, I believe they were molded
pots. I don't know how they done it, but they looked t' me like
they'd been molded. And we'd put our blackberries and apple butter
and pumpkin butter and such as that in those. Momma'd cook it
and fix it like she wanted it, and she'd put it in them jars, and
she'd put on a layer of cloth, and she'd cover that with some flour
starch made out of homemade *wheat* flour. She'd just have a *big*
bowl of it. And she'd put a layer of cloth and tie that down. Then
she'd take a layer of paper and put on there and smear it with
enough starch t' seal it, and then another layer of paper and more
paste—it was *thick* paste, too. I don't know how many layers she
did put on [each one] but seems to me like they was about six or
eight layers. Then she'd come down on the rim of the thing [and
draw the layers down over it] and tie that up with good strong
string. Then she'd smear *that* with that paste. And when we'd go
t' open one a' them jars, we'd just take a knife and just cut it out
[inside the rim] just like you do a tin can. I don't think they held
any more than a gallon. And we had *several* of them.

Then we had fruit cans out of clay. They had a mouth on 'em
big around enough to where we could get our hand down in there
t' wash 'em. They come up straight and then come in and had that
big mouth on top of there, and you could tie a string around there.
Whenever we used them jars for canning and used what was in
them up, we'd take them jars out t' th' branch between the house
and the spring and we'd put 'em in the branch and weight 'em
down with rocks—put rocks on the inside of 'em t' keep 'em from

washing away—and let 'em lay in there till all that stuff washed off of there so we could wash 'em.

And then we had churns just pretty close t' th' time that we moved down here to Georgia. Somebody from down in here [in Georgia] brought some churns up there t' th' store and sold 'em. I think the Tarp Dorsey family brought 'em up there. I know of them a-going up there several times after we come t' Georgia, and I'm satisfied that's who brought 'em. And my daddy went and got some just quick as he found it out. And we used them for milk and for pickles and pickled beans and kraut. And then he got ahold of a great *big* old jar. I think the bottom was about as big around as a churn, and it come up thisaway [with broad shoulders], and it had a pencil rim around it where you could tie a cloth on it, and Momma used that t' pickle in, too. It was a big *round* jar [not tall and straight like a churn]. Well, somehow 'r 'nother that jar got broke. I don't know whether it froze with the pickle beans or kraut one in it or not. But anyhow it got cracked all t' pieces. And my daddy was s' hard up that he took them pieces of jar and he took wire and he wired that jar back together. He had a pair of pliers, and he just put a wire everywhere it needed t' be—some come up this way and some'd go around—and he wired that tight enough that it didn't leak. My mother used it the year before we left there and it never leaked *one bit!* I think she left it there, though. I believe she give it t' one of Poppa's aunts.

We dried apples. Whew! Cut and dried apples till I declare I just thought I was turning *into* one! Had lotsa dried fruit. We peeled 'em and took the core out and put 'em out on a thin board in the sun. Slice 'em thin as we could with a knife and place 'em where they wouldn't stick and rot, you know, or mold. And when they begin t' get kinda dry enough t' move, you know, Momma'd stir 'em and then they'd finish drying. Then we'd put 'em in a great big long sack we called a meal sack. I don't know where they got 'em, but we had great big long sacks that we took the corn and wheat t' mill in, and she'd put it in one a' them. She had a chair in the room where we slept in the corner that she packed that stuff up in. And she also dried sweet potatoes. She'd boil the sweet potatoes and skin 'em and slice 'em as thin as she could and put them out on them scaffolds t' dry. Now you talk about something good t' eat in the wintertime. That's right! And she dried pumpkins. We'd set of a night and cut the pumpkins—you have t' cut it [in round slices] so it'll hang on a stick, you know. Had a rack built up before the fireplace that had poles on it, and we could just slide them pumpkin rounds on, and when that heat'd begin t' get on them pumpkin rounds, they'd just *droop!* When they was dry, we'd pack them up the same way. Then we'd kill hogs, and when Momma'd boil backbones and spareribs there'd always be some grease left in the bottom, and she'd fix some dried pumpkins and throw them in there and cook it. Oh boy, you talk about good eating, we *had* it. We don't have nothing good t' eat like that now.

We didn't have no root cellar. We put the potatoes out in the garden in mounds—sweet potatoes in one and Irish potatoes in another. We'd heap up a mound of dirt where the water wouldn't get to 'em, and dig a trench around it and away from it so the water would run off. Then we'd put straw on there and put the potatoes on that straw and then put more straw over the potatoes and throw dirt up over that. Then we put up four posts and covered that with boards [like a shed roof]. We done our cabbage the same way. They kept good, but I remember one year they froze. We didn't have any potatoes then. When they first froze, we had t' eat potatoes just as hard as we could 'fore they soured, and after that we didn't have any more till spring unless somebody give us some. It was a *cold* winter that winter, I remember.

And we had a big popcorn patch. My oldest brother claimed the popcorn was his, and we was curious about it, you know, and me and him took a peck of it t' mill one time on an old two-wheeled cart and the man ground it for us and we thought we was gonna have some good bread! [laughing] I don't think it made too good a bread! [laughing]

And all that that we raised is what we lived on—that and the chickens and eggs, and the milk and butter from our cows. We could sell a few eggs and things to get stuff we couldn't make ourselves. I know we had bought knives. They had a wooden handle and the blade was metal. And the forks was the same way. Now, I don't know where they come from. And the spoons, we bought them from the store. Little spoons and big spoons. They mighta been bought with chickens and eggs. I don't know. I know we never did sell no butter nor no milk 'cause it was all devoured *there.* And we had a little cash sometimes. My daddy would get out and he'd haul lumber for the sawmill people, you know, that was sawing it. Had a pair a' mules and a wagon—first pair a' mules he ever had—and he'd haul lumber t' town for them where they could ship it. He'd have a little cash money that way. But that wasn't used to buy food or seed or any of that. We had all that t' do ourselves. I remember we saved seed of *everything:* pepper, tomatoes, beans, all that. [To get tomato seed], Momma always cut hers twice across and just raked the seed out. See, they're in quarters in there, and they have old jelly-looking stuff on 'em? She washed 'em, got that stuff off of 'em in water, and then strained that water out on a rag and then she put that rag out t' dry in the sun. Then she'd take the seeds off. Oh, yes. Had *plenty* of tomato seeds from one year t' th' next. Didn't have no trouble with diseases or nothing. And she'd tie them seeds up in a rag and hang 'em up in the kitchen mostly behind the stove. That's where she had some nails fixed t' hang 'em. Do the same with pumpkins and beans and everything. Always pick the best tomatoes and the best pumpkins and the best ears of corn and save the seed from them.

And then when the gardens were in, we had t' make sure that nothing got that food before we did! My mother had a mole trap and, boy, she kept that thing set every day. When she'd catch a mole, she'd reset it. But groundhogs? I don't remember being bothered with groundhogs. I don't know what one looks like! Now crows, they'd eat your corn up as fast as you'd plant it if you didn't scare them away. Sometimes we'd put up a scarecrow, but the crows didn't bother us too bad because they was a big bunch of us and we was just about all over the place and kept 'em run off. And we never had beetles. We never had a bean beetle till we come t' Georgia.

Then Momma wove cloth, too. She had all that t' do. She was raised up to it and she had it t' do. She's sheared many a sheep. I don't think we ever kept more than four or six at a time, but that made just about all the yarn that Mother needed to work up into stockings. Law, I was glad when we got to where we didn't have to wear them stockings in the spring of the year. Them wool stockings nearly eat my legs up! And my daddy would wear wool stockings the whole year 'round, summer and winter. I asked Momma one day, I said, "Why don't he pull off them old wool socks and stop wearing 'em out in the field like he does?"

"Well," she says, "he said they was just as cool on his feet as cotton." That's the idea he had about it, so he just wore his wool socks.

Then mostly what she wove for us was blankets for the beds. Her and Grandma would make 'em up together. They would help one another. They had two great big walnut trees, and Grandma used the green walnut hulls to dye the thread to make the cloth. I think they always come out brown. And they dyed with indigo blue sometimes. I remember Grandpa wearing them old jeans britches and jeans coats, and I tell you, they was so thick you couldn't tell where the thread was at. I don't see how they done it. And it was all wove on a homemade loom. I don't know who made the loom, but it would take up half this room. It got left behind when we moved t' Georgia.

Between work, we went t' school. We had a five-months school up till the year I left there, and they got it up t' seven months then. That was in nineteen and twelve. I think we had two months in the summertime, and then the next three months in September, October, and November. It was usually out about Thanksgiving week. [We had a break, though] 'cause we had t' stop out and pull our fodder. Everybody pulled fodder. The school was there at Union Church. The church and the school was built on the same grounds [but different buildings]. At first it was just one-room, and they enlarged that one room as population begin t' increase, you know. They built an "L" onto the end of the old one, so then you had one room for up t' th' third grade and then when you took up the fourth, you went t' th' other room. They had two teachers then.

I didn't have any trouble with any of my subjects. It was always easy for me. And they was one that couldn't learn nothing, and she'd sit down and copy what I had on my tablet and she'd hand hers in. And she was up with me. If I was wrong, she was wrong too! [laughing]

And we had fun there. They'd give us plenty a' time t' play. We'd have morning recess and dinner recess, and we usually built play-houses out in the woods in the fall of the year in October when the leaves was pretty, you know. We'd string leaves—take little sticks and pin 'em together—and go around our playhouse about knee high, you know, and leave a door and a window, and take rocks and get moss and put on 'em for the chairs. Oh, we had a good time.

After we come t' Georgia, I took the seventh grade at another little country school over here for *two* years. And I thought *surely*, then, I'd got through the seventh grade! [laughing] And that's as high as it went. Then if you went t' school any more, you had t' get a way t' go t' Cleveland, Georgia. They had a high school up there. A lot of boys would walk and go, you know, but the girls didn't. Or they might go and find a boarding place and board up there and go t' high school. Quick as they got through high school, a lot of 'em went t' teaching. And a lot of 'em went t' teaching when they got through the little country school we went to. But that was the end of my schooling.

Now when we come to White County, Georgia, in 1912, I was

fourteen years old. Poppa took a notion to come to Georgia and let us kids raise cotton and get rich! And oh boy, if *we* didn't get disappointed! Here in White County, now, raising cotton! And the very best of it didn't get no more than about [18 inches] high. Well, it'd get sometimes [about 36 inches], but it didn't have very much on it. And my mother didn't want t' move down here. She *begged* him not t' do it. And my granddaddy begged him not t' do it. Says, "You're a-ruining yourself now by giving up what you've got here and going somewhere where you don't know how t' do like they do." And it was the truth. He didn't know a thing in the world about raising cotton. Somebody had told him it was easy! I guess it was his cousin. He had one cousin down here, and he had come t' visit that cousin, and I guess he persuaded him t' buy that place next t' him.

Well, if Momma hadn't a' signed the deed for him t' sell the place up there, he *couldn't* a' come, and she come pretty near not doing it. But he just kept on and kept on at her till she just finally give up.

So he just come and bought the place and made arrangements for somebody t' clean the house out. And then we come. And we didn't find it very satisfactory. We have talked about it since then, and my sister said she didn't see *what in the world* Daddy meant a-selling that place up there and coming down here t' nothing. Now, we had a good orchard there. We could raise enough t' eat. Had stock and barns and everything was just fine. But no, he wanted t' change things.

We come on the train from Prentiss. That was the depot station. We got on the train there and come t' Clarkesville and stayed in an *old* house over there that night. It was night when we got t' Clarkesville and got off. And we brought our cooked food with us. And me and my sister was talking here a while back. She said that was the happiest time she thought she'd ever had [laughing]. She didn't know then what we were getting into! We had our supper and our breakfast, you know, with us. We had boiled ham and all kinda sweet bread and stuff t' eat, and biscuits. And I think we even brought some milk. And we just fared fine. And coffee. They had coffee and they made coffee. And I remember the house like t' caught afire that night. They had a great long pole a' wood in the fireplace [sticking out into the room, and the fire came down the pole] and it had burnt off to the jamb where the wood floor is, but we got it out. It didn't burn much. And me and my sister slept in a box of bedclothes. Some of 'em slept on pallets on the floor, but we got in a big box that we had our bedclothes packed in and slept in there. And it was cold that night, too, but the next day was warm and pretty and sunshiny.

They left most of our furniture up there. Brought a few chairs and the bedsteads. The dining table we had—left it up there. Somebody was gonna get it. They didn't sell it. They just left it there for some of 'em t' come and get. And my mother had a dish cabinet that my daddy had made out of poplar wood. He'd made it himself. Left it. And I just worried myself t' death over that little old cupboard we had. What little furniture we brought, my daddy made two trips with a wagon.

Then he sold all the corn he had up there before he come down here. I know they was several of 'em come and bought corn till he sold all of it. And so the year we moved here, we about lived on soup beans. Had a big sugar barrel made outa thin staves, and we had that barrel two-thirds full of dry soup beans. Me and my sister picked most of 'em and shelled 'em too. And we eat soup beans all summer. And boy, they was good too. We didn't get tired of 'em. We was hungry! [laughing] We had brought three or four hams of meat with us, and we had 'em all eat but one, and if somebody didn't steal that last ham we had! Momma claimed she locked the smokehouse, but Poppa told her she surely didn't or anybody couldn't a' got in there.

So we just worked and worked and cleaned up a place t' live there where the home was that he brought us to, and it was a mess. And the land was just a rock pile. Nobody hadn't tended it, only just a few little spots around—the very best spots that they was on the place. Well, he took a notion he'd have us to help clean up that land, and us girls went t' work! Worked in cotton and peas and corn. Stayed in the field most of the time! [laughing] But I never could see we was getting anywhere! Now that's the truth. As young as I was, I couldn't see we was getting anywhere. But Poppa just made out like he was just well satisfied with it.

I never did figure it out. He sold that sixty-five acres in North Carolina out when we left there, just by little lots, you know. And I don't think he ever did get very much out of it. I don't think it was fifteen hundred dollars in all. And he bought this place that we come here to for fifteen hundred dollars, and he had to borry money from the government to pay for it. And when he died, it was still not paid for. He lived seven or eight years, and then he died with cancer, and he still thought when he died that Momma would go ahead and finish paying for the place. That they would

just work on just like they had while he was alive. But it wadn't a-
suiting them. Well, I had married Cheever by then, and my mother
and my sister sold that place and paid it off and they got out and
went t' renting. My younger sister, then, she went to the cotton
mill at Habersham. She worked over there two or three years and
then she went off t' school at Berea College in Kentucky. Two of
my sisters went there, actually.

And that place we moved to when we first come to White County,
there's no house on it now. Everybody that's moved there has moved
away, and it's growed up in some of the *prettiest* grass you *ever* laid
your eyes on. It's great big high grass. You see little bunches of it
here and yonder, but that was just a field of it—or was when we
was over there here about a month ago. It looked like it had been
sowed. I don't know whether it's what they call bear grass or not,
but people gathers it and makes dry flowerpots [arrangements] out
of it.

And the homeplace in North Carolina, we was up there first of
October of this year. We go up there every once in a while. But
we don't find any relatives up there anymore. We just have one
cousin living there now, and his family is gone and he's the only
one that's left there. And the old house is gone. Not a thing left.
Just the land, and the land don't look like it did then to me. They've
built, I think, about seven new houses on it, and it don't look like
the same place. Some of the roads look natural, but they've built
new highways, you know, now everywhere.

Now Cheever was raised in White County, and he was raised hard.
He'd tell me about things he'd do when he was at home, just a
boy—that they'd send him out t' cut wood by hisself, and he'd keep
the cookstove wood up, and a lot of the firewood. And he'd carry
that wood in on his arms, and he had a stiff arm—it wouldn't bend
in the elbow. He fell off a little old limb on a tree and broke it,
and his daddy never did have anything done with it. Never did take
him t' no doctor t' get it straightened or nothing, or fixed. And it
just growed that way.

I met Cheever over at Zion Church where we went to Sunday
school and church. Him and his folks went to Mossy Creek Church,
and they would visit and go to other churches, you know, and he
was visiting over at Zion one Sunday with his sister, and he told
another girl that he'd like to meet me. "Well," she says, "I'll arrange
it."

Directly she come around and got me and took me around and

PLATE 33 An old photograph
shows Cheever and Arie in front
of their kiln.

introduced me to him. That was fine, you know. So the next Sunday
he wanted to date, and he got the date, and he just kept a-coming
and kept a-coming, you see, till we got married! [laughing] I was
about seventeen. The first two years we was married, we lived in
the house with [Cheever's] father and his three sisters and two brothers. I was just one of the family. "You do as I do." It wasn't an
easy life. Everyone farmed to raise food. [Pottery] was the way the
family got their money to pay the tax and buy extra [things]. From
what I understand, the way they got into pottery first was that old
man Davidson came up and showed them all he knowed about pottery and got them started in making it. Now Cheever's father never
did make any. He built the shop for [his children] to work in. Where
the chimney is up there was where the first kiln was built. The shop
was there too, but the first shop he built was too small for them
to work in, so I think they tore it down and built another one [that
was] bigger.

   [At this time] Cheever didn't turn any, either. [While his brothers
were there] Cheever helped make the balls of clay and he would
grind the clay in the pug mill and keep all that work up. Then his
sisters would help put it in the kiln. And if they was any to set
out to dry, they always put it out in the sunshine to dry. They didn't

have no stove in there like Lanier's got in there now. Lanier never carries a piece out to dry. He just sets it up on the plank there and builds a fire in the stove there. But they would help carry that stuff out every morning that it looked like it wasn't going to rain and that the sun was shining, and then bring it back in that night. Then, if it needed any more drying, they'd help take it out the next morning. Finish drying it.

Cheever didn't make pottery until after we was married. When all his brothers left home, there was nobody left but him to do anything there in the shop. He just took over the shop and went to work. The first time he made pottery, he told me he was going to get him some clay and he was gonna make him some ware. They called it ware [back then]. And I said, "Why, you can't make that stuff. I've never seen you make a piece in your life. You've never tried to make it."

He said, "I'll show you." He went in [the shop] and made a kiln of ware just as pretty as you've ever seen.

In 1919, we built this house here and moved into it. Cheever [and his father] still had the pottery going, and once in a while they hired other people to turn for them. "Daddy Bill" Dorsey had a pottery near here—that was Cheever's uncle. Married his aunt. He didn't make ware, but he hired people to, and when they had slack time [they'd turn for Cheever if he needed them]. Old man Hewell was "Daddy Bill's" steady turner then, and he turned some for Cheever. Javan and Willie Brown did too. They were working for "Daddy Bill" and somehow 'r 'nother had some slack time, and they come up here and wanted t' turn for 'em up here. That was 1921, the year that my youngest boy was born. And they did come— Javan and Willie both, I believe. They were fine people. But their ware was so *thick* it didn't suit the Meaderses. They wanted to turn a big amount in a day and they just throwed it up and it was so thick you couldn't hardly lift it. It needed t' be lighter, 'cause it's heavy at the very *best*.

Then there was Mr. Jim Brown [father of Javan and Willie], and he had three or four boys and two girls to support, and they moved in a house down here with Q [Quillian]. They took part of the house and Q kept the other half of the house, and they stayed down there for a year, I believe.

And then they had another old man by the name of Page Eaton. He was a Irishman. Little short cut-off fellow. They had him hired, and he was a good turner. He didn't turn like the Browns did. They built him a little log house out over a little ways from the shop for him and his wife to live in. And she wanted t' keep a little old dog all the time—kept it in the house with her. That dog got out one day and Cheever done somethin' 'r 'nother to it. Hit it with a rock or something. Anyhow, he nearly scared it t' death! It went running back t' her, and she never *did* know what was the matter with that dog. And he never did tell her! [laughing] But Cheever just scared it nearly t' death. It hadn't been out *much*, you know!

Well, then the Depression come along. I still say we didn't suffer during the Depression for we didn't have anything, so we didn't have anything t' lose! [laughing] And when the Depression come on, he was selling jars for ten cents a gallon. That was a three-gallon churn for thirty cents. A four-gallon'd be forty cents. Somebody come along and told him one day, said, "You'll be a-taking less than that for it 'fore long. Now just wait and see."

"Well," he says, "when the time comes that I have t' take less than what I'm a-gettin' *now*," he says, "I'll *quit*." Well, he didn't quit. He just kept on. He *had* to. We had to live, and we had to have a *little* money. [And he still had a market.] He'd put on a load of pitchers and churns and jugs and take 'em out over the mountain yonder 'round Blairsville and Hayesville and Murphy and around in there, and he could bring back groceries instead of them. Sometimes a little extra money, too. Casey [Cheever's brother] helped. Casey hauled his pottery on a wagon over the Blue Ridge Mountains into Rabun County and even back up into North Carolina and South Carolina. They'd be gone sometimes a week at a time. Casey was always into the hauling business.

I don't remember Cheever actually hauling any himself on the wagon, except once or twice, and he didn't take it very far. He happened to be able to get ahold of an old truck, and that's how he hauled, mostly.

I remember one trip him and Quillian made with a load of ware. They left home one evening, and it was awfully cold. We thought it was gonna snow, but we didn't know. And I took a mattress off one of my beds and let 'em have it t' sleep on while they was gone, and if they hadn't took it, I guess they'd have froze t' death. And they slept in an old storehouse over there that night, and they had a good fire. They said they didn't suffer a bit. But I know how it blowed snow here. It come up out of the east, and that was the biggest east snow I ever seen in my life. Our house didn't have anything but weatherboarding on the outside of it, and didn't have no ceiling in here, and why, that snow would just come in through them little cracks [in the board roof] like they wasn't nothing there!

Who-o-o-o. And I went up to his daddy's to stay all night while he was gone. I could a' stayed at home, and lots rather done it, but Cheever made me promise t' go up there and stay all night and I did. And next morning it was snow on the ground and it was snowing that morning when I come back down here t' milk the cow. I brought one of the younguns with me—I had two then—and I brought one of the babies with me and set him down in here and I thought, "Well, he can stay in here until I can go milk the cow, surely." But we didn't have any fire built down here and I got uneasy about him and I just left the cow and didn't milk her at all and come back and got him and pulled back and went to the fire with him. I said the cow could just go till some other time! And she did.

Then we was able to sell some at the shop. This little old road was nothing but a dirt road at that time, but people would come by and stop sometimes. I remember one time—I'll never believe it was anybody else but President Roosevelt and his wife, 'cause I'd seen her picture too much, and his too. And they come along one cold morning. I was out down there boiling clothes, and I had my second girl out there on the porch. She was just a little thing, just big enough t' reach up t' th' banisters, and I had her fastened in with a little fence around the porch.

And [the lady] walked up and says, "What's the matter with [your little girl]?"

I says, "She's a-wanting out!"

"Well," she says, "she's *out!*"

I says, "She's not out on the *ground*, though." I says, "That's where she's a-wanting!" [laughing]

And she wanted to know what I was cooking down there. I told her I was a-boiling clothes. Had my battling stick pushing 'em down in the water letting 'em boil. Well, I understood her to say she'd never seen 'em washed that way. But I would think she *had*, as old as she was. I don't believe they was any washing machines at her young age. But they might of had a different system of it. I don't know.

Well, she come on up here then, and they was a pitcher a-setting there, and she said, "Where'd you get that pitcher?"

I says, "We *made* it."

And she says, "You make it in here?"

I says, "No." I said, "My husband makes 'em up the road yonder at a little building."

And she says, "You want to sell this pitcher?"

PLATE 34 "I rolled the grapes out on a board with the washing-machine roller and cut them in little squares about so big and then I'd roll them around in my hand. I cut the leaves out of the clay with a sharp-pointed knife. I put cobalt glaze on the grapes and on the leaves I put cobalt and chrome glaze."

I says, "Yes," I says, "I'll sell it to you. But," I said, "you can get more of 'em at the shop."

Says, "I want *this* one." Says, "What'll you take for it?"

"Well," I says, "a quarter, I guess."

"A *quarter!*" she says. "Why, that's just like giving it away!"

Well, it was, and she gimme more'n that for it. She gimme fifty cents for it! She just doubled it! So I don't know whether they stopped up there or not, but it sure did look like them. I'll never believe it was anybody else. [It was the beginning of the Depression]

PLATE 35   Chet Welch arranged a collection of Arie's work
on the back steps of her house for this portrait.

and I just figured they'd went down to Warm Springs, you know,
and spent some of the winter down there. But they didn't tell me
who they were. She was driving. They had a little dog. He was
leading the little dog and brought it out there and give it some
water. I remember seeing him walk back out toward the car. It looked
just exactly like him. Had on a big overcoat, and she had a big
fur coat on.

Now, I didn't know a thing about pottery before me and Cheever
was married. Right after him and me was married, I started helping
some around there. I helped 'em up there doing the things that
had to be done, like I'd carry the [green] pots out to dry, and carry
'em back in, and help load the kiln. But mostly, while Cheever was
making pots all the time, I was doing what had to be done in the
garden, and raising corn and all that—and children. I was in the
field most of the time while Cheever was in the shop, and when
bean picking time came, I'd can and pickle beans and kraut and
all that.

I did everything on that farm but plow. I've never plowed. I'll
tell you a little story about plows. My sister-in-law over here has a
son-in-law, and he was raised on a farm. And they was gonna plant

PLATE 36   A closeup of Arie's
peacock jar.

'em a bean patch down below the road yonder. And that son-in-
law hitched up the mule. Done all right hitching the mule up by
his wife helping him. And he got the plow and went on down there
in the field and tried to plow and just tried to plow and he tried
to plow. So he went back up there to the house where his mother-
in-law was and he said, "I just can't get that plow to go in the
ground to *save my life!*" He says, "I have tried and tried."

"Well," she says, "you and me'll go down there and I'll see what
I can do to help you." And she went down in the field to help
him see what was the matter, and she got down there, and he didn't
even have a plow point on! Trying to plow with that old round

nubby wooden thing! [laughing] She said she believed that was the hardest laugh she ever took in her life!

Anyway, I did everything *but* plow. We even raised cotton. We tried raising cotton every year after we married, and when the cotton would get grassy and needed hoeing pretty bad, Cheever had me and the younguns over there hoeing cotton. Well, I couldn't see we was doing any good with that cotton at all—and after all that work. So finally one year we made a bet, and we kept track all year of what we put in that cotton in seed and supplies and time, and we figured at the end we'd made twenty-five dollars all told. That was the end of that. Yeah, and we *didn't* do any more cotton after that, either! So I went t' work in the shop with him. I says, "We're gonna do *one* or the *other*." I says, "We'll work in the shop all the time, or," I says, "we'll work in the field all the time." And I says, "That takes you out a' th' shop!" He couldn't stand that. He *had* to work in the shop, you know. Cheever said a lot of times that he'd rather be a potter than do anything else he had ever done. I told him one day, I says, "I believe you'd work in that shop if you *knowed* we was gonna starve to death!" [laughing]

So I helped him a whole lot then. My oldest girl tended to the little ones while I was up at the shop, and then when they was in school, I could work in the shop, too. Cheever would make the big pieces and I'd decorate them for him. Now, I never took but one art lesson in my life. When I was about twelve years old, our teacher had finished high school down there at Franklin, and he come up there and got the job of teaching our school, and he had, I reckon, took art, and he wanted us to do things, you know. And so he give us a art lesson one day. Set objects up and let us draw 'em on paper just like they looked t' us. Well, by the time they all got one drawed, they didn't look alike! Looked like different things. But we tried it. Well, I always did like t' draw things. [But there weren't any other potters decorating their ware so she'd have patterns to go by.] Nobody there never had made any decorated stuff until I went t' making it. I just had it in me. I just wanted to do it. So that was just my own origination.

[But I still hadn't made any pots myself.] I'd go in the shop, and I could see all kinds of things in my head to make besides churns and pitchers. Oh, I could see vases and all kinda pretty bowls and things. And just t' watch 'em make a churn or anything else, why, it looked like it would be easy to make the other stuff, but they just wouldn't never get into it. One day I went in the shop, and the first thing that caught my eye was the prettiest little bowl.

It was sitting on the end of one of the boards, and it caught my eye, and I thought it was beautiful. I said, "Who made that pretty bowl!" They was three of 'em in there, and they got t' looking around and saw what I was looking at, and boy, they commenced t' laughing. They just laughed and laughed. Turned out it was a bed chamber! Cheever's brother had a five-gallon churn on his wheel he had just turned, and he got t' laughing so hard he hit that and just tore that churn down.

But I knew they woulda been a market for vases and things if they'da put it out. We just didn't put it out. We coulda sold a lot more than we could make. [But I couldn't get them to change.] I tried t' be boss of it, but I didn't do very good at it! [laughing] So I just kept quiet. My family was all pretty high-tempered, but my daddy taught me how t' hold it down. He told me it made me ugly! [Said softly, confidentially with a laugh] So I didn't say anything. I'd just stand and watch him a lot of times when he didn't know that I was watching him, to see what he done, and I seen how it was done. And the day I was sixty years old was the first time I put my hand on the wheel and tried to make anything.

It was along in the fall, and the weather had begun t' get cold. He just couldn't stand the cold weather, and he had quit for the day, and I just decided, "Well, now, while he's not working in there is a good time for me to get in there and see what I can do." I just wanted to get in there on that wheel so bad I couldn't hardly stand it. Just seemed to me like I couldn't keep my hands off that wheel. But I didn't attempt to while he was up there. So that day right after dinner, I pulled out and went up there and picked me up some wood as I went on and built me a fire in the little old stove. It wasn't too cold, but I didn't want t' stay in there without any fire. And I got me up some scrap clay that he'd throwed back and wadn't a-gonna use and I decided, "Well, I'll just work it up like he does. Do the best I can with it and put it on the wheel."

Well, *I* didn't have any trouble in centering it like a lot of people has. It just went right on with me! [laughing] But I couldn't get it into me how in the world he brought it *up* that way with his *hands.* Didn't take me long t' learn it, though. I found out you had t' put the elbow grease to it! That you had to *make* it come up there.

So when I went t' work in there, he come *right back* and we worked till the weather did get so cold that we couldn't stay in there. And next spring we went at it again along in February. At the first, I was just making some flat pieces. That was all that I could make. I couldn't bring [the ball of clay] up like he could, so I would make

PLATE 37 In 1968, when we first visited the Meaderses, Arie was still working up her own clay . . .

PLATE 38 . . . and turning ware daily.

flat plates and flat dishes. He watched me cut them off the wheel and every one of them would crack. I asked him one day, "What's the matter with this stuff? Is it me or the clay?"

He says, "It's you."

"Well," I says, "now what do I do to it that makes it crack that way?"

He says, "You watch me cut one off the wheel and you'll find out." He says, "You've got to keep that wheel going around as that wire cuts it off the wheel." I got to doing that and he was right. Then I learned how to pull the clay up. After that, we worked about thirteen years together until he got disabled to work.

It didn't seem to bother [Cheever] when the boys didn't want to make pottery. He just liked to get in [the shop] by himself. He didn't mind me being in there helping him but he just didn't want the boys in there. And they didn't want to be in [there] either. They'd rather have done anything in the world than [work in the shop]. They'd just nearly take a fit when they was called on to help set [the pottery] in the kiln.

But they would get in [the pottery] when Cheever wasn't in there and they would make a lot of little stuff and mess with the wheel.

[Cheever] said they'd tear it up every time they got in there.

The only one of [the children] that wanted to work in pottery was Lanier. I think he liked [pottery] from a child on up. He made a kiln of ware—churns and pitchers—and sold them when he was about sixteen years old. He had a lot of drawbacks, though. The rest of the Meaders family would come in and hinder and talk when they should have been somewheres working. Now, when you're making pottery, you don't want to be bothered.

That's why, when the pottery began to get well known, it made it hard on Cheever. In one way it was a help, because we sold more. See, this was the highway people began to travel to Florida on after it got paved and all, and people from New York and New Jersey and all up in there begin to come by, and they would pass and see them churns a-setting there and they'd have t' stop and *look* at 'em. One winter we unloaded the kiln and put the ware out on the ground and it snowed and the snow covered it up? Well, those people would come by there and stop and they'd scratch that stuff out of the snow to get it. So that kinda encouraged him a bit. But the bad part about that was that people would come along and want to take his picture, and he felt they were just taking up his time and it would be worth nothing to him. Why, it would just aggravate him to death. He said he could be making some [pottery] while they was talking to him and taking up his time. He had just kind of backward feelings about things like that. [He wasn't a person seeking publicity.] That was entirely out of his mind. He didn't think his stuff was that good. He thought the other fellow's stuff was probably better than his.

Like when Doris Ulmann come to make his picture, that made him mad. It'd tickle me t' hear him go on that way. It was *fun* to me t' have my picture made. I didn't care! And I seen one of Cheever's pictures up at Cullowhee, North Carolina. The oldest daughter was a-standing with her back t' th' camera looking up at her daddy just like she was saying, "Well, Daddy, what are you so mad about?" He was so mad he coulda bit a tenpenny nail in two! I could tell when he was mad, and he showed it in that picture, too! [laughing]

Then the Smithsonian came down to film him in '66. When they was down here making the picture, he was sick and he hadn't wanted me t' let 'em come. He said he just didn't want to fool with them. I told him to just take it easy and take it quiet. I says, "Cheever, it won't hurt you for 'em to come." It could be done without him having to do any of the work, and it was. I says, "I'll get Lanier t' do whatever it is that they want you t' do." And I says, "You just

PLATE 39   "To make the rooster, I started
with [clay cones]. I made [the base] one day
and let it harden till the next morning. And
then I made the body. I let that harden; then
I put the neck on. I put it right on there and
got enough slush out of the slush box to
soften it so it would stick to it. I just took a
ball of clay and worked its head in. [The head
and neck] was fresh made when I put them
on. Then I rolled some clay out to make the
gills and the comb.

"To make the tail, I rolled a piece of clay
out flat—used a washing-machine roller to do
it."

stand back." And I says, "It don't make no difference if they want
t' make a picture of it." Lanier had to take his place and pass as
him in making a churn, and oh, he just couldn't stand it t' save
his life. But he *did* get in there and turn some t' show 'em that he
did make it. He died the next year.

I've seen the movie. I went up to Washington and it was shown
in some room, a library they called it. I didn't know where I was.
[The occasion was the showing of the rough-cut version of the Smithsonian film about the Meaderses at the American Folklife Center
of the Library of Congress on their "Meaders Pottery Day" on March
17, 1978.] John Burrison took me, and Lanier went with us. Cheever
never got to go. That is what hurt me so bad, to think the likes of
that was going on and he couldn't get to see it. He would have
liked it. He didn't like Doris Ulmann taking his picture, either, but
after that book [Allen Eaton's *Handicrafts of the Southern Highlands*]
came out with that picture in it, he felt a little proud of it then.

After Cheever died, I worked on with Lanier for a few years longer.
I got started making owls when I saw the Pogo comic strip in the

PLATE 40 "The swan was just an idea I got in my head. I made two of 'em. Both of 'em cracked, but the other one wasn't as bad as this one. When I pulled it together, I pulled too hard."

Atlanta papers. And I made quails. I made some pottery hens and roosters that went in the Smithsonian. And I put leaves and grapes on Lanier's pots—decorated them for him. They all sold good. There's a lady up in Pittsburgh that come down and got a U-Haul load. She never had seen any made before, and her and her husband come down here and they got a U-Haul load and took it back up there, and she put it in a building—what we'd call a smokehouse— and she made a picture of them unloading it in that place and sent us a picture back. Well, last year her daughter come down here and brought a jug that she had got at that time and she says, "Mother has still got every piece of that ware." Now that was *last year*. She's getting pretty old, too. She ain't as old as I am, though!

But I reckon if they can do it [buy ware up and hold it] and they've got the money to put out t' buy it, I don't see anything wrong in it. I'd do it myself if it was me! I don't see a thing wrong with it. [The fact that others make the bulk of the profit off it]— well, goodness gracious. It's that way with everything that you buy and sell. Why, my goodness, you can't expect anything else.

PLATE 41

PLATE 42

PLATE 43

But they do tell a lotta big lies about it. Somebody went up into a gift shop somewhere—I don't know where it was at—and said they seen this piece a-sitting up there, way up high there, and it looked like a old piece, and that's what they was a-hunting—old pieces. And they thought *it* was a old piece. And oh, that feller told 'em it was *no telling* how old that thing was! "Why," he says, "you can *look* at it and tell it's been made a long time!"

And he says, "Well, I'd love t' get it down where I could see it good. I can't see it good up there." And they got it down and turned it up and there was Lanier's name on the bottom! He just started signing 'em in the last few years.

I'm not able to work in the pottery anymore. My legs give out. And I'm a diabetic, too. I thought when I had t' quit up at the shop that I was done for, but I wasn't. I says, "There's something else I can do besides work in the shop." And I says, "I can sew." So I just went t' sewing and crocheting and doing things like that. I don't do any more crocheting. It like t' put my eyes out. So I just quit doing that. Well, I'd got all I *wanted* anyhow. I'd learned how t' do it! I didn't care much about it, then. And so then I went t' doing other kinds of work—making pillers and cushions and things like that.

The children gave us a anniversary party when me and Cheever was married fifty-five years. In all, it was right around sixty years we was together. And I think he did have a good life. He got t' do what he wanted t' do! Back then we thought we were just the poorest people in the world. But when I look back, we had just as much as anybody.

When I was just a girl in North Carolina, I remember I'd wonder when we'd buy churns how in the world they made it. I just couldn't figure it out to save my life. I thought they'd wind a rope up or something or another, and then pack the clay, maybe—or whatever they made 'em out of. Didn't even know then they was made out of clay! Found out all about it, though. That was one good thing about the move to Georgia.

Interviews with and photographs of Arie Meaders and her work were by Bert Davis, Stephanie Short, Ronda Turpin, Chet Welch, and Rhonda Young.

Cheever and Lanier Meaders

The Old Ware

The largest pieces Cheever turned regularly for his area customers were six-gallon churns, and six- and seven-gallon jars for pickling beans or kraut or beets. These larger pieces each required twenty-two pounds of clay, and they were turned in two pieces (the top quarter first, and then the remainder, after which the two pieces were joined together on the wheel), both because it made the job slightly easier, and because if the churn were turned in one piece, there might not be enough clay left at the top to ensure the proper thickness of the upper quarter. (In the following chapter about Burlon Craig, plates 249–259 show him turning a large jar in two pieces, using a nearly identical process.)

Each churn had a shoulder and a wide flange inside the mouth to accommodate the churn's lid (which Cheever also made out of clay). The pickling jars, on the other hand, had almost no shoulder but rose nearly straight from the base to the narrow rolled lip which allowed a cloth to be tied tightly over the top.

Starting about eight o'clock in the morning, Cheever could turn seventy-five to a hundred gallons' worth of such large ware in a regular eight-hour day. He would weigh out and wedge four to five balls of clay at a time, turn those, and then work up more clay. After eating supper, he often would go back to the shop that same night and add the handles.

In addition to these large vessels, Cheever also regularly made three- and four-gallon churns, and one- to five-gallon jugs with narrow necks for liquor or syrup.

The smaller pieces he produced included what Cheever called "fruit cans." These were turned straight from base to top and had a flange that held a lid; they were produced in quart, half-gallon, gallon, and two-gallon sizes. Used to can fruit, they were sealed by pressing a cloth soaked in beeswax over the mouth and down into the flange or lip, and pressing the lid down onto the cloth. They were very popular at the time, and Arie remembers her mother filling such jars with apple butter, pumpkin butter, cooked apples, and blackberries. In the same four sizes were what Cheever called "broad-top pots"—the equivalent of today's buckets—used mostly for milking; and pitchers, for which there was a tremendous demand. Also he made the wide-mouthed, straight jars that Arie described as being used "to strain the milk up in so the cream would rise.

PLATE 44   Wig purchased the jar pictured here at an antique shop
in North Carolina for the Foxfire collection, not knowing who made
it. When it was shown to John Burrison, he was sure it had been made
by Cheever. We took it to Lanier to find out:
Lanier: "Who did John say made this?"
Wig: "Cheever."
Lanier [smiling]: "He did. He did. This is one of his earlier ones.
You see, it's kind of heavy here in the bottom? Well, he quit that after
he got a little more experience, but there was a reason that he would
do that. You know his elbow was broken on his left arm, and it was
stationary. He couldn't bend it. It was just frozen in that shape. And a
lot of times, he couldn't reach down in there. It probably bothered
him a lot of times, but he didn't say nothing about it. And he just
couldn't pull the clay out.
   "Another way you can tell is the way this top is shaped [with a broad
lip so a cloth could be easily tied over the top]. And the next thing is
the handle. He never put a straight handle on in his life. He just couldn't
do it—or he didn't want to. Or something. If you'll look at that—if
you can see it; I can—when he put a handle on, he'd always do *that*
to it [pushing upward on the base of the handle with his thumb]. Can
you see that thumb mark right in there? That little depression right in
there? He'd always put his thumb against it [and push up] and it would
compact the clay in this curve up here. If he didn't do that, the handle
would always crack right where it comes over here [at the top]. And
he didn't care if that made it a whole lot more crooked than it was!"
[laughing]

PLATE 45   The Cheever Meaders jar is the second from the right.
John Burrison thinks the two churns were made by Wiley Meaders. When
we showed them to Lanier, without telling him John's suspicions, he
said, "Well, the same man made both of these. Now this one [second
from the left in the photograph] is the first one I've ever seen marked
like that—marked [with the rings] that high up before. And this kiln
drip . . . It's pretty hard to tell actually who did do it. That pot is
light. Really, it's too light. This could be a Meaders. It could be a Wiley
Meaders pot. It could be. I guess it is. But still, this top and all, it's
lacking just a little bit. This rim in it is not deep enough, really. It
looks like one that he would have made in his earlier days, and I would
have to say that's what that is.

"Now, who did John say made it?"

When we asked Lanier why the potters didn't sign their work, he
said, "Just didn't take the time. It wasn't necessary. Never no necessity
for it. Now, without that, a collector don't want it. If it's something
that he can't prove what he's got, well, he don't want it."

Of the jug on the far right, Lanier said, "That's a syrup jug. Now
this handle, nobody around here ever put handles on like that. It could
be a Dorsey or a Craven or a Davidson. There's a lot of resemblance
of the Cravens in that."

Then we'd take a spoon and we'd cut it 'round and skim it off
into the churn into the milk that was milked the night before that,
and that would make a churning. And they'd be two gallon of it,
or two gallon and a half. So we'd make buttermilk there, and butter
too."

Cheever disliked making the smaller pieces, though, because, as
he said, "In the kiln we could of burnt a four-gallon churn" (in
the space taken up by a one-gallon pitcher). He also disliked making
face jugs, although he made a few of them to satisfy people's re-

PLATE 46   The same jars, turned to show their opposite sides.

quests. But they were "too much work. Time I make one, set it off, and get it decorated and fixed up, I could turn two pitchers."

Lanier can still, and sometimes does, turn the same shapes, carrying on the tradition. A large percentage of his time, however, is spent turning the face jugs for which he is renowned, and which have undergone a steady evolution from the rather primitive ones we took to the Smithsonian festival, to what can most nearly be described as the pieces of sculpture he shapes now.

The Clay and the Mud Mill

The clay Cheever used was dug from several different locations near the shop. In the early 1920s, for example, it came from the Cooley property, and Cheever paid the owner a dollar a wagonload for it. Later, he began hauling it in two-ton loads by truck from the Frank Miller property for fifteen dollars a load.

In nearly every case, Cheever had to dig a pit several feet deep, removing the overlying soil to get to the clay deposit beneath. He told Ralph Rinzler, "Yellow clay is always finer than white or blue clay. I try to get clay that's got as little grease in it as I possibly can. . . . Sometimes I throw it out [of the pit] a month or two months before I ever haul it out. After I get it up there, it's ready for grinding."

Up until 1960, the clay was ground in a mud mill—sometimes called a pug mill—pulled, in later years, by his mule, Jason. It would take roughly an hour to grind or process a millful. Edwin talked about the mill and its function in a recent interview we did with him for this book:

"It's not a pug mill. It's just a clay conditioner. What it does, we call it grinding. It takes the hard lumps out of it and just makes it all even, just like if you was making bread. It cuts [the hard lumps] in two as it comes around and just continually mixes it all together till it gets it all just the same firmness all the way through. It just conditions it so you can use it.

"It would take about an hour to condition it with a mule. When we were boys, we'd just hitch him in there and we'd tie the line around the post to the staff up there, and he'd just foller right on around. Had a thing we'd tie the bridle to, and he couldn't go *out* [away from the mill]. He could go *in* [toward the mill], but he never would go in. He was trying to stay *away* from that thing. And it'd work just fine. But they was one thing about them old mules. They soon learned whether they was anybody right behind them or not, and if they wasn't, they'd stop. When we was little, we'd have to walk behind that mule. His name was Pledge, and he'd stop if we didn't. So we'd go a few rounds—get over where he could see us and go round and round, and then we'd ease over a little where he couldn't see us and go a few rounds, and as we come to the corner of the shop there, and the door, we'd slip in the shop and he'd just keep going. He thought we was still behind him? Just keep a-going? Daddy'd *laugh* about that. Oh, we had some fun, I'm telling you. It was. We didn't know it back then, but now we *see* it was."

PLATE 47   On a visit in 1968, the mud mill—or pug mill—was still standing, though unused. Of the more formal name, "pug mill," Lanier says, "That all comes out of college and places like that. They didn't know what it was and they just give it a name. Course, it had been named 250 years ago, but them old names wasn't *adequate* for it!" [laughing]

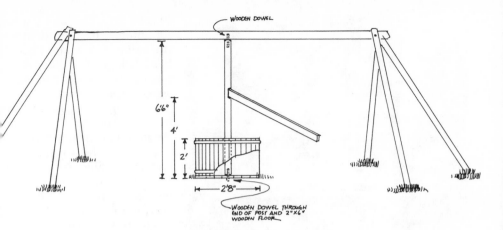

WOODEN DOWEL

6'6"

4'

2'

2'8"

WOODEN DOWEL THROUGH
END OF POST AND 2"×6"
WOODEN FLOOR

PLATE 48

PLATE 49 When the mill is constructed, a hole is drilled into either end of the vertical pole or "staff" Lanier is pointing at. Into each hole, a white-oak pin or dowel at least an inch and three-quarters in diameter and six inches long is inserted. The end of one pin goes through the flooring of the mill, which is made of two-by-sixes and two-by-eights resting flat on the ground. The end of the other pin goes into the horizontal pole overhead. In this way the staff is held in place, but it can still rotate.

PLATE 50 The wooden be[ar]
the mule is harnessed to wh[ich]
the mill is in operation is visi[ble]
here. Lanier's right foot rests [on]
one of two wooden counters [on]
which the finished clay [is]
blocked up before being carri[ed]
into the shop. As the mule tur[ns]
the mill, Lanier says, "You ca[n]
imagine all the squeaky nois[es]
and everything. It sounds l[ike]
old screaking doors on [a]
hainted buildings. Just re[al]
creepy. Real ghostly-like."

The two students in the ph[o]tograph are Greg Strickland a[nd]
David Wilson.

PLATE 51 Looking down into the mill, half-filled with leaves, two of
the nine oak pegs are visible. There are three rows of three pegs each,
staggered so that no two run the same course. "Those pegs are mostly
flat on the bottom and rounded off on top and that gives the clay upward
lift. When them things go around, they leave [an open] place behind
them, and the clay rolls back into that open spot and then another
peg comes along and cuts it again and keeps it rotating all the time.
[You have to be careful because] you can get too many of them things
in there. You can put so many pegs in there that it'll choke itself. It'll
just pick up *all* the clay and just slide it around and around in one
lump. Now that's what happened [in the motor-driven mill with a metal
shaft and blades Lanier had built to replace the wooden mill], and me
trying to get that old boy not to do it that way. I tried to explain him
how to do it, but he can only do things *his* way. You can't tell him
how you want anything done or you get him all outa sorts and he can't
do it at all. But he put too many teeth in it, and I had to take a hacksaw
and saw some of them out."

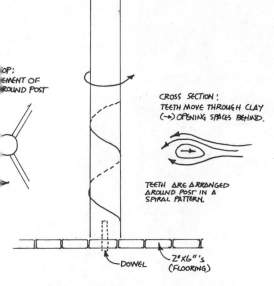

OP:
EMENT OF
ROUND POST

CROSS SECTION:
TEETH MOVE THROUGH CLAY
(→) OPENING SPACES BEHIND.

TEETH ARE ARRANGED
AROUND POST IN A
SPIRAL PATTERN.

DOWEL   2"x6"'s
(FLOORING)

PLATE 52

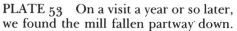

PLATE 53   On a visit a year or so later, we found the mill fallen partway down.

PLATE 54   Several months later, it had collapsed. Now it is gone completely, but Lanier talks occasionally of reconstructing it. He has used one so many times, however, that he's not sure he'll ever actually run one with a mule again. As he says, "I'd like to see someone hook a Jersey milk cow to it, or four or five goats or something like that; but I've seen all I want of one run by a mule. Besides, I don't like to work that good."

PLATE 55　A tractor-powered mill stands outside Lanier's shop now. Clay is dumped into the hopper on top and fed in between two horizontal metal rollers that crush it into powder. Then it is mixed with water in the motor-driven mill in his shop (described in the caption for Plate 51).

Lanier: "I'm using two kinds of clay now. I bought two loads of Ocmulgee clay at thirty dollars a load, and I bought a couple of loads from Banks County, and so now I believe I've got all the clay I'll ever need. I mix them together—three-fourths Ocmulgee clay and one-fourth Banks County [feldspar-based] clay, and that works awful good. It works good on the wheel, and it fires good and glazes good."

Turning the Ware

Inside the shop, the tools and equipment Lanier uses are basically the same ones Cheever used. Though the treadle wheel he turns ware on is not the same one Cheever employed, it is the same style. The homemade ball opener is Cheever's (used to open the ball of clay and set the proper thickness of the bottom of each piece), as is the set of scales, made from a wooden beam and various pieces of cast-off junk for weights. As Cheever described it to Ralph Rinzler,

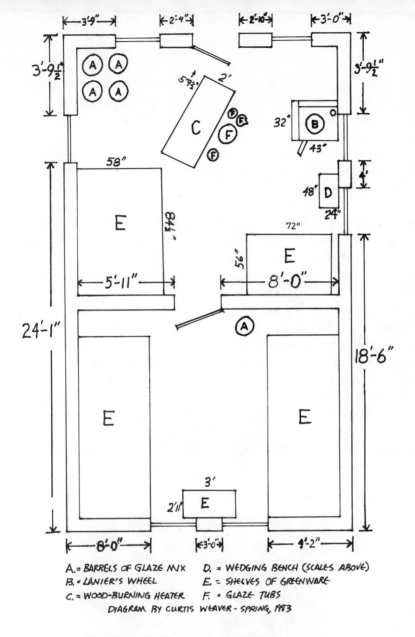

PLATE 56 Floor plan of Lanier's shop.

"That piece hanging down for the weigh balance come off a road scrape that broke down out there and they throwed it out in the field. We just got that and made us a weight." The other weights are made up of such items as a ballpeen hammerhead, "a plow point from a one-horse turning plow, a piece of the wing that come off a one-horse turner, and a gopher point that went on a single-foot. I picked up all that junk to put together and I had my weights like I wanted them pretty quick." Cheever used the scales, of course, to weigh out the amount of clay needed to accomplish the various pieces he was making: twenty-two pounds for a six-gallon churn, ten pounds for a one-gallon piece, and five pounds for a half-gallon piece.

To turn pieces to the proper height, Cheever used what he called a "measuring stick," or height gauge, still in use today. When making a piece, he set the tip of the pointer at the height the piece should be when finished: twelve inches for a one-gallon piece, fourteen inches for a two-gallon (which also had a greater diameter), and so on. The combination of the proper amount of clay, turned to the proper height, and old-fashioned experience generally guaranteed the results. No gauge was needed for the diameter of each piece—that was pure experience alone.

Cheever's iron lifters, used to transfer the finished piece from the wheel's headblock to a drying shelf after the piece had been cut from the wheel with a piece of wire, were made in a local blacksmith shop following a pattern conceived by Bill Dorsey. Lanier still uses them today. He also still uses the smoothing chips that smooth the outside of the vessel and can also inscribe the incised line or lines around its shoulder, as it is turning on the headblock.

And so if Cheever were able to return to his old shop, he would see much that he recognized and would probably take much satisfaction in the fact that what he left behind is not gathering dust.

PLATE 57 The scales Cheever described are the same ones being used today.

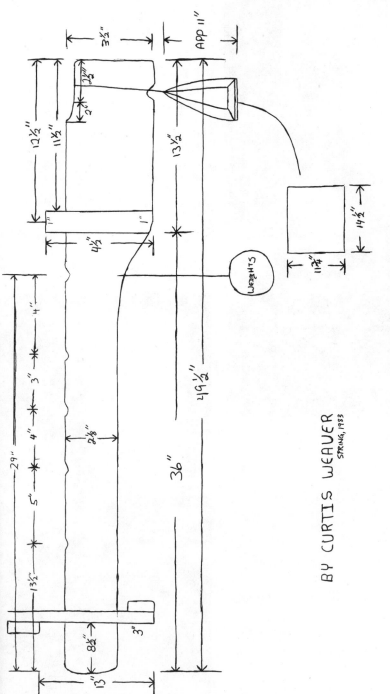

BY CURTIS WEAVER
SPRING, 1983

PLATE 58 Cheever's scales.

PLATE 59 These two photographs, taken in the late sixties, show Lanier opening a ball of clay on the wheel with the ball opener. The same ball opener and wheel are still in use today.

PLATE 60

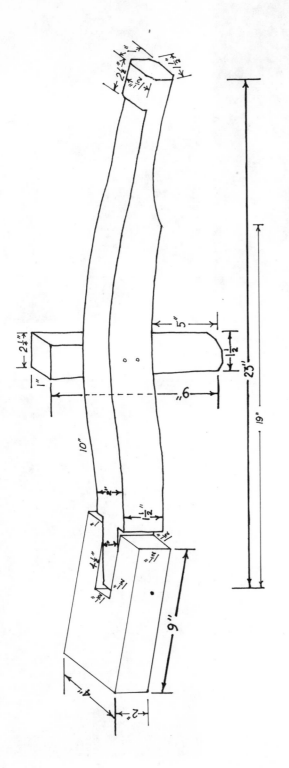

DIAGRAM BY JERRY TAYLOR

PLATE 61   Lanier's ball opener.

PLATE 62 Lanier shaping a vase in the late sixties.

PLATE 63

PLATE 64

PLATE 65   A photograph of Arie taken at the same time shows the simple but efficient height gauge she and Lanier employed. When in use, to indicate the height a gallon piece should be, the pointer was set at twelve inches above the surface of the wheel, and the piece was turned to the pointer's tip.

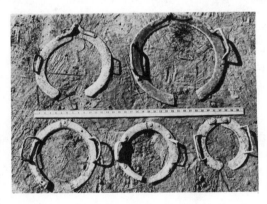

PLATE 66   These lifters, made by a local blacksmith, were used by Cheever and are still in use today.

Glazes

Though Cheever at one time turned flowerpots that were not glazed and were therefore porous, nearly all his other ware was glazed so that it would hold liquids and not seep or leak. His earliest glaze, which he called his "Shanghai" glaze, was made simply of "settlings"—silt that had been deposited over the years by a stream flowing into an abandoned millpond nearby—ashes and a silica-bearing material such as sand or, later, powdered glass, and water. The ashes acted as a melting agent and helped hold the glaze on the pottery. Cheever preferred the hardwood oak ashes from which his neighbors had already leached the lye to make soap. These ashes did not burn his skin as those still containing lye did. In addition, since pine ashes "flowed" on the pottery too much—required more settlings, and thus also required more kiln heat to melt because of the additional settlings—he felt the hardwood ashes were the best choice. The proportions, according to Cheever in the interview with Ralph, were three measures of the ashes to one or two measures of settlings (depending on what type of ashes were used), and enough water to make a thick, smooth liquid that was ground between the glazing rocks two or three times before being used. The result was a brownish glaze. When discussing the proportions, Cheever offered a useful caution, warning that the proportions differ according to a number of variables. "A fella's just got to be his own judge about it." If it was made too thin, however, the glaze would not coat the ware evenly.

Sometimes he also added a measure of white sand to the glaze (according to Cheever, three of ashes, one of settlings, and one of white sand). Arie described where he got this sand:

"He has used that white sand in ash glaze too. Used to go right over yonder in the woods the other side of the creek yonder. They was a path that went out through there—used to go to the old Northwestern Depot. That was the train that went to Helen during the time that Matthews Lumber Company was up there. It was built for that. Well, after all that quit up there, then, the railroad was tore out and done away with. And he used to go over here and get some of the prettiest, whitest sand, and it was fine, too. And after a rain, you could go and rake up just a whole lot of it. It'd wash in there, you know. And that made pretty glaze."

For a dark reddish brown or black color, a measure of iron sand was added—a dark sand that accumulated in a ditch beside a road about four miles from his shop.

As glass became available, a measure of powdered glass was often substituted for the measure of sand, since it melted at a lower heat. As Arie said, "I'd go around to the neighbors' and pick up all the broken fruit jars and bottles they had, and after they found out that I wanted to use it, they'd pile it up for me—heap it in a box. He was lucky one year. They was a Coke truck turned over at the end of the road and broke a great big pile of bottles there, and he used that." He broke the glass up as much as possible by putting pieces in a metal crankcase cover and beating them with the end of an iron rod. The rest of the job was accomplished between the glaze rocks.

When the commercially produced Albany slip became available to Cheever in the early 1900s, he sometimes used it in place of the settlings. He might also use whiting in place of the crushed glass. But despite the fact that these ingredients greatly simplified the task of making glaze, he also continued to employ the others, for there were sometimes disadvantages in cutting corners. The disadvantage he found with Albany slip, for example, was that it did not flow as easily as the Shanghai glaze and thus did not run and fill any imperfections or porous areas in the walls of the ware.

He expanded his glaze repertoire even further with a grayish glaze made of lime, clay, and white sand. He explained to Ralph how the lime was obtained:

"Above Clarkesville, over there, they had a big lime kiln where they burnt it. Well, if it stayed out in the air long enough it would do what they call 'slaking,' but if it didn't, they'd have to bring it in and spread it out and put a little water on it and it would go to smoking and smoke just exactly like something that caught afire.

PLATE 67   On an early visit, Foxfire student Greg Strickland helped Lanier dig settlings. When we showed this photograph to Lanier recently he said, "This was going down in the pasture over there and digging our settlings. There used to be an old millpond over there, and all the silt washed in from off the hill up above and settled into it. It was real fine clay, and it had good melting properties, and that's what we used to make the glaze out of. That, ashes, glass, and flint sand. Then we'd grind it in that rock out there and make it into the glaze. That made a 'tobacco spit' glaze that was black striped stuff."

PLATE 68   The glaze mill, still in use in the late sixties when these photographs were taken, is no longer usable as the action of the top rock turning in the bed stone has now worn through the bed stone itself. When first put into use, the top surface of the bed stone was completely flat. Lanier: "That thing *wore out* [concave] that way. When that [glaze mill] was first started, this [top] rock was just set right flat down on the other one and clay packed around it to hold [the glaze] in. And then the top rock just wore its way through the other one."

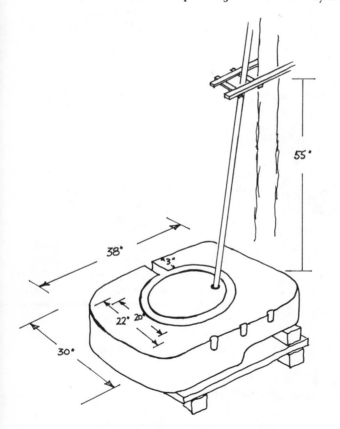

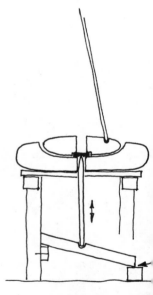

DRIVING WOODEN WEDGE UNE
END OF BEAM RAISES TOP RO
INCREASING GRINDING DISTANC
BETWEEN ROCKS,

PLATE 69   Lanier's glaze mill, no longer in use.

PLATE 70 "What I'm pointing at here is the hole for an iron shaft that goes down through this bottom rock. That shaft was a brake rod off a wagon."

PLATE 71 "This end of the shaft up here was sharpened. This iron cross just sat on the end of that point, and the [underside of the] top rock, you know, had them depressions cut out in it [in the shape of a cross] and the cross just fit in them flush.

"Now the bottom end of that shaft sat [under the mill] on a wooden beam, and one end had wedges under it. If the top rock was too tight—too close—why then you'd just tap those wedges and raise it up a little bit. So that shaft and cross is to hold the top rock off the bottom rock a little bit just like on a gristmill. If the top rock is too close, the glaze won't go down in it, and if it is too far open [apart], it won't grind. It has to be set just right."

The groove cut into the far side of the bed stone is where the ground glaze runs out.

PLATE 72   To grind, the top rock was set in place and a flowerpot with the bottom knocked out of it was set over the central hole in the top rock. With clay packed around its base, the flowerpot acted as a funnel for the raw ingredients of the glaze to be poured into. Those ingredients usually included settlings, ashes, sand, and/or glass in a water base. If glass, it would have been pulverized already ("We beat the glass up with a long iron rod and mostly main strength and awkwardness"), but between the grinding surfaces of the two rocks it would be powdered even further.

PLATE 73   "You see that iron rod I've got there? I've got that top rock prized up and I'm pouring water under it to unstick it. After it's used, there's always some glaze that's left in there, you know, and it dries out and sticks and you have to loosen it before you can grind again."

PLATE 74   Then Lanier would pour the glaze mixture into the flowerpot funnel . . .

PLATE 75   . . . and grasp the wooden pole and begin to spin the top rock. The glaze would flow out the groove cut in the bottom rock "in little squirts." If the rocks were too far apart, "It wouldn't be grinding the stuff that went through it. When you feel of the glaze, you can tell whether it's ground or not. If it's coming out too coarse, why then you have to let the top rock down. Just ease the wedge out a little bit [from under the beam the iron rod rests on at the bottom] and take another iron pin or something—whatever you want— and chug down on the end of that thing in there and that would let it down a little. And a lot of times, you wouldn't have to mess with the wedge. Just [making a tapping motion] tap it down."

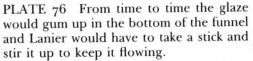

PLATE 76   From time to time the glaze would gum up in the bottom of the funnel and Lanier would have to take a stick and stir it up to keep it flowing.

PLATE 77 "There I'm mixing glaze—dipping it up and pouring it back out. That's the best way to do it—dipping."

PLATE 78 When the glaze is the right consistency, Lanier eases a dried jar into the tub . . .

PLATE 79 . . . and spins it several times to coat the inside and outside completely. Then he sets it on a counter to dry before firing.

PLATE 80 "That's a base for a lamp I turned. You see where the glaze is squirting out at the back? That's where the hole is to run the cord out of."

PLATE 81 When glazing a piece with a small neck, like a face jug, Lanier submerges the jug completely, lets it fill partially full with glaze . . .

PLATE 82 . . . swirls it around to coat the inside completely, and then pours the excess out.

PLATE 83 Lanier's face jugs have undergone a steady evolution in the sixteen years we have been visiting him. Compare these, made in October of 1982 and awaiting the glazing process, with those in Plates 23 and 24.

PLATE 84 When the glaze is dried, Lanier scrapes it off the bottom
of the ware. Since the inside of the ware is glazed, the pieces will still
hold liquid. "I scrape the glaze off the bottom of the jugs before I
put them in the kiln so sand and stuff won't stick to the bottom. Leave
that glaze on there and when it's melted, it'll pick up a ton of sand
right quick."

And you'd see that rock begin to fall all to pieces. Well, after it quit smoking, leave it alone a little bit and that was your lime just as fine as it could be. But you never saw anything smoke so in your life. You couldn't lay your hand near it. It'd burn it. Well, after a while all that smoke'd quit, and then you had some good lime."

When Lanier took over, the glaze mill was still in operation and he continued the ash glaze tradition as well as experimenting with glazes of his own, such as one that combined ashes, Albany slip, and whiting. Later he made one of the same clay from which the ware was made, and Albany slip mixed with ashes and whiting. Either that later glaze or some variation is the one he still uses, though the continuing experimentation that takes place around an operation like the Meaderses' may have already made that statement false.

Kilns

As with the glazes and the ware itself, kiln design is subject to constant experimentation and changes as old kilns give way and are replaced. Despite the numbers of kilns that have been built at the Meaders operation, and the resulting years of experience, the new experiments sometimes do not work. In Lanier's newest kiln, for example, built in the late spring of 1983, the curve of the arch is a perfect half circle (much like the prototype in the kiln that immediately preceded it) rather than the squat semicircle of the earlier ones, and this seems to work well; but the two draft holes in the firebox end have proved to be too small, and Lanier was about to enlarge them as we delivered the manuscript for this book to New York.

Cheever's kilns, like Lanier's, were usually of the railroad tunnel variety, built on top of the ground with sidewalls eighteen to twenty-four inches high. The arch was built first, and the front—or breast—end and the chimney added last. The approximately 400 gallons' worth of ware they held was loaded through an opening in the chimney end (which was closed with bricks and clay when the kiln was being fired) up until the time he built his final kiln. On that kiln, he decided to both load and fire through a door at the firebox end, a change he seemed to like. A new kiln could usually be built in four days to a week, and the amount of time it would last depended on factors such as how often it was used—but usually two years or more. Often the same homemade clay bricks that were used in the early kiln were recycled in the new, supplemented as needed by commercially produced red clay bricks (not firebrick).

Cheever also once tried a groundhog kiln (the same basic design, but set into the ground so that the top of the arch is nearly level with the top of the ground as in Burlon Craig's kiln), but though it worked, the design was not used again.

Another aspect of kiln design that has undergone some change is the opening through which the fuel is added to the fire in the firebox. In Cheever's early kilns, the wood was loaded through the sidewall of the firebox, allowing him to use longer slabs to fire with. A door in the center of the firebox's front wall was also tried, but it required shorter, four-foot slabs. It must have been satisfactory, however, as every kiln built at the Meaderses' since Cheever's death has had the same feature.

Lanier's first kiln, built after Cheever's death, was the same as Cheever's last kiln (railroad tunnel, sidewalls, arch made using Cheever's old arch boards, and fired through the center of the firebox end), but Lanier returned to the door in the chimney end for loading and unloading ware. Lanier also tried electric oil furnace blowers with fuel oil to supplement the pine slabs (which were still required at the end of the burn to raise the kiln temperature to the proper heat required to melt the glaze—about 2300°). This innovation made firing easier—an important factor since Lanier had just had a heart attack—but he has since returned to burning exclusively with wood, and to loading and unloading ware through the firebox end.

In all these kilns, the ware is placed on the sand-covered ware floor with the larger pieces at the chimney end to keep them from blocking the heat or being damaged by the flames. Shorter ware is placed behind the low protective firewall that separates the firebox itself from the ware floor.

When firing—a process that takes ten to twelve hours, depending on the clay and the weather conditions and the wood—either hardwood or green pine slabs from a local sawmill are used in a low fire to temper the ware gradually. The amount of wood and frequency of adding to the fire is increased as time goes on until the final "blasting off" phase, where pine is used exclusively to create the intense heat needed in the last hour or so. A removable brick near the bottom of the chimney affords a peephole through which the potter can see both the ware itself and—if used—the cones, each made of a flat piece of clay with a finger-sized lump of dried glaze. When the glaze is melted and slick, the ware is finished and the firing stops. A day or so later, after the kiln and ware have cooled, the ware is removed for sale.

PLATE 85 Kilns are frequently dismantled, redesigned, and rebuilt in any operation like the Meaderses'. As Lanier said, "Most of the brick in his [Cheever's] kiln, he had used them over and over and it seemed like it never hurt them, but they were homemade bricks and they were made out of clay that would take it." Of the kiln designs, he said, "It's all just by golly and mostly hope you hit it. [You don't have to worry about them drawing from the fire pit end through the kiln to the chimney.] They always draw *too* well. The next one I build, I'm gonna choke it down. Have three flues in the chimney all the way up to the top. Really it'll just be three chimneys, and each flue will have one. And that'll be the last chimney I'll ever build. I won't never need another one. I really don't need the one I've got. What I'm saying is, one more building'll do me as long as I'll ever be able to do anything."

In this photograph, taken in the late sixties, the remains of Cheever's last kiln, looking from the fire pit down the inside left wall toward the chimney, reveal some aspects of its construction. The wall then, as in the kiln Lanier is using currently, was the length of one brick wide. The bricks were turned a different direction in alternating courses, and placed so no seams matched [see Plate 87]. After the wall was about eighteen inches high, arch boards were set in place, the row of log and rock backing was set to brace the base of the dome, and the dome was built.

PLATE 86 One of the old arch boards used when constructing a kiln's dome. Of the number needed, Lanier said, "Well, it really don't matter as long as they're not too far apart where the dome'll swag down. They can be close, or they can be six feet apart, but not more than six feet."

Strips of wood are nailed to the top of the arch boards to form a solid roof, the dome is built of brick over that, and then the arch boards and strips are removed.

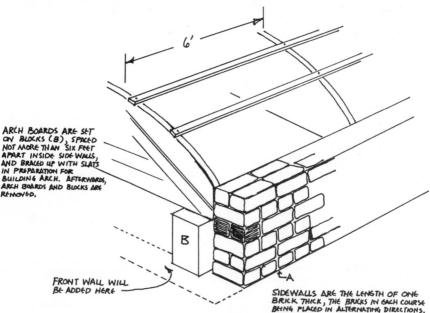

ARCH BOARDS ARE SET ON BLOCKS (B), SPACED NOT MORE THAN SIX FEET APART INSIDE SIDE WALLS, AND BRACED UP WITH SLATS IN PREPARATION FOR BUILDING ARCH. AFTERWARDS, ARCH BOARDS AND BLOCKS ARE REMOVED.

FRONT WALL WILL BE ADDED HERE

SIDEWALLS ARE THE LENGTH OF ONE BRICK THICK, THE BRICKS IN EACH COURSE BEING PLACED IN ALTERNATING DIRECTIONS. PERIODICALLY, HALF-BRICKS ARE USED (DARKENED) TO OFFSET A COURSE AND BREAK A WEAK JOINT (A).

PLATE 87

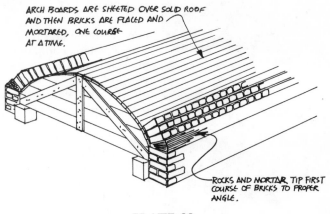

PLATE 88

PLATE 89   In July 1983, Cleater Meaders, Jr. (yet another potter in the Meaders family; his father, who was also a potter, was Cheever's brother) built a kiln for himself patterned after his father's. The design and construction techniques are very similar to those used by both Lanier and Edwin for their kilns.

In this photograph, the sidewalls (which are seven courses of brick high and 10′ 9″ in length) are complete, and Cleater is constructing the arch, or dome. The arc for the plywood arch boards was determined by the arc that a logging chain assumed when hung against a piece of plywood and allowed to droop from the two points Cleater had established as the length of the base line (55″) to the point he had selected for the height of the arch (23″). Note that on top of both sidewalls, one row of bricks laid end to end serves to tip the first course of arch bricks up.

PLATE 90 The bricks Cleater used were firebricks he had obtained from a kiln used once by a brickmaking company. The cement mixture he used was nine parts of white sand, four parts of masonry cement, and one part regular cement. The cement was placed between each course so that it was thickest at the outside edge, serving not only to help tip each course up but also to keep to an absolute minimum the amount of cement showing inside the arch. The bricks were also cemented edge to edge except between every fourth and fifth brick—left uncemented to allow for expansion during firing. As each course was completed, Cleater simply laid several more pine strips on top of the arch boards, not nailing them down, and continued working toward the center from either side. Note that every other course begins with a brick split in half lengthwise to stagger the joints.

PLATE 91 With the last row of bricks hammered down into place to wedge the arch, Cleater cemented over the top of the last five courses and signed his name and the names of his children in the wet cement. After the cement set up, using a crowbar he simply knocked out the columns of loose bricks supporting the arch boards. As the four arch boards were removed, the strips of wood they had once held up fell to the ground inside the kiln and the arch stood alone.

PLATE 92   With the arch boards removed, Cleater had room inside the kiln to build the flash wall. The base of the wall was made of three courses of bricks laid flat, set so their edges paralleled the sidewalls and only their ends were visible. The next courses (each one brick wide) were laid on that base, their bricks set end to end as seen in this photograph. At the top of the flash wall, as an experiment Cleater left a row of openings, knowing that if the pots behind it got scorched, he could always go back and fill the openings easily before firing again. Then he shoveled earth and a layer of sand in behind the wall to form the ware bed.

PLATE 93   Next, Cleater built the breast end of the kiln. In this photograph the draft holes and the door have been established, and the finished flash wall is visible behind. During a test firing after the kiln was completed, and with the door blocked except for the firing hole, Cleater showed us how he could regulate the intensity of the blaze simply by inserting bricks into or removing them from the two draft holes.

PLATE 94 With a piece of heavy angle iron placed across the top of the doorway, Cleater was able to finish the end. The two blackened bricks whose ends are visible at the top of this photograph are two of four bricks that Cleater salvaged from his father's kiln and set into his own for good luck.

PLATE 95 The breast end complete, Cleater moved to the other end of the kiln to begin the chimney. The inside wall was kept solid up to the top of the ware floor.

PLATE 96 Then Cleater, with six columns of bricks each four bricks high, established the five flue holes. He also, at this stage, created the two-brick-high peephole in the outside chimney wall through which he would be able to observe the ware during firing.

PLATE 97 That done, Cleater finished the chimney, keeping the walls two bricks thick until the chimney was nearly to the roof line of the kiln shed. Then he stepped the thickness down to one brick and tapered the walls in to close the opening slightly. Several weeks later he burned a kiln of ware, and we were there to get this photograph.

PLATE 98   The kiln Lanier was using in the late sixties. "That picture was made from the chimney looking toward the fire pit. There's the back wall of the fire pit—you know, the flash wall that keeps the flames from hitting the pots.

"This kiln didn't have a row of [keystone-shaped bricks] down the center of the dome. There was supposed to be, but there wasn't. We just packed that with old pieces of shards that we drove down into it that kept it from caving in."

PLATE 99   The inside of the same kiln, looking toward the chimney end. The kiln was loaded through the center opening (a person is visible, squatting down, just beyond it).

PLATE 100 David Wilson helping Lanier load ware into the kiln pictured in the preceding two photographs.

PLATE 101 Lanier setting the ware in preparation for firing. Then, as now, no ware was stacked. "There's just one layer of glazed ware."

PLATE 102 Looking from the fire pit toward the chimney through the loaded kiln.

PLATE 103   Before the firing, Lanier made up a set of cones. "I make them out of the glaze and set them in the bottom of the chimney. That's to tell when it's done. They melt at about 2300° F. I roll them out after the glaze has dried out enough to roll."

PLATE 104   A set of cones after a firing.

PLATE 105 Before firing the old kiln, Lanier would brick up the door in the chimney end through which he had loaded the ware.

PLATE 106 Then he would seal the door over with red mud.

PLATE 107 One brick in the chimney door was left loose so that it could be removed during firing in order to observe the cones.

PLATE 108   During this period in the late sixties and early seventies, Lanier used a combination of pine slabs . . .

PLATE 109   . . . and fuel oil to fire the kiln. Here he checks the level of oil in the storage tank.

PLATE 110   The oil burner was placed just outside the kiln at the fire pit end. "I used mostly wood to start with, but when it come time to have to stand up here and poke wood to that thing, at that time I wasn't able to do it. I was trying to get over that blasted heart attack, and it seemed like it just wouldn't go away. So at that time I needed all the help I could get on it, and that oil was one way of doing it. I use just wood altogether, now. I'm feeling the best I've felt in twenty years."

PLATE 111 The burn begins with slabs of pine thrown off the storage pile toward the kiln . . .

PLATE 112 . . . and cut up into smaller lengths with a chain saw. "The length I cut the slabs into just depends on how long the pieces are, and whether I can saw three [equal] pieces out of it, or two."

PLATE 113 The kiln is heated steadily for hours until time for the final "blasting off" phase. "There at the last, I was throwing wood, oil, and everything I could throw at it. Right along there, there was some hard going."

PLATE 114 During the "blasting off" phase, when the temperature inside the kiln is at its highest, flames shoot out of the chimney into the night sky.

PLATE 115   The end.

PLATE 116   A day or so later, after the kiln has cooled off, the bricks are removed from the door and the finished ware unloaded. In this photograph, taken in the mid seventies, Lanier had rebuilt the kiln and had left a larger door in the chimney than in his previous one.

PLATE 117   The kiln Lanier used until the spring of 1983. This kiln's dome was arched higher than those of previous ones, and it was loaded through the fire pit end instead of the chimney end.

PLATE 118 Looking down the outside of the dome toward the chimney, the increased curve of the dome is visible; in this case, in Lanier's words, a "half circle. And it don't need all them braces on the side of it to hold it up. If it's a perfect half circle, that thing will hold itself up."

PLATE 119 Nevertheless, as in previous kilns, Lanier had the base of the dome securely braced. In this case, mortar was used between the bricks in the dome instead of red clay mud. It burned through and dropped out in many places. When the kiln was being fired, Lanier said, "You can see through every crack in it. It just takes a little bit more wood, and it really don't matter. The fire is still confined in it, and that's what you want."

PLATE 120 When the chimney on Lanier's kiln partially collapsed in April of 1983, he removed it. Without the chimney, the construction of the end of the arch was easily visible . . .

PLATE 121 . . . and one could see how the sidewalls and arch were braced.

PLATE 122 Between the vertical log posts and the kiln's sidewall, and behind the brick column visible here, is a long trough filled with dirt for insulation against the sidewall.

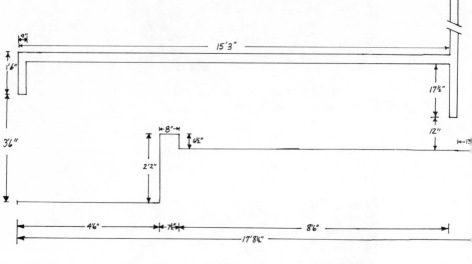

DIAGRAM BY CURTIS WEAVER
FALL, 1982

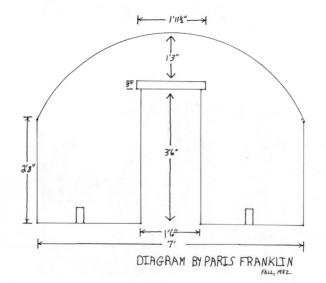

DIAGRAM BY PARIS FRANKLIN
FALL, 1982

PLATE 123   The front of Lanier's old kiln.

PLATE 124   Curtis Weaver measuring the inside of the kiln Lanier
stopped using in 1983. Beyond him, the flues in the base of the chimney
are barely visible. In this case, instead of three large flues as in the
previous kilns, Lanier had a row of smaller ones across the entire end
[see Plate 125].

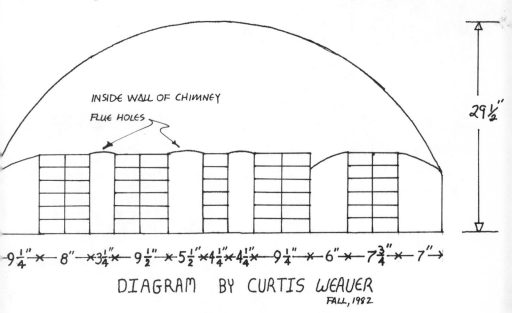

INSIDE WALL OF CHIMNEY

FLUE HOLES

$29\frac{1}{2}''$

$9\frac{1}{4}''$ $8''$ $3\frac{1}{4}''$ $9\frac{1}{2}''$ $5\frac{1}{2}''$ $4\frac{1}{4}''$ $4\frac{1}{4}''$ $9\frac{1}{4}''$ $6''$ $7\frac{3}{4}''$ $7''$

DIAGRAM BY CURTIS WEAVER

FALL, 1982

PLATE 125

PLATE 126   The fire pit end.

PLATE 127   To fire the kiln, Lanier bricked up part of the fire pit door after loading the ware in, making sure to leave two small draft holes in the bottom.

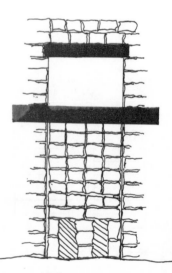

PLATE 128   The door was bricked partway up, and then a steel beam was fitted into place on top of the last row of bricks. The remaining hole is the one through which Lanier shoved pine slabs during the firing.

Richard L. Trusty

PLATE 129

PLATE 130 After a recent firing, Chet Welch, Milton Brock,
and Curtis Weaver help unload
the ware. Of the face jug in
Chet's left hand, Lanier said,
"That jug there looks like somebody's in real misery!"

PLATE 131 If there are beads
of glaze left around the bottom
edge of any of the pieces, Lanier
grinds them off before selling
the piece.

PLATE 132 Two ash-glazed
pitchers from a recent firing.

PLATE 133 Ready for sale:
face jugs, pickling jars, dishes,
bowls, and pitchers.

PLATE 134   The new kiln Lanier built in the spring of 1983.

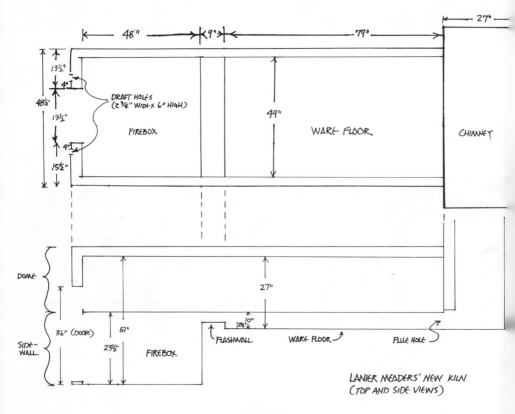

LANIER MEADERS' NEW KILN
(TOP AND SIDE VIEWS)

PLATE 135

PLATE 136   The new chimney
is stepped in in two places. At
its base, the three removable
bricks are visible. When these
are slipped out, the holes afford
Lanier a view of the ware and
cones inside the kiln when it is
being fired.

PLATE 137

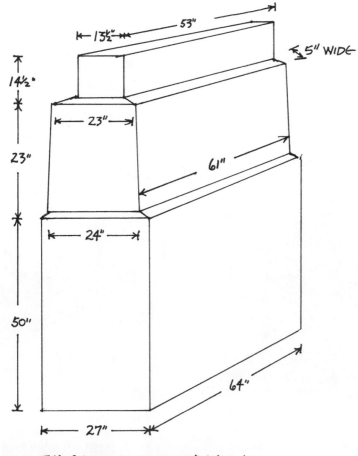

THE CHIMNEY ON LANIER'S NEW KILN

PLATE 138

PLATE 139 The arch of the new kiln is a perfect half circle.

PLATE 140 Dirt is piled up against part of the sidewall.

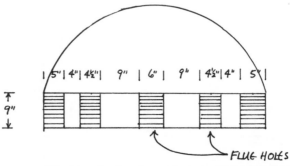

| 5" | 4" | 4½" | 9" | 6" | 9" | 4½" | 4" | 5" |

9"

FLUE HOLES

THE CHIMNEY END (INSIDE) OF LANIER'S NEW KILN

PLATE 141

PLATE 142 On either side of the door, at the base, a draft hole is visible. Lanier has found that they are too small and plans to enlarge them before he fires the kiln again.

PLATE 143 The front wall of the new kiln is braced by a horizontal log held tightly against it by cables with turnbuckles tied to the log posts that support the roof.

Edwin Meaders

Arie Meaders and John Burrison thought that we should interview the latest member of their pottery-making family. As Edwin had no phone, we took off for Cleveland, Georgia, not knowing whether he would even be there. As we pulled up into Edwin's drive, we could see smoke billowing out of the kiln chimney and a surge of excitement came over us. I had never seen pottery being burned in a kiln and neither had Wig. Through all of the excitement we managed to keep our cool, meet Edwin, and then scramble for the cameras and tape recorder.

Edwin was very hospitable and welcomed our company. Meanwhile, I could hear the roar and crackle of the fire and was ready to see the main attraction.

Edwin led us around to the kiln and the air around us increased to about a hundred degrees. To Edwin, the heat was nothing since he had been firing since six o'clock that morning. Edwin kept feeding wood into the kiln like a fireman on a steam locomotive, with little time to rest. Every time I looked

PLATE 144 Edwin Meaders with one of his roosters.

PLATE 145 Denise Dixon, Edwin's twelve-year-old grand-
daughter, is learning how to turn pottery. Here she and her
five-year-old brother, Dennis, hold three of her pieces.

*at Wig, he would say with a smile, "This is great! We've lucked up!" I
kept telling him it was because I came along.*

*To say the least, the interview went great and on the way home we felt as
though we had done a full day's work.*

*A couple of weeks later, we again decided on the spur of the moment to
ride down and get Edwin to go through the steps involved in making one of
his roosters. Once again, we were in luck. Edwin was in his shop and within
a few minutes was ready to begin making one for us. The cameras were snapping*

as Edwin worked diligently to show us how the three pieces he had made several days earlier fit together. Since we still wanted to see the pieces actually turned, Edwin dug off a chunk of clay and began turning the basic pieces. I was very impressed, since Edwin had worked all day and still had the energy and the willingness to make the parts for another rooster for us.

During the first trip I had failed to capture all of Edwin's moods, expressions, and gestures on film, so on our second trip I was especially striving for good photographs. Edwin was a comic, and at certain points throughout the interview I was so tickled that I could hardly hold the camera steady long enough to take a picture.

Interviewing Edwin, taking and printing the photographs, and drawing the diagrams was a great pleasure. I received an even greater bonus by having the opportunity to go to New York for four days to present my material for this chapter to Loretta Barrett, our editor at Doubleday.

Overall, the interviews with Edwin were hard work, but during our two visits we had some good laughs, and I met a talented man whom I will never forget.

BERT DAVIS

Photographs and diagrams by Bert Davis, Bruce Lodge, and Adam Wilburn, with additional help from Chris Hogelin, Ronnie Welch, Scott Shope, and Richard Trusty.

[Cheever] was already making pottery when I was born. Now, he was happy with that. And he'd talk about all the time—what time he wasn't whistling and singing! [laughing] You could hear him whistle all over the country.

I was the youngest boy. All of us would get in there—you know, kids play. [Cheever] never would say nothing. My uncle, Q, was the one. He worked there and he couldn't *stand* for us to be in there. Just a bunch of kids. It was aggravating, I can look back and see now. We was bad to aggravate him, too. You know how kids are.

[Cheever stayed in the shop instead of farming because] he tried to farm and work at that too, and both of them didn't work good together; so we always just got out and done the growing of the food and he just went ahead and worked in the shop. [The reason is] really, to tell you the truth, he wasn't prepared to work in the wintertime so he *had* to do the most of his work in the summertime while it was warm and while he could. That old building they had was just an old log shop daubed with mud, you know, and he tried to make it in the wintertime but [the ware] would freeze before it got dried. He had a fireplace, but it didn't do no good. The air would come through them old cracks in them logs till you just couldn't save [the ware]. I'll tell you what happened one time. It's the truth. You see that old chimney yonder? That's where the shop was. All right. Mother and Daddy had been making churns for about a week. The weather was pretty, but it was wintertime. And back then, you didn't know if it was coming up a cold spell. When it come, you knowed it was there. We didn't have no weather news back then—didn't have no radio or nothing like that to go by, you know—and a man just had to almost *guess* at it. So we had that shop half full of churns. It started turning cold, and Daddy quit. He said, "We better get up some wood to burn in here to keep this stuff from freezing." There was dead pines up on the hill there, and we started cutting that wood to haul in here to build a fire, and you know what? While we was over there [cutting wood], it turned so cold just in two or three hours that that stuff froze and cracked in that shop before we ever got the fire [built]. He says, "They ain't no need to build it now." So there was about a week's work gone. Well now, that's the way it was in the wintertime. So he'd grind [that clay] over and start making again, and it might freeze again. He was just taking a chance every time he done it [that it might not] get dry enough to [be able to be burned in the kiln].

We even tried building a fire out in the middle of the shop there, and that still didn't do it. Daddy worked hard. He wanted to work. But back then people didn't have things to do with like we've got now—didn't have no heaters and things like that—so he just quit making it in the wintertime. And in the summertime, when he wanted to farm, he had to make pottery, so that's what made that [situation], you see?

Well, they was enough of us to do all the working in the fields that needed to be done. They was four boys, and they was two girls old enough to work. And Momma, she really made us get it out there. She'd work along with us, you see. So there was enough of us to take care of all that without him out there. So he'd stay in the shop and work the whole summer.

Course, even when we was boys we'd go help him to dig clay and tote wood and soak clay and put it in the mill and grind it. We would help make the glaze. We never did use ashes out of the kiln to make our glazes with. Old slabs is so dirty that they've got too much dirt in them for glaze. When I was small, people would give us their ashes. They made soap, and they had these barrels, and they'd put their ashes in them barrels and pour water over 'em and run the lye off. We'd rather have them than ashes that had the lye still in them, you know, 'cause you go to glazing with them and that lye and stuff'll go to eating your hands up. It was bad. So we'd get those ashes where they'd made soap. We'd have to take a chisel and chisel them ashes out of those barrels—that was the hardest stuff you ever seen in your life—but they wasn't no lye in them and they didn't burn your hands.

We helped with just about all of it. We'd make up balls, help put [the ware] in the kiln, help burn it. We done the whole process, just like Daddy, except turning. But I'll tell you what, though: I got to where I could even make pottery at a young age. [At first] we'd watch and figure it out. He'd *tell* us a whole lot, but he never did show. It was there for us to see. But he would *tell* us—like something would work or something wouldn't work, you know. I remember all them things just as well as if he'd told it yesterday. And it worked out just that way, too. He already had it figured out there, and what he told me has helped me a whole lot here. It was all things that was what I'd call logical. When he would tell you something, it was just like he said, 'cause he'd tried it already. That helped me a whole lot when I got ready to go. Like he'd tell me about how thick to make a bottom, and how it would do if you made it too thin or too thick, and it worked just exactly like he said it would.

So pretty soon, then, we was turning too. We'd turn ours when he wasn't turning. We'd make stuff and sell it—little old pitchers and jugs. People'd buy that. They was just as anxious to get it then as they are now, but it didn't bring much—maybe five or ten cents apiece. But that was big money back several years ago. And so I helped with the whole process. A lot of it was hard work, but I got a big kick out of all that. It was all fun. I'll tell you, though, back then a person couldn't see the fun he was having. Have you thought of things in the past like that? [Hate it at the time and find out you] enjoyed every minute of it? It was just right. It couldn't have been better. [laughing] So that's the way that was.

I went through the tenth grade. I didn't say I *learned* anything! [laughing] Course I think I know about as much as some of them that graduated. I could of went on, but I got started in school at a late age. I never got started in school till I was nine years old, they tell me. They said I was always so small they was afraid for me to go to school. I was always little-bitty. But I went through the tenth, and I decided that what I was gonna do didn't require any schooling at all, 'cause I wasn't gonna do anything! [laughing]

So I stayed there at home and helped Daddy till I married. I even helped Daddy haul in those later years. I'd drive a truck for him. It was a '31 Chevrolet. He could drive, but he never did want to go out and drive on the road. Around the house, he'd drive— haul wood and things like that. Anyway, most of the time we'd go up in North Carolina with it—across this mountain to Blairsville, Hayesville, Murphy, Andrews, Bryson City—all them places back in there. I don't reckon they was nobody back in there that was making it. There was several potters, but they was far away and they never did bother us. Then later, Daddy got to letting the customers haul it themselves. He'd just sell it to them and let them just come here and take it on home.

He *used* to haul it in wagons. He was all the time talking about his wagoning, you know. They'd haul them churns on wagons, and he was just a little kid then. The other boys was all grown and he was just a kid going along. They'd get started out with a mule and they might be gone two or three weeks at a time. They wadn't in no hurry back then. I've heard him talk about all that before they was any cars. Pretty slow travel. Three mile an hour! Couldn't put up with that three-mile-an-hour travel now, could you?

By the time I got a few years on me, it seemed like everybody right along about then was wanting to drift away from it or something, and the demand for what Daddy was making—the churns and pitchers and jugs—the demand for that was done gone. This glassware and so on had come in here, and that changed Daddy. There wasn't nothing but a churn and a pitcher and a jug worth anything to him, and you couldn't hardly get him off of it. He'd call anything else "junk." And you couldn't get the idea in his head that this other stuff was in demand. To him, it was just *nothing*. You know how them old people were. You couldn't change them off. It's like trying to take a man out of a buggy and put him in a airplane. It'd be about the same thing.

[Then Arie started making] and he thought she'd gone crazy. Aw, he really didn't think that, but when she got started up there, he'd *watch* her, you know. He'd slip and peep in that window. She *knowed* he was. But they all thought she was crazy for making that old stuff. First kilnful she made after she learnt to make it, and they got up the wood and burned it, heck, it was gone in two or three days. Well, it didn't take Daddy but just a day or two to make up his mind and he got right back in there. He had just got discouraged at it, is what it was, with them churns and stuff not selling anymore.

So then she'd draw stuff and have him to turn them things, and they was just making all *kinds* of stuff. They just worked together real good there. [And she had the time to give to it by then.] The kids was all taking care of theirselves and she didn't have all the responsibility. When we was coming on [growing], she didn't never work in the shop. She had to stay at home and work in the gardens and the corn and the cotton patches and do all the canning and all the housework and all that. But after all us kids got grown and got up and on our own, why then she didn't have all that responsibility and she could do something, so she come up there [to the pottery shop] and started that. She learnt to do it in just a few days. That's the part that was so grand about it. Course she had seen it since they was married, and all she needed was just a little experience. She's eighty-six years old now, and you wouldn't think that. She done a lot of things a lot of people wouldn't have done.

Course, by then I was married, and I wasn't making pottery at all. [Lanier stayed with it] but I worked at a lumberyard for years. Then I'd work at the poultry dressing plant awhile, and then go back to the lumberyard, and then back to the dressing plant. Finally, about three years ago [1979], I got tired of it all. They run me around there like I had rollers on me. I made up my mind I wadn't going to hurry anymore, and I decided I'd just stay here and work then. [The reason I stay is] I make more money here. Good reason, isn't it? There's people just begging for this pottery, and I mean just all the time. I didn't know there was a demand like that till I got started back. I didn't really know, you see? That's part of why, way back yonder, I quit.

Now, when I first started back I didn't have any trouble with making things. All that stuff just come natural to me, because I had been around it all my life. I'd growed up in it, and I haven't forgot *one* part of it. It's still with me. It don't never go away. But I didn't know where to sell it at. I didn't know who bought it. I didn't know where to go out here to sell anything. After I found out who bought it and where to sell it, why, it wasn't no problem. They just come to me. I didn't have to go to them at all. When I got started, I'd burn a kiln and it'd not stay here two or three days till it would all be gone. You couldn't find a piece of it. That's just how fast it goes. The only way I can keep any of it is to hide it. And then I have to lie to them, and I don't want to lie to them! So I just set it back out. That's right.

I don't make my stuff exactly the old way, but a lot of it is close. I don't use a mule to grind my clay with, and I don't mix that kind of glaze now for my stuff 'cause I haven't got any glazing rocks or anything like that to grind it and make it like it ought to be. So I just get Albany slip, whiting, feldspar, and clay and mix it myself—but the amounts are a secret! And the roosters I make aren't just like the ones Momma used to make. I tried to make my roosters like she did, and I never *could* get mine like hers. I tried and tried, but they just wouldn't go that way for me. I'd make the awfullest-looking things you ever seen! When I just come back to my own imagination, why then, that's the only way I could do it. I mean I could see the picture of it right there [in my head]. You know how it is. I've got it right there!

And I don't know whether I want to say it or not, but I've got orders now for all the roosters I can make. I'm behind now to where I don't know whether I'll ever catch up. I'm glad I've got plenty of sales, but I don't know if it's good to be behind like this or not. If you'd hear how the [customers] talk, you wouldn't think it was. There was one feller—I had just burnt a kiln of roosters and they was still hot, and he wanted some of them. And I told him, "You'll just have to wait till they get cool." He said he wasn't gonna wait till they got cool. He said, "I'm gonna get 'em *now*." He got out there and he got a darn pole and he rigged him up a wire on that thing and he went to hooking them roosters out of there. Had to hold them with a rag after he got them out, they was so hot. But he was gonna *have* some roosters. If they'd been too hot when he got them out, they'd have cracked, but these had cooled down just enough. If they're cooled down to where you can't hardly handle them without burning yourself, they'll be all right. I usually wait till they're cooled completely, though. But that man wouldn't wait. That's the way some of them are.

Most of them tell me to call when I've got their order finished. I call from Mother's. I haven't had a phone in six or eight years—maybe longer'n that. Them kids run the bill up about a hundred dollars one month, and I *told* them, I said, "Now, we ain't gonna have no phone if you do that again." Well, they done it again? We ain't got no phone.

I've been thinking about putting one in 'cause it's pretty hard to get along without one now. Sure is. But I don't know . . .

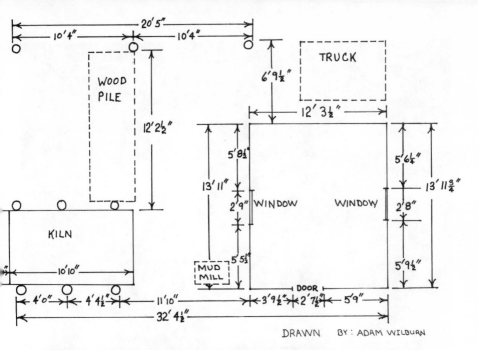

PLATE 146   Diagram of overall layout of Edwin's operation.

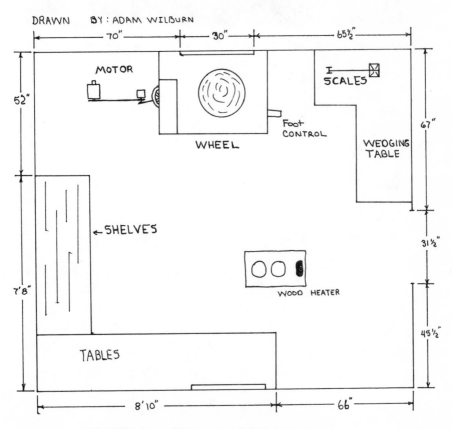

PLATE 147   Diagram of Edwin's shop.

PLATE 148 One pair of Edwin's scales is modeled after Cheever's.

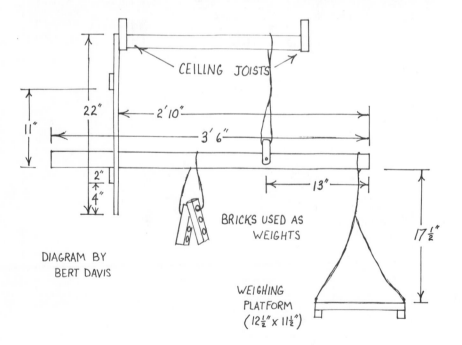

CEILING JOISTS

22"

2' 10"

11"

3' 6"

2"

4"

13"

17½"

DIAGRAM BY
BERT DAVIS

BRICKS USED AS
WEIGHTS

WEIGHING
PLATFORM
(12½" x 11½")

PLATE 149   Diagram of scales.

PLATE 150 Edwin's motor-driven wheel and his ball opener, or "bottom gauge." Edwin says, "I call it a 'bottom gauge,' not a 'ball opener.' I don't need it to open the ball. I can take my fingers and do that. I need it to give me the thickness of the bottom."

PLATE 151

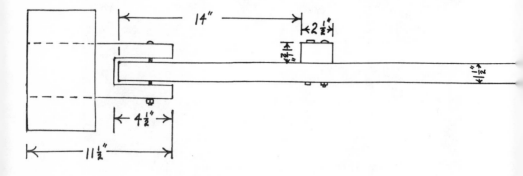

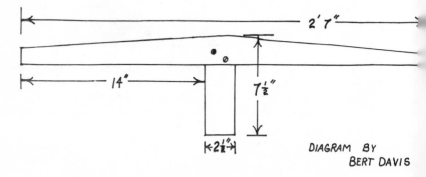

PLATE 152   Diagram of ball opener.

PLATE 153   A pair of Edwin's metal lifters . . .

PLATE 154   . . . and a pair of his wooden ones.

PLATE 155   This series of photographs, taken by Bert Davis
and Bruce Lodge, details Edwin's entire process for making a
rooster. First he weighs out the clay he needs. It takes approximately 9½ pounds to make each: 2 pounds for the base, 3 pounds
for the rear part of the body, 3 pounds for the breast and neck,
and 1½ pounds for the head, comb, gills, and tail.

PLATE 156 First Edwin turns the base and the two main body parts. To form the rear part of the body, he starts with a dough-nut-shaped ring of clay. He pushes through all the way to the top surface of the wheel so that it will have no bottom.

PLATE 157 He then draws the ring up into a jarlike shape . . .

PLATE 158 . . . pulls it in at the top when it is tall enough . . .

PLATE 159 . . . pinches off the knob of excess clay at the top . . .

PLATE 160 . . . and closes the hole.

PLATE 161 Then he smooths the outside of the bottomless, hollow dome and, using lifters, eases it off the wheel and sets it aside.

PLATE 162 Using the same process, he next shapes the pieces for the breast and neck . . .

PLATE 163 . . . but he draws the top portion up into a cone . . .

PLATE 164 . . . and then, as before, lifts it off and sets it aside.

PLATE 165 In shaping the base, again he begins with a bottomless ring . . .

PLATE 166 . . . raises the walls . . .

PLATE 167 . . . and pinches in the top. Edwin uses no height gauge for these three pieces, but he does have one horseshoe-shaped piece of heavy-gauge wire. The space between the ends indicates when the widest portion of each piece is the proper diameter. It is barely visible being used in Plate 166.

PLATE 168 The three main pieces are allowed to dry overnight to become firm enough that they can hold their shapes as they support each other's weight.

PLATE 169 The next day, Edwin mixes up a double handful of raw clay with enough water to make a sticky clay "mush"—the glue that will hold the pieces together.

PLATE 170 He then washes his hands, takes 1½ pounds of raw clay (5 pounds for three roosters), works it up on his wedging table (Edwin calls this process "working a ball"), and rolls it out in a long roll.

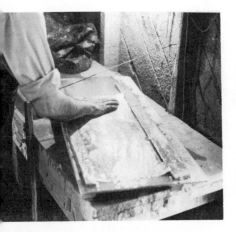

PLATE 171 Spreading a sheet of damp oilcloth on a board . . .

PLATE 172 . . . he slowly flattens the roll out, first with his hands . . .

PLATE 173 . . . and then with a wet rolling pin. He works very slowly and deliberately to keep the clay from cracking. When it is almost the proper thickness, he lays another damp sheet of oilcloth on top, continues pressing and smoothing, and then, grasping the top edges of the two sheets of oilcloth with the clay sandwiched in between, turns the whole slab over. Peeling off the top layer of oilcloth, he moistens his hands and smooths out the numerous hairline cracks in the clay, presses the slab again with the rolling pin, replaces the oilcloth, turns the slab over again, and repeats the process three or four times. When he is finished, the slab is approximately ½″ thick by 6½″ wide by 18″ long.

PLATE 174 The battered, three-year-old patterns Edwin uses for the tail, gills, and comb are made of synthetic leather.

PLATE 175 Taking the pattern for the tail first (which really only establishes the width of the tail's base), he cuts the tail out of the slab with a knife . . .

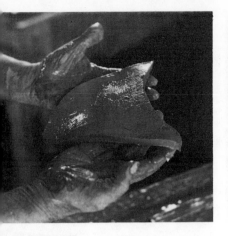

PLATE 176 . . . lifts it away, and sets it on a board covered with fresh newspaper so it can dry slightly and stiffen up.

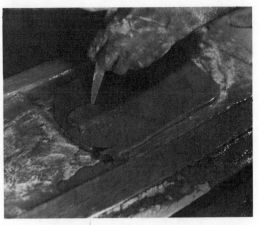

PLATE 177 Pressing the remaining slab so that it is slightly thinner, he then cuts out the oval for the comb, but he does not, at this point, shape the serrated edge.

PLATE 179 . . . pulls the excess clay away from the comb, and sets the comb aside on a board covered with newspaper.

PLATE 178 He removes the pattern with the point of his knife . . .

PLATE 180 Next he takes all the excess clay, wads it up and reworks it into "handling clay" that is softer and even more uniform, flattens it out into a slab using the same process as before, and cuts out the two gills.

PLATE 181 He places the gills on a board covered not with newsprint, but with slick enameled magazine paper that keeps the gills smooth and will not tear when it is lifted. He covers the gills with a damp cloth to keep them soft. If the gills are too thin, after they are mounted on the rooster they will pull together at their lower edges, both as they dry and when they are fired. If the proper thickness, they will stay flared slightly apart and will not warp together.

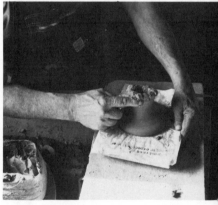

PLATE 182 Now, as the tail and comb are stiffening, Edwin takes the base and slices off enough clay to slant the top edge.

PLATE 183 Then he covers the top edge with balls of his clay "glue."

PLATE 184 Taking the rear part of the body, he tapers both the inside and outside bottom edges so there will be more surface area for the glue to adhere to . . .

PLATE 185 . . . and presses the piece firmly down onto its base.

PLATE 186 Now begins a lengthy smoothing and mounting process. Using the glue that has squeezed out around the seam, supplemented with fresh glue as needed, he slowly connects the two pieces.

PLATE 187 Next he slices a large slanted piece out of the breast portion . . .

PLATE 188 . . . shapes and trims the edge slightly . . .

PLATE 189 . . . applies a ⅛" to ¼" layer of glue to the rear body part . . .

PLATE 190 . . . and presses the two body parts together.

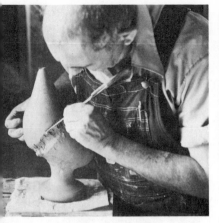

PLATE 191 At the seam, all the way around the body, after some minor trimming to make the two pieces fit together more perfectly, Edwin takes the point of his knife and makes a series of closely spaced long gashes. These cuts scored into the seam knead the edges of the two pieces together and guarantee there will be no air bubbles trapped in the seam.

PLATE 192 The resulting groove is then filled slowly with small balls of clay glue, each one being worked into the groove and smoothed out to eliminate air bubbles and irregular surfaces.

PLATE 193 Edwin also adds additional glue to the breast and blends it smoothly into the base.

PLATE 194 Now, some forty minutes into the assembly process, the tail is reshaped. Edwin removes an arc-shaped piece from the base . . .

PLATE 195 . . . and cuts out triangular pieces to indicate feathers. As he works, Edwin says, "I'm gonna change this style of tail. I can make it look more real than it does. But all this work is the reason I don't even like to hear roosters crow. If I had better sense, I wouldn't do this."

PLATE 196 The tail set aside again, he takes a nearly double handful of fresh raw clay, wedges it, pats it into a ball, and pulls it out into a roll. Then he smears soupy, clay-laden water onto the neck ("If you wet it with clear water, it'll crack"). He hollows out one end of the new roll with his knife, adds a little glue to the neck . . .

PLATE 197 . . . and sets the head into place.

PLATE 198 He turns it so the rooster appears to be looking off to one side . . .

PLATE 199 . . . and then smooths, glues, and shapes the new addition to the body.

PLATE 200 Next, the feathers are cut into the comb and it is set aside to continue stiffening.

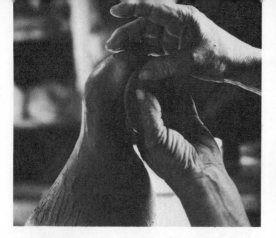

PLATE 201 A deep groove is cut into either side of the neck, and the two gills are pressed and glued and smoothed into place. The seam where each gill joins the neck is treated the same as the seam joining the two major body parts.

PLATE 202 When the gills are attached, they are flared apart slightly so that as they dry, they will hang down straight rather than pulling together. Then a groove is cut into the top of the rooster's head to accommodate the comb.

PLATE 203 With the statement, "Now I believe I'll crown him," Edwin adds the stiffened comb and glues it into place.

PLATE 204   He drills holes for the eyes with the point of his knife . . .

PLATE 205 . . . and adds a small clay eyeball to each hole. "I believe he's gonna be goo-goo-eyed!"

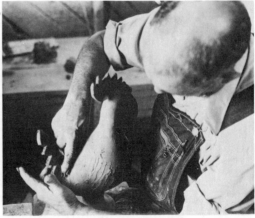

PLATE 206   Last, he places an arc of glue where the tail goes, curves and sets the tail in place . . .

PLATE 207 . . . adds glue to the seams, and blends body and tail together. He sets it aside, then, for at least three "good sunshiny days" before final trimming, shaping, and drying. Making the roosters three at a time, he can make eighteen on a good day. He fires sixty-four at a time in his kiln.

The Kiln Firing

Edwin's railroad tunnel kiln is one of the tightest, neatest structures we found. Though small (the ware floor measures only five feet square and holds an average of about 80 pieces), it seems efficient and relatively easy to fire. It was built in the late 1960s out of "regular old common red brick." The sidewalls are approximately fourteen inches high, and are the length of one brick wide. Like the sidewalls on Lanier's kiln, the bricks are laid in alternating courses. Outside each sidewall, however, at each of the four corners, Edwin built a square brick column, and then ran two-by-ten boards (backed up and supported by the same poles that support the roof over the kiln) horizontally the length of the kiln outside the brick columns, to create a long channel parallel to each sidewall. These two channels he filled with dirt to provide additional insulation against the sidewalls of the kiln.

When he built the arch, he followed roughly the same procedures used by Cleater and shown in Plates 89–97. He set the arch boards in place, leveled and straightened and braced them, and then decked them over solid with slats. For the first course, to get the upward tilt of each brick correct, he set the end of each brick in the course straight down against the slope created by the arch boards, and he filled the space created between each brick's bottom side and the top of the sidewall with cement. From that point on, he used "clay and old red mud" between the courses. He did not use a line to keep the courses running straight the length of the dome. As Edwin said, "When you put the mud on them [for the next course], and you push the end of that brick right straight down against the boards, it'll just keep it spaced just right, and keep the curve right, and you just come right on over." For the final course, rather than using a row of keystone-shaped "wedge" bricks, Edwin says, "I beat bricks out with a trowel and cut them off and put them in there and I got pieces of old jars and clinched that row— tightened it—where the dome would stay up there. When I got done with it, the boards wasn't hardly touching. I made it so tight [the dome] had done rose up off them. Didn't have no problem getting the [arch boards and slats out from inside]."

Then he added the chimney and the breast end. The inside of Edwin's chimney has no central divider but is open all the way across. He is worried the opening is wider than it should be, because in the last phase of firing, when the flames periodically come out of the chimney, they tend to come out at one side or the other instead

PLATE 208   Edwin's kiln.

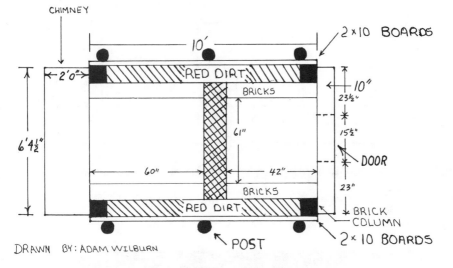

CHIMNEY

2 × 10 BOARDS

10'

2'0"

RED DIRT

BRICKS

10"

23½"

61"

15½"

6'4½"

DOOR

60"

42"

23"

BRICKS

RED DIRT

BRICK
COLUMN

DRAWN BY: ADAM WILBURN

POST

2 × 10 BOARDS

PLATE 209   Floor plan of Edwin's kiln.

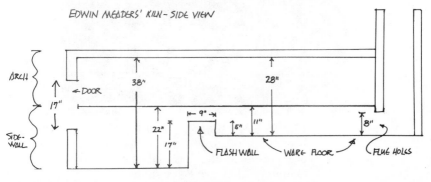

EDWIN MEADERS' KILN - SIDE VIEW

ARCH

DOOR

38"

28"

17"

22"

9"

5"

11"

8"

17"

SIDE-
WALL

FLASH WALL

WARE FLOOR

FLUE HOLES

PLATE 210

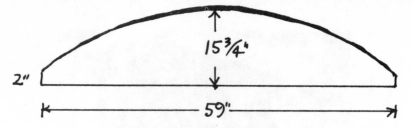

AN ARCH BOARD USED IN MAKING EDWIN'S KILN

PLATE 211

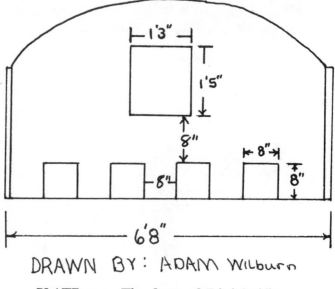

DRAWN BY: ADAM Wilburn

PLATE 212   The front of Edwin's kiln.

PLATE 213   In the back of Edwin's kiln, the seven flue holes are visible at the base of the chimney. They are 8″ high and are spaced 3¾″ (the width of one brick) apart.

of escaping evenly all the way across the opening. He has thought about adding a course of bricks to the top, the ends of which would protrude over the opening to choke it down somewhat, but has discarded the notion, believing that that will not solve the problem ultimately. "I don't know whether that'd do any good or not. I kinda believe you've got to [start choking the chimney in gradually from the base to the top as you build it]. Otherwise, the flames are just gonna be going hard against that [lip extended over the top course] and that ain't gonna hold back much. The flames'll just push a little faster out of that, you see? I don't believe it would do a whole lot of good.

"I always thought the more air it had, the better it'd burn. Well, it will burn faster, but you've gotta hold that heat back there some for it to burn right. That's one reason why I leave those two flue holes in the front closed up and just leave two open. With all four open, it just don't burn right."

It usually takes Edwin an average of three weeks to turn enough ware for a burn. When Edwin loads his kiln, he crawls over the fire pit to the ware floor and has someone load the pieces in through the loading door. "If I ain't got nobody to help me, I just lay me some boards over each side of the firebox and set my stuff on those boards and then crawl in and set them [on the ware floor]. I have the stuff that's left setting right outside the door, and when I get the boards unloaded, I reach out the door [from inside] and put them on the boards and then set them [on the ware floor]. I do the same thing over about twice and I've got it finished.

"I set the small pieces in the back [near the inside wall of the chimney] where the fire goes down through them vents [in the base of the chimney's inside wall], and then in the middle I've got the bigger pieces, and then down there at the firebox end I've got smaller pieces again [so they can be protected behind the flash wall]. That keeps them from getting too hot down at this end, you see? I've got that flash wall there, and they're sitting just behind that. If there were big ones there [and they stuck up over the top of the wall] that blaze'd burn the glaze off the top of them."

Edwin uses pine slabs cut into four-foot lengths for firing, and uses an average of three-quarters of a cord per burn. He says he uses pine simply because "it does better" and is easier to get. "I don't know of noplace where you can get oak or hardwood slabs nowhere. I would use them if I couldn't get the pine, but I can

PLATE 214   His shop from the outside with smoke from the kiln's chimney rising behind it.

PLATE 215   Edwin fires with pine slabs. A portion of the loading door is bricked up during burning, leaving a hole through which he shoves the slabs. The metal plate resting against the kiln covers the hole when wood is not being added.

PLATE 216   Edwin checks the kiln every ten to fifteen minutes.

PLATE   217   Through   the loading door, he can see both the fire and the pots on the ware bed beyond.

PLATE 218 A view of the chimney end of the kiln during the final hour of firing.

PLATE 219 Two of the draft holes in front of the kiln are left open during firing.

PLATE 220 During the final phase of firing, Edwin goes to the chimney end, removes two loose half bricks in the chimney wall, and checks to see whether or not the ware is completely fired.

PLATE 221 Looking through the hole in the chimney, Edwin can see the pots beyond.

PLATE 222 Rather than using cones, Edwin throws in a chip of wood. It ignites immediately and its glare reflects off the melted glaze. If the glaze has melted all the way down to the wares' base, Edwin stops firing.

PLATE 223 Satisfied that the burn is complete, Edwin replaces the two bricks in the chimney, stops firing, and waits for the kiln to cool.

just get the pine easier. It was even hard to get pine this winter. It's been so wet, they couldn't get logs into the sawmill so it hasn't done hardly any business this winter. I guess they'll go at it again, though, when the weather opens up a little."

When he starts firing, he closes all four flue holes up at the breast end until he gets a bed of coals "started in there" in the fire pit. Then he opens the two middle holes and leaves the two outside ones closed. The length of time it takes depends to a great extent on the weather conditions, but the average burn is nine hours. On the day we watched Edwin burn, the wind was blowing so hard that it had had a genuine effect on the nature of the burn, causing the flames to surge and whip around inside the kiln instead of heating the ware steadily and consistently. Edwin said several times, "The wind is so bad today I wish I hadn't started burning at all. If I'd known the wind was gonna blow like this when I started out, I *wouldn't* of started. Today, with the way the wind is, it's gonna take ten or eleven hours to burn this, and I'm gonna burn a whole lot more than three-quarters of a cord of slabs. My cousin helped me burn one time up here and the wind was blowing from the south a lot harder'n it is today, and I'll tell you what, we like to *never* got that fired. We like to *never* got it hot enough. But we just kept on till it finally got hot."

Another factor affecting the burn is the nature of the wood. The fact that the wood was slightly damp on the day we were there complicated matters further. "I believe my wood got wet the other day when that blowing rain come. I usually stack it in the chicken house green and let it get dry as a chip before I use it, but that rain come the other day and blowed in on it and I imagine it took up some of that moisture. [This wood] just seems like it ain't got no pick up and go like it's been a-having."

Almost every ten minutes during the final several hours of the burn, as the heat waves coming from the chimney began to subside, Edwin removed the metal door that hung over the loading hole and added six or eight more slabs, sending fresh smoke and some flames out the chimney. He was careful to shove the slabs in at an angle, because "I have to watch about letting the wood go over the flash wall and over on my stuff. I ain't certain that I ain't pushed some over on it already." And he only rarely added enough fresh slabs to cause flames to shoot out the chimney in some of the more spectacular displays pictured in this volume. "I [often] never get the blaze out the chimney. Just take my time and not rush it. You have to stay with it, though. I can leave it for ten to fifteen minutes

PLATE 224

at a time at the beginning when the fire's not too big—go in the house and eat me a bite or get a drink of water. I can be slack with it then for about the first six hours and just piddle around, keep a little wood thrown or walk around, take it easy; but after I get it so hot, I've just got to keep that going and not let it cool down. I have let it go down, but it takes a while to get the temperature back up, which is aggravating. It won't *hurt* it, but it takes too long to get the temperature back up.

"And you can fire too long. You've got to watch it. I was working on the truck here one day—something on the clutch went wrong and I had to fix it—and I'd come up here and fire and go back to working on the truck, and I looked around and I'd fired *twelve* hours! I just forgot and it absolutely burnt the glaze off some of it. That was the easiest kiln I ever fired in my life, though. I just wasn't *firing,* I was working on my truck. That ware passed, but it wasn't like it ought to be. Had the glaze burnt off the top and it had run off the bottom some and I had t' work on it a whole lot. It didn't suit me, but they bought it."

Ten and one-half hours after Edwin began the burn we observed, it was finished. He left the metal door in place and let the fire begin to die down. Thirty-six to forty hours later, he would open the door. "I've got a stick that I stick in there and hook it out [rather than] crawl in there and hand it out." The contents of this burn (pitchers, jugs, and small pots with rolled clay grapes on their sides) would be picked up by the craft shop that had ordered them. Meanwhile, after several days off Edwin would be at work turning more ware.

BURLON AND IRENE CRAIG

On John Burrison's recommendation, we also interviewed Burlon Craig and his wife, Irene, who live in the Catawba Valley of North Carolina. There were several reasons for the interest in Burlon, one of them being that he is the only potter John has met who uses a water-powered glass mill for pulverizing the glass he uses in some of his glazes. Another reason is that he is the only folk potter still using a traditional groundhog kiln and traditional turning techniques and designs in a part of the country that is dotted with the remains of what used to be a thriving pottery center.

Burlon was born in the Catawba Valley on April 14, 1914. As a boy, he got to know many of the potters in the area, including Harvey and Enoch Reinhardt (who had learned how to turn pottery from their father and uncle), Bob Ritchie, James Lynn, Mac (McGruder) Bishop, the Propst family, the Leonards and the Ritchies, and the Browns in the Catfish section of Catawba. All were turning at about the same time, and all were getting their clay from the old Rhodes farm there in the area. Of course, the competition was fierce. As Burlon said, "They would go to some store and the man would say, 'Well, I've been buying from Mr. Propst. I'll just wait on him.'

"'What are you paying him for a gallon?'

"'Ten cents.'

"'If you'll buy from me, I'll let you have it for eight cents.' The man would be looking for a bargain and he'd buy that because it was all good stuff. I've seen this done when I was a boy. Then the merchant would usually sell it for fifteen cents a gallon.

"Then they hauled a lot of their pottery back here thirty or forty miles back into these mountains. They'd have their covered wagons and pack the ware in straw. They had places where they could pull in and camp along the road and feed their team and cook their supper and breakfast and go on a little farther the next day.

"The T-Model had come along when I got into the business, so I missed all that wagon stuff, but I've heard it was a lot of fun. I

PLATE 225 Burlon Craig applying a handle to a five-gallon jar he has just turned.

think it would be fun *now* if you could keep from getting blowed off the road!"

At the time, Burlon's family was not involved in pottery at all. "My father was named Major Craig. He was a farmer and a preacher, so we lived on a farm. Lots of hard work when I was growing up. We raised and picked a lot of cotton. Course, we had a lot of fun. Had our old swimming holes we went to on Sunday. Played a little baseball. They always bought these thick heavy socks and you could ravel that thread out when the foot of the sock was wore out— take the leg and ravel that thread out and make a ball out of it. That's where we got our balls. And we would cut down a little hickory sapling and hew it down small on one end like a baseball bat. And we made our little wagons. I've made a many of them. Pull 'em uphill and ride down. It was a lot of fun. And a lot of hard work.

"Eventually my father and another preacher moved to Wilkes County, North Carolina, but that was about the time I got married so I wasn't involved. He was also a good carpenter, and they built several churches around over Wilkes County. He died there in a little place called Cricket."

When Burlon was still just a boy he started helping James Lynn, who had a pottery operation nearly on the spot where Burlon's is now. He was getting older, and Burlon helped him get his wood and dig and grind his clay. Lynn didn't have a mule, so Burlon would take his father's mule and grind Lynn's clay on his pug mill when he was just ten or eleven years old.

Lynn asked him to go in partners with him before Burlon had even learned to turn. "That was along about October or November after we'd gathered up the crops on our farm. I was about fourteen years old, and I said, 'I'll tell you what I'll do, Jim. I'll try it till next spring, and if I'm not turning out some stuff that I can get a little money out of, I'll have to stop and help Daddy farm.' So by next spring I was turning out some sellable stuff, so I stayed on with him for a couple of years till he got sick and too disabled to work. He had cancer and died, and the shop closed. Until then, though, we split the profits fifty-fifty.

"Then I went to work for Harvey and Enoch Reinhardt for about one summer." After that summer, in the 1930s, he worked for Seth Ritchie and Floyd Hilton. Ritchie had two turners—Burlon and another man. "They paid me two cents a gallon. I got ten cents for turning a five-gallon piece. They was selling it for about ten cents a gallon. They dug the clay, dried it, ground it, glazed it and burnt it. I didn't do anything but turn it."

At about the same time, Burlon got to know Casey Meaders (brother to Cheever Meaders, the father of Lanier, a potter who lives in our area and who is also featured in this book). Mac (McGruder) Bishop, a potter, had moved into the valley from Georgia, and when Casey Meaders decided to move from Georgia too, Mac helped him find a location for the pottery operation he wanted to set up. It was set up about thirty miles from Burlon's present location because of the availability of good clay. Later a brick company moved in and used all the clay up, and Casey died. Burlon got to know Casey because a friend who was a highway foreman would hire Burlon to run a motor grader, and he'd time his run so that he would go past Casey's place at dinnertime. The two of them would eat together and spend an hour or so under the shade trees in front of his place, talking. Casey wanted Burlon to work with him, but at that time Burlon was already committed.

Burlon went into the Navy during World War II, and when he got out of the Navy in 1945, Harvey and Enoch Reinhardt had split up and Harvey had built a new pottery operation. Burlon bought him out, and Harvey opened a barbershop in Hickory, North Carolina, and later moved to Florida where he died. Until then, Burlon had never had his own pottery shop. The operation he bought from Harvey is the same one he still operates today.

The wares Burlon has made over his career have changed, of course, with the wishes of his customers. When he was working with James Lynn as a boy, the ware was nearly all strictly utilitarian:

"Back then about all we made were pitchers, milk crocks, churn jars, and storage jars like those five-gallon ones with two handles on them that I make now. And a few bean pots were made. When I was learning, most of what I was turning was gallon milk crocks and stuff like that. They're easier to turn. People used them back then to go in the box they had built in their spring to keep their milk in. That was before the refrigerator days. People made their own lids for the jars. They'd take a cloth and lay it over the crock and then put a wooden lid on it so that spring lizards and bugs couldn't get in the milk. Then they'd have a two-gallon crock to keep their cream in, and when they churned that into butter they had what they called a butter crock that they kept the butter in. All that went in the spring box.

"Later I got to where I could turn those storage jars. They were used for making wine and putting up sauerkraut and cucumber pickles and stuff like that. They had a large mouth, and they'd tie a cloth over the mouth of the jar and then lay a wooden board over the top of that. The small-mouth jars we also made were used to put vinegar in. People back then would make cider, you know, and let it ferment and make their own vinegar. Also we sold a lot of one-to-five-gallon jugs to these people up here to put their whiskey in, and they had a small mouth. That's what the bootleggers wanted so they could close them up easier. What we called molasses jugs were just like them only they had a little larger mouth, because in the wintertime and cool weather that syrup got thick and it wouldn't run out too good. But just the opening was all the difference there was in them.

"And we had what they call the buggy jugs too. You know, where you put your feet in the buggies, those sides wasn't built up too high, so we made a one-gallon jug that was just a regular jug with the small mouth and handle—just a regular jug, only it was squashed down low and wide. People could put their liquor in that and hide it in the buggy between their feet, you know what I mean. If you had a big tall jug and was riding along the road and the sheriff come along, he could see your jug. So they wanted them low so they could put it between their feet and then put a lap robe over their legs to hide it from the law. That was back along when there was no cars. They was getting a few T-Models in the country, but people still used buggies, and some guy that liked a little drink would take his buggy jug and hitch his old mule or horse to the buggy and go to a guy's house and get it filled up. I never did make too many of the buggy jugs, but I know when they was being made and I made a few of them.

"Some of those guys that liked to take a drink would get special jugs made, too. I know a preacher—he's a good friend of mine—that used to drink. That was back before he got reformed and became a preacher. And he had Casey Meaders make him a three-and-a-half-gallon jug that was marked three so he could get three and a half gallons of liquor put in it but only pay for three!

"Now I never seen old man Lynn ever make a face jug. After I got to where I could turn jugs, I made a few alone. But you didn't have no sales for stuff like that. Once in a while people would come here from Charlotte, going to the mountains in the summertime after they began to get good cars that would run. Might sell a face jug or something like that that you didn't have, but most of the market was for stuff that people had to have. They didn't have the money to spend for anything else."

It is the remarkable snake jugs and face jugs Burlon makes now, however, that customers demand. And it is these items, as well as the Reinhardt swirl-type ware that he alone among the mountain potters still makes, and the traditional techniques he refuses to give up that have earned him a tremendous amount of publicity, a constant stream of visitors, and nearly immediate sales for everything he makes, whether flawed or not. In fact, a large percentage of the phone calls he gets are from collectors and customers who want to know exactly when he is going to burn his next kiln load so they can be present when he unloads it and be first in line to select the choice pieces for their collections:

"The only time when that gets to be a problem for me is when you get the publicity and the people coming and you've got nothing to sell. Then it's not helping you any. Of course, now, don't get me wrong. I'd rather see it that way than not be able to sell the stuff at all. I'm not grumblin' about it, but [if too many people come] it doesn't help you any."

The fact that so many people are now collecting the works of potters like Burlon led us to ask him whether he collects himself—and elicited the following fascinating piece of material:

PLATE 226   The front yard and porch of Burlon and Irene's
house is a mass of plants growing in pots they have made.

PLATE 227

"I have collected some—not a lot. I've got some of the Jugtown at Seagrove, and I've got a piece or two that old man Seth Ritchie made back when he was turning and I worked with him. And I've got a churn or two that old man Jim Lynn made—the man I was working with when I learned to turn. I've got a good many of Lanier Meaders' face jugs put away. I wanted some of his stuff to put away and keep it. And I've got a few pieces of the Reinhardts'—I guess I could still find them.

"I used to have a lot of that Reinhardt swirl pottery. What I had at that time I guess now would be worth two or three thousand dollars, maybe, for last Saturday over at that flea market at Hillsville, Virginia, I seen a little old monkey jug for sale that the Reinhardts had made and the price they had on that was two hundred and eighty-five dollars. All mine got stolen, though. There used to be a little building set out here that I built and ran a little store out of at one time. Finally I quit fooling with that, and I had that pottery in there—used it as kind of a storage place. And I collected salt and pepper shakes. They weren't worth no money, but I collected them—had an old candy showcase out there setting full of salt and peppers. I went off here one weekend camping, and I come back and someone had gotten all my old pottery and my salt and pepper shakes. They was all gone—every damn one of them. [laughing] I guess they must have taken a tow sack and throwed them in and carried them out.

"But some of that old pottery has really gotten valuable. Over where my daughter lives, they have a little auction sale over there, and she said that there was a ten-gallon jar over there the Seagles had made—it was stomped [stamped or initialed]—and it sold for $950. It was a jar just like I'm makin' in there only it was bigger and had four handles on it. She tried to get me to guess how much it brought and I said, 'I don't know. Maybe $400.' She said, '$950,' and I just couldn't hardly believe it. But then a guy was here last week and he was telling me about seeing this same jar sell for $950. I said, 'It'd be my luck if I'd pay that for a jar to drop it and break it before I got it to the car!'

"And he said, 'Well, that ain't the whole story.' He said the boy that bought it sold it for $1,250, and the man he sold it to sold it for $1,400. Now I don't know whether that part's right, but I'm satisfied that the $950 is right, for my daughter and this guy both told the same tale in here in the shop.

"I've got people that's got a lot of my stuff, and they're buying it as an investment—no doubt about it. They would never want that much to keep just for themselves. And I *hope* it's a good investment for them. And I think it is. Someday I'm not gonna be a-makin' no more, and now as soon as I make the last piece, why then the price of my stuff will go up. Now, you wait and see if it don't. That's my idea now, and I believe I'm right on it. I'm not gonna be like Enoch Reinhardt, though. He's the one that made that monkey jug I was talking about that was down at the flea market. The Reinhardts only made about seven years, and Enoch was still a-livin' up until a couple of years ago. He wasn't making any more, but while he was still living the stuff he had made brought an awful price. He had sold everything he made, though, and when people began to get interested in it he got out and got to buying it all up and paying about ten times or maybe twenty times what he had sold it for. Now what about that?

"And I told my wife here one day—we was talking about it, and I didn't have any of my stuff to amount to anything except maybe a couple of pieces that I had made—and I said, 'Well, I'm going to keep me a little bit of mine.' Said, 'I'm not going to do like Enoch out here done and have to get out and buy it up and pay an awful price for it.' I know I saw him buy back a swirl bean pot—pretty good-sized pot—and pay $50 for it, which was a bargain for it at that time, but when I worked for him I saw 'em sold for a dollar apiece. I could have bought fifty of 'em easy for fifty dollars back when I was working for him, and he would have been glad to get that.

"Lots of the stuff that was made wasn't signed, but people that I worked with like Jim Lynn and the Reinhardts, I can take one look at it and tell whether they made it or not. And my stuff, why, it could be settin' out there on that porch and I could tell from here whether I made it or not. I was up at Maggie Valley [North Carolina] here a year or two ago and I stopped there at a little flea market, and they had a pint jug that I'd made. As soon as I saw the jug, I knew I'd made it. Well, the man there was trying to sell it to me. I didn't say anything at first. He kept on telling me how old it was and that crap, you know. Said, 'That was made about 1850,' or something like that. He was wantin', I believe, ten dollars for it. I finally told him, 'Well, I won't give that for it.' I said, 'When I sold it, I probably got two dollars for it.'

"He said, 'Where'd *you* get it?'

"I said, 'I *made* it.'

"He said, 'Aw, you didn't make that jug.'

"I asked him where he got it, and he said he got it from a banker in Gaffney, South Carolina. I don't know how it got down there or how come a banker with it. He could have been here to my place and got it. But that's what that man said—some banker in Gaffney. But I didn't try to convince him anymore that I'd made it. I just told him what I told him and walked off. I don't think that he believed me.

"Another guy tried to sell me one for old stuff that I had *stomped.* It was a little snake jug with two little snakes on it. Had 'B. B. Craig' on it. I said, 'That's not old. There's the man's name on it.'

" 'Oh,' he said, 'he's been dead a *long* time.' [laughing]

"I didn't tell him right then that I made it. In fact, I hadn't aimed to tell him at all till he kindly made me mad. When he made me mad, I told him right there. I said, 'Why, I *know* the man that made that.' I said, 'That's not old.'

" 'Oh yeah?' he said. 'That man's been dead for a hundred years.' He kept on and he kept on. I'd started to walk off, you know. And then he said, 'You better *get* that jug.' Said, 'That's *real* old.'

"I just turned around and went back to him and I pulled my driver's license out and I said, 'I *made* that jug,' and I said, 'here's my name.' I said, 'You compare them initials with my name and see if that ain't right.'

"He looked at it and he looked at me a little bit. He never would admit, though, that he thought I made it.

"But I've studied about that. I don't know whether he was trying to gyp me or whether he had gotten gypped. That's the thing about a thing like that, you know. Somebody could have gypped *him.*

"That happens *a lot.* I know there was some people from down at Fayetteville come here, and they had got ahold of a piece of my pottery somewhere'r 'nother, and they found out where this place was. Well, they come here. And I was mowin' the yard out there. The wife, she come out here and was a-waitin' on them. And they kept *looking* out at me, you know. It was a man and his mother. Directly they said to my wife, 'Why, he don't look like he's eighty some years old.'

"My wife said, 'Why, he's not!'

"Said, 'Well, we bought a piece of pottery from a man,' and he said, 'He'll probably never make no more.' Said, 'This'll be worth a lot of money.' Said, 'He's probably up in his eighties. He probably won't never make no more.'

"But that's sort of funny, you know, some of the things you run into like that. Some people will lie their grannies for a buck. I can't do that. I can't see it. Money's not *that* important. You've got to have it, but it's not that important to lie about. But a lot of people will. They'll tell you anything."

About his visitors, Burlon said, "Well, the old-timers enjoyed visitors, and I do too. Of course, they didn't have too much tourists then. It would tickle them to death for somebody to come by from Charlotte or somewhere and stop in. They got a kick out of that. They really enjoyed it. Some of them didn't always tell the truth, but they'd tell them a tale or two. I do too, but I always try to keep my tales down to the facts!"

Another measure of his popularity is the fact that he and Irene are often asked to attend folklife festivals and demonstrate. They agree to several of these per year, and they have worked out a system for demonstrating their skills:

"[When I demonstrate] I take enough clay to make one example of every kind of pot I make, and I work that same clay over and over. I turn a pot of every kind and set it out where people can see it—like a jug, a pitcher, and a jar—and then when I make another pitcher, I tear that first one down and rework the clay from it into something else. I don't have to haul a lot of clay around that way. Then at the end I break it all down and bring the clay back. I don't try to bring back green pieces. I tried that one time and found out it'll damage in hauling—you bump it, you know—and you not know it and then it'll show up bad in the kiln. So I don't try to bring the pieces back whole. I break them up and bring the clay back."

During the 1981 Smithsonian-sponsored Folklife Festival in Washington, D.C., Burlon and Irene were featured. It was an experience he talks about with awe:

"They estimated at five-thirty Saturday evening on the Fourth of July, there was a half a million people on the Mall. I wish you could have saw those grounds the next morning when we went over there and worked. It was covered up with paper, shoes, coats. They must have all got drunk and went off and left it. They had these guys out there raking it up in what I call a windrow—raking it up in long rows like hay. They had this big truck come along with a big sucking thing sucking it up in a big truck. That was the awfullest mess I've ever seen. There was a nice bunch of people up there though. They treated us awful nice."

They also demonstrated at the 1982 World's Fair in Knoxville, in the folklife area—twice.

"When I went to the World's Fair to demonstrate, some of them people had them *Foxfire* magazines with me in it, you know, and the first thing they asked was, 'Did you bring the little dog? Did you bring the little dog?' You know, his picture was in the magazine and they had seen it." [laughing]

PLATE 228 Vance Wall, one of the students involved in the interviews for this chapter, trying to make a pot on Burlon's wheel.

PLATE 229 Wig, Burlon, and Eddie Clark, another student involved in this chapter, reviewing an article that was previously printed in *Foxfire* magazine (Volume 15, #3, p. 200) about Burlon, and adding new material for this chapter.

PLATE 230 The dog—ever-present company.

What about the satisfaction he gets from his work? "Well, you've got to do a lot of work that you don't want to do. That burning is hard, but the hardest part of it really only lasts three hours. The rest of it's not too bad. And when you open up the kiln and you've had a good burn and there's some pretty stuff in there and it turns out good, why, then you get a lot of kick out of that. That's a pleasure. That, and the turning, I enjoy. This will make about the fifth kilnful this year, and it will probably be the last one this year. I'm not going to make as much as I have been. I'm cutting down. I'm not gonna *quit*, but I am going to cut down. I feel like that I might last longer if I take it a little easier, you know what I mean? I'm sixty-eight years old, and I'll be sixty-nine next April, and when you get up around seventy, why, you're pretty lucky to have good health, you know, the way I look at it. As far as I know, there's not anything wrong with me, and I can do a day's work about as good as I ever did; but I used to could work all day and run around all night, but I don't want to do that now. If I work all day, I want to sleep, you see what I mean? But I still want to make some and *will* make some as long as I'm able. I know I will. I'll never quit. I like to fool with it too good. But I am going to cut down maybe to three or four kilnfuls a year."

And health hazards? "You just have to keep the dust down to a minimum. About all the potters that I knew lived to be up in their eighties, so I don't see where pottin' had killed any of them. Something's gonna take you away from here sometime or another anyway!"

We also talked with Burlon's wife, Irene, who paints flowers and other designs on some of the pottery Burlon throws:

"I was born not far away, over in Rutherfordton County. My mother and daddy came to Catawba County when I was five years old and I've lived in the community around here since. My husband and I have known each other from school. We've lived in a lot of different places, but we've owned this for about thirty-six or -seven years.

"I never did work in pottery. I've seen it a lot and been around the pottery shops, but I never did work in it before I met him. But after we married, my children and myself had to help him work. We used to get out and help him get his wood. And we've helped him with clay. I still go with him to get the clay.

"And then I decorate some of the pottery. You see, you have to take the pottery when it gets thrown and dry, and you take whatever you're gonna decorate it with and make the flowers or whatever.

PLATE 231   Irene Craig and two pitchers she decorated with flowers.

Then it's to be glazed and then fired so the decoration will show
up. He always fixes my colors. He can fix me up a little bit and I
can make blue flowers. I can make white flowers. But he's got to
know what kind of clay for me to use.

"I decorate a lot of the little bowls and a lot of vases. Then I
do sets of those canisters. I put little flowers around the lid.

"Then also, for the last long time, I've handed the pottery to
be fired into him in the kiln. There's nobody to help you do nothing
no more. It's just a lot of little jobs to be done. I can stamp the

pottery with his stamp. Then a lot of times people want us to put their children's names or something special on a piece before it's fired, and I do that. Just whatever's to be done.

"The day we sell, I do all the counting. I count up all the bills and collect the money and I keep a record of it. He hardly ever counts a bill unless it's just somebody that comes and buys a piece. In fact, he's not sold enough himself the last couple of years to even know what the prices are. I keep all that.

"Back in the Depression when times was hard, you couldn't make a living at nothin'. You couldn't sell stuff at all, hardly. But now you can sell anything you make. It don't make any difference what it is, it'll go sooner or later. We have a good business now.

"And I'm pretty proud of all of it! Now and then you'll have some pieces that something will happen to, but not many. When it turns out nice, I'm proud of it.

"We have five children. We have three boys and two girls. Donald can make pottery. He's the baby boy. But he got both legs messed up in Vietnam and he just can't stand up long. They all have their jobs that they make money at without working hard like we do. They'll never do this. It's a lot of hard work, but it's a great thing to learn. It can be a good sideline. We've made good money on it for the last few years. But there'll be no one else making it here. Burlon is the last one and there'll be no one else. This is the last groundhog kiln they are in operation now. There won't be nobody else here when we quit."

[Note: After checking this article for accuracy before publication, Burlon and Irene sent us a note with the news that their daughter, Colleen, has now learned how to make pottery. Irene wrote, "Her Dad has helped her on lots of things, and she can make small pieces now. She is doing real good. Hopefully she will carry on with pottery making."]

Interview and photographs by Vance Wall, Eddie Clark.

Terminology

The terminology Burlon uses is somewhat different from that used by potters today. As he says, "These modern potters say 'throwing pots,' but I say 'turning.' I guess I'd been turning ten or fifteen years before I ever knew what 'throwing' was or what it meant. I never heard the word when I was starting out. And all I ever heard the wheel called was a 'turning lay.' Or 'potter's wheel' sometimes, I guess. And it's a kick wheel. That goes without saying. That one in there that I use is actually a treadle kick wheel. You actually kick a wheel underneath on some of them, you know, but this one has a treadle that you pump with your foot and that's a big difference than the kick wheel. And it's a lot easier, I think, than actually kicking the wheel. I couldn't turn like that.

"And I notice a lot of these potters now say 'pots' all the time. But we always called it 'stoneware'—or else 'jars' or 'churns' or whatever you were making.

"Now with the kiln, I call the front of the kiln [opposite the chimney end] the 'breast,' and I call the wall going across the kiln inside the front the 'inside breast.' What people today call the 'flash wall' is what I've always heard called the 'fire wall'; and what they call the 'fire pit' we always referred to as the 'ash pit.' That's actually what it's for, you know, to hold the ashes. The 'bed' is where you set your ware in the kiln, and the 'arch' is the dome of the kiln. We always called it the 'arch,' and that row of bricks that goes down the center of the arch that holds the arch up is made out of 'wedge bricks' because that's what they do. They wedge it up. And when you build that arch, you use 'arch boards.' That's all I ever heard 'em called.

"We load the kiln through the 'loading hole.' That's the hole in the chimney where you load the kiln through and unload it. You fire the kiln through the 'fire holes' in the breast, and the holes in front of your breast where your kiln gets its draft are the 'draft holes.' And that's it."

The Clay and Mud (or Pug) Mill

"[For turning] I mix what we call 'short' clay with my good clay. You find that at the edges of the clay deposits. If you notice in plowing a field or anywhere you're working where there's clay, it will be different in the center of the patch than it will be around the edges. Well, one won't turn by itself—it's not as good or as tough a clay—and the other [from the center of the pit] turns good by itself but it won't stand up in the big stuff I make. You can't turn it out thin like you can if you add some of the short clay from around the edges of the pit to it. So you mix the two together in the right quantities to get the right combination, and you do that by experimenting with the two clays. That's something you've just got to find out yourself by experimenting. [I can't give you a formula

PLATE 232   Burlon stores his clay in open bins behind his shop.

PLATE 233

for that because the clay you'd be using from your pit would be different from mine and would have different characteristics.] So you've got to experiment to get the right combination so that when you go to making pots, the clay will turn good and stand up too."

Burlon digs his raw clay from swamp bottomland north of Lincolnton and stores it behind his shop. When we asked him if there was any danger of running out, he grinned and said, "There's probably a hundred acres of it there. The man who owns it dug a half-mile-long ditch through there to drain the bottom right above the swamp. When he was through, he called me and said, 'Come down here, Burl. Let me show you something.' It was solid clay. He said, 'I just wanted to show you this so you wouldn't be worried about running out.' "

Burlon uses about six tons of clay a year. He and his wife drive a ton truck to the edge of the swamp, and Burlon wades in with two buckets and a shovel. He fills each bucket with clay, hauls the buckets to a wheelbarrow waiting nearby and dumps them in. When the wheelbarrow is full, he rolls it out of the swamp to the truck, unloads it, and then goes back for more.

One of the first pug mills Burlon used was the mule-drawn mill belonging to "Uncle" Seth Ritchie, for whom he worked briefly in the early thirties. After Ritchie died, Burlon and Vernon Leonard, a neighbor, rented the shop from Ritchie's wife and made some

PLATE 234   Uncle Seth Ritchie's pug mill.

pottery there, continuing to use the pug mill shown in Plate 234. The boy standing beside the mill is Paul Leonard, Vernon's son.

Ritchie's mill had wooden knives or blades mounted horizontally in the vertical wooden shaft. The box that held the clay was square, and so as the shaft turned, clay was forced into the corners and left there. Later, Ritchie replaced the wooden shaft and blades with a metal shaft and metal blades made for him by a local blacksmith. He continued to power it with his mule, however.

The first pug mill Burlon made for himself was a wooden tub made like a large barrel with ribs and hoops. It had a metal shaft and metal blades, and a wooden sweep. He used a mule to turn it until "it got too expensive to feed the mule just to grind clay with, so I got to working on the power pug mill turned with my tractor." This mill, the same one Burlon still uses today, was built of metal scraps and salvage parts that he scavenged for the job. It has a large cast-iron wheel, for example, which Burlon calls a "pulley," that came out of an old water-powered Delco light system. "I went and talked to the boy and he said, 'Well, the old waterwheel is rotted down and the pulley is half covered up with mud. You can

PLATE 235   Burlon's tractor-powered pug mill.

PLATE 236   PLATE 237

PLATE 238   Inside the pug mill's tub, the top horizontal bar has three
metal knives that extend vertically downward. The second horizontal
bar, mounted on the central shaft at a 90° angle to the first, barely
scrapes the bottom of the tub and has four metal knives that extend
upward. These slice in between the tracks the leading three blades have
made in the clay. The capacity is roughly 150 pounds, or three balls
weighing forty to fifty pounds each.

have it if you go down there and dig it out.' I went down and got it out and used it and it worked just fine. I had other pulleys around here, but they would run it a little faster than I wanted it to run, and if it runs too fast, your clay won't grind. It will sling it all out. And the faster you run that thing the more heat there is, and your clay gets warm. And the hotter the clay is, the longer you have to let it age. Right now I can grind mine today and turn [pots] tomorrow, where if the clay got hot I would have to let it lay for several days and age before it would turn."

The mill also makes use of a truck's rear axle, a fifty-gallon steel drum that "I set on some rocks and then I built a wooden frame around it and poured cement under it and around it and let it set up and then took the frame down," and the metal blades that slice and blend the clay as the tractor pulls the belt connected to the pulley wheel.

Any clay left to dry around the edges inside the drum is always broken up and soaked and ground in with each new batch.

The Ware

As the market has changed, the ware Burlon makes has undergone a steady evolution away from the exclusively utilitarian items like churns and pitchers and crocks to the snake jugs and face jugs and swirl ware so in demand today. He still makes the utilitarian items, along with canister sets, mugs, birdhouses, and other items that customers request, but the output of any average 500-gallon burn will be heavily tilted toward the collectors' preferences. These include monkey jugs [jugs with one handle, two separate interior compartments and an exterior spout for each], and ring jugs [circular, doughnut-shaped jugs with one spout]. Burlon says people used to want the monkey jugs so they could carry both whiskey and chaser in the same vessel, and the ring jugs so they could hook them over their saddle horns, but he doesn't know what people want them for today.

Because the face jugs are so popular, we asked him especially about their origins: "The old-timers told me Africans made them to put on the graves of loved ones to keep the evil spirits away. When they brought the slaves over here, the slaves started making a few and then the white people did and that's the tale! I've seen the old potters like the Reinhardts and the Hiltons make a few, but until recently there wasn't much sale for them."

In addition, not many potters like to make them because it is a

PLATE 239   A variety of "green" pieces awaiting glazing and firing.

PLATE 240   Two of Burlon's magnificent glazed jars. The vertical stripes are the result of placing strips of glass on top of
the handles just prior to firing. As the kiln's heat melts the glass
strips, the molten glass runs downward through the glaze.

PLATE 241 An occupied, unglazed birdhouse. The small
hole beneath the entrance hole
is for a wooden perch (which
most nesting birds remove and
discard).

PLATE 242 A variety of finished ware in Burlon's shop. It includes
face jugs, face pitchers, canisters, unglazed birdhouses, and glazed
"swirl" birdhouses (one of which, strangely, has a snake on its lid).

rather time-consuming and tedious job. "There was a friend of mine down at Raleigh. Him and an old retired potter was making some real nice fancy stuff together. They weren't making any old [type] stuff. Some people wanted this old potter to make some face jugs. He said, 'Hell, no! I'm not makin' them things.' Said, 'I'll make the jug. If you want a face on it, you put it on yourself.' And he wouldn't make one. Never did make it."

Burlon says that despite the time it takes to turn some of the types of ware he makes, a good potter should still be able to turn a hundred to a hundred and fifty dollars' worth of ware a day. He always makes time, however, for the experiments he envisions. "I always try it if it's something I want to try on my own. I take the time to do it. That's the only way you can work it. Just go ahead and do it and forget the rest."

A DRYING SHELVES   F WEDGING COUNTER   J. WOOD STOVE
B POTTERY DRYING ON FLOOR G BENCHES   K. STOVE PIPE
C TABLE   H GLAZE MIXING BOX   L. CHIMNEY
D BURLON'S KICK WHEEL   I TOOL SHELF   M STORE ROOM
E CLAY STORAGE

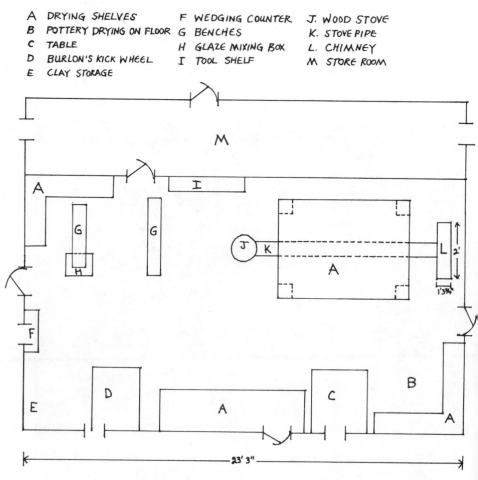

PLATE 243   Layout of Burlon's shop.

PLATE 244　When Burlon is ready to turn a piece of ware, he first weighs out the amount of clay he'll need on a seventy-five-year-old set of scales that were first in Seth Ritchie's general store and were later moved into his shop. Ritchie gave the scales to Burlon when he knew he was going to die, along with a wheel and some drying boards.

PLATE 245　He then wedges the clay repeatedly to remove any air bubbles and debris.

PLATE 246 At his wheel, the wooden gauge has been raised to the proper height for the piece he is about to turn, and set with a metal C-clamp.

PLATE 247

PLATE 248 Rather than actually kicking the flywheel, Burlon has only to pump the wooden shaft (lower right) with his foot to make the wheel turn.

PLATE 249 Pumping with his left foot, Burlon centers the ball of clay on the wheel and lowers the ball opener to open it up for turning.

PLATE 250 Closeup of the ball opener.

PLATE 251 He lowers the ball opener far enough into the clay to set the thickness of the jar's bottom.

PLATE 253

PLATE 252 Then, grasping the edges with his hands, he begins to bring up the jar's top.

PLATE 254 The top complete, he cuts it loose from the mound of clay and sets it off to one side.

PLATE 255 With the remainder of the clay, he shapes the bottom two thirds of the jar. As he turns, he says, "On these big pieces, when you start drawing the clay up it really takes pressure. I'm beginning to feel it in my right arm. Seems like it's getting weak on me. I may have to quit some of this big stuff before long."

PLATE 256 The bottom complete, he replaces the severed top and blends the two pieces together into one.

PLATE 257

PLATE 258 Slowly and deli-
cately he forms the neck and
closes the top at the exact height
designated by the gauge.

PLATE 259 While the wheel is
still turning, he uses a stick or
marker of some sort to scribe
decorative lines into the shoulder of the jar. Then he cuts it
loose from the wheel at the base
with a wire and, using a pair of
wooden lifters, moves it to a
wooden base.

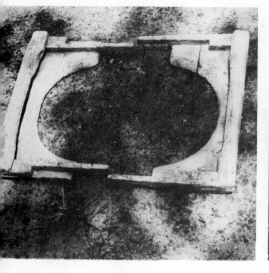

PLATE 260 Burlon's wooden
lifters separated . . .

PLATE 261 . . . and closed.

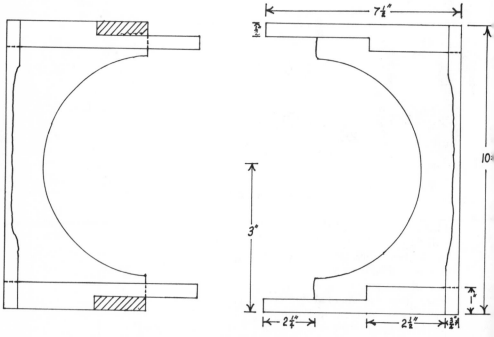

PLATE 262

PLATE 263   Then he attaches
the two handles. Note the pairs
of wooden lifters on the walls
behind him.

PLATE 264

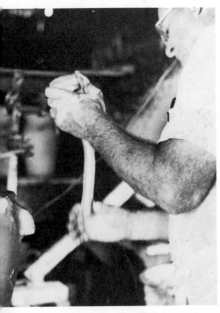

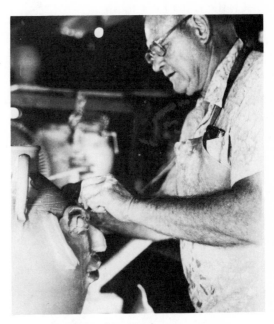

PLATE 265   Sometimes Burlon stops here and sets the jar
aside to dry, but to this particular jar he has decided to add a
face. Taking a moist lump of clay
and drawing it downward into
a long strip, with two fingers he
clips off the pieces he will need
for the nose and eyes.

PLATE 266   In the same manner, he makes and adds eyelids,
eyebrows, lips, and ears.

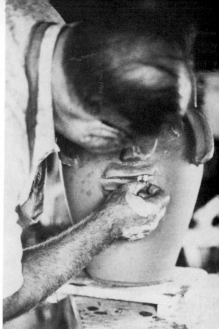

PLATE 267 Taking an old china plate and a pair of metal pincers, he snaps off a piece of the china for a tooth.

PLATE 268 One by one, he makes and sets the teeth into place between the clay lips.

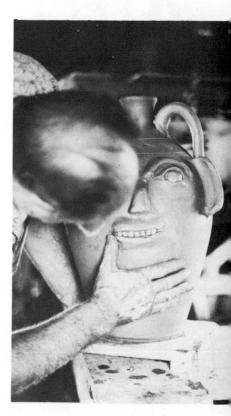

PLATE 269

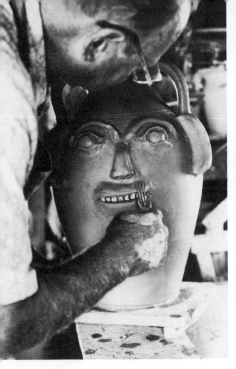

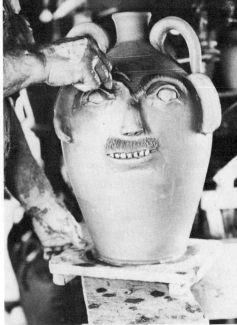

PLATE 270   As finishing touches, he takes a fork and scratches a mustache into the damp clay . . .

PLATE 271 . . . and eyebrows.

PLATE 272   Then he sets what used to be simply a twenty-pound lump of clay aside to dry.

The Glazes

Burlon uses two basic glazes. Both require pulverized glass. To obtain this, he takes soft-drink bottles, breaks them up, and puts the pieces into an open wooden box with a metal bottom at one end of his glass mill. The metal bar on the end of the mill's horizontal water-powered beam smashes down into the pieces of glass approximately twice a minute, and gradually the shards of glass are reduced to powder. Burlon can load the mill in the morning, return to his shop and leave it working by itself all day, come back in the evening and dump the contents of the box into a bucket, return the larger pieces to the box and add new ones, leave the mill working all night, return in the morning to dump and reload, and so on until he has enough for a batch of glaze. At this point he sifts the contents of the buckets to separate the powdered glass from chunks that are still too large to use in a glaze, and returns these pieces to the mill for further processing.

One of the glazes Burlon makes produces the dark green cast that most of his pottery carries. A normal batch consists of five gallons of sifted oak ashes from the wood heater in his shop, five gallons of sifted glass, and three to three and a half gallons of dark-burning clay slip. If he senses that the ashes are too weak, he may add an extra gallon of ashes. The glass itself, of course, is clear. It is the additional ingredients of ashes and a dark slip that give the glaze its greenish cast. The ashes are used not for the color they impart to the glaze, however, but as a flux—to make the glass melt at a lower temperature. The slip helps keep the glaze from running off.

Sometimes Burlon also adds a little feldspar or a half pint of powdered flint to a gallon of glass to keep the glaze from running. "That flint is just powdered quartz rock. You can get it from anybody that sells pottery supplies. I went to the plant at Spruce Pine, North Carolina, up there where they make it when I got my last batch. I got two hundred pounds. Lord, that will last me a lifetime, no more than I use it.

"It's snow-white stuff. All these commercial glazes have flint in them. There's aluminum in that flint and that aluminum is what keeps your glaze from running so bad. You've always got a lot of aluminum in your clay anyway, so for years I didn't use no flint at all. I just added enough clay in slip form to the glaze so it wouldn't run. Then I got to using a little flint—more or less experimenting with it, was all.

PLATE 273 Burlon with one of his favorite types of bottles for glaze purposes. At right is John Fiant, a student from the Conrad-Weiser High School in Robesonia, Pennsylvania, who spent a week with us during the first time we interviewed Burlon.

"Before we could buy that powdered flint, we used to beat some of those rocks up ourselves. I never did beat much of it, but I have beat a little of it. You didn't use much, so you'd just take a couple of flint rocks and put them down in the hottest part of the kiln when you're burning it. Heat them up in there and then after they're cool, you can beat them up easy.

"Old man Lawrence Leonard put beat-up flint rock on his kiln floor instead of sand. Whenever he got ready to change that—just like I change the sand in my kiln when it gets glaze and stuff on it—he'd take new flint rocks and build up a fire outside around them with slabs and get them good and hot. Then he would take

PLATE 274   Burlon inspecting a bucketful of pulverized glass from the mill. It will be sifted and the larger pieces returned to the mill for further processing.

PLATE 275   On our first visit the stream that operates the glass mill had flooded, turning the mill askew.

PLATE 276   Burlon showed us how it operated, however, and we were able to get some measurements. The slab nailed on top of the horizontal pole (and on which Burlon's left hand rests) gave a bit of needed extra weight to that end of the mill.

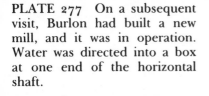

PLATE 277 On a subsequent visit, Burlon had built a new mill, and it was in operation. Water was directed into a box at one end of the horizontal shaft.

PLATE 278 The weight of the water in the box causes the opposite end of the shaft to rise, like a seesaw.

PLATE 280 Eddie Clark and Vance Wall at work measuring the new glass mill, between strokes.

PLATE 279 When it rises, the water pours out of the open box, the weight of the water is gone, and the far end drops, sending a metal bar smashing into the wooden box filled with glass. The water refills its box and the process continues, over and over, automatically.

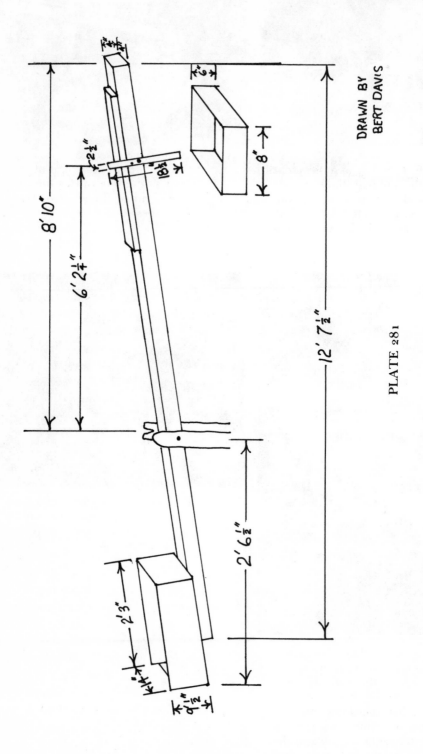

DRAWN BY
BERT DAVIS

PLATE 281

a sledgehammer and beat them up just like he wanted them and use that for the bed of his kiln."

The second main type of glaze Burlon makes is a clear glaze made for use on his swirl pottery so that the two colors of clay will show up through the glaze itself. The swirl pottery itself is made by an intriguing process that requires two types of clay: in Burlon's case, the regular dark-firing clay that he and his wife dig from the nearby swamp, and Tennessee ball clay which burns white. To make a quart piece, Burlon uses one pound of each. He slices both balls of clay, stacks the slices in alternating layers, and then balls the resulting lump up just enough to center it on the wheel and turn it. "You don't want to work it after you've got it laid together, for if you do, it'll blend all together and won't show up as a swirl.

"As near as I can find out, Samuel Propst started that swirl stuff. I've seen him turning it. Some books say Harvey Reinhardt started it, but that's absolutely wrong. Both the Reinhardts is dead and gone, and I don't mean no harm by what I'm saying, and I don't know whether they come right out and said it or not, but they wanted to leave the impression that they was the ones who started making the swirl. But they wasn't. I saw about four turners turning swirl before either one of the Reinhardts ever learned to turn. So I think that should be clarified. A lot of this writing leaves the impression that the Reinhardts started it, but that's wrong. They *did* turn a lot of it, though, and it brings a lot of money now. If I'd been dirty enough to do it, I could've got ahold of their stamp and turned a lot of swirl and stamped their name on it and sold it and got by with it and nobody would've ever known. I could've done it a long time and never got caught up with, and I could've got rich off of it."

When glazing his swirl ware, in order to keep the glaze basically clear so the two colors will show up, Burlon uses the same ingredients in the same proportions as his other glaze—ashes, powdered glass and clay slip—but he uses a white slip like kaolin or Tennessee ball clay instead of the dark slip. "That's the way I do it. Don't use a dark slip. See, both the kaolin and the Tennessee ball clay burn light, so you can use either one. We used to could get white-burning clay locally, but it's all used up now. The kaolin I use comes from the Harris Mining Company up here at Spruce Pine."

To make the glaze even clearer, Burlon has recently begun substituting Epsom salts for the ashes. "Now, that's something that I don't believe many potters know about, but it'll hold that glass up there really better'n ashes, and it makes your glaze clearer too. And you don't have to use an awful lot of it. I think I use maybe two big spoonfuls to every five gallons of glass I use, and it really works.

"That's something I learned by experimenting. I learned that because I had burnt one kilnful where I had tried some of that Epsom salts in the glaze I had on the swirl pots, but I hadn't put any in the [green] glaze. And that time when I burned, it seemed like that [green] glaze didn't want to stay up there. It wanted to settle some on me. And I thinks, 'Well, now, that Epsom salts worked on your swirl glaze. Why wouldn't it work on this other? I'll try it and see what it does.' So I just added a couple spoonfuls the next time I burned and it worked. Course, no reason why it wouldn't. If it worked on one, it'd work on the other. Now I don't intend ever to quit using ashes in my [green] glaze, but it used to be that if I thought I didn't have enough ashes in it, I'd have to go back and sift some more through a fine sifter to add to it. Now I just throw a couple spoonfuls of that Epsom salts in there instead of adding more ashes, and it works. Holds it right up there.

"I'm gonna experiment again next time and use a dark slip and put no ashes in it—use Epsom salts instead—and put it on a few pieces just to see what it looks like [even though I don't intend to stop using the ashes]. I never burn unless I have at least half a dozen experiments. Something new. Try some new color glaze or something. Change *something*. Every time. I have for years. Some of it works. Some of it don't. Something you're *sure* is gonna work— well then, that's what won't work. That's what'll mess you up. I made some stuff here one time, experimenting with a new glaze, and I was *sure* that would work. I glazed about twelve or fifteen pieces, and that was the awfullest-looking stuff you ever saw. It was almost the color of a shotgun barrel. Oh, it was sorry-looking stuff. I won't try that again. I'll know. See, I write it down every time I try something. Then if it don't turn out like I think it ought to, why I grab that paper and wad it up and throw it in the stove so I won't get ahold of it no more!"

Burlon glazes the pots when they are completely dry and he has enough made to fill the kiln. He waits for a day when the atmosphere is dry and the sun is shining, because on very damp days he has had problems with the bigger pieces falling apart when he takes them out of the glaze.

To glaze, he submerges the pots completely in the mixture, one at a time, letting the glaze run inside and swirling it around to coat the inside of the vessels, and then pouring out what's left.

The Kiln/Firing

After glazing he loads the kiln, which was built in the thirties out of bricks made by the Reinhardt brothers, who had had so much trouble with bricks they bought that they decided to make their own. Not knowing how, each time they fired a load of pots they added a few bricks they had made to the load to try them out. After they found what they believed to be the right formula, they made 125,000 of them and fired them in a kiln for fourteen days and nights with two people working at night and two in the daytime.

Burlon watched the bricks being molded and fired. The clay that was used was a white sandy variety from a nearby farm that was ground in a horse-drawn pug mill and then molded in dampened single-brick wooden molds, the bricks being set out to dry on twenty-foot scaffolds.

The kiln built from those bricks is the one Burlon still uses with the exception of the chimney [which, though lined with the hand-made bricks, has a layer of commercial bricks on the outside] and the front end. The main body of the kiln, however, is the original. Burlon says that the kiln is quite satisfactory, but if he were ever to build another, he'd build it on top of the ground to help counteract the dampness inside, and he'd build it with vertical walls to raise the dome up off the ground a little—even if only eighteen inches—to give a little more room inside.

The ware floor of the kiln is three to four inches deep in sand, and beneath that is red clay. Though the ceiling of the kiln is level, the floor slopes up slightly toward the chimney end. Burlon says, "I don't think that has anything to do with the drawing. I don't know that, though. I never fired a kiln with a flat bed. I would say it's raised up so your pottery would get the heat better than if it was level. I think that's the idea, but I'm not sure."

The kiln is loaded through the door in the chimney end, with the regular churn jars and thick face jugs closest to the fire. Next comes the ware glazed with any glaze that melts at a lower tempera-ture. The big pots are placed in rows that run the length of the kiln, with the smaller pots set in between them to minimize the wasted space.

Before firing, the door in the chimney end is bricked shut and the kiln is fired with pine slabs through the three open doors at the opposite end. Firing takes ten to twelve hours, depending on how fast the kiln is heated. He and one helper begin in the morning, raising the temperature in the kiln gradually until "blasting off" time. By then it is dark, allowing Burlon to gauge the temperatures

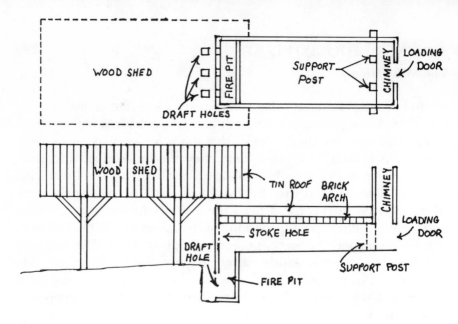

DRAWN BY
BERT DAVIS

PLATE 282   Floor plan and side view.

PLATE 283   Burlon's kiln from
the chimney end.

better; and for this last two-to-three-hour period of maximum heat
he works alone, burning the last of the three cords of pine slabs
required as rapidly as necessary, to keep the heat at its peak. He
works alone then, because in the final firing phase "you've *got* to
know what you're doing." He does not use cones or other devices
to help him keep track of the temperature. Instead, he sets a three-
gallon jar in plain view at the chimney end and watches the glaze,
as well as the smoke coming from the chimney. He is not sure how

hot the kiln burns, but he recalls that once he got into an argument with some men who, after he told them that he thought the kiln burned at about 2800° F., brought some cones that would melt at 2400° F., placed them in what they knew would be the hottest part of the kiln, and let Burlon fire it. The cones almost melted away. As Burlon says, "What was left was almost like the end of my thumb."

After firing, he covers the top of the chimney and the draft holes and fire holes to close the kiln up and then lets it cool off for two to three days before opening it up and unloading the ware. Then he usually goes in the house and lets his wife handle the sales to the collectors and retailers who have gathered, awaiting this last step. Sometimes forty people will be in the yard. "It nearly always looks like a camp meeting around here. Everybody has their pile. Sometimes they have even been known to take some off somebody else's pile. There have been some hard feelings here over that a couple of times. I try to keep that down if I can. I don't like that. That don't help my business none."

Luckily, most of what Burlon fires turns out successfully, so everyone goes home with something that pleases him. Once he hurried a firing because there was a storm coming up, and in rushing the job he got the kiln too hot too fast and two eight-gallon jars blew up. Another time several pieces came out with damaged bottoms because he fired them before they were completely dry. Since then, however, nearly everything has turned out well.

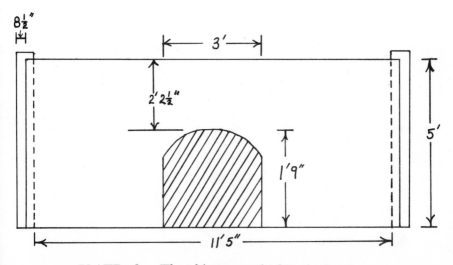

PLATE 284   The chimney end of Burlon's kiln.

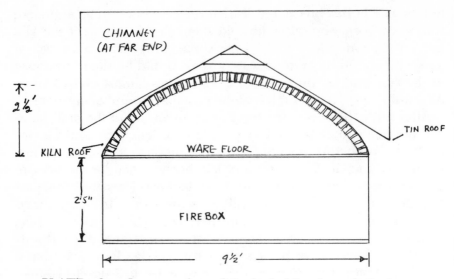

PLATE 285   Cross section of Burlon's kiln through firebox.

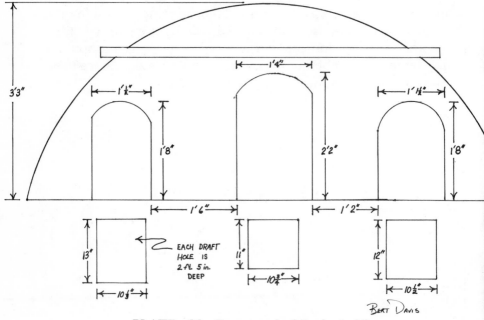

PLATE 286   Breast end of Burlon's kiln.

PLATE 287 Burlon's kiln from the breast end, showing the holes through which he fires it and the three corresponding flue holes.

PLATE 288

PLATE 289 Inside the kiln, looking toward the breast end.

PLATE 290   Arch boards used in the construction of the kiln's
dome.

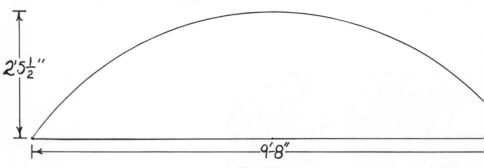

PLATE 291

PLATE 292 On edge, a regular brick and a
wedge brick.

PLATE 293 An old photograph in Burlon's collection shows
the kiln being fired. Note how the door in the chimney end is
bricked up.

NORMAN AND IRENE SMITH

Norman Smith

Norman Smith is one of the few folk potters left in the country who still grinds up the raw clay he uses with a pug mill that was originally horse-drawn. His shop was easy to find, once we got onto the right road, as it sits right beside the main highway and the yard is filled with wares that are fired and ready for sale. The pug mill dominates the operation. For the first years of his work, he operated it with horses. One after another, however, each horse got worn out and had to be replaced. There were five in all, one of which couldn't even pull the mill's horizontal arm if the mill was more than half full of clay. Finally Norman switched to tractor power, even though it wasn't any faster, partly out of frustration and partly because of an attack of conscience. As he told us, "I'll never get to heaven if I work any more horses!"

He was born and raised in the area around Lawley, Alabama, where he and his wife still live today. It was a tough existence as the family struggled to survive on their small farm, and few of the children were able to get much of an education. As Norman recalls:

"Didn't ever go to school but maybe a week or two at a time. We'd try to go to school regular, but we had to wade the creek or swim to get over to the schoolhouse way back up in there. We'd go over there nearly every morning and I'd slide off into the branch. Fall in. I just couldn't walk a footlog. [Especially when] icy weather come. But we'd get across it and we'd walk on up to the schoolhouse, and I'd done have wet feet. Get up there and I'd be a-crying my feet was hurting so—freezing. She'd put me right by the heater and wrap my feet up and everything. We finally never did go much. My mother died about that time. But I had four brothers, and my oldest brother did make a schoolteacher. He didn't have nothing but an eighth-grade education, but he stood an examination and he passed it all right. He got $45 a month for teaching and paid $5 a month board. He taught fifty-six years. After my mother died, my dad married again and had a bunch of children—had nine children with his last wife. I don't see how he ever lived through all them hard times! [laughing]"

When Norman was twenty-four, he moved to a small farm and began his own pottery operation with his wife, who helped him

PLATE 294 Norman Smith standing near his kiln.

dig the clay, load and unload the kiln, and market the ware. In the early days of his pottery business he sold the churns he made for ten cents a gallon, fifty cents for a five-gallon churn. When he had someone working for him, he'd pay him two and a half to three cents a gallon to turn them. He sold the ware by hauling it with a horse and wagon, and later a Model T truck, to merchants in cities in Alabama and Georgia. More recently, most of what he sells is to people who come to his shop. He is still somewhat bemused by the change in his customers from housewives needing utilitarian objects to tourists whose motives for buying are somewhat different:

"[Those pitchers with black glaze] didn't get hot enough or it'd be a pretty glaze. But I've sold a lot of it. Most people want it to look old, and they pay a good price for it, too. Some people would get my ware, and they had a mud hole they'd put it in, and after they got it [dirty] like they wanted it, they'd load up and take it to Florida. Gallon jugs sold for eight dollars apiece down there in

PLATE 295   "People don't realize the work I've done."

Florida a long time before I ever went up from [charging] a dime.
My wife'd fuss at me about that all the time. But I'd sell them for
a dime apiece, and have sold some low as eight cents a gallon.
Now I get from a dollar to three dollars [a gallon]."

Working in the relative cool of the mornings and evenings when
the weather is hot, he still makes pots, the vast majority of which
are not glazed. He talks seriously about giving it up. On our last
visit, however, he had a kiln load of greenware ready to be fired,
but he had been unable to find anyone willing to help him with
the hot, dirty task. He has no apprentices, no one to take over the
business. And the emphysema he now has as a result of working
in dust and dirt and smoke for sixty years has made it almost impossi-
ble for him to carry on alone. As he said, "You might think I'm
exaggerating, but I've made some pretty stuff—churns and pitchers

PLATE 296   Ricky Foster (left) and Wig interviewing Norman in the open porch outside his log studio.

PLATE 297

PLATE 298

and bowls—but I've about quit now. I might make another kiln
[load]. I can't hire a hand. I can't pay them what they can make
now. They get good pay unless they don't know much, and I don't
see no use in cutting [what they can make] when they can make
better [elsewhere], 'cause the way things is, they just have to have
the price. I used to work for a dollar a day. Had a brother-in-law
farmed for another man for fifteen dollars a month. They was a
lot to think about back yonder. You never was old enough to know
much about it.

"But I ain't gonna do too much more pottery making, 'cause I
just can't do it. My leg's been awful bad, and with emphysema and
ever'thing . . ."

And so, by the time this book is published Norman's operation
may well be finished. We hope not, because it's a special one. And
we prefer to remember the answer he gave us on our first visit,
when we asked him how much longer he planned to make pots.
That time he smiled his slow, quiet smile and answered, "I'm going
to quit when I get to be a hundred!"

*Article and photographs by Ricky Foster, Chris Jarrard, Pat Marcellino, and
Chet Welch.*

[My dad] had worked a few days around a pottery lot cutting wood [and doing odd jobs like that], and that got him a little interested. He always wanted to [make pottery himself]. Back when I was ten years old he made a saucer and put it in the wood stove [to bake it]. He got discouraged, though, and he didn't never try it no more for a long time, but it got me to thinking about it. Of course, I'd eat a lot of dirt in my life. I had done a lot of farming with my dad.

Then my daddy-in-law [to be], Tobe Terry, got to talking about pottery. He was talking with my dad and they was drinking together and one thing and another. They'd made a little whiskey together but my dad always drank it up and they couldn't sell none! [laughing] But they got to talking about pottery. They knew where there was a wheel that somebody had used years before close to Centreville, Alabama. He thought he knowed something about pottery, and so he talked to my dad and got him interested again. [They got that wheel] but it was too high, so they went on and got another wheel, and I got the high one and put it up, and I'd take it over and play on it every day. That was in about 1921.

Everybody told them, "Takes four years to learn to be a potter." And I said to myself, "Oh well, take four years—maybe I can learn by that time." [laughing] I learned from that time right on. No trouble for me. I got a nephew up yonder said, "Generally you can't learn it without some sort of talent to begin on." That's what people said I had. But I don't think I had the talent. It was just getting at it, staying with it, playing at the wheel. I was bad to eat dirt anyhow. It didn't hurt me.

So I taught myself. Tell you what a man said. He was from south Alabama. He was retired, I believe, from the Army. He got started turning and coming up here. One time I made him mad. He said I didn't make him mad, but anyhow he asked who I got to teach me how to turn. I said, "Nobody. Turned all by myself." He said, "You *had* to have somebody!" I said, "I absolutely did not."

So I went to making stuff and we was selling it. It wadn't too pretty. Little churns just so big around and so high [about one gallon]. But we sold them. They'd use them for milk just the same [as big ones] or to put up lye soap in.

Then we finally got some potters from Randolph County in Alabama, and they come down and worked about two months. That was Charlie Brown [originally from Atlanta] and Ralph Phillips.

Charlie was so poor he had his shoes sewed up with string. I was turning a little bit but not too good yet, so we just got them here more or less to help us out so we could have something more [to sell]. Charlie Brown, he was a fiddler. He wanted to teach us to play the fiddle. Said he'd teach us how. I wouldn't care [mind] to learn. I'd love to be a musician of some kind, but I just done gone too far now [to do it].

It wadn't too long [before] I was turning eight- and ten-gallon vessels. I turned two twenties in my life. I turned them in three pieces. One of them busted just a little bit. [You always get a few pieces that split.] There's a "fire split" and a "charm split" and "cool cracking." A charm split is when it's cracked in the mouth. If it goes any further than that, it'd be called a fire split. If I'd a-saved [and sold] all the stuff that was cracked a little, I coulda been independent now [laughing], but we'd throw them out there and fill up ditches with them even if there was just a little old crack in the mouth. Now then, people buy them even with a crack in the bottom! [laughing]

Anyhow, me and my brother Oscar was turning. My father and father-in-law never learned how. They'd get up wood [to burn in the kiln] and help out around. Oscar cut wood too sometimes. He was a good hand to cut wood. Cut enough in half a day with an old crosscut saw that he had broke in two [so one man could handle it]. He'd get out there and work. He was stouter than I was.

Then I done all the glazing too. My brother nor Dad nor none of them didn't do that. I could glaze 'em pretty fast and they would set [load] the kiln. We made an ash glaze. We always used ashes out of an ash hopper where they'd dripped the lye (to make lye soap). They'd save 'em for me. Give 'em a churn or something for 'em. And we'd use that. The ashes would be rotted already where they'd stayed there so long. I don't know whether pure ashes [would work] or whether they have to be rotted some or not. You can try that if you ever want to. But we used them and mixed them with water and strained them through flour sacks [into a tub] and then let that settle and get thick. It had to be as thick as your fingernail on the ware to be thick enough. I'd always stick my finger in the glaze, and if I couldn't see my thumb hardly, it was all right. I don't think we mixed anything else with it then. Except sometimes my dad went over there to a gully and got some sand out and put in that. Course, ashes is mostly sand anyhow. But we always heard "sand and ash" glaze. I guess that's what my dad was making when he added sand to them. And it was pretty. The sand and all the ashes melted. But I never did get him to show me just where that sand was at.

Later we did put Albany slip in there with it and that'd help out. Make it stay on the ware better. And then we used salt, too. It makes a pretty glaze. Different colors. Pretty. Now I just use Albany slip altogether whenever I glaze. That ash glaze is so much trouble to work up.

In 1932 when I married, my wife and I come to this farm here. It didn't take any time to move the four miles over here. We just had some household goods and that high wheel. It wasn't no trouble. When I first left from over there, I'd walk from here over yonder to turn for Dad, but having to walk four miles I'd be nearly give out for the day—then walk back. And I couldn't make it. I had some stuff turned and I told my dad to go ahead and burn it and they could keep [what they made from selling] it. The rest of that first year I just farmed, and I was about to starve to death along then, farming. Y'all don't know the tough times [we had] back then. Finally I decided to start my own pottery to see if that would help. It was snowy weather and cold. We'd gathered the crop. My wife helped me build a kiln in the snow. We was *trying* to get things started. That spring, when I got set up, I worked out there in the field still, and then what time I might have been fishing, I made pottery instead. I just stayed at the wheel what time I wasn't doing nothing [on the farm]. Did most of my pottery at night and cut hay and got the field work done and built up my land [during the day]. My wife said it's no wonder I can't work now. I worked my darn self to death back yonder. But I enjoyed it.

We tried about everything in the world here. The first shop I built was right down there, and water'd seep up and get all in the ground. Started losing stuff. Sometimes I'd get a churn dry and put that churn on the ground and water would seep up and get the ground damp. Burn one of them where the bottom had got damp and take it out and the bottom drop off of it. Dug a ditch behind the shop to drain it and it would come a rain and that mud would slide back in there. So then me and this common [hired] hand built this log shop I have now. It's better, but termites are about to eat it up! Been in this shop about forty years.

Then I used that first kiln for about a year but never did get to where I could burn right. Dampness would seep up in there, too. Start a fire, and if you hadn't burnt in it for quite a while, dampness from the bottom of the kiln would steam up through and it never would get hot enough. So I used the bricks out of it to build a round kiln. Built a chimney right in the middle. But I couldn't burn it like it oughta be either. Too many fireboxes on it. Five. You'd have to stay up with it day and night. It didn't work.

So then a half-brother, Ewing, helped me build another one. I had it started. Fact of the business, I've built several kilns here, and that's what's the matter with my emphysema now—building these kilns over. I was in dust so much till the next day I'd spit up that stuff. Sometimes they'd be too damp, or the draft wouldn't work right or the blaze didn't work right or the bricks couldn't stand the heat and some of 'em would melt out. I got some brick at an iron-ore furnace one time and they was supposed to be fire-brick, and I thought the fella sellin' 'em to me was honest, but they wasn't no-count. They'd just crumble. The stuff was mushed together just enough to stick 'em together. So I've tried just about everything in the world. The very *first* kiln we ever made when I was with my dad was covered over with rocks! But it'd fall in. Just didn't manage it right. It was daubed with mud. First brick we got was from Bibb County, Alabama. They sold brick for eight dollars a thousand that they'd got for coal ovens—ovens they'd burn char-coal in. And they'd come to pieces sometimes.

The last one I built I got my brother Clement to help put it up. I don't remember the year, but not too many years ago. It's manufac-tured brick—common brick—and it's not as good as it ought to be. Firebrick's the best. A kiln gets pretty hot.

In the early days of his pottery business, rather than relying on customers to come by his shop, he and his brother or wife would take the finished wares to merchants in nearby cities and sell them. It was a hard way to make a living. They'd leave about daylight, but even so, sometimes when they got to a store, they'd find that another potter had gotten there ahead of them and the merchant had bought all the pottery he needed. Another thing that made the work frustrating was that merchants were very picky, and they'd never buy a piece of ware that was even slightly chipped or cracked. And then often, when he finally sold out, he'd have to buy fertilizer or supplies for the farm and he would get home with no money at all. On top of all that, he had to contend with situations like the following:

One time my brother and I took a wagon apiece [loaded with pottery] and went to Birmingham. We'd go around them corners and those old crazy mules would go a-skipping and slipping. [A policeman] came up to us and said, "Y'all going to have to get some shoes put on these mules," and we told him we didn't have enough money. [And we didn't.] People just don't realize [how hard it was].

Thirty years ago I drove to Birmingham with a T-Model truck

load to sell and a policeman stopped me again. I said [my pottery was stuff you make your ownself and I got a right to sell it anywhere]. Argued with him some. He said, "You mind going down to city hall?"

I said, "No, I'll go." I said to my wife, "Come on." I said, "Y'all going to bring us back (to the truck)?"

He said, "Yeah."

I didn't ask him if he was going to put us in jail. I went down there and they questioned me a lot. Said the law doesn't matter what you're selling. You had to pay a license. But anyway, I talked him out of it. [We just didn't have the money.] They said, "You go back home and don't never come back to Birmingham and you'll be all right." I was scared to go back there for a while, but I finally went to going back pottery selling. [You had to watch out all the time, though, because they were always waiting to catch you.]

I went driving up the road one time [with another load of pottery] and I was about a quarter of a mile away from the place I was headed to and my truck broke down. I walked up there to a garage— or somebody took me—and left the truck standing on the side of the road. I told him what I needed. He said, "Well, I'll go get it and we'll try to fix it." He went and got it, and I said, "I ain't got the money to pay you now."

And he said, "Don't I look at your face [and know I can trust you]? We'll fix that truck." [Turned out] I had enough money—it wadn't very high. Four or five dollars or something. I gave it to him. I banked on selling something to spend the night. I slept in the truck. I went clear to dark and hadn't sold a thing. Didn't have enough to buy breakfast with. Got up the next morning and got out there and sold a little bit of stuff. Soon as I got it sold, I headed home. But I went a long time that time without eating.

And another time, me and my wife left here; drove plumb down to Georgia and went over in there and went up on one store where the man was nice to us. I said, "Are you from Georgia?"

He said, "No, I'm from Alabama."

I said, "I thought so." Every dang one of them [Georgia merchants had] been halfway bawling me out, but he was nice. I went on plumb over into Atlanta. Me and my wife camped out, and they was some fellers knew where we might sell something. I still had a truckful. It was a Model T truck. I drove on over there to Stone Mountain and I finally got eight dollars. We drove on back to Atlanta and I drove up on that little place in the middle of the street—you know, where the lights are. Tried to sell some stuff and couldn't. We came

PLATE 299

on over to the other side of Atlanta, spent the night, had a box of crackers and sardines, and when we finally got home I had a dollar left. But we had a heap of fun.

[It was hard, though.] I've seen myself lying in the grave when I was driving at night. But I got by. I never did get no school. I've lost a lot of what I would know if I'd kept studying. My brother said, "Take and read the signs on the road and you'll get to read a little better." He'd been [to school] enough to where he could make out a bill, but I never could make out a bill. I had all that trouble to go through. I don't know. I'd go through it again if I had to.

Course, it's made me sick. I've got emphysema now. It's caused from this clay or something. It's best not to be in too much dust. Every time I clean my kiln out, I go to the house the next day and spit out all that stuff from my lungs—black stuff, ashes. It's a wonder I've lived as long as I have. But I have. I'm thankful for that.

Irene Smith

Irene Smith was interviewed for this book by Janet Crowder, who teaches at the American Studies Center in Tuscaloosa, Alabama, and her students, Allison Ingram, Wendy Dollar, Jennifer Jolly, Peter Weisberg, and William Baker.

I was just raised out on a farm, in Perry County, Alabama, and I grew up there. They were four of us girls and three boys, and the three brothers would plow and the four girls would hoe in the cotton patch. And when the cotton grows up, you know, and it's ready to open? We really enjoyed that—picking cotton. You don't see any more of that around now, hardly ever. But when I do, I just *wanta* get out there and pick some of that! It's just what you're raised up to do.

I went through the sixth grade. Back then that was as far as you could go. See, we were raised on a farm, and the reason I didn't go [on to another school] was 'cause I didn't have the clothes like the others had, you know, and I wouldn't go 'cause it was embarrassing to me [laughing]. But I shoulda went on anyway. And I think Norman said all he went was three months. Back then, you know, it was really rough. He said his daddy would make them stay out of school and work in the fields, and they *wanted* to go, but he'd make them stay out and work in that field!

But that's all we knew of back then. Everybody farmed, you know, all around. But some didn't have to work as hard as others [so it was easier for them to go to school]. I know us four girls worked harder than most other girls on a farm, 'cause a lot of times the others had off all day on Saturday and Sunday, too, and we only had off one day and that was on Sunday. We thought we had the meanest daddy *ever was* 'cause he made us work on Saturday!

Norman and I married April 13, 1940. I met him here at the pottery. [We didn't really date] 'cause you only had one day off and that was Sunday, but we'd go to church together. That'd be about it. But when we married, I was twenty and he was thirty-five. I'll have a birthday next month—the eleventh of December. And we've been living here in this old house about forty years. We used to have cows and I'd milk them. I never loved butter, but I loved to churn because I wanted to see how much butter I was going to make! But we don't have cows anymore. There're several around that *do* have them, but we don't. It takes a lot of work to keep the fence up and all that, so we don't. We had them all the way back in the woods, though—had big fences put up? About the only farm animals we have left now are those chickens out there, and I've just got those chickens 'cause I just *like* them. My mother used to have a lot of chickens. She'd sell a lot of chickens. And we still have a garden, grow vegetables. We always have plenty of those.

And we've always worked in the pottery together since we married.

[When Norman started] he just found a hunk of clay one Sunday, he said, and just got interested in it, and from that he learned. But he said he did that a lot on Sunday just trying to learn? Then he got to where he used to make several hundred pots a day. Nowadays, sometimes he goes out there and makes about forty, and sometimes less and sometimes maybe a little more. He used to turn three and four hundred gallons a day. Just turn them up and down [stacked mouth to mouth] or either set them up straight in one stack to dry.

I told him, I said, "It's hard on you to stand up and bend over to stack it," so I said, "let me do that." You know, it's hard work, but after all, I enjoy it. I help put it in the sun, and after it gets so dry, you've got to clean the bottoms of it off, and I usually do that. And I help a lot glazing the little things. I used to try to turn on that wheel, but it makes me dizzy! [laughing] I don't know why. It's the wheel, you know, that's turning that makes me dizzy. I have made little churn lids and things like that [but not much].

The first kiln we built was a *huge* kiln. It was round. It took a couple of months to build that one. But it didn't work out good. We were gonna use coal to fire it with, but that coal wouldn't heat it up, so we finally cut our wood shorter and used that to fire it with; but that way the glaze still wouldn't melt right like it should.

The last kiln we built, we were the only two that did it. It was along about this time of the year [November] and I'm sure it took a couple of weeks, maybe three or four weeks. We hauled those bricks from Selma, by truck. Then we'd go dig red clay and we'd work it up with water [to mortar the bricks together], and it works real good.

We used to dig our pottery clay all back over here in those mountains, but it's so hard to get to, and there was so much dirt that had to be moved; so my son-in-law had a jeep, see, and one Sunday afternoon we went back *this* way in the forest and we found this clay, and you don't have to move but just a teeny bit of dirt off it, so we go back there now. Then after you dig the clay, you back up to the mud mill. There's a soaking box there. And you fill it up full and then you bring water to cover it over and let it soak overnight, and then you dig it back out of there and put it in the mud mill and you mix so much water with it. You've got to grind it with a tractor? And then when you finish that, you have to just dig it out and carry it in the shop.

We used to have a big white horse, and we used it to grind the mud. It's been about twelve to fifteen years ago [that we changed to a tractor]. We had stalls up here next to the woods and we'd keep him in there, and I used to grind that clay all the time, but now, I don't now. I've got afraid of that thing. I'm afraid that lever pole or something might break [so Norman grinds it now]. But I used to love to grind it.

After it's ground up and you've carried it in the shop, then you have to work your own balls, you know, when you take it in the shop. Get all the little rocks out and the air bubbles. And if you're going to make a large piece, it takes so many pounds of clay, so you weigh out what you need. [If you leave an air bubble or a rock] it would show up on the out edge someplace. 'Specially if it was in a churn. If it was in a churn or glazed pitcher, one, it would show up.

We've always used wood to fire our kiln. Sometimes in the back [chimney end] of our kiln it won't melt glazed pieces, so we stack a lot of flowerpots and those big urns back there, and then we start on our glazed pots [and come toward the fire end]. That white [Bristol] glaze won't work in our kiln now, so we have to use all brown [Albany slip] glaze. [And to keep the ware from cracking], see, you have to put a fire in the kiln one day after you get the kiln set to warm it up, you know; Norman is bad about putting too much wood in it [too soon] when he's firing the kiln the first day. He breaks a lot of them doing that! But after they're fired and set outside, we never have had any to get broke out there. We've had some real bad weather, but we never have had anything broke from that. I've always thought about it, you know. We used to buy a lot of cement stuff, and I always thought, well now, if it was a storm, it could turn those tops off those birdbaths, but it never did.

Back then, after we had a load of stuff fired, we'd go out together to sell it. We'd go to Birmingham. Spend a day and spend the night. Sometimes we'd sell out real early. Sold to all the hardware and dime stores. Places like that. Yeah, we used to travel a lot, but we don't no more. Go to Selma, you know, if we take a notion to go somewhere, and be gone the whole day. But not much. Once we went to Georgia with a load of pottery, you know, and we had this old truck and it broke down? The radiator got to leaking. We was close to some people's houses, so Norman went out and asked the lady did she have any Octagon soap? Y'all probably don't know nothing about Octagon soap 'cause that's what they used years ago? To wash clothes with? So they gave him a bar of Octagon soap and he packed it in those leaks in that radiator, you know, and fixed it with it? But that was *so tiresome* going on trips like that! Sometimes [we sold a lot] and sometimes we didn't. You know, there were a few years back there when times was so hard, you know, people didn't have the money and they wouldn't buy it hardly at all. But it's different now.

Now people come here and buy what they want. We don't have no special buyers. It's usually people from most anywhere. They've been to town to buy their groceries and they come back through and stop. We don't advertise. People knows about it. Or, you know, like here in this little community—people that had relatives living way off, they'd come to visit them on their vacation? They'd take a load home with them. It'd be something new to them. [They've come from] California. Sometimes people have been here before and found where the place was at. Then they would come back.

Now there was a man come the other day from up about Birmingham or somewhere, and those little gallon churns, I was getting three dollars apiece. And I said, "We don't make enough [of them] to sell wholesale anymore." He said he thought that three dollars was too much. I said, "No it's not." I said, "I wouldn't go and dig the clay for less than three dollars 'cause that's *hard* work."

I don't think he was really interested in [the fact that we dig the clay and do it all by hand and all]. He was wanting it cheap where he could make some money off of it, and I said, "I'll tell you what. We have to work *hard,* and if anybody makes some money off it, *we* should be the ones," you know? I enjoy it, but like I said, it's hard. I drive this big truck out here under the shed that Norman bought from one of his brothers about twelve years ago. It's as easy drove as a car, and I learnt [how to drive] it all by myself. But I drive it about eight or nine miles way back in the forest— some of the hills way up like that [steep], and I load that clay. I hold out real well with that shovel loading that clay, and I enjoy it, but I work—and it's hard.

[What keeps me going is] setting that kiln and firing it and then taking it out and seeing how pretty it's going to be! That's what I enjoy. Especially when something turns out pretty. Actually, I'd rather work out there than here in the house! [laughing]

We had four daughters, but I don't know whether they'll carry this on or not. When they were little, they'd help take the pottery to the kiln, and after the kiln was fired and it was cool enough to take out, they would help. And they were good about helping to put it out in the sun to dry [before firing]. They'd even try to make something. I really wanted them to try to learn. Even this grandbaby of mine, she goes in there and turns that wheel alone and tries to make things. But I don't know whether they'll actually carry it on or not.

Now Mary Ruth, she and her husband, Cecil, live right across from the pottery, and she can make pretty little pieces: candle holders and piggy banks and little pots and things like that. She's the oldest, and they have a woodworking shop, and she weaves bottoms and backs in those rocking chairs and straight chairs? She went to work at a garment plant about two weeks ago, and when she comes in, after she eats her supper and all, she goes out to the workshop and she weaves bottoms and backs. It's real interesting. And they have put a pottery wheel up out in their workshop now, and Mary Ruth has turned a lot of little pieces? And Cecil, her husband, he's trying to learn. They work at it a lot at night; and Cecil said to her one night, he said, "I don't think I can ever make anything only candle holders!" [laughing] Now he can *make* candle holders! But they're the only ones learning. The one next to the oldest one is Linda. She lives in Illinois. She's a telephone operator. And Shirley. She stays at home. She's the one that's got the little girl in school. And Pat, that's the baby one. She works at the same garment plant where Mary Ruth works.

But we see them a lot. We're a real close family. We always have our Christmas dinners out at my daughter's in the big workshop. And I see [the children that are here] every day, most of the time, and every night. They all just made a habit of coming in here at night to visit with us.

PLATE 300   Norman's studio, kiln, and storerooms are all under one roof. Taken from the highway, this photo shows the finished ware scattered in the yard, the supply of wood for firing the kiln (center, right) and the pug mill (center, left).

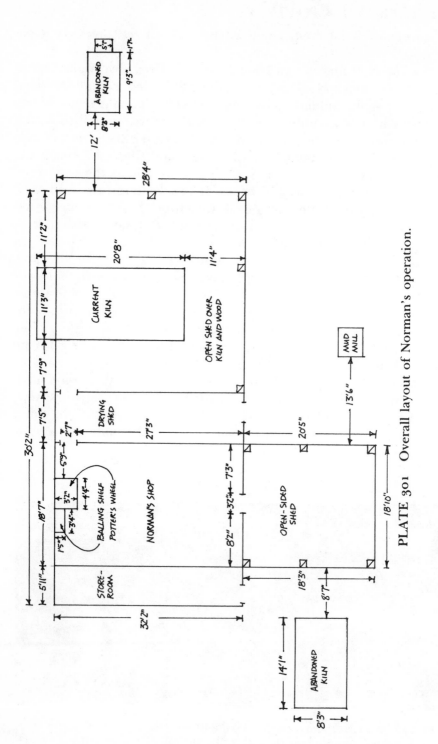

PLATE 301 Overall layout of Norman's operation.

PLATE 302   The collar used by
the last horse to turn the pug
mill hangs unused, the horse
having been replaced by a tractor.

PLATE 303   When preparing
clay, Norman puts as much raw
clay as he needs into the mill
from the pile beside it, wets it
down, and makes about 150 rev-
olutions with the tractor.

PLATE 304

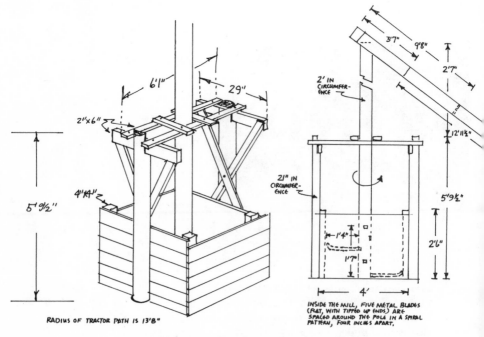

6'1"

29"

2"x6"

4"x4"

5'9½"

RADIUS OF TRACTOR PATH IS 13'8"

3'7"

9'8"

2'7"

2' IN CIRCUMFERENCE

12'11½"

21" IN CIRCUMFERENCE

5'9½"

1'4"

2'6"

1'7"

4'

INSIDE THE MILL, FIVE METAL BLADES (FLAT, WITH TIPPED UP ENDS) ARE SPACED AROUND THE POLE IN A SPIRAL PATTERN, FOUR INCHES APART.

PLATE 305   Norman's pug mill.

PLATE 306

PLATE 307 Looking inside the mill, the placement of the metal blades around the shaft can be seen.

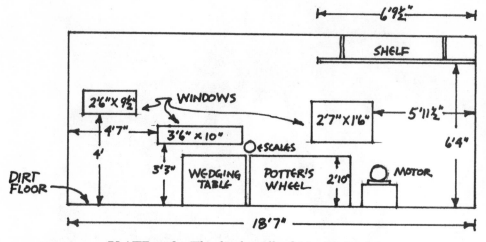

PLATE 308   The back wall of Norman's shop.

PLATE 309   Norman's wedging table and his electrically powered wheel
stand against the back wall of his studio.

PLATE 310   Metal lifters hang on the wall above the wheel.

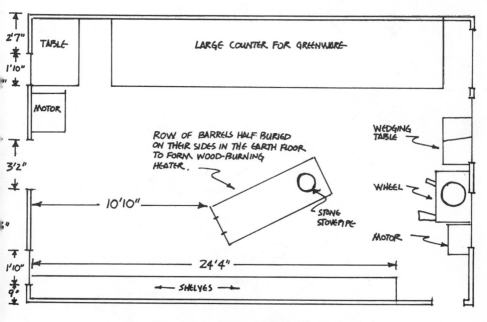

PLATE 311   Floor plan of Norman's shop.

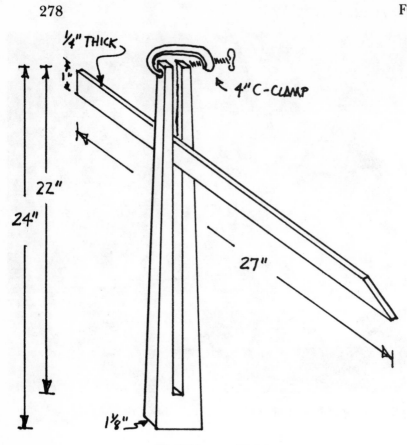

PLATE 312   Height gauge.

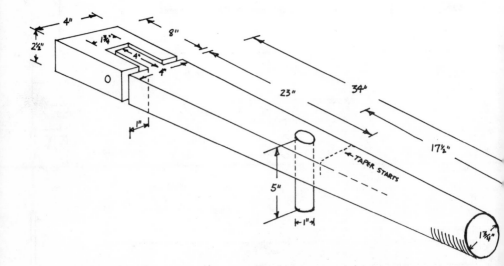

PLATE 313   Ball opener.

PLATE 314 After weighing the amount of clay he needs, wedging it, and opening the ball of clay, he turns a jug . . .

PLATE 315 . . . and attaches the handle.

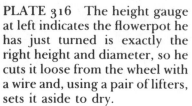

PLATE 316 The height gauge at left indicates the flowerpot he has just turned is exactly the right height and diameter, so he cuts it loose from the wheel with a wire and, using a pair of lifters, sets it aside to dry.

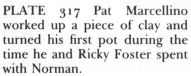

PLATE 317 Pat Marcellino worked up a piece of clay and turned his first pot during the time he and Ricky Foster spent with Norman.

PLATE 318   The walls of Norman's studio and storage rooms are lined with stacked green flowerpots and planters drying and awaiting the kiln.

PLATE 319   PLATE 320

PLATE 321 Norman's glaze
mixed and held in the wood
barrel altered to serve that pu
pose. In the background is or
of Norman's old kilns, used or
briefly and then abandoned.

PLATE 322 Several aba
doned kilns—experiments th
were never satisfactory—dot th
site.

PLATE 323 A second abar
doned kiln, its walls supporte
by brick columns braced b
wooden poles foreshadowin
the design of the kiln Norma
uses today.

PLATE 324   On Norman's current kiln, brick columns are built
out from the sides, backed by the poles that support the shed
roof over the kiln. The dome of his kiln is higher than average,
so Norman can stack his ware higher and keep from hitting
his head. He can nearly stand upright inside.

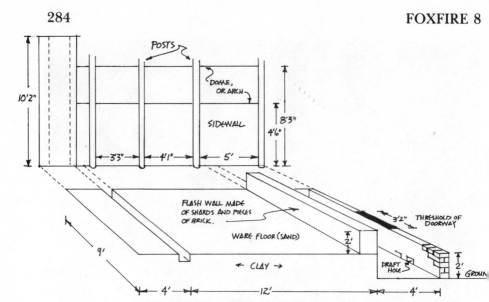

THE WARE BED IS BUILT UP TWO FEET ABOVE GROUND LEVEL SO IT WILL STAY DRY. SINCE THE KILN
WAS FULL WHEN WE WERE THERE, WE COULD NOT GET INSIDE, BUT NORMAN TOLD US THE FLOOR SLOPES
DOWN SLIGHTLY TOWARD THE CHIMNEY END, AND THAT JUST IN FRONT OF THE INSIDE CHIMNEY WALL IS A
SHALLOW TRENCH, EIGHT INCHES ABOVE WHICH IS A ROW OF TEN FLUE HOLES SPACED FOUR INCHES APART.
HE LOADS HIS UNGLAZED POTS, STACKED, IN THE REAR AND HIS GLAZED WARE BEHIND THE FLASH WALL.

PLATE 325

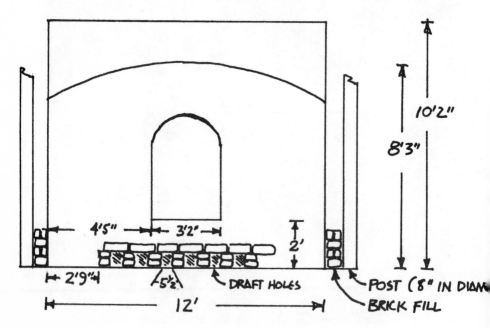

PLATE 326   The front of Norman's kiln.

PLATE 327 Norman loads the ware and fires the kiln through the same door, because "that's the way I learned." He has seen kilns with a door in the side of the firebox so that longer wood can be pitched in, but he likes his way best. Unglazed ware, since it won't stick together, is stacked as high as five pieces high in tight rows that run lengthwise in the kiln. The flash wall is visible in the foreground of the above photograph.

PLATE 328 To fire, the loading door in front is bricked up, leaving an opening through which the four cords of pine slabs needed for the 2400° F. burn will be loaded.

PLATE 329   Test pieces can |
inspected through a hole in th
chimney. He can also tell if th
kiln is hot enough by looking
the door. ("When you get yo
ware started meltin', it shine
It looks right pretty som
times.") The kiln gets so ho
"You'll be settin' right there ar
hear them bricks crack and po
You'd think the kiln was falli
in." To help hold the chimn
together, Norman set strands
barbed wire in the wet ceme
of each course of bricks. B
cause of a central wall, it is real
two chimneys in one, two bric
thick at the bottom and one
the top. As holes and cracks a
pear, he redaubs with clay.

PLATE 330   He leaves his fir
ware outside in the grass awai
ing buyers. When we asked hi
about theft, he said, "So far
ain't been bothered too bad

THE WILSON, HEWELL, AND BROWN POTTERIES

The three potteries discussed in this section and the families who own them have all been in business in their present locations (or nearby) for more than forty years. They have all undergone gradual transitions over the years, to keep up with trends of customers' demands, fuel shortages, and automation.

They all had several things in common that were apparent to us as we interviewed them. They liked the ways their fathers and grandfathers had made pottery and they wanted to hang on to the methods and even the machinery used, though they are all having to figure out ways to increase production to keep up with the increasingly automated competition.

None of these traditional potters that we have interviewed consider themselves "studio potters." They are "production potters." They are making a quality product that there is a ready market for and they want to ask a moderate price for it, so their goods will turn over.

The Wilson Pottery has been in operation in Lula, Georgia, a small north Georgia town, since 1954. Hallie Wilson moved his shop from nearby Gillsville at that time, and brought with him several of the potters who turned for him there. He and his wife, Monteen, still live next door to the ever-expanding business. Their youngest son, Ricky, twenty-two, still lives at home and Wayne, Jimmy, and Jackie live with their families close by, coming to the pottery each day. All four of the sons are capable potters, though only Jimmy and Wayne turn on a regular basis. And all four have various responsibilities in the business. Their sister Doris Reeves and her husband do the bookkeeping for them.

Mr. Wilson is retired from the business, but is as busy as ever, driving truckloads of pottery and other freight to customers as far away as Myrtle Beach, South Carolina, and the mountains of Georgia, North Carolina, and Tennessee.

The Hewell Pottery in Gillsville, Georgia, is a family pottery operation with several of Maryland "Bud" Hewell's sons still working there. Harold Hewell, his wife Grace, and their only child, Chester, and his wife Sandra are now the owners. Harold's brothers Carl and Henry work there. Harold's and Grace's house is directly in front of the pottery, and Ada Hewell, Maryland's widow, lives next door. There are several other family members involved in shipping, waiting on customers, bookkeeping, and all the other aspects of running a thriving business.

The grandsons of Davis P. Brown, Charlie (thirty-three) and Robert (twenty-nine in 1982) are carrying on the pottery tradition of their grandfather, Davis Brown, and his brother Javan Brown. Davis and Javan Brown founded Brown Brothers' Pottery in 1924 in Arden, North Carolina, a town just outside of Asheville. The pottery is the oldest continuously operated business in the town. Rob and Charlie now own the business jointly, and they and their mother, Mrs. Lewis Brown, and Rob's wife, Joanna, are the only people who work there regularly. Mrs. Brown, who also looks in on Mrs. Davis Brown throughout the day, helping her as needed, pours the molds for the many odd-shaped pieces that require this different process. Joanna assists Mrs. Brown in that department and also works at other places in the pottery. She often makes the features for the face jugs and waits on the many customers who come in to buy, to browse, or just to visit. Lewis Brown, retired because of his health, comes around quite often, assisting with turning and occasionally helping repair machinery.

Life at Brown Pottery still revolves around Mrs. Lewis Brown, now unable to be at the shop very much. And it is her daughter-in-law (Charlie and Rob's mother) who cooks those big noontime meals for all the family, in addition to her own housekeeping chores and her work at the pottery.

Stephanie Brown, Charlie's eight-year-old daughter, is in and out of the shop whenever she is not in school or visiting friends. She is already proving her adeptness as a potter, the eighth generation of Brown potters.

Although Charlie and Rob can be found at the pottery most of the time, they do maintain "hobbies" that also keep them busy. Charlie is a member of the local fire department and an emergency medical technician for the rescue unit. Rob maintains an aviary at his house for injured birds and nestlings that have fallen or been blown from their nests. He gets calls at all hours to come rescue birds, usually hawks and owls. Two of the owls he had at the time we were visiting were nestlings found on the Blue Ridge Parkway. He will care for them until he can let them loose in the wild, if possible, or turn them over to some facility that will care for them permanently.

PLATE 331 Charlie Brown showing Foxfire student Melanie Burrell how to turn. Potters at all the shops we visited were eager to show us how the wheel worked.

The Browns are able to meet the demand for their pots and casseroles by using several methods of production. Rob turns face jugs, pitchers, bowls, some of the mugs, and small vases on the standard potter's wheel. Charlie "jiggers" many types of casseroles, and explained this method to us and a third method of making pottery at the Browns'—by pouring a liquid slip into molds to make odd-shaped dishes, vases, and florists' pieces.

Robert has an electric motor operating his potter's wheel, but he and Charlie still use their grandfather's foot-operated wheel when giving pottery demonstrations in schools, at crafts fairs, and when they were at the Smithsonian's Folklife Festival in Montreal, Canada, for six months in 1971.

Their products are on display in the Smithsonian Institution in Washington and are for sale in the gift shop there. They are rated with the best of the traditional potters, and have maintained their family's tradition of making pottery for seven generations, longer than most pottery families in the United States.

All the material in these three sections was collected by Melanie Burrell, Carla Houck, Tammy Ledford, Alan Ramey, Cheryl Wall, and Chet Welch.

THE WILSON POTTERY

Monteen Wilson

We talked to Mrs. H. A. (Monteen) Wilson about her role in the Wilson Pottery. Hallie (H.A.) Wilson worked for Maryland Hewell before he and Monteen Skelton married. H.A. would deliver pottery for Mr. Loy Skelton, Monteen's father, who owned a pottery. Monteen would visit relatives who lived in Gillsville, where the Hewell Pottery was located. They just came to know each other from being at the same gatherings and with the same people.

Monteen Skelton Wilson learned to turn at her father's pottery. After she and H. A. Wilson were married and when their children were small, she turned some whenever she had time, wherever her husband had a pottery. She can turn up to a seven-pound ball, usually making strawberry jars. She started turning regularly about five years ago, although she is not doing much of it right now:

My daddy, Loy Skelton, was a potter. My mother was Eva Carpenter Skelton and we lived in Cleveland, Georgia, right down from the Meaderses. I was born and raised in the Center Grove Community near Cleveland. Lanier Meaders and I were in the same grade together at Mossy Creek and at Cleveland High School.

My daddy had his own shop down below Center Grove Church. I started working there when I was real little, probably five or six. When he loaded the kiln and opened it to unload it, he had all us children down there to help him. He ground his clay with two mules. We had a great big old clay mill. One mule couldn't pull it alone. The mules were hooked up to the mill like they would have been hooked up to a wagon. We had to get behind them and drive them.

My father ran a full-time farm and a full-time pottery with two potters turning, and he trucked the pottery to other places to sell. He fired the kiln and sold the pottery, but he never did have time to make it himself. Will Hewell and his sons, Mark and Arlin, worked for my father. Occasionally my father would kick the wheel for Mr. Will when they had a big order to get out.

PLATE 332   Mr. and Mrs.
H. A. Wilson.

My brothers, Ray and Crawford, both learned pottery there. Ray
was a potter in Gordon, Georgia, before World War II. He was
killed in the war. Crawford worked some at Gillsville after he was
grown and then later gave up pottery. He now works in a bank at
Cleveland, Georgia.

Mark Hewell never married. He came to work with my husband
when we first opened a pottery operation and stayed with us thirty-
two years, until he died. Everywhere that we moved, Mark moved
with us, building himself a little house nearby, living there and eating
at our house. He was about two years older than Hallie.

Arlin Hewell, sometimes called Caleb, and later his son, Billy Ray,
also worked for us, until Billy Ray's untimely death and, later, Arlin's
retirement.

When my husband and I married, he was working for himself.
He didn't have his own pottery shop, but he had his own trucks.

All our children, two girls and four boys, have helped load and
unload the trucks and the kiln whenever they were old enough to
handle it. They all began their pottery making by making balls for
the potters. The boys all learned to turn, but neither of the girls
did. They both went into office work and Doris, along with her
husband, Reeves Hill, does the bookkeeping for the business now.

The boys have bought out their father and are equal partners
in the business, although their father still hauls for them. Wayne,
the oldest, was born in 1940; Jimmy was born in 1945, Jackie in
1948, and Ricky in 1956.

[Editor's note: From *A History of White County, 1857–1980*, page 390, second printing. No author listed. Copies available from White County Historical Society, Cleveland, Georgia.] "About 1918 and 1919, Loy Skelton built a pottery shop to help supplement the family income. A Mr. Will Hewell did most of the pottery making. During this time Loy bought a Model T Ford truck to carry his finished pottery for sale and to our knowledge, this was the first Model T in the county.

"In 1922, Loy swapped the Model T for a 1920 Dodge with screened sides so he could carry pottery into nearby states. During the Depression he would have to swap pottery for things to be used on the farm and in the home.

"At this time there were no funeral homes in our county. The Dodge truck was used to carry both whites and blacks to the churches for burial.

"Eva died October 5, 1956. Loy died July 6, 1974. Both were buried at Mossy Creek Church Cemetery."

H. A. Wilson

I was born and raised over in Gillsville, Georgia. I lived there until I married and had two or three kids. I left down there in 1941, and have hardly ever been back.

Farmers then could not even make a living to pay for the fertilizers. My father was a blacksmith shoeing mules and beating out plows for a nickel a plow in Gillsville. We had another boy staying with us, George. Mr. M. [Maryland] Hewell had a pottery, and he said one day, "Would George or you like to come over and work some?" He didn't say how long: a week or what.

I said, "Man, I would, if my daddy would let me." So I went and asked my daddy. I told him he'd give me a dollar a day, so Daddy said, "Go ahead." So I went over there and worked four years for him. I was sixteen years old when I started.

That was M. Hewell. That's the way he listed his business at that time: "M. Hewell Pottery." Maryland was his name and they called him "Bud." He was a fine fellow. He used to make some beautiful churns. He made up a [glazing] machine. He had these pins in the shaft. When it'd pick up this pin, it'd drop, and it'd pick up another and drop, and beat that glass. We mixed that up into his formula. He used ashes and powdered glass and clay. The clay was made up into a slip and was used in there to keep the glass where it wouldn't slide down when it melted. It was a very pretty glaze.

Later we used red lead in Albany slip glaze to make it melt quicker. We didn't have to go so high in heat with the kiln. That was forty, fifty years ago, and nobody knew there was anything bad about [lead] in pottery. We ordered the lead in little ol' packages back then. You could buy any amount you wanted to. That's been a long time ago. We wouldn't use that now, though, with [the way the] government checks us.

I think Mr. Hewell had worked some over there in White County, either for the Meaders or my daddy-in-law [Loy Skelton]. They did some of that glass glaze over there and then he went over to Bud Johnson in South Carolina and worked several years and came back and built a little pottery shop over in Gillsville, over in the field near his house. He must have learned that glass glaze from Bud Johnson, but I don't know. He might have figured it out for himself. I know he built that [glass] beater himself. I *beat* that stuff!

You ought to have seen me putting that glass glaze on for him. First we poured the glaze into the churn [to be glazed]. We would fill that churn and shake it around, then pour it out in a tub. We had a plank right across there and we'd turn that churn up on it, over that tub where we wouldn't waste that glaze. We'd dip that

churn down in the tub, come right around—man! I got to where I
could just lay it around there and never waste a drop. I've glazed
a-many of them.

So I was making a dollar a day when I was working for M. Hewell.
That was big money at that time. Course we had to climb a 'simmon
tree to eat breakfast every morning back then. Y'all don't know
nothing about that!

In a period of about four years, I burned about 365 kilns for
him. Sometimes we'd fire three kilns a week, usually two but sometimes three. I done the firing and most of the setting and glazing
and beating of the glass.

And my brother went to hauling and selling churns for him. He
bought a truck and he done a good job of it. But there wasn't any
money. The churns he was hauling, we were having to sell for eight
and ten cents a gallon. Now you could get a dollar and a half a
gallon for them. We was delivering a three-gallon churn for about
twenty-four cents up to thirty and now you can get six and eight
dollars apiece for those things. He hauled them all the way to Rome,
Georgia. Think of the idea of making a churn here and putting it
in Rome for eight cents!

And we used to buy that good cordwood for two dollars and a
half a cord. You could *burn* a kiln with it. Now you can't get nothing
but slabs. We're using slabs on this wood kiln here to burn. Anything
that's unglazed, all you want to do is bake it anyway [so it's okay
for that], but when you're glazing like for a churn, the last hour
or hour and a half it's got to have a real draft of heat. But you
can't get that type of wood now to burn at all. I've never done
any glazing here [at Wilson Pottery] at all. We just make flowerpots,
strawberry jars, and planting pots.

After I worked for Hewell, I went over to the Holcomb Pottery
and worked three years for him. He let me have a little more time.
See, Hewell had three or four turners and it kept me busy sunup
to sundown keeping the clay fixed up for them, but Holcomb was
just doing the throwing there himself and I had more time to get
in there, and the first thing you know, I was making churns and
pots.

One day I got a call from W. P. Ferguson in Gillsville. He had
borrowed some money from my father-in-law, Loy Skelton, and built
a little kiln down there in Gillsville, and he got scared he wouldn't
be able to pay it back. He wanted to sell me the old house, the
kiln and the pottery. I said, "Man, I ain't got no money."

But he said, "I owe your father-in-law. You can pay him." So I

PLATE 334 A churn and a milk pitcher that H. A. Wilson made as a young man. Mr. and Mrs. Wilson still own them.

called my father-in-law and he said, "Buy it." (He had a pottery over there in White County.) So I went down there and stayed, oh, almost two years and built up a pretty good little business. I took a chance and done real good. I think I bought it for about $1,700, and built a room onto the house, and about the time I wanted to get out of there and get out onto the highway, some guy come along and I sold it for $3,200.

I probably never would have had a pottery [of my own] if it hadn't been for W. P. Ferguson calling me. He's dead now. Boy, he was a good potter. He could really make 'em. He wasn't no higher than you are [5'6"] and he could make a pot taller than he was. He could just keep going up and piecing that thing. He was one of the best.

[After I sold out] I went off down to Flowery Branch. I was just riding by and they were auctioning a little house sitting there—about four rooms and about an acre and a half of ground. I told the old boy [who was driving] to stop and see what that old thing was going to sell for, and I popped out there and somebody bid it up to $2,400. It was right on the highway to Atlanta—good spot but didn't have quite enough land. But the old auctioneer knew me and said, "Ah, Wilson, you'll give $2,410, won't you?" I said,

PLATE 335 H. A. Wilson with
Cheryl Wall, Foxfire student, inside the pottery shop.

"Yeah," and he knocked it off on me. So I went down there and built a kiln and a pottery and had about three or four boys turning, and my, it was just like a gang of bees there on the weekend—all that Atlanta traffic [heading] for the mountains. I didn't have no problem selling anything. I even went to buying pottery from others [to resell].

Stayed there about a year and a half, and this man come along there and I was in the bed sick, and he'd sold his place over at Buckhead. He said, "Would you be interested in selling this business here?"

I said, "I haven't ever had nothing I wouldn't sell."

He said, "I'd like to have it."

I said, "Man, you don't know nothing about this stuff. You'll go broke. You might do better than I could do, though."

"Well," he said, "I've lost my shirt several times, but I'd like to buy it. Give me a price."

I had about $6,500 in it. I said, "You can have it for $13,000." He bought it.

So I moved about a mile up the road from here [in Alto, Georgia]—place with eighteen acres, a little fishpond, a nice little house and all—and I bought that property for $7,000 and today it'd bring fifty. The boy I bought it from owed some money and had to sell it, but about fourteen months later this boy's father came over one night and asked if I'd be interested in selling. I hadn't even spoken to my wife or kids [about selling]. They liked the place fine. But I said, "Man, I haven't ever had nothing I wouldn't sell." He said, "Well, I'd like to keep it in the family."

I said, "You can have it for $10,500." So he just plopped me out $500 to hold it and he got it.

Back when I had a pottery place in Flowery Branch, a dollar a day was [usually] all you could make. You appreciated that. I run up on a man in Walhalla, South Carolina, and he was selling dishes. They was made up there in Erwin, Tennessee and they were hand-painted. He was selling them so cheap. I said, "Man alive, if you had them things down in Georgia—"

He said, "Well, young man, if you'll help me go and sell them, I'll pay you well."

I said, "Come on down the road," and we went down to Palmer's Hardware in Gainesville and sold them the whole truckload. He said, "I'll give you five dollars a day and your board if you'll go over with me and work."

I went to Tennessee and stayed about six to eight months. People couldn't believe I was getting five dollars a day, but I was.

I was still fooling with dishes [when we moved up here] and I went to work for Carolina Provision, a wholesale grocery company. I'd have pottery in my car on every trip going around [to call on grocery stores when I was selling for Carolina Provision]. My boss come out one time and wanted to go with me to get a cup of coffee. He saw all that pottery. Said, "Wilson, what *have* you got back here?"

I said, "Oh, that's a little pottery, dishes I've got." There were a lot of women buyers up there in them grocery stores. The grocery salesmen really got mad at me, but I'd just laugh it off. I'd give those women a piece of pottery, a nice plate, and shoot, they'd hold me an order. I had it made. [laughing]

Eggs got short one time. It's been twenty-five years ago, and they got scarce. Hoffman Brothers at Lavonia was a *big* supermarket. Mr. Hoffman wanted to know if I could find some eggs around. Well, I knowed my daddy-in-law had plenty of 'em. He was raising eggs and had a egg-house. I asked Mr. Hoffman, "How many do you want?"

He said, "Twenty-five cases, if you can bring them in that car. I'd take more, but that'll be all you can bring."

So I just pulled down to my daddy-in-law's and got twenty-five cases of eggs, and piled them around in that Plymouth car.

Well, my boss wanted to go get a cup of coffee that evening. He said, "What in the world have you got in that car?"

I said, "Some eggs. I'm taking them to Hoffman Brothers." I said, "Boss, you don't know how big a order I'll get by accommodating that man. He ain't got no eggs down there."

He said, "That's fine, Wilson. I'm not complaining. I'm glad you're doing it."

So I come into a big order. He seen I was doing the right thing. I took him those eggs and that man ordered fifty cases of Hunt's peaches from me on one order for that.

But carrying that pottery around—my boss couldn't understand that. After a while he found out, though. They sent me up there to Toccoa one time. We had a new brand of flour, Light Flake. Well, this flour salesman rode with me that week and I talked to him as we were riding along store to store. I said, "I'll tell you what I can do. I've got three or four stores where I could have a flour sale on Saturday if you'll furnish me with plates." I had the plates, but he was going to buy them. I was selling the plates, too. "If you'll furnish me about two hundred dinner plates, I'll sell two hundred bags of flour, twenty-five barrels at least, on one day. I won't let no other brand of flour go out of those stores, I'll assure you." And I didn't.

He said, "Yes, sir, go right ahead. I'll furnish you *three* hundred if you need 'em."

So I set up a big display at the front of the store, and as each lady picked up a bag of flour, I gave her a plate free. And one lady had another brand when she came by there. I talked her into trying my brand and getting a plate, and she put that other flour back on the shelf. I had to send back for more flour.

I was picking those plates up in Ohio and around about, you see. There was nobody, Hewell or nobody else in this pottery business, even fooling with anything, only what they made, till I brought that load of dishes in.

I traveled five years. I sold to all them stores from Clayton all the way to Franklin. I was living back up here at Cornelia, and one day I was down here [selling to a grocery store] and the old man there said, "Why don't you buy that [property]?" There was a little old four-room house and a little old barn right there, and

the boy was up in Michigan that owned it. There was about nine
acres of it [and it was for sale] for $3,500. I said, "Write and tell
that boy to come down here. I might just buy it." He came down
and I bought it for $3,000.

I went down to Gillsville and ran Perdue Pottery for five years
before I built my pottery up here. I lived here then but hadn't built
a kiln. Perdue retired and wanted me to take his pottery over, and
Javan Brown was working for me down there. I run it five years
and then came back here and built this pottery in 1954. You should
have seen it. I put up a little wheel in the little barn out there.
Wayne, my oldest boy, learned on that wheel, and Caleb [W. Arlin]
Hewell turned for me. I still had the place leased down at Gillsville
when I started in this little barn here.

[This land] goes all the way out through there. I started in and
I built this little old pottery building here. Then I [added the others].
Javan worked here for me for about a couple of years. [He designed
and helped build] the kiln we use now. He's dead now. He was
one of the best. His son's got a pottery now up in Asheville. But
he worked for me for several years, and then his brother Otto, and
Jimmy. Both of them is dead.

Then I had a Nance man to come in here and work for about
six or eight months. He was a good thrower. He could fill that
rack up in one day. He has a pottery up in Mayfield, Kentucky.
He makes all these chickens and ducks, and then he makes strawberry
jars and pots, too. He has a gas kiln and all, and he has the power
lays.

Marcus Hewell, a nephew of Maryland's, turned for me and made
pots. I learned him to turn this pottery. He just stayed with us
from the time he was a young man on until he died several years
back. He was just a couple of years older than me. My father-in-
law [Loy Skelton of White County] and his father, Uncle Will Hewell,
used to be together. Uncle Will worked in my father-in-law's pottery
quite a bit.

Arlin [Caleb] Hewell, Marcus's brother, made pottery for me for
about fifteen to twenty years. He had a boy named Billy. They all
made pottery. Billy's dead and Arlin is still living but he's not able
to work any longer. [See family tree in the Hewell Pottery section.]

Five or six years ago, I added that last building. Our first years
here, we only done about $85,000 [a year] but it's got up to quite
a bit now. I've just got two boys turning, but we're doing all we
want. And we're still in the old-time way here. [And we've made a
few changes.] Used to, we kicked it—used a kick wheel—and used

PLATE 336 Mr. and Mrs. Javan Brown in an old photograph probably made at a pottery owned by Mr. Wilson.

PLATE 337 A chimney top made by Javan Brown while he worked at Wilson Pottery. Note the "E. J. Brown" signature on the upper left side, standing for Evan Javan Brown.

a mule to grind that clay. We do the same way now except we have a power mill for the clay and a power "lay" [lathe or wheel] for throwing.

It fell right in my category to buy and sell the pottery [for Wilson Pottery]. I can sell flint rock. [My boys and Marcus and Arlin Hewell did most of the turning.] And my wife did a lot of throwing here until I let this place go. She made a little half-gallon strawberry and a little planting pot called a stump pot. They were a little different shape from what any of them make here now. Some man come in here the other day wanting to know when she was going to make some more. Says, "I want five hundred if she ever makes any more." I don't know if she's ever going to make any. She was pretty good, though.

And now Wayne, my son, has built a little gas kiln. Nice little outfit. He's making some. That striped strawberry is some of his work, and those little jack-o'-lanterns. Things like that.

In 1975, I let my boys have [the business]. I was supposed to have retired but I've been doing more trucking for these boys than I had for myself. I'll take a load of our pottery, and pottery and other giftware we've bought, down to Myrtle Beach, and I'll buy a load of stuff down there to haul back this way. Sometimes I'll come all the way home in one day; sometimes I'll lay over in Camden, South Carolina, and come in the next day. I don't have to touch a piece of stuff when I go down there. They do all the unloading. I was in Gatlinburg last Monday with a load. Up in the mountains, I have to do my own unloading. I'll go back up to Gatlinburg and through Tennessee again in the spring. I was supposed to have retired but I can't set down.

The demand for this kind of stuff [unglazed flowerpots and strawberry jars] is so much greater than [for glazed] churns now. We don't have to glaze this and we're getting more [money] for them. There's a lot more work in making those churns. [For a time, there was little demand for the glazed churns.] We could get more money for churns now, though, but [the flowerpots] are selling a lot better. We don't have the type of clay or the type of wood that we used back when we made churns. We had good cordwood back then. Of course, they could make [the churns] with this gas kiln, but they'd have to have the Albany glaze. With this rough clay we've been using, one little bitty pinhole and you put kraut or pickles in it, it'd go to leaking and you'd be in trouble. So we just went to buying churns somebody else makes. We still sell churns, but we don't make 'em.

PLATE 338

PLATE 339   One of the electrically powered potter's wheels at Wilson's. The wooden bar at lower left, pushed down by the potter's left foot (operating like the accelerator in an automobile), controls the speed with which the wheel turns through a system of gears.

[Our potters] don't have no time to make face jugs. We've got some boys that could make one, but they don't have the time for that.

We buy thousands of those little four-, five-, six-, seven-, eight-, nine-, and ten-inch flowerpots out of a Marshall, Texas, pottery. We can buy them and make more than we could if we made 'em. We don't make a nested pot. We do make a planting pot, a strawberry jar.

You get ahold of a new item all along. You take that little kettle pot with the legs, like a washpot. Used to, we couldn't make enough of them. It takes so much time we don't make many of them now. We still make a few for somebody that's a good customer, if they

PLATE 340 Fired pots that will be sold as they are exhibited here or packaged and shipped out.

PLATE 341 A close-up of several types of pots made by Wilson's. Note the tall, graceful Rebekah pitchers, left rear, the popular jack-o'-lanterns, and the strawberry jugs, right front.

order some. We don't make pottery on the scale that the Hewell and Craven Potteries make. We're just a small operation.

We make [our money] on what we buy from imports and pots we purchase from other potteries. We buy a lot of stuff from brokers in New York and Chicago [and then truck that out to buyers through the Smoky Mountains and down to Myrtle Beach]. There is still a demand for handmade stuff, too, and what the boys here make sells fast. Pottery continues to be a good business when everything else [in the economy] is bad.

Jimmy Wilson

All the potteries are related in a way. Daddy started working for the Hewells at Gillsville and the Hewell that runs it now, Harold, was working for his daddy and he married our cousin, Grace Wilson; and the Craven, he's kin. In a way, it's all kin one way or another. It goes back.

Daddy's done a lot of different things, but he just loves to buy and sell. He's always been the wheelin'-dealin' type. Here, instead of being the maker of the pottery, he's always been more or less the salesman. If it wasn't for us kids growing up and getting in the business, he'd probably have sold this place many years ago. I've got three brothers that work here. Me and Wayne started in here and learned to turn [when we were young] and we've stayed with it longer than anybody. When I was seven, eight, nine years old, I didn't have a choice about [working around the pottery], after school and in the summers.

Javan Brown was one of the reasons that I decided to learn how to turn. He worked for us [Wilson Pottery] for three or four years and I worked his clay for him. Javan's brother, Otto, and Otto's boy, Jimmy, worked for us too, when Daddy had the place at Gillsville. He had about seven turners working for him at Gillsville. The place was on the right side of the road just before you get to where Craven's Pottery is now. That's all been torn down now. Javan lived in one of Daddy's houses while he was here. He would wear a white shirt and tie, and when he would leave work [at the end of the day], there wouldn't be any clay on him at all. He wouldn't get dirty or anything. He's the best turner that I believe I have ever seen. He was fast when he was turning, too. He helped me. He worked with me and showed me a lot of things, even though he didn't have a lot of patience. It worked me to death trying to keep up with him. You know that big pot up at Brown's Pottery? [See Plate 407.] He turned that just to show people he could do it.

PLATE 342   Jimmy Wilson stacking in a display area pieces that have
just come out of the kiln.

When Javan was here, we had a better clay than what we have
now, though. The clay we were using when he was here has run
out. That clay hardly ever had a rock in it. It was a lot different
from what we're using now.

Now my boy, Brian, is learning how to turn. He's left-handed,
though, and you really have a problem [turning left-handed]. The
wheels are set up for right-handed people. You could reverse it
but when you're learning how to turn, it's like having two left hands
anyway. Jackie, my brother, is also left-handed, and he doesn't turn
much anymore. It's hard to learn.

Wayne, one of my brothers, has a girl and a boy and they're
both right now interested in turning pottery. It's a lot easier to
start when you're young. You've got more patience. It's really harder
to do than it looks like.

The skill of handmade pottery is something you want to pass
down, whether [your children] stay in the business or not. My boy
has plans to do something else, but I would like for him to learn
that skill anyway. If you learn the skill [of turning pottery], it's just
something you can always do later on. I'd like to think that fifty
years from now [this pottery would still be in business], and my

PLATE 343 Gary Wilson, Wayne's young son, turning.

PLATE 344 Jimmy Wilson at the wheel. Note the balls of clay on the table. Each of these will be made into a pot like the one behind the clay.

PLATE 345   Pots drying in one
of the rooms of the pottery.

son would have the skill to be a turner, and perhaps someone would
be interviewing *him* on the pottery business.

Me and Wayne make these five-gallon strawberry jars and planting
pots and jack-o'-lanterns. But now we're so far behind [on filling
orders] that we really don't even work on the orders anymore. We
just make whatever we want to, really. Like on this [five-gallon jar].
Wayne will turn about a hundred of these this morning. He won't
work but half a day. It's rough on your arms and your legs standing
there that period of time. Then I make a lot of jack-o'-lanterns.
They seem to be a big thing with us. I've probably made a hundred
thousand jack-o'-lanterns in the last three or four years and I've
got more orders now than I've ever had. I fill up one whole room
with newly turned pots and then I move to the wheel in the other
room and turn in that room. As the pottery dries, we put it in the
kiln to fire it. We just continue going back and forth from one
room to the other. One week's work will go in one of our rooms
in the shop, so a week's work is a kiln of pottery. Lots of times

we have people who come in to see the operation. They'll stay half a day or more with us. They just can't believe that we make this many pots in a day's time, that they're not molded [or factory-made]. I don't take up that much time with them when they come. I just try to be polite and let them look around.

I enjoy making pottery. I really don't have any favorite piece. Anything that's hard to make and I learn how to turn it, I feel good about that. The Rebekah pitcher is hard to make. Or I find it hard to make. We make ours in one piece, not two pieces. We got the idea for the Rebekah pitcher we make out of the Bible. We may have a different style but that's where we really got the idea for it. We've been making them for as long as I can remember. I don't know who designed them originally, but whatever turner makes one will create his own design, being handmade.

We don't put our names on our pots because it would bring in more business [than ever] and we don't need it. I could tell my pot or I could tell his pot from somebody else's pot anywhere. Every turner's got his own special mark. I could make that five-gallon pot like [the one Wayne Wilson makes] but mine wouldn't look nothing like his. To you it would, of course. You couldn't tell them apart. But every turner's got a little touch of difference. The inside ridges, maybe, or the way he pulls up with his fingers. I pull mine different than he does.

We still do a lot of our work by hand. Other places have hammer mills and all like that, but we still wedge the clay by hand and burn wood in the kiln, the same old way. A lot of people call it "wedging clay," but we always called it "beating balls," and there's other names for it. I call it hard work. We mix clay every day. Burn the kiln two times a week, on Tuesday and on Friday. That's about twenty-five hundred to three thousand gallons a week that we make. That's probably fifteen hundred to two thousand pieces. That's with two people turning full time. We've got another boy who's learning how to turn now, and he's working part time. We set the kiln on Wednesdays and Saturdays. Just a continual thing. That's because with this drying system we have [and the use of the Ohio clay], everything that we'll make here today will be toted out with these other racks and we'll dry it overnight. It could go in the kiln the next day if we wanted it to. But used to, it'd take two, three, four weeks to dry this stuff. Lang Griffin, an engineer who lives up at Lula, Georgia, came up with the idea of this heating system to dry the newly turned pots faster before they're put in the kiln. The ware must dry very slowly for at least twenty-four hours before this drying process is

PLATE 346 Jackie Wilson bringing newly fired pots out of the kiln.

PLATE 347 The kiln being fired. This view of the wood-burning kiln shows the firebox. The twin chimneys are at the other end of the kiln, creating drafts through the kiln and over the ware. Many times ware nearest the ceiling of the kiln will be scorched because of excessive heat. For each firing, therefore, already scorched pots are stacked into the kiln in those places most vulnerable to too-high temperatures.

PLATE 348 A section of the system devised to conduct the excess heat from the kiln to the rooms where newly turned ware is drying.

PLATE 349 A view of one of the pottery rooms where ware is drying. A fan at the center of the room brings hot air from the kiln.

started. We burn our kiln at eighteen hundred degrees Fahrenheit. Even after a load of pots is removed from the kiln, there is still a lot of heat in the bricks. Lang designed a system for us using big round pipes [about twelve inches across] hooked right into the kiln. They have an on/off valve and a huge fan at the pottery room end. After the ware has set for about one day, we turn the valves on and direct that heat from the kiln into the pottery room. The fan is turned on to circulate the hot air. If you close the doors it'll get so hot that you can hardly walk in there, but it will dry that wet ware out overnight. The next day it will be dry enough to go in the kiln. That is something we've been working toward to use during the winters especially. Before this we were running gas heat wide open and there's a lot of money in gas. That ware would still be wet and take up to two weeks to dry. Now we can dry it in two days with this invention.

We've got a mixture of four clays. We've got two different types of clay from Banks County, a clay from Madison County, and Ohio clay. That mixture gives us the body and color we want. Georgia clay gives the color of our pots. The Ohio clay helps the pottery to dry faster so it won't blow up in the kiln. See, any pot that goes into the kiln with any kind of moisture in it will blow all to pieces. We haul the packages of Ohio clay ourselves from Ohio in one of our tractor-trailers. We pick up there every week and we just bring back a load whenever we need it. We get most of our clay out of Banks County and Madison County [Georgia]. They deliver it to us in a dump truck. [We don't dig that local clay ourselves.

We hire people to dig it.] We get it up about every two to four years. Get a hundred loads at a time. It usually takes a whole month when we get it up, because all the potteries go in together—Cravens, Hewells, and us. The lady that owns the clay has it up for sale. We buy it from her and pay her so much for the clay. Then we pay drivers so much a load to haul it. We use a bulldozer and stack the clay up behind the shop. When we get it piled up back there, it looks like Stone Mountain. It's a big pile of clay.

Javan Brown built our present kiln in 1964. It took about two weeks. You don't find many people that'll do anything on this stuff anymore, so if anything breaks down or tears up, we usually have to fix it ourselves. We can get about eighteen hundred gallons in it. We'll get about two hundred and fifty of these five-gallon pots in the kiln at a time. We put pots that have already been through the kiln and were scorched up on top of the kiln closest to the heat. [This blocks the flames from scorching a new set of ware.] If we don't have [the burned pots] there, the good pots will crack and scorch. But we like a wood-burning kiln the best. I guess it's because we've been using it all these years. Today now, it's actually cheaper to operate than [gas- or coal- or oil-fired kilns]. We used to think it was old-fashioned [to use wood] but it's not as old-fash-

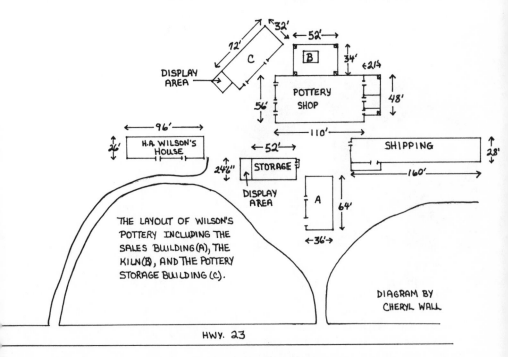

PLATE 350

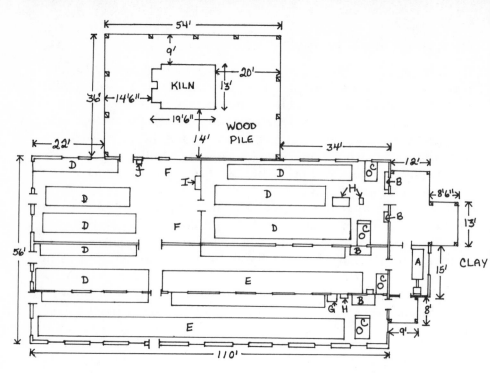

PLATE 351

A—Clay mill
B—Wedging table
C—Potter's wheel
D—Pots drying on racks
E—Pots drying on racks hanging from ceiling

F—Pots drying on the ground
G—Electric kiln
H—Heaters
I—Fan
J—Fan for blowing hot air from kiln into drying room

PLATE 352 Jimmy and Jackie Wilson unloading the kiln. This photograph shows the arched brick-lined interior of the kiln and the Wilsons' method of loading. The scorched pots can be seen at the top rear of the kiln.

PLATE 353 An exterior view of the kiln showing one of the chimneys at left and the arched, clay-covered main section of the kiln. The firebox (which cannot be seen) is to the right. The entire structure is covered by a high tin roof, open at either end. The pottery shop is to the left of the kiln and gives easy access from the drying rooms to the kiln.

PLATE 354 Jimmy Wilson emerging from the kiln with a load of jack-o'-lantern hats.

PLATE 355 A view of the kiln showing the twin chimneys.

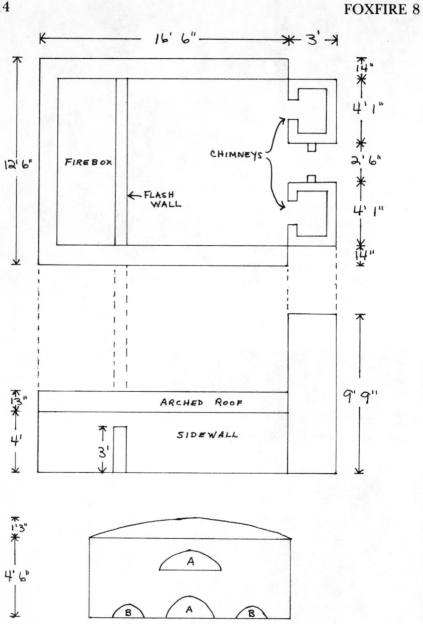

A - LOADING HOLES FOR FUEL
B - DRAFT HOLES

Diagram by
Kim Hamilton

PLATE 356   The kiln used by the Wilsons.

ioned as it used to be. The kiln has to be between eighteen hundred and two thousand degrees [to bake the pots]. You can tell by looking when it's hot enough. It usually needs to burn for fourteen hours. I usually start the kiln up at three o'clock in the morning, and then usually it burns to five or six o'clock the next afternoon. We start off at just a slow heat and that's when I do most of my turning. I make my pottery early in the morning. Then every ten minutes or so, I add wood. It works up to the hot heat that it has to get to and after that, someone has to stay right with it [to maintain that temperature]. We get it up to eighteen hundred degrees and hold it at that heat for about four hours. You hold it by not adding as much wood, just enough to keep the fire maintained. [I learned how to fire the kiln] just by doing it. It's really not hard to learn. We've got a peephole in the kiln door that we look through to see the pottery. When they get white hot, you know it's about two thousand degrees Fahrenheit in there.

The pottery business has speeded up a whole lot from what it used to be. An old-time potter might make only a few five-gallon pots in a day's time, where we'll make a hundred or a hundred and fifty in half a day. All the old turners used to be real slow for some reason making pots. But the price setup is different, too. Where I'll get five dollars wholesale for a five-gallon pot, someone like Lanier would be getting fifty dollars for it. He does different type work from what I do. He makes face jugs and he glazes all his ware. I've got some pieces at home that I made and had had glazed [at other potteries], but I had to get someone else to do that for me. We're just not set up that way in our business and we sell to a different type customer, too. We're set up to sell so many pots and we just don't think about doing the [type of pottery he does]. We could do that type of pottery, but it's just not what we want to do. And we can make more money off ours now anyway. Used to, we weren't able to do that when we first went into this business. At that time the pay was much lower than it is now and we didn't have people to make [pottery] for us. A turner today makes between six hundred dollars and seven hundred and fifty a week. Back when Daddy first opened this place and Mark [Hewell] was working for him, Mark was probably making fifty to sixty dollars a week. Back then that wasn't bad money, but still that wasn't enough.

Those clay pots we get out of Marshall, Texas, and other places [to resell] cost us much more in freight than they used to. The pots we get shipped in here cost more than we have to charge for ours. Our handmade pottery has been the same price for the past four or five years, and you know how everything else has gone up in that time. Still, we're making a good profit on the whole because there are fewer potteries than there used to be. Unions and cost of labor have forced many of them to shut down.

Our sales are our business. There's a lot of money to be made in handmade pottery. We went in the direction of sales some years ago instead of [primarily pottery making], so we're just tied up with it now. We've got four tractor-trailers that haul pottery, and we have two people that drive for us. Half of our sales don't even come into our building. We just handle the paperwork on them and ship [the goods] on to other parts of the United States. We don't ever touch that. And we've got jobbers and distributors in different places that sell the stuff we make and haul to them. Most of it goes to tourist areas like Gatlinburg [Tennessee] and Myrtle Beach [South Carolina] and different places in Florida. Most of our stuff is sold out of state. And it's on display in various places. I guess we've all got pieces up there at the Smithsonian. Actually, I'd rather see it setting at somebody's house than up there.

Michael Crocker

Michael Crocker, involved with the wholesale supply aspect of the Wilson Pottery, worked there for about nine years. A few months after this interview, he changed jobs and is now turning for one of the mass-production potters in Hall County.

I've lived right up here about two hundred yards behind the shop all my life. I started working down here when I was in the eighth grade. I just picked it up. When I started turning, I'd get a little ball of clay that weighed two pounds [and turn a pot]. Then when it got dried, I'd cut little holes in it. A board Jimmy puts five five-gallon pots on I used to put fifty [of those little] pots on. That's how I got started. But Jimmy and Wayne are the ones that turn the most. There has been a lot of good turners down the line in the Wilson Pottery.

Part of what we sell we make ourselves, and the rest we buy from other manufacturers and resell. Our next order, for example, will be imported from Taiwan. It will consist of wood bowls and bamboo baskets, which we sell to greenhouses and florists. Because they are imported, we can sell an eight-inch wood bowl for forty-five cents. An eight-inch clay pot, something we manufacture here, we have to get seventy-five cents for.

PLATE 357 Ricky Wilson (left) and Michael Crocker stacking planters ready for shipment.

We import so much because we can buy and sell those items cheaper, and we can get all the quantity we need to supply our orders to greenhouses and florists. We have to supply the demand to stay in business. Wayne Wilson will talk with a broker overseas and he'll set the shipment up with a manufacturer's agent. He'll contact the freight liner. The broker will call Wayne back and negotiate the deal until they can agree on the prices. Prices are usually pretty good because labor is so much cheaper in Taiwan. One five-member family in Taiwan will get about three dollars a day. One adult gets about a dollar a day. That's the wages. The ones that really make a lot of money over there are the brokers, not necessarily the manufacturers. We also import from Hong Kong, China, the Philippines, and Mexico.

The order will be shipped into the port of Savannah [Georgia] and it takes sometimes two to three weeks from Taiwan to Georgia. The ship can't always dock right away and the liner must pay $300 per minute while in port, waiting to be unloaded. Therefore they want to get in, get their freight unloaded, and get out of there. The [people at the port] stack those shipping containers up like eight-track tapes on the ships, using a huge crane. When the people at the port unload [our order], they'll contact us, telling us our shipment is ready to be picked up. They wait until it has cleared customs before calling. That sometimes takes up to twelve weeks, or it may go straight through with no problem. They have assigned drivers [who can haul our shipment to us], or we can send someone from here down to pick the loads up.

Usually Wayne has another order placed and on its way before we even sell half of what we already have, because you can't tell

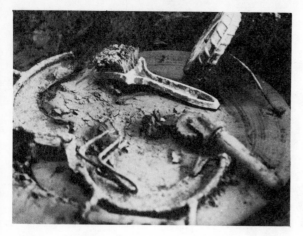

PLATE 358 The designs on these pots are made by such unlikely instruments as the wire brush, the toy tractor tire, and the metal roller shown here.

how long an order is going to take to get here, and we always have a lot of customers needing their merchandise. You can lose a lot of money waiting for an order to get here.

This past week I called in an order to Roseville, Ohio, for a forty-five-foot trailer load of crocks and red clay bowls. They are stamped in a press mold up there. Some of them are cheaper than what we can hand-make, plus we don't make enough of some sizes to supply the demand. Therefore we go ahead and buy through another pottery manufacturing company.

We're set up with a driver right here. He's a local driver that's been driving for us for years—named Bobby Ferguson. I'll call the manufacturer and set up the order with him and ask when he'll have this order ready. He's usually got the order stocked up, so we don't have to wait long. Usually I'll call an order in one day and have it set up for pickup three days from that date. It takes about ten hours for our driver to get there to Roseville. He just backs into their dock and gets out and watches them load his trailer. Then he drives on back. Lots of times the driver takes a load of beef or something else in that direction. He'll take sixty thousand pounds of cows and unload and get that freight collected, and then get our load on the way back.

On this particular load that he's picking up this week, half of it is already sold to a customer, so the driver will go directly there and unload his order. Then he'll head on in here. We'll unload the trailer tomorrow and the next day, and then the trailer will go back out Monday morning.

We order from different people, but not necessarily every time. We ordered a load of standard red clay pots from Marshall Pottery yesterday. Ricky Wilson and I just went out back and looked at the stock. We've probably got a hundred and fifty pallets in stock

PLATE 359 Jimmy Wilson, in the truck, and Melvin Crocker loading a truck with their ware. This particular shipment was to be delivered to Myrtle Beach, South Carolina.

right now, and a trailer will only hold about fifty-two pallets. We just went at random, and if we had three pallets of standard red clay pots we ordered three more, because six is a good stock to keep. We supply 350 or more florists, and they all use different sizes of clay pots, but mostly the six-inch size for cemetery and hospital orders. Therefore we try to keep a good inventory of that size. We order some items as people request them, and we keep some items available that we know we'll sell on a regular basis.

Usually we'll go through a catalog and just use our own judgment on what a good item is, what we think the market wants to buy, and what we think a good competitive price is, and then we'll sit down and make the order out and send it in. How that item sells determines how many more of that line of merchandise we'll stock.

We sell to florists all over the southeastern United States. We ship UPS, or customers drive here to pick up their orders. The savings they get by buying here will pay for their trip. They can take off work all day, stay in a motel and then go back, and still save money. Florists are not the only people we supply. We supply some of the largest greenhouses in the Southeast. There's one man who comes every three weeks. He buys twenty-five hundred to three thousand dollars' worth of merchandise every three weeks for one greenhouse. We probably supply two hundred greenhouses, but some of them won't buy but fifty dollars a week. Anyone that wants a better deal, a better supply, a better variety, can come here and usually get what they want.

THE HEWELL POTTERY

Ada Hewell

I've lived in Gillsville [Georgia] ever since I was about eleven years old, and I married Bud [Maryland] here in 1910. My husband's daddy, Eli, was a potter all of his life, and his daddy, Nathaniel, had a pottery near Winder, Georgia. Eli had moved to Gillsville and bought a place, and when Bud was still a boy he had learned how to make pottery. They said when he was sixteen he was making six-gallon churns. Course that was before I knew him. They thought it was too hard a work for him to be so young, but it never did hurt him. And he never did any other work except make pottery.

After we married, Bud worked for many different potters. He never had his own business until he was about thirty or thirty-five years old. He worked for his daddy, and he worked some for his uncle, Henry Hewell, who ran a pottery right out this side of Winder. We went to White County and worked for a Meaders that was kin to Cheever right in Cleveland. And at one time he worked with his brother, John Hewell, there at Gillsville. There just wasn't enough work, though. My husband could make three or four hundred gallons a day if he tried, but [the old pottery operations were] just small little log places. They wasn't big shops like they are now. They'd get them filled up [with ware] and they'd lay him off. They'd have the yard full of burned stuff and the warehouse full of raw ware and didn't have nowhere to put no more. So then we went to the other side of Anderson, South Carolina. My husband worked for a

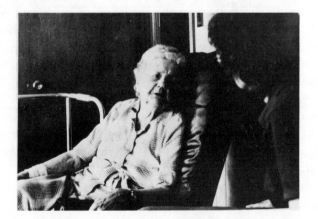

PLATE 360   Mrs. Ada Hewell.

PLATE 361 Maryland (Bud) Hewell.

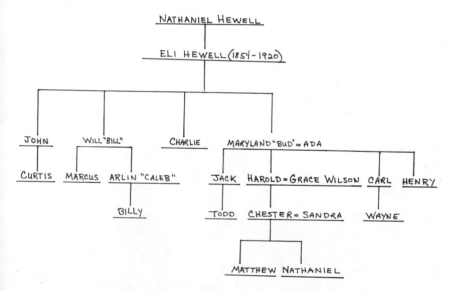

NATHANIEL HEWELL

ELI HEWELL (1854 - 1920)

JOHN   WILL "BILL"   CHARLIE   MARYLAND "BUD" = ADA

CURTIS   MARCUS   ARLIN "CALEB"   JACK   HAROLD = GRACE WILSON   CARL   HENRY

BILLY   TODD   CHESTER = SANDRA   WAYNE

MATTHEW NATHANIEL

PLATE 362   Nathaniel Hewell lived and worked in the area of Statham and Bogart, Georgia. Eli Hewell moved to Gillsville, Georgia, about 1890. He was married twice and Maryland is a son of his second marriage. Eli worked for a potter named Addington in nearby Maysville, and later started his own shop. This shop was then run by his oldest son, John, and was in existence for fifty years.

Will Hewell worked for the Skeltons (Mrs. H. A. Wilson's parents) at Mossy Creek, White County, Georgia, and later also for Maryland. Will's sons, Marcus and Arlin, and Arlin's son Billy worked many years for Wilson Pottery.

PLATE 363   John Hewell's pottery about 1907.

PLATE 364   John Hewell's pottery, showing John and Maryland
(Bud) Hewell.

PLATE 365   Pots displayed outside old pottery, not identified.

Johnson [as a potter] there. We were in South Carolina for two or
three years, and Harold, the one who owns our pottery now, was
born while we were there. But we never made nothing. It was real
cheap working then at a cent and a half a gallon [turning for someone
else]. You can just imagine how many gallons we had to make [to
make a living] 'cause we didn't own anything in the business. So
it wadn't much money, but I reckon it beat farming.

Now what they made then was churns, flowerpots, pitchers. They
used to make a lot of jugs for syrup and whiskey and everything.
And they made what they called fruit cans then. That was a little
jar that would hold about a half a gallon, and they made a lid for
it out of pottery. They had to put something on it to seal it—I
don't remember what. The top went down [on it] just like the first
little churns. They made a lot of those way back.

Later they got to where they made a lot of different sizes and
shapes of vases. They were making vases when Harold was just
little, some of them holding five gallons. You saw the Rebekah
pitcher on the porch? [That was one style they made.] I remember
the first [vases] we made that we realized we had anything out of
it [potentially profitable]. He had his uncle's shop rented back over

here in the country about two or three miles. He made a solid truck-load of vases of different shapes and sizes and sold them up on the railroad up here—the Tallulah Falls Railroad—and we lived on [the money from that] all that winter. We put the money in Frank Martin's grocery store over here in Gillsville and we lived off that that winter. That truckload. We sure did.

Finally he bought down here [about a mile away from the present Hewell pottery operation] in Gillsville. He put up a little old log shop, and he worked there for hisself for thirty-six years. And I tell you, it was hard work then. Well, it's still hard work, but it seems like it was harder then than it is now. [When it was cold] sometimes it got so bad that they couldn't make pots. They'd have to keep fires all night in the shop, and it took so much wood to keep the fires [going] all night that they'd maybe have to stay out a week or two. I just hated it when it was rainy and cold. When you have that clay on your hands and your arms, it would just make them chap open and they would just be rough and sore. And then hauling that pottery by team—with a wagon and mule—and digging that clay just by the shovel out of those pits they found around here. Now that hauling's done by truck—my husband, I reckon, owned the first truck around here that pottery was moved with—and that clay's dug by machinery.

It's changed so much. At first Bud had to push that [potter's wheel] with his foot. Then he sat down and drawed [the plans for

PLATE 366   John Hewell's sons and a worker at the old Bud Hewell pottery.

PLATE 367 Chester Hewell: "[That mill wheel] is what they used to grind the glass glaze with. They had an old thing to beat the glass up to a fine powder and then they ran it through the stone, like you were grinding cornmeal. They would run the whole mixture through there. It served as a ball mill. A ball mill is a thing that tumbles and mixes different types of clay and glazes together to make it a body of its own."

a power wheel] and carried it to Slacks up here at Gainesville and had it made. He had the first power wheel around here. And he had just a brick kiln like they have down there, but he burned wood. See, they wadn't no gas here then. They called it a groundhog kiln. It wadn't a big one like Harold has now, but it was built like Harold's is—just out in the open. They built it theirself.

And every evening when [my children] came home from school, they'd grind the clay [with the mule]. They'd grind every day until maybe sundown from right after school broke, unless it was freezing weather or something like that. That mule would stop still and not move nary another track [unless you stayed right behind him]. I've seen Henry put a blindfold on the mule so he could run to the house, and the mule would think he was still behind him. He had to go round and around that mill with that mule—right behind him. Sure did. They gave that [type of mill] up a long time before my husband died.

He had to make his own glazes, too. He didn't put glaze on the flowerpots, but the churns, pitchers, and jugs he did. He used glass.

PLATE 368 A finished bird-house made by Carl Hewell, ready to be taken off wheel.

He went to Gainesville to the Coca-Cola and hauled the broken bottles down here and he had a thing made that went up and down and beat that glass, and he had to sift it then in a sifter like they used to sift cornmeal or flour or anything, and mix that with some clay and ashes and water and then grind that. Had a thing [with mill rocks]. It went through them rocks and it ground that all up good. It's a lot different from the way it used to be. A lot different.

We had seven children—three girls and four boys—and six of them are living. The baby girl died from diabetes. The other two girls live in Chattanooga. They both were registered nurses. And all four of the boys are pottery makers. The oldest, Carl, will be seventy his next birthday. He makes the birdhouses. He lives right over there, and turning pottery is all he's ever done. Henry stayed in the Marines twenty-eight or thirty years. He knowed how to make pottery, and when he got out he came right back here. He lives in Commerce, and he comes up here and works with Harold every day.

And Harold is the one that owns it. Harold moved up here before his daddy died. He raised chickens [up here] and was making pottery at the same time with his daddy [at the old shop]. Harold went in business with Bud when the war was over, you know. They took in the big old barn and put in more wheels and everything. Then when Bud retired, he just rented the thing to Harold. Harold tore down the old kiln and built the kiln arch over after Bud rented it to him. He had the arch built over and put firebrick in it. Then, when he got rid of the chickens, he went to making pots up here [at the present location]. He tore down the old kiln down there and moved up here. He used some of the old brick from that kiln in the kiln they've got now.

Grace is Harold's wife and she turns a lot of pottery. My husband had a half sister, Catherine, and she would round the ball and pull it up so high and then her husband, Charley Ferguson, would take it and shape it and make it, and [while he was doing that], she'd go to his wheel and do the same thing. They went backwards and

PLATE 369 Matthew Hewell smoothing a pot he has turned.

PLATE 370 Two workers at Hewell's Pottery moving pots to kiln for firing. This gives an overall view of the pottery shop.

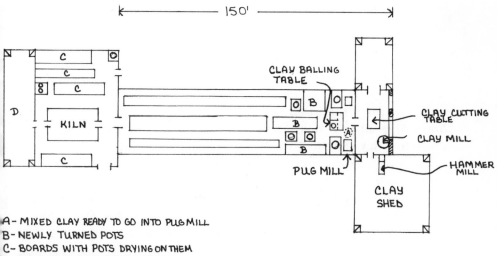

|←————— 150' —————→|

CLAY BALLING TABLE

CLAY CUTTING TABLE

CLAY MILL

HAMMER MILL

PLG MILL

CLAY SHED

KILN

A- MIXED CLAY READY TO GO INTO PLG MILL
B- NEWLY TURNED POTS
C- BOARDS WITH POTS DRYING ON THEM
D- FIRED POTS READY TO BE SHIPPED
☐ POTTERS' WHEELS

DIAGRAM BY
KIM HAMILTON
CARLA HOUCK
CHERYL WALL

PLATE 371 Layout of the pottery shop.

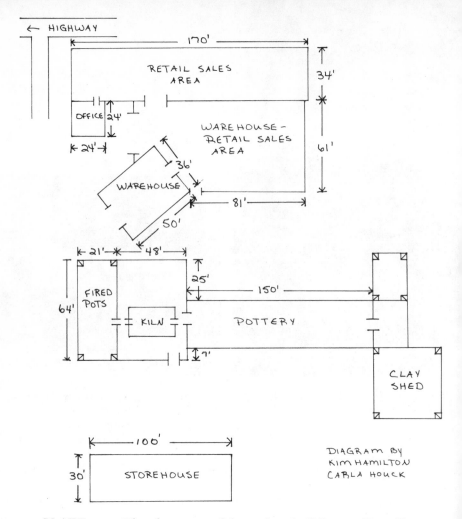

PLATE 372   The placement of the various buildings at Hewell's Pottery.

forwards. But Grace does her own rounding the ball and everything. She works all day at it. Lord, she's going all the time. I told her the other day, I said, "You gonna quit that some of these days."

She said, "Work never did kill nobody!" I think you can do enough to hurt yourself sometimes.

Chester is a potter too. He is Harold and Grace's son. He has two little boys, Nathaniel and Matthew. Those are the great-grand-babies. And Matthew turns now. And Todd, another grandson, is a Hewell, and he turns. So there's lots of family still in the business.

Bud had a stroke and was paralyzed for four years before he died. I lived down at the old place until after he died. Then I moved up here. I couldn't have lived down there by myself. I enjoy it up here. I couldn't be happier anywhere else than I am up here. I know they are [family members] right around here and if I need anything or anything gets wrong, they'll be some of them [to help]. And I have my own home. Nobody can say "Move." It's mine so long as I'm here to use it. Nobody can say "Move" or "Pay your rent." I don't owe nobody nothing.

I hardly ever go down [to the pottery] anymore. I haven't been down there but twice since it's been up here. Henry was in California in service, and when he came back he made his wife some pots to put flowers in. He wanted me to go down there one Sunday to look at them. He carried me down there. I couldn't walk by myself. And then last year my daughter from Chattanooga was here and Henry's wife came up from Commerce. I have a wheelchair now, and they put me in it and rolled me down there. I saw Matthew turning some.

Henry Hewell

[When I was being raised] we had a place about a mile down here and my father [Bud] owned the business. [We still used a mule to grind the clay, but that was] more than thirty years ago. I'd say we used the mule up to 1940. You had to stay behind the mule most of the time. We'd play tricks on him and sneak off for a Coke or something, but he'd get wise and stop.

[When I was young] there was some five to eight years that we used a glass glaze. We'd beat up Coke bottles. And then we used Albany slip or Sadler's slip. That's when people used to have milk cows and used to put up kraut and pickles and stuff. Every family had a cow and they needed a churn or two, and they needed two or three pots for pickling and sauerkraut and that sort of thing. Now times have changed. Nobody has a cow. Times change. I guess we quit making [glazed ware] in the early forties. The war changed a lot of things. [Even then] we made a few [unglazed flowerpots] but not near as many as we did just the churns and glazed ware. People didn't have five or ten bucks to put into flowers. People who grew them, grew them in tin buckets and everything else. A few people would buy flowerpots but not too many. It was mostly milk vessels and [ware for] more utilitarian uses around the house.

[I turned] up until I was seventeen or eighteen years old. Then I was a hired gun for the United States Government—you know, the U.S. Marine Corps. So I've only been back [in Gillsville] about ten years. It's like riding a bicycle or swimming. Once you learn, you don't forget. It takes you a few days to get back into it. The

PLATE 373   Henry Hewell.

PLATE 374   An old photograph showing (left to right): Eli and Frances Hewell; Lon and Eva Hooper (Eva was Eli's daughter and Bud's sister); rear: Maryland (Bud) Hewell and his brother, John Hewell. Made at John Hewell's pottery. Note pug mill at right.

muscles in your hands get tired [at first]. There's a lot of pressure on that [hand] when you're making pottery.

I have used a [kick wheel]. My brother had one that he used for several years after we got the motorized wheels. I have made some on it, but when I really got going I had an electric-driven wheel. I came in just about the change of the thing, but I can very well remember when everybody was using the kick wheel. I was just a little guy then. My father, Bud, had one driven by a gasoline engine—one of those old hit-and-miss gasoline engines. He operated for several years on that. Then they had electric motors that they came along with. By the time I got going, they had electric motors hooked to most of the wheels.

The clay we use now is all alluvial clay that over a million years or more has settled down with sand shifting over it, grinding it down into fine particles. Therefore it comes out usable clay. It's usually found in swampy areas because the runoff brings all the sediment in there and the weight on top of it keeps a certain amount of pressure on it.

We call the clay by where we get it. We call some of it Chambers clay because we get it from Mr. Chambers. We call some of it Grassy Knob clay because that's a place up the road here they call Grassy Knob. We use approximately five percent of Grassy Knob [clay]. That gives a very red color. Then we use about ten percent of a clay from Ohio. The rest of it is a clay we get around here. This mixture just makes a better product.

[The work we do now is unglazed because] this is all for flowers or growing plants. You don't want to glaze stuff you're gonna grow plants in. For flowers, the pot must breathe. Some air will go through this unglazed pot. It makes a lot of difference. Plants don't grow in a glazed pot anything like they will grow in this pot.

PLATE 375   Clay for pottery piled up outside the Hewells' shop.

Everybody contributes something [to the making of the pottery]. It's a selfish thing. A person is just trying to help himself out [when he comes up with something], but it helps everybody else. I use that little gadget to make a design in some of the pots. It's made from a caster, like you'd put on a bed or other piece of furniture. We went down to the hardware store and got a set of casters. That was a small contribution I made. Somebody may pay an extra quarter per pot for that design being on it.

Grace Hewell

I got married [to Harold Hewell] in 1949 when I was sixteen years old, and I always said, regardless of who I marry—if I marry a mechanic or whatever—I says, "I'm gonna do what he does." So I married a potter and that's what I wound up with [but not on purpose . . .]. I'd never been in a potter's house or anything. When we was dating, I think I went down there *one* time. I don't know why I didn't go [more often]. I just didn't go. I guess I was young and I just didn't want to go to his mama and daddy's house. That was probably it. But anyway, we got married when we was sixteen, and after we got back off our honeymoon, the first thing I wanted to do when he went to work was go with him. So I went with him and they made pots! Then they was making churns and jugs, and they was making some log planters and things like that to plant in.

So I said, "I believe I can do *that.*" My husband laughed and said, "Why, you can't do that, Grace!"

And I said, "Well, you don't *know.*"

He said, "You ain't never been around it enough."

Well, he was working with a comb—scratching them logs with a comb—and I just took it away from him and I just went to scratching them blame things like everything. Them men stood back and just died a-laughing at me. And that's how I got started. I really just went into it. They just thought I couldn't do it. They didn't mean they didn't *want* me to. They just thought I *couldn't.*

Now Harold's sister did handle [put handles on] some washpots and his mama handled some churns, but now that's all they could do. His mama could handle churns but she never learned to put a handle on a washpot or things like that. So one day his sister was handling some pots and she was in that old log shop—that's where we made them back then—and I said, "Let's you and me go to Commerce."

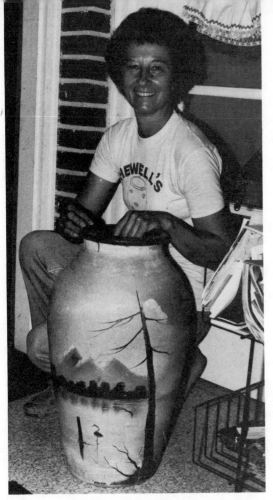

PLATE 376 Grace Hewell: "We've got a big old urn Harold's daddy made on the wheel. This artist painted it in watercolors for my mother-in-law. She gave me the vase and I'm real proud of it."

She said, "I haven't got time." Says, "I got to work, get all these pots done."

I says, "Well, what if I help you?" I says, "Then we can go, can't we?"

She said, "Yeah, but Grace," said, "you don't know how."

I said, "Yeah, but you can't tell. I might can do it." And I just picked me up some handles and went to puttin' them things on just as fast as I could put 'em on. I was just layin' them handles on! It was my brother-in-law's pots I was handling, and he went to the house and told my husband's mama, said, "Grace is down yonder just a-handlin' them pots to beat the band, but there's just one thing wrong with it. She's puttin' one up a little higher than she's puttin' the other." And Mrs. Hewell says, "Well, why don't you *tell* her?" Said, "She don't know the difference. She hadn't never done none of that." Says, "Why don't you tell her and they can put 'em right." So they told me and that's how I got *my* job. I just dove in and went to work.

Then one day after my son Chester was born, I decided I wanted to learn to turn. So my husband there again says, "Ah, you can't turn."

I says, "Ah, you don't know." And I just went in there on a wheel nobody was a-usin' and I made me up, I think, six balls. Well, I made little old pots out of them things and I thought I done real good. Well, they did too. The next day I went in there and I made me up a dozen and I turned them real quick and I done real good. Then next day I made me two dozen. The next day I made me three dozen. And the next thing I knowed it was up in the hundreds. And that's how I learned. I wanted to, and it was just interesting. And the first little old pots I made on the wheel sold, too. Fifty years from now, I'd like for my great-grandchildren to know how many pots I made in a day and see if they could make that many. I sure would. Two days last week, I turned a thousand and fifty each day. I usually make three to four hundred jack-o'-lanterns every day, then cut the faces and rub the pots smooth for all I've made and the ones Harold's made. My cousin, Brenda Turpin, also cuts [jack-o'-lantern faces] and finishes up the pots for us.

Now my son Chester was not interested [in learning how to turn] at *all.* When he was little, he would go out and play with his little red wagon—play out in the sand and all. Then he went through high school and then he went to Lanier Tech and took a course in welding and got him a job in Atlanta welding. Then he got married. When he got married, he says, "Mama, can I come back and learn to make pots and work with you and Daddy?"

I said, "Why, sure you can." So he left [Atlanta] and come back [to Gillsville] and therefore he likes it. If we'da *made* him done it, he wouldn't have liked it. I'm just so proud it worked out like it did. He come back and learnt real quick.

[Harold and I do all the buying for the floral supplies and gift items we sell in the shop. We got into floral supplies because] we just saw that pots and flowers go so good together. We go to gift shows and there are also salesmen who come here. Harold and I went to Chicago this past year. The gift shows are in Chicago and St. Louis, Missouri and Atlanta. We go a lot of places.

[Occasionally] we have a trailer load of pottery and giftware come on a boat direct from overseas. All of our Italy pots come by boat into the Savannah port and then are "piggy-backed" here on tractor-trailer trucks.

We get a lot of [flowerpots] from Marshall, Texas, and Ohio. One day this week, [a truck from the Marshall, Texas, pottery] was

PLATE 377   View of Hewell's Pottery and Harold and Grace Hewell's house at left.

here and they delivered us a load of pots and picked up a fired load [of our pots]. Then they were going on to pick up a load of blankets [somewhere else]. See, that makes [their truck] pay both ways.

[Some of our clay] comes from Grassy Knob, up here between Gillsville and Lula. The Wilsons get the same clay we do. We use the same diggers, same trucks. [We didn't get any clay last year], but year before we got worlds of it. We've even got clay stored over at Chester's house—a different kind of clay that we're not even getting now. Someday we'll need it. It takes a lot of clay. If there's been a lot of rain and the swamps where we dig our clay are real wet, we might not be able to get in there and get it out. You have to stay ahead.

We like working on production because that's what we've always done. [Hewell's] has always been a production line. Our business has been great! It really has been good. I'm hoping we'll be in [our new pottery building] by December or the first of the year [1983]. We're all excited about that. It's going to be real nice. We may have two [shuttle kilns]. [We fire our present kiln] one to two times a week, but we'll be firing every day [with that second kiln].

[For the new pottery], we've got two more boys learning. They are cousins of ours. We're in the process of getting more [people]. We're going to get every turner we can get ahold of everywhere. We are hoping to get bigger. And Matthew's learning. He's Chester's oldest son. When he was two and one half years old, he'd come and say, "Granny, let me set in your lap and make a pot." And I always just took time whether I had time or not. I'd set him up in my lap and let him make a pot. So it got to where every day he was over here. He just learnt *real* good. He'd pay attention to what you said, and him that little. He'd pay attention. So he's been makin' stuff we can sell for a long time—ever since he was about four years old. And what time he wasn't here learning to turn in my lap, he was setting right there watching me.

The last time he and Nathaniel, who's five now, came down to the pottery, they wanted to see how much clay we had gotten and how much had been done on the new pottery building down there. I heard Matthew telling Nathaniel last night, "Nathaniel, don't you know that one day Granny and Paw-Paw are going to get old and die, and we're going to have to run the pottery building?" He said, "Now you're going to have to get busy and start learning how to make some pots." They were just as serious. They didn't know I was listening to them talk.

Nathaniel said, "Okay, Matthew. I'm gonna learn to make pots. I'm just practicing on chickens now. I've got plenty of time. I'm gonna make pots." The first thing Nathaniel does when he gets home from school and comes over here is get a piece of clay and make a chicken and go to playing with it.

If we hadn't started back [rebuilt] after our old pottery burned, Chester probably wouldn't have been in the pottery business now and our grandsons wouldn't be in the pottery business. I feel like we done good by keeping on. We've got a lot of people in jobs and it's kept our generation [of potters] going. And I love it. I work every day. I love it.

Chester Hewell

I guess I sort of influenced myself [to become a potter]. I'm a welder, too, and that's a big help in fixing the equipment. I make about anything that we produce except the birdhouses. Carl [Hewell] makes them most of the time. I may make strawberries for a month or I may make an assortment of stuff every day. It's according to how much of the stuff is sold. Sometimes all of us are working on the same order, and then again maybe we are all working on different orders. I made the first jack-o'-lantern here. I've got it up at my house. It looks a lot different than these we do now, the way they cut the teeth out and the shape of it. I like to make them about as good as anything. Them, and saucers you put plants on.

Now by the time I really got started, things had changed almost completely. I can remember the wood-fired kiln and the big long lines of slabs to fire it with, but I can't remember too much about it. And I never saw any of my people make pottery on anything but an electric wheel. I had to go to Lanier Meaders' to see a kick wheel. I hadn't ever saw one. I haven't ever made a pot on one

PLATE 378 Two views of the pug mill.

PLATE 379

and don't intend on trying! I have done some wedging by hand, but there is a lot of work in wedging clay. We haven't wedged any clay in eight or nine years. It would cost a lot of labor now to have someone wedge it. [We have a machine that compresses the clay into "logs" and we make our balls from those.]

We still use some old-time stuff. Some of those lifters were made at Bagwells' Barn. That was a place that made the Bagwell wagons.

PLATE 380   Wire frames used to cut clay into uniform slices from which the balls of clay are made.

PLATE 381   One of the pot lifters at Hewell's. "I don't know how old those are. There ain't no way to tell, but they're very old. They were hanging in the shop with all the other lifters when the pottery shop burned, but were salvaged. I make the lifters myself now." (Chester Hewell)

PLATE 382   The conveyer belt bringing dry clay into the clay mill to be mixed with water and packaged Ohio clays.

PLATE 383   The view of the clay mill from the other side.
"Our clay mill was made at Crosley Machine Company, Trenton,
New Jersey, and then it was shipped to Detroit, Michigan, and
was used in crushing carbon. Next it went to Missouri and I
think it was used for crushing clay there. It came to Georgia
in 1951. We went and got it, brought that thing in here on a
Ford one-ton truck. The motor runs to a jack shaft which is a
speed reducer. That, in turn, runs the flat belt over to the clay
mill. The mill came with a big flat pulley on it. That's the reason
we use such a long, flat belt. The motor runs off of a fifteen-
horsepower, three-phase electric motor. Occasionally we have
to do something to it, but it's very little you have to do to ol'
Dugan. That's the clay mill's name. Some of the boys working
here named him Dugan. Ol' Dugan will kill you if you stay with
him long enough. He's hard work! If you just visit him daily
for a while, he's not too bad, but if you stay with him very
long, every day all day, he's rough. We've had to put new gears
on him because they wore out. Not much more, though." (Chester Hewell)

PLATE 384   The motor, jack shaft, and belt running the clay
mill.

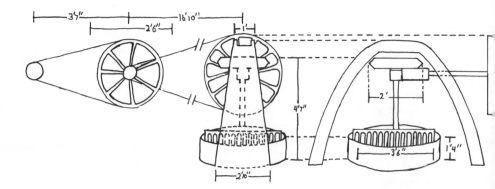

DIAGRAM BY
ALLAN RAMEY

PLATE 385   Diagram of clay mill.

PLATE 386   Matthew Hewell turning in foreground; his father Chester in the background; eight-gallon strawberry pots made by Harold Hewell in front of Matthew.

PLATE 387   A strawberry jar in use.

It was a real old blacksmith shop in Gainesville, Georgia. The lifters have buggy hinges on them for the hinges.

And we didn't used to have any way to beat the clay up, but we have an old hammer mill out there now. It makes the clay a lot smoother and better the way we do it now. It knocks all the rocks out of it. J. Merritt, in Lizella, Georgia, made that hammer mill. That mill's probably sixty or seventy years old. They made hand-turned pottery down there a long time ago, and that's where that mill came from.

So we still use a few pieces of old equipment, but most of that stuff is gone now. And so are some of the old practices. My grandfather, Bud Hewell, and his brothers worked out a formula for a good-looking, workable glaze, for example, but I don't think my daddy or any of my uncles know how they made it exactly. I've got them old glass-glazed pitchers at my house that they made way back then, but I didn't see it done.

And these eight-gallon strawberry jars are extremely hard to make. Daddy even makes up to a ten [-gallon size]. I don't think we have any right now, but it ain't been very long ago he made some. Every time he makes them, he says he ain't going to make no more. They're real hard to make. Very few people can make them over an eight or ten. It's hard work. There's a lot of weight. So these are gradually getting gone too. They won't be here much longer. There won't be anybody who can make them that big. I can't make them.

But we have a good operation that's much more efficient now, and that's why we're still in business. We've been making pots for years, and we've worked out standard measurements for each type pot and each size pot. Daddy [Harold Hewell] designed [the kiln we use now]. That is a one-of-a-kind kiln out there. It will hold from fifty-five hundred to six thousand gallons of pottery. We know how long to burn it and we watch the temperature. We check it every hour. When it gets up to seventeen hundred or seventeen hundred and fifty degrees Fahrenheit, we just hold it there for about three hours. Then we let it cool a couple of days. Right there is something that *hasn't* changed in a long time—the way we close up the kiln. [We seal the door] with red mud or red clay. It's just red dirt is all it is.

The pots turn red when they're fired because the clay's got iron in it and the oxygen in the air in the kiln changes the color of the clay. When it's fired, that's called an oxidation process. Most of the time the clay that's got [iron] in it is yellow-looking when it's dug. Most of the clay that's fired to a white color will be a blue-colored clay to start with.

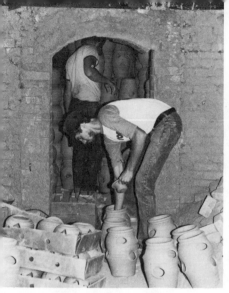

PLATE 388   Some workers at Hewell's loading the kiln.

PLATE 389   The kiln being sealed up before being fired. Note how the pottery is stacked in the kiln.

PLATE 390   The kiln sealed and ready to be fired.

PLATE 391   Chester Hewell at his wheel.

Very few pieces [I make] have a name or anything on them. I don't mind marking them, but when you get done [making them], you're so glad to get through you don't [bother]. So it don't have no name on it. We just figure that every extra process it has to go through would mean it costs more money [to produce]. So we leave out as many [extra steps] as we can. But I could recognize what I make, probably.

I like the work. I might [still be turning fifty years from now]. I ain't nowhere near wore out yet, so I better be. Let's see, I'd be about eighty-four years old, so I'd still have a long time to live. I ought to. I might retire when I get to be about a hundred, and not do nothing. There ain't no doubt about it. Hard work'll make you live longer. I don't care what you're doing. Work'll make you live longer. You take, on the average, people that have worked real hard generally live longer than people that just don't never do nothing.

I'd like to see [the Hewell Pottery] about four times as big as it is, or twenty times bigger. I'd like to see it continue to grow. One thing for sure, I'd really like to see it still here in operation and my sons or nephews or some other Hewells running it just as long as it's still in operation.

THE BROWN POTTERY

Louis Brown

Our business here is not really a big business, but it's a big operation. I was about nine years old when I started working in it. Every day when I got off from the school bus, I'd come in to the shop. We worked until around nine o'clock at night and then we went home and did our lessons. We always had homework. Next morning, we was out on the road at seven o'clock. And if we happened to miss the bus, we walked. That's the way we went—rain, shine, sleet, or snow. We never had a day off back then. And we didn't get rich, but it was a living and you didn't go hungry.

Coming from the early twenties and growing up through the thirties, everything was changing. This highway out here was just barely eighteen feet wide, but it was paved. I can remember when I was a kid and we'd be out playing. A lot of times I could hear horses trotting on that pavement. People still had horses and wagons. We could hear them horses just clattering, coming down the hill. And there were T-Model and A-Model Fords and old Hupmobiles and Essexes and automobiles of that type. I was raised with that. I was used to that kind of thing. [laughter]

We had a 1925 International truck that we used for the shop here, and that thing would get about twenty miles per gallon in gas. It had heavy, wooden-spoked wheels and balloon tires on it. The earlier models had solid tires. That was the biggest truck around here then. That truck would haul a full cord of green pine wood.

A T-Model Ford truck would only haul about three quarters of a cord. It would have to be an awful good T-Model to haul a cord.

[Before we built the pottery shop and this kiln in 1939 and 1940, we only had a shed-type building.] If you were to see an old picture of this place, you'd see a great big bank up there by the side of the highway. It was about five feet high and all down in here [where the present pottery shop is] was swamp. There used to be a well right out there and the water'd come right to the top of the ground. We'd just dip down in the well with a bucket and carry the water right over and pour it in the clay mix. The well was right there near where that wall is now. We dug that bank off and hauled the dirt back here and dumped it, to level this off [where we built the pottery]. We didn't have bulldozers and stuff like that. It was wheelbarrow and shovel.

We used to have a groundhog kiln out in back and I had helped [my father] built it. Then I helped him build the big round kiln that we tore down when we built this one. It was a kiln the same size and type as this one, but it was outside. Then we built this

PLATE 392 Front view of Brown's Pottery. Note large kiln chimney at right.

PLATE 393 Brown's Pottery is located along the main highway through Arden, North Carolina.

PLATE 394   Louis Brown.

one in this building here. We had carpenters working to build the new shop [at the same time] my father and I were working on the kiln. They put a roof over there where the kiln is and the rest of the shop was still wide open. [When we started working in the new pottery], concrete trucks were still coming in here to pour the floor. We had to move stuff out of the way so the trucks could get back in to the section they wanted to pour next. We had decided if we were going to build a building like this, we had to put a good foundation in it.

This kiln is a round, downdraft kiln, and it's one of the best-built of its type that I've ever seen. It's really got what it takes. It took us three weeks to build it, and we *worked*. We didn't fool around. It's got lattice floors and channels for that fire to go in under the brick, and we did get some help there digging the ditches for the channels in the foundation, but every brick in this kiln was handled by me and Daddy. There wasn't anybody else here, not even a carpenter, that handled a brick that went in this kiln. We put every brick where it was supposed to be. All the brick that was in the other kiln was used in this one, but [in addition], this one is also lined with a solid firebrick lining. Everybody used to dream of building a firebrick-lined kiln, but most of the potters didn't have the firebrick. We got ours shipped in from Missouri, so there's special bricks in this kiln. If I'm not mistaken, Daddy said that in all, it has 28,000 bricks in it. It has enough brick in it to build a house.

[Another thing that makes it different from the old kiln] is that this one has more insulation. It has two walls, and it is twenty inches thick all over, and there is sand poured between two walls of the kiln that serves as insulation. It goes all the way to the floor. The inner and outer walls were built and sand poured in. This insulation serves to hold the heat inside the kiln and make it so it won't be too warm on the outside. For reinforcement, it's got expansion bands around it. Expansion bands are cables around the kiln and when you put enough heat in there, they're gonna expand and tighten up. They pull pretty tight. [The cables] run all the way up the sides of the kiln, about a foot apart. They're buried in that sand [between the kiln walls]. Whenever the kiln expands, it can't bulge out, so the heat raises the top of it. It'll rise about six to eight inches at the top whenever there's high heat. I've seen fire blaze out of the top of the chimney when we were burning with good split pine wood. The fire goes under the [kiln through several channels] and out through the chimney. And it's a big enough kiln that you can walk around in it. You may have to stoop over in places, but it's

PLATE 395　A view of the center of the kiln floor. This is the only area of the floor that is solid, and is the coolest part of the kiln. Note how the bricks have spaces between them as they go out from the center. The lattice floor of the kiln is eighteen to twenty-four inches above the actual dirt bottom of the kiln. There are channels running under the lattice floor to a tunnel at the rear of the kiln which goes into the chimney, creating a draft for the kiln fires.

PLATE　396　The　firebrick-lined ceiling of the kiln.

PLATE 397 The entrance to the kiln. This kiln has not been fired for a number of years and has been used for storage. The Browns do intend to start firing it again in the near future and use it instead of the smaller electric kiln now in use.

PLATE 398 A view of the kiln showing the domelike top. Note the expansion bands and cable.

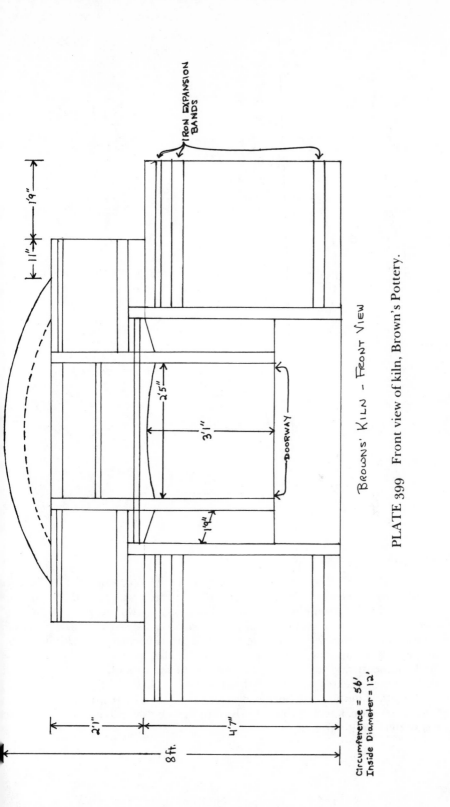

BROWNS' KILN – FRONT VIEW

Circumference = 56'
Inside Diameter = 12'

PLATE 399   Front view of kiln, Brown's Pottery.

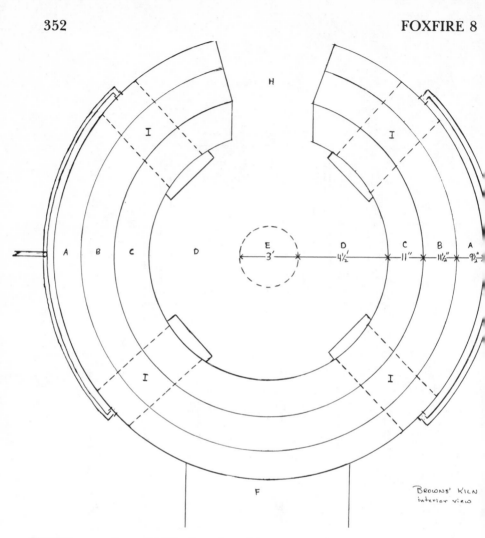

PLATE 400   Brown's kiln, interior view.

A. Outer wall, 9½″ thick, made of bricks from the old kiln; B. Middle core 11½″ of sand between outer and inner walls; C. Inner wall, 11″ thick; concret wall with firebrick forming inside lining. (Plate 397 shows the walls at the kiln entrance.); D. Floor made of firebrick and elevated 24″ above dirt base. Channe are constructed beneath it, creating the draft from fireboxes to chimney. (Se Plate 395.); E. Center of kiln floor, solid to the dirt base and the coolest sp in the kiln, measuring 36″ across; F. The exit of the tunnel, or channels, goin to the chimney creates a hump behind the kiln; G. Gas lines, now used fc firing the kiln. There is one burner every 13 feet. (See Plate 403.); H. Doorwa 37″ high, 29″ wide, and 11″ thick; I. The four fireboxes that have been converte to gas outlets (Plate 402.).

PLATE 401 A rear view of Brown's Pottery showing the large kiln chimney at left. The vibrations from fast-moving trains occasionally cause pottery in the kiln to fall.

PLATE 402 One of the four fireboxes, seen from the kiln's interior.

PLATE 403 Charlie Brown demonstrating how the gas will be piped in when they begin firing the beehive kiln again.

six feet high in the center. It's big enough that I'd say it will burn four or five thousand pieces of different sizes in one load. You can turn some of the milk churns upside down and use them as the floor for the next pots. If you get the glaze on the tops and the bottoms wiped off, you can just keep loading.

We used to burn this kiln about three times a month. You can see that that gave you very little time for a cooling-off period. Just as quick as we'd get one load of pottery out, we'd go in and start setting [the next load in]. We had another kiln [load] made and setting on the floor ready. Soon as we got that kiln empty, we started again. And that's the way we went. We'd be burning two, and sometimes three, times a month. If you had any repairs to do to the kiln, you had to do them just as quickly as the kiln got cool enough to do it. Like if you need to reline the fireboxes, you do it then.

[To close the kiln after it's loaded], you build the door up with brick the same way that wall is right there—a solid brick wall. You leave a peephole in your door. Then when you learn to fire this kiln, even if you don't have an instrument or a cone to go by, you can just look in [through the peephole] and know what's going on.

When we were firing with wood, we'd stack the wood by each firebox, then walk around and keep the fires up. If you burn with oil, you set your burners and wait awhile. Then you reset them, step them up, and equalize them. When we used oil, we figured that it took 250 to 300 gallons of oil to burn a load in the kiln. [Natural] gas was regulated the same way as oil. We figured 25 pounds of gas pressure, divided between the four burners, about six pounds at each burner. When we went to gas [from oil], the gas that we used was cheap enough to be competitive with oil because the gas companies wanted to get the oil business. So when we went to gas, prices were about the same as oil. Then when the gas went up, oil went up and everything else, of course. In 1939 a lot of people still heated with fireplaces [and wood], and oil wasn't that plentiful [in our area]. It was a lot more expensive than a lot of things, but was also cheaper than a lot of other things. Each time as we went from wood to oil to gas, we went to a better fuel.

One person can fire this kiln, and usually the man that burns this kiln stays with it from beginning to end. It's no problem, except that most of the time you're thirty-six to forty-eight hours at it and you get tired. One time I stayed with it fifty-four hours. And you have to watch what you're doing. When I was a boy and would go to my uncle's, he'd say, "How about relieving me?" I'd relieve him, half a day at a time, or all day, or maybe burn it all night. Everywhere

I ever went as a kid, everybody knew I'd worked around this stuff and they could turn me loose with it. There could be a grown person to go up there and they wouldn't even risk *them* [firing the kiln], because you can lose everything you've got if you burn a kiln like this and make a mistake. If you *do* make a mistake, you just hope you're making a little one. Or maybe a train would come along and shake everything you had here, and when it did, sometimes part of the pottery would fall. When the firing was finished, you'd start at the peephole and take a hook and start jerking those hot bricks out to tear the door down; and all the time you'd sweat it out because you might have an order in there that you were hoping you didn't lose. Something might have fell over that was in that order. If there's a man with an order he was expecting at a certain time, it might be three weeks before his order could get to him [if an accident happened in the kiln].

But this kiln is in excellent shape, especially when you think of the times we've fired it. It shows you the way people used to have to do. [They built things to last], not like the modern things they've got now. And life is so much faster now than ours was. It's harder and harder for young people to get into this business because they don't have the time to apprentice long enough to learn it. They've got to start earning a living right away and have a big paycheck to apply to the expenses of rising prices. They can't take the time to learn something like this because with the changes in cost and everything, the dollar value is so hard to keep up with.

Charlie Brown

All of Grandpa's brothers were potters. Grandpa [before coming to Arden, North Carolina] had a pottery down in Atlanta somewhere. Grandpa came to Arden because of the clay. He found clay up here. He was just traveling looking for clay. And wherever Grandpa went, Javan and the rest of the family followed. So Javan and Grandpa came here in '23–'24 and started Brown Brothers Pottery, and they ran it together. That vase was made in 1925. My grandpa and Uncle Jay [Javan] made it. It is 6'2" tall and 9'8" in circumference. It weighs about 500 pounds. Took about a week to make it. They started out on the wheel. They built it as high as they could on the wheel and then built it in sections from there. They would work so high and then it would get soft and they would stop and let it dry a little and then go on. They made it together right after they got up here. I think they made it just showing people what they could do.

PLATE 404   Charlie Brown.

This was the only pottery in this community for years. As it got built up, Otto, Rufus, Bobby, Willie and the other people in the family came up and worked. At one time they had twenty-six people working here. The pottery even had its own ball team, and they always talk about the baseball team that Grandpa had. Just about all the team worked in the pottery. They must have been pretty good. I don't know how he kept that many people busy in the pottery, though. I don't know what they all did. I never asked. But I suppose he had like two or three potters, two jiggering, somebody doing clay, somebody doing casting, somebody setting the kiln, somebody packing, somebody doing the books.

I do know what they made, though, and it was all utilitarian. Every time you see a picture of these old, old potteries, you see the old-timey churns and crocks and all that. That's because people made their own butter, stored their own milk, made their own pickles—pickled beans, kraut—they made everything in those old crocks. And along with them, all the old potters made jugs for liquor, pitchers for milk and water, washbasin bowls to wash in, teapots, and stuff to cook in like bean pots. And they were made real simple. They used that old sand and ash, or Albany slip glaze. They weren't pretty. A few potters got fancy, but we sure didn't. We had to make a living.

PLATE 405 Davis Brown, about 1940, in the present Brown's Pottery.

PLATE 406 Davis Brown at foot-powered wheel in the 1950s.

PLATE 407 The tall vase made by Davis Brown and Javan Brown in 1925, on exhibit in the Brown's Pottery display area.

PLATE 408   Davis Brown with chimney tops made for a large
office building in Raleigh, North Carolina. (See Plate 337 for
a picture of one made by Javan Brown while at Wilson Pottery.)

I know they made a good product, though. About three years ago I was in the back, working, and Mom came back there and said, "I got a lady up there that's got a casserole that's broke—wants to talk to you." Well, you got a bad deal when you've got somebody that's got a broke casserole.

So I come up and was trying to make the best out of a bad deal. Uncle Jay was here. I said, "All right, who's got the cracked pot?"

And this lady who looked exactly like Lucille Ball said, "I do, and it's not a damn bit funny."

I said to myself, "Oh, God, right here in front of Daddy and Uncle Jay and everybody." So I said, "Ma'am, can I see it?"

She pulls this bean pot out of a bag. I was trying to get together what to say to the lady, and Uncle Jay said, "Yeah, we made that one."

I thought, "Boy, you're a whole lot of help."

He looked at it and said, "Davis made that one." They could look and tell who made what. Robert and I can too. I can tell if he made something or if I did. So he said, "Davis made that one."

I said, "Well, ma'am, how long have you had that one?"

She said, "Well, I'm going to get to figuring." She had bought this casserole in 1927 and had used it continuously since '27 and had cracked it.

I said, "Well, ma'am, I can't fix it. You heard my great-uncle say my grandpa made it, and he's been dead for years. I would like to have it. I'll give you any new casserole dish in the shop if I can have the old one."

She said, "No, if you can't fix it, I'll take it back to Cincinnati." She said, "I'll keep it."

I said, "All right."

She said, "Give me your card and I'll leave it to you in my will."

I said, "Okay."

So I gave her my business card and that was it. So the next year I didn't hear from her, but the second year she came walking in. I was back in the back, working. She said, "Do you remember me?"

I said, "Yeah," 'cause I mean this woman could pass for Lucille Ball.

And she said, "Well, I got home and got to thinking about it, and that pot doesn't mean anything to anybody but to me or to you, so here it is." So she gave it to me, and I gave her a new bean pot. I've got the old one. There it is. And [that style bean pot] is what Robert is making back there now. We still make them.

And the way she remembered what year she bought it, 1927, is

PLATE 409 The bean p
made by Davis Brown a
bought in 1927 by the wom
who returned it in 1979 becau
it was cracked.

because it was the same year the elementary school opened here, and she was here for the opening. They had come out and watched Grandpa make [that pot], and they come back in a few days after he had glazed and fired it and picked it up.

But she wasn't complaining about the product. She just wanted us to fix it so she could keep on using it.

About the only major change they made in the [product line] happened during the Depression. At first times were pretty hard, and Grandpa even went a couple of places and built kilns for other potters for extra money. He kept the pottery going here too, though, and in the thirties a man came here from New York who had heard about the family and heard we could produce the product he wanted and got us started in this French-style cookware. He had imported it from France, but he could buy it from us and ship it to New York cheaper than he could buy it in France. Grandpa still had twenty-six people working here, and using our clay and our glaze, they started making that cookware and shipping it up North. That was steady work—especially during the war when everybody turned in their metal pots and pans and used clay cookery [as part of the war effort]. I've got the poster on the wall. It was a big deal. Then after the war it kind of slowed down. But before and during the war, this major buyer took almost the whole output of the shop, and that extra [business] is why we rebuilt the shop in 1939. By

PLATE 410 Pottery from France brought to the Browns to use as models for making similar cookware.

PLATE 411 World War II poster urging people to reserve "all precious metals for war use" and use pottery cookery instead.

that time, Dad was working here, and that's when he and Grandpa built that new kiln. And by then, we were coming along too. That's how I got started in this business. You just grow up in this and that's the influence. We weren't made to do anything. This is what we wanted to do. [When we were little] they made us a wheel just to keep us out of their hair, really. Back in the fifties, people would watch us turn and then they would come up here and look around at all the stuff [for sale], and we'd have ours there [priced at] ten, fifteen, twenty-five cents apiece. I can remember making two dollars a day during the summer when I was a little kid. Two dollars' worth of candy was a whole lot of candy back then.

When Grandpa saw that we were trying really hard on the wheel, he would come over there and help us, and even today, as long as I've been doing this, and as many pieces of pottery as I've seen, I can stand for hours at a time and watch someone turn. You can always learn something. You can just learn the different ways of moving your hands. Everybody does it different. Everybody ties their shoes different, but as long as you get your shoe tied, that's what is important.

Javan was still working here when I was coming along, too. He was a wanderer, and he drifted in and out—worked for other people sometimes—but he was here a good bit. Back when we had a lot of people here, Granny cooked a full meal every day for Grandpa and everybody down here at the shop. I mean that was biscuits, cornbread, cube steak and gravy, mashed potatoes, green beans, sliced tomatoes, and iced tea—a full meal. Javan ate with us every day when the pottery was going strong, and no matter what Javan ate, he had those little green peppers that are so hot you can lay them on the floor and heat the building with them. He would eat two of them, anyway. He ate *hot* peppers. I believe he could have ate fire. I can eat hot stuff, but Javan was unreal.

He worked in a white shirt and tie and a dark pair of pants— worked in a suit. He wore an apron, and he was as clean when he left as when he came in the morning. And he put out a tremendous amount of pots. He put out as much as probably any two people would at one time. He was real small—5'4" and 100 pounds. I think the most he ever weighed was 130 or something like that. It wasn't much. But when he was seventy and I was eighteen, he like to have killed me. He worked me to death. He made twelve-inch pots every day, and I made up the balls of clay for him. A ball of clay weighed about thirty pounds. And I couldn't keep up with him. He had no choice but to slow down. But he was easygoing. He and I got along

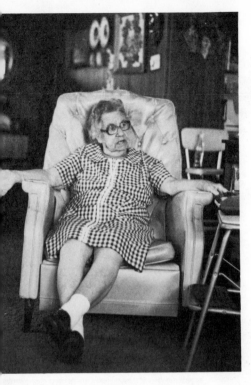

PLATE 412 Mrs. Davis (Ella) Brown at her home near the pottery.

better than any of them. He and I got along real good. Both he and Grandpa were really good, great people. They were good at what they did, and they enjoyed it and enjoyed helping other people with it. And they both made pottery right up until the end. Javan kept on even when he was sick. He had his wheel in the living room of the house, and he worked right there until he went to the hospital in Valdese, North Carolina. He died in November 1980, so he's not been gone long.

Grandpa worked until the end, too. He made churns up until the late fifties, and crocks. He quit making them because he got sick. He fell in the front door over here with 200 pounds of clay in his arms and it hit him across the abdomen. He started getting sick then. They thought he had an ulcer, but he probably ruptured something, but he wouldn't go to the doctor. So then as he started getting sick, he started just letting people go. He would discontinue stewpots, then discontinue soup pots, until no one was left steady but Granny and Grandpa. So then he just kept getting continually sicker, and they kept treating him for an ulcer. Dad worked here up until '57 or '58, and then he went to work for a truck line as a diesel mechanic and he'd work here at night and on his days off. Grandpa kept going, though. I've got a bean pot in there on top of the Coke machine that's one of the last pieces he made. It was

PLATE 413 This is a churn made by Brown's Pottery many years ago and brought in to show the Browns one day when we were there interviewing them. The man who owns it now is a friend of the Browns' and had recently purchased the churn at an antique shop.

PLATE 414 Davis Brown in the late 1960s.

PLATE 415 This photograph shows Davis Brown making a type of small pot many years ago . . .

PLATE 416 . . . that is still being made by his grandson, Rob.

PLATE 417

in the last big kiln he fired, and that was late '66 or early '67. He died on July 4, 1967. Dad took over and ran the shop when Grandpa died. Then Dad had a heart attack a couple of years after that and he had to retire. That's when I took full control, and Robert and I own it together. Slowly we've brought back just about every line Grandpa made. All the molds and the standards and everything were stacked back, and we just brought them out. We still make the old-time liquor jugs, and the milk or tea pitchers, and we primarily produce cookware, dishes, mugs, beer mugs, coffee mugs, some vases, bunches of face jugs, batter bowls, dough bowls—that kind of thing. [Some things we used to make that we don't any longer] are strawberry jars, flowerpots, washpots, and birdbaths. Now, that's all Wilson makes and you can't compete with him on prices, so we specialize in cookware. He specializes in the other. It works out better. I like those boys down there. They're good people. They crank out some stuff! But this specialty keeps them going, and the cookware line keeps us going. It's pretty famous. It used to be Good Housekeeping approved and all that. So I went on the reputation [for a while while things were slow]. Then the superior product—and it is a great product—is what brought us back. Hopefully we're stepping [production] up, but everything's slow right now.

We've got a good system worked out here, and we have special techniques for everything. Robert loads the mill and I grind the clay. I'm not crazy about finishing, so Mom and Johanna [Rob's wife] do that. They put all the handles on, and they put our stamp on the bottom that says, "Browns Pottery—Arden, N.C." They also wait on customers. I like to jigger, and my favorite thing to make is coffee mugs because they're so fast. I like to see how fast I can make them and how many I can make exactly alike. Ultimately your goal is sixty an hour. I make about forty an hour. I make them all alike. We've been making the same kind of mugs that Grandpa made, and we haven't changed them.

Rob usually turns the face jugs. Robert, Daddy, and I used to take turns putting the faces on. Right now Johanna has been putting the faces on. It's fun, but it's pretty well time-consuming. I'm not sure where that face jug idea came from but I've heard that [in the past] when a face jug was made, the people would carry it and put it on a grave and it [was supposed] to stay there for one year. During that year, if it was not broken or gone at the end of the year, the closest living relative would go get the jug and break it and there'd be a big celebration. But if that jug was broken or gone during that year period, there wouldn't be any celebration because the dead person's soul [was thought to be] wrestling with the devil.

PLATE 418   Demonstration of how a ball opener works and then the pot being brought on up by hand.

PLATE 419

PLATE 420

PLATE 421 Brown's Pottery pieces are either stamped or handwritten on the bottom with the pottery's name and address.

PLATE 422 Unglazed face jugs. Because of the demand for them, there were no finished face jugs in stock.

PLATE 423   An example of a decorated jug done by Rob Brown.

Robert also does [the scenes on the sides of some of the pots]. He draws it on with a pencil and then cuts it away with tools. He's been doing that for quite a few years. We've got some pieces up at the house that were made probably in the twenties or even earlier that someone painted on. I don't know who. And I've got a set of vases that I guess my great-grandma or somebody made. She put leaves, grapes, and all on them. So decorating them is not a new idea with us, either.

The only thing that varies much in our routine is the speed. It's harder to work in the summer when you've got tourists in, for example, because you've got to quit and run up here and wait on them. So we don't get as much made then as during the winter when nobody is in and we just make a lot of stuff. Then, all these racks will be full and pots will be up and down the sides here with just room to walk down through here. Sometimes we even set [raw ware] over in the display [area] over there. There's never enough room. We added that concrete block building out there a couple of years ago. We built it for an office, and now it's got about 50,000 pounds of clay in it!

Clay is another thing that hasn't changed much since we took over. As a boy, I can barely remember going to Morganton to dig clay. We went quite a few times when I was little. The best I can remember, we drove to a cornfield to get it. There was a lot of pine trees and it was hot. I was a little kid, but it was impressive.

[While I was still young, we found a new site and] pretty much all my life we've dug clay in the same place that we dig it now. It's about four miles from here in Fletcher, North Carolina. We have a deal worked out with the owners that we've been able to [maintain] for thirty-something years with no problem, as long as we fill the holes back and landscape [where we dug] each time.

We usually go once a year. We used to dig it by hand, but the cost of manual labor and the laziness of the people stopped that. Now we use a backhoe. It's a sedimentary-type clay about an eighth of a mile from Cane Creek, which is a small river. We go through about thirty inches of topsoil to where the clay starts, and the deeper we go, the grayer and better the clay gets. We use that gray clay, not the red. The red is dirt here, not clay. It comes out in chunks, and we put it inside here in the bin. We fill the bin up completely in the fall of the year for the winter. The bin will be full, and the clay goes to the top of the walls. We pack it as high as we can. We have two-by-six lumber across the front to form a solid wood wall except for an eighteen-inch-high space across the bottom. That's where we shovel the clay out from—shovel out from the bottom of that thing and the clay keeps falling down. When there is no clay up against the walls, we take the two-by-sixes down and work our way back into [what is left]. That clay in the back corner has been in here a year and you can see that it's still wet. It just holds moisture even on this floor. That's why we have that heat duct. If we get low on dry clay, we just shovel about six inches thick of clay in here for overnight and with that heat blowing and hitting it, it will dry out enough for about a thousand pounds—which is a little more than we use in a day, depending on what we're making.

And we don't have to add anything to this clay but water—that's how good it is. The only impurities in our clay is what the city puts in our water. I tell everybody that. Our water here has a lot of chlorine in it and that's the only thing. Just straight clay and water. We make everything out of it—big pieces, small pieces, cookware, dishes.

To process it, we shovel the dry clay onto the dry pan [sometimes also called the "duster"]. These wheels above it weigh about 3,000 pounds apiece. They run over the dry clay and crush it. In the bottom of the pan there are little slits that are real narrow, and as the pan turns under the wheels, the clay is crushed fine enough to go through those slits. The clay falls onto a tray underneath. There's a bar under there that pushes it off as the pan turns, and the clay goes into this tray that has a stainless steel screen-wire bottom. What is fine enough falls through the screen, and what is still coarse comes out here and is shoveled back in and recrushed until it is fine enough. It's a real dusty process, so we have these fans pointed at the machine. You can't see back here without those fans running.

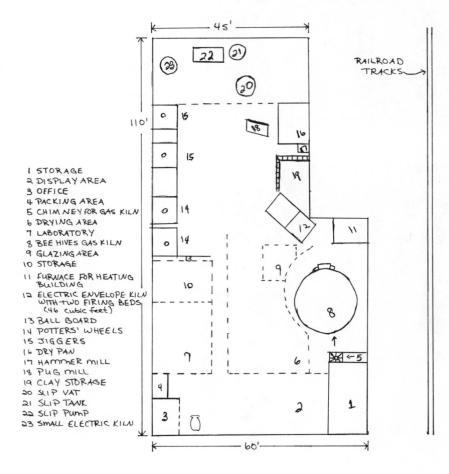

BACK

1 STORAGE
2 DISPLAY AREA
3 OFFICE
4 PACKING AREA
5 CHIMNEY FOR GAS KILN
6 DRYING AREA
7 LABORATORY
8 BEE HIVES GAS KILN
9 GLAZING AREA
10 STORAGE
11 FURNACE FOR HEATING BUILDING
12 ELECTRIC ENVELOPE KILN WITH TWO FIRING BEDS (46 cubic feet)
13 BALL BOARD
14 POTTERS' WHEELS
15 JIGGERS
16 DRY PAN
17 HAMMER MILL
18 PUG MILL
19 CLAY STORAGE
20 SLIP VAT
21 SLIP TANK
22 SLIP PUMP
23 SMALL ELECTRIC KILN

RAILROAD TRACKS

FRONT

PLATE 424   Floor plan of Brown's Pottery.

PLATE 425 Charlie Brown shoveling the dried clay into the dry pan to be crushed. There is also an old hammer mill in the shop that was once used to crush the clay. It operated like an old corn-grinding mill. Charlie told us it is no longer used because his grandfather thought it was too dangerous, and so built the dry pan.

PLATE 426 View of the 3,000-pound wheels in the dry pan.

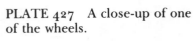
PLATE 427 A close-up of one of the wheels.

PLATE 428 Rob shoveling up some of the ground-up clay that needs to go through the dry pan again.

PLATE 429 The powdered clay is dumped into the pug mill from the box above it. The dry pan is directly behind it, making this a very efficient operation.

PLATE 430 Water is added to the powder as it is moved down the pug mill's trough by the action of the twisting blades.

PLATE 431 Charlie Brown overseeing the pug mill's operation.

PLATE 432 Charlie lifting out dampened clay as it reaches the end of the trough. This clay is not completely mixed and will be returned to the far end of the trough to be run through again.

When you get your bin full underneath, you have about enough dust to run 500 pounds of clay through the pug mill or to make slip or whatever you're going to do with it. The pug mill is where you mix however much water back with the clay that you want. This is all old machinery Grandpa Brown made from just whatever he had around. That's a piston out of an old T-Model Ford running the duster. In the pug mill, one full mill of dust will make about 500 pounds of wet clay. You just let it start grinding the clay, and it works its way through to one end and you just cut it off and keep throwing it back into the mill until it's the right consistency [for use]. You can tell by the way it cuts how good it is and if it's ready to be used. If you're going to jigger, for example, you want it real soft so when it hits that mold and you start to pull it out, it's going to spread real fast and easy. If you're going to use it on the wheel, you want it stiff so it will stand up and not flop over. So we grind it according to what we're going to do with it.

After the clay is made up, if you're going to use it on the wheel, we bring it up to the ball board and work it on the wire to work all the air out of it. We call it "working on the ball board." The college term is "wedging." After you work it on the wire, you weigh each individual ball so they're the same. Then you have a gauge that you set for the height pot you're turning, and turn each piece right up to the edge of that gauge.

After we make it on the wheel, we set it on the boards, and the

PLATE 433   Clay that is ready to be pounded into balls and turned on the wheel being taken out of the pug mill by Rob.

PLATE 434   The ball board, with scales for weighing balls of clay in the background. There is a piece of wire tightly strung from the wall to the front edge of the counter over the flat piece of plaster material where the clay is worked. A ball of clay is first weighed for the amount needed for the specific piece to be made. It is pounded onto the flat surface, then cut in half by the wire and pounded together again. This is done several times to ensure that all the air is out of the clay.

PLATE 435   A close-up view of the scales.

PLATE 436 Greenware on drying racks, stacked up and ready to be put in the kiln.

PLATE 437 This electric kiln is used at the present time. The ware is placed on the racks of a movable cart (foreground). The cart is mounted on tracks and rolled into the kiln. The doors on either end are closed and bolted for firing.

next day after [the pots] set overnight—or even later that same day, depending on the heat—someone will put the handles on and take and finish the bottom edges where it's a little rough where it came off the wheel. Whoever's doing it will smooth them down with his thumb or a finishing tool. Then we stamp our name in the bottom. Then it goes over here in these drying racks and it will stay anywhere from a week to two weeks before it's dry enough to go in the kiln. Then it comes back here again and we glaze it, wipe the glaze off the bottom, and put it in the kiln and go from there. It will be fired and then back to the front to sell. We don't bisque-fire anything. We glaze everything as greenware and do one firing. We also use jiggers and molds. We use them because of the time they save. We've got to make a living. If we don't sell, we don't eat. It's just basic. You've got to turn it out to get it sold.

When they first set the shop up, Grandpa had a mold-maker work-

PLATE 438 A view of the variety of pottery and cookware in the Brown's Pottery display area. The strawberry jars on the floor at far left are made by the Wilson Pottery. The large crocks on the floor in

ing here full time. Now we use a couple of mold-makers that work over in Tennessee. That's an art in itself. You make the block and case first—that's the master mold you make a mold in. The block is the inside piece and the case is what goes around it. Then you make the molds out of pottery plaster. It's tougher than, say, molding plaster [and it needs to be because] every time you cast, a tiny part of the plaster [wears] away and it just slowly wears bigger. What happens is that you pour the mold full of clay that's just a little thicker than liquid. It's called casting slip. The plaster absorbs water, and as it absorbs the water, it pulls it out of that clay. The more it pulls, the thicker the edge gets. When it gets out to the right thickness, in three or four hours, you pour the excess out. Then the plaster just keeps right on absorbing water, and the clay, as it dries, shrinks enough overnight that it pulls away from the mold and turns loose. We just lift this ring off the next morning

the center of the photograph are trucked in by Wilson's and sold by Brown's because of buyer demand. All ware on the counters is made at Brown's.

and reach in and lift it out. Then the mold has to be set up so air can circulate through it and dry it out so it can be used again.

We use the molds for shapes like chicken roasters that you can't turn on a wheel because they're oblong or oval. We don't have the facilities to hand-make [those items]. That's just too much time and too much work [to be profitable].

A lot of people add stuff to their slip so that it works faster. You can make your slip real heavy or real light by adding silicate. We don't, though, so our molds stay wet longer. It weighs out the same. We do it that way because that's the way Grandpa did it. In the fifteen years that he's been dead, we've added maybe five new items. We've changed colors just a little and put in the electric kiln and that's about it. This is exactly the way Grandpa did it—everything.

We also have molds for big things like birdbaths. We've got one

PLATE 439 Molds with pottery slip poured into them. The slip is made from the same clay used in the turned pots, with more water added to give a liquid consistency.

PLATE 440 The slip will dr enough in twenty-four hours fo the molds to be removed.

PLATE 441 Johanna Brown removing a pottery piece from a mold.

PLATE 442 For sale: rabbit that were made in molds.

birdbath mold that I'm not man enough to carry around by myself. When it's full of clay it weighs about 200 pounds, and it takes both of us to lift it off. We also make exceptionally large flowerpots and planters with molds. You put the soft clay in there with your hands and pack it. Then we have great big knives and we've got a thing that fits up in the ceiling and we put a rod in it and we walk around it. It makes them. We use a block and tackle to lift those big molds.

We use jiggering for making big flat pieces like Spanish rice dishes and quiche dishes where you have to take the time to get the clay all the way across. See, there is a lot of flat surface in this mold, and you have to take the time to pull the clay all the way out and make sure each of these is full of clay. If it's not, when you take it out of the mold there's a big old gap and you've got to take the time to patch it with your thumb and do all that. That takes a lot of time and that's what you don't want.

That jigger wheel up front turns very, very fast. If a mold goes in sideways and comes back out, you best be getting out of the way because you're gonna get hit, and if a thirty-pound mold hits you in the chest at that speed, you've got broke ribs.

We still make our glazes. We don't use sand or glass glazes, or Albany slip, but we still use the old iron oxide glazes. They are basically the same old thing. They are all lead-free. Most of them are just made from local minerals. We use a red iron oxide from up North; feldspar out of Spruce Pine; flint out of West Virginia; whiting out of north Georgia. We've got all the old formulas, and we've not changed them that much, but we have to change them some because every few years the chemical companies change their products so we have to vary [the formulas] a little.

When we glaze, we just wipe [the ware bottoms] and carry them straight to the kiln. Glaze has a tendency to flake off if it sets on [the ware] a long time. And we don't have enough room to have a whole bunch of stuff glazed up ahead [anyway]. The more you handle it, the more chance you have of flaking the glaze off. After it comes out of the kiln, it goes straight to the front.

PLATE 443 Charlie Brown's specialty is the jiggering of pieces that would be difficult to turn on a conventional potter's wheel in the quantities put out by Brown's Pottery. Here he holds one of the jiggering molds.

PLATE 444 Charlie at the jigger wheel, demonstrating how a jigger "knife" compresses the clay into the mold. He trims off excess clay before he removes the knife and sets the mold on a shelf to dry.

PLATE 445 An overall view of the jigger wheel with knife in place. To the right of the wheel is a steel structure in which one of the ends of the knife's handle is inserted. The chain is threaded through a pivot point attached to a beam in the ceiling, and provides a counterbalance for the knife as the potter exerts pressure on the opposite end of the knife while the jigger wheel turns. The mold shapes the dish or pot on the outside and the knife shapes it on the inside, the distance between the two being the thickness of the dish. The knives and jigger molds are paired to give uniform sizes.

PLATE 446 Three sizes of wheels the jigger molds are placed in.

PLATE 447 Empty jigger molds on the shelves, drying. At the end of the nearest shelves, jigger knives of varying sizes are hung. The knives and molds are numbered so that they match.

PLATE 448 A better view of the jigger knives.

PLATE 449   A close-up view of one of the knives, fitted into the handle that is fitted into the steel structure (see Plates 444 and 445).

PLATE 450   The reverse side of the jigger knife.

PLATE 451   Stephanie Brown, Charlie's daughter, age eight (1982), is the eighth generation of Brown potters. She practices her pottery making whenever she has time after school and during the summers.

COCKFIGHTING

PART I: BREEDS, BREEDING, SELLING, RAISING, COMBS, CONDITIONING, FIGHTING, AND THE LAW

Cockfighting. The word itself has a sinister ring. Intermittently over a three-year time span, spurred on by students like Richard Jones who themselves raised gamecocks, and students like Kelli Allred who were curious, and the fact that the raising and fighting of such roosters was and is so widespread throughout the mountains, we began to explore the subject. It had come up frequently in conversations with contacts, almost as an aside. Joe Farmer, for example, the gunmaker we interviewed for *Foxfire 5*, said, "Back over where I was born, they used to have a place over there they called the Chicken Fighting Ridge. They used to fight there a whole lot." And Jake Plott, a nearby [fur buyer] we have interviewed several times, told us, laughing, "When I first commenced fooling with chickens, I'd heard of gaffs, but we didn't have them. A bunch of us boys would just get together and fight the hell out of the chickens and jump up and down and holler and laugh. We didn't have any money much to bet back then. We'd fight them and bet pocketknives and all that kind of stuff, you know. We used to make homemade whistles, and we'd say, 'I'll bet my whistle against yours,' and all that."

Others had told us incredible stories, in the context of interviews concerning other subjects, about game roosters that had killed hawks or dogs or even foxes that had tried to invade their territories and carry off hens or chicks.

Finally, such bits and pieces got the best of us and we began to collect material in earnest. Kelli Allred broke the ice with a series of three interviews which she introduced as follows:

"When the topic of cockfighting was mentioned in class, it first struck me as something I would never be interested in. Yet, the more I thought about it, the more it intrigued me. It's something completely different from anything I've ever done. It also didn't seem to be a girl's sport, so I was challenged.

"After I had started thinking about it, my first thoughts went in

PLATE 452   Often when riding down a secondary road in the
rural South, the casual traveler will notice a row or two of small
structures in a field and not even know what he is passing. These,
for example, stand beside a back road northwest of Greenwood,
South Carolina.

PLATE 453   These are in a yard in Young Harris, Georgia.

PLATE 454   Closer examination will reveal that each houses either a proud fighting cock and its hen, or an individual cock tethered to its pen just out of reach of its neighbor.

PLATE 455   The roosters preen and strut and crow, making obvious the origin of the expression "cocky."

all different directions. I had an idea that the fighting itself would
be bloody. I wasn't looking forward to that. What seemed more
important were the reasons behind the fight. I knew that cockfighting
was a sport dating back to ancient civilization, so there had to be
a reason for its lasting so long.

"For my interviews, I started on familiar ground. The first interview was with an old friend of my family. I expected a good story
from him. Then I went to a raiser, and two trainers. Expecting rough
men was my first mistake. These people were some of the warmest
people I've ever met. They went out of their way to make sure
that every step was clearly explained.

"As for the cocks themselves, they were beautiful. They came in
all colors of the rainbow. You could almost feel some kind of dignity
that they inherited along with their fighting instinct. The grooming
they were given was amazing. There wasn't a spot of lice on them,
their feathers weren't even out of place. Every person I talked to
would say one thing which says it all for gamecocks, 'A game chicken
is the gamest thing on the face of the earth.'

"The fighting is refined to an art. Men who fight cocks are honest.
The rules are followed, no questions asked. It is orderly and struc-
tured.

"When I got finished, I started thinking about how I felt about
cockfighting. With each person, I was careful to go over the controversy around cockfighting. Yes, it's bloody, but I just think of it as
a part of life. If the cocks were in the wild, they would still kill
each other because a cock will not stop fighting until dead. The
steel just makes it quicker for one to be killed. These animals are
loved. They are fed, trained, and fought by men who have great
pride and love for their chickens. If they have a short life, at least
it's a good one. If I've learned a lesson, it's that controversial subjects
will never seem the same to a person if he can take time to look
at both sides."

The sport of fighting roosters has apparently been practiced since
before Christ and has had a long history since then. Some writers
claim that the wild gamecock was domesticated by the Chinese as
early as 1400 B.C., and a mosaic of two cocks in battle was found
in ancient Pompeii. According to an article in *National Geographic*,
"Cockfighting was a popular pastime in England during the reign
of Henry II but it was put down as unlawful in the reign of Edward
III and again in 1569 by Henry VIII who, however, built a cockpit
in Whitehall Palace. The sport was revived in the reign of Elizabeth.

James I and Charles II entertained guests at cockfights." (*Races of Domestic Fowl*, MaJull; April 1927, pp. 349–52.)

In an unpublished paper entitled "Gamecock—The Feathered Spartan," by Benjamin Hill of the Biology Department at North Georgia College in Dahlonega, Georgia, from which the above information was taken, Hill also writes that cockfighting was enjoyed in this country by George Washington (who once stated that he had attended a church vestry meeting and a cockfight in the same day), Thomas Jefferson, Benjamin Franklin, and Abraham Lincoln who sometimes acted as a referee at cockfights. Andrew Jackson supposedly had his own pit at the White House. Hill also notes that the University of South Carolina's mascot is a gamecock because General Thomas Sumter, a Revolutionary War hero and famous South Carolinian, was given the nickname "Gamecock of the Revolution" because of his courage.

And it goes on. One has only to glance at any of the magazines devoted exclusively to cockfighting (*Feathered Warrior*, DeQueen, Arkansas; *Grit and Steel*, Gaffney, South Carolina; *Sabong*, Rizal, Philippines; *The Gamecock*, Hartford, Arkansas; *Game Fowl News*, Madison, Connecticut—now defunct—) to see how well-entrenched, long-lasting, widespread, and avidly followed is the custom. *Grit and Steel*, for example, was first published in May of 1899 and has been around ever since. On page 19 of the November 1971 issue, the only issue we happened to have handy, Col. John H. Hempel wrote, "I have been a chicken 'NUT' since boyhood. I started out fighting bantams with the neighborhood kids at about ten years old and graduated to gamecocks and gaffs at fourteen . . . I went into the Army in 1937 and fought cocks in almost every place the Army sent me for the next 26 years. I am a veteran of both World War II and Korea. I found game chickens in Belgium, England, France, Japan, Mexico, and everywhere I was stationed in the States. Throughout my extensive travels, I have met hundreds of fine cockers and, I hope, have learned a little from a lot of them.

"I retired from the regular Army as a colonel and have devoted most of my time since to my game fowl and loafing."

The magazines are filled with articles about breeding, conditioning, penning, and healing of roosters, their histories, profiles of leading or emerging cockfighters, obituaries of noted "cockers," letters from readers, announcements of upcoming derbies from scores of "game clubs," and the score sheets from recent derbies or matches. Equally fascinating, however, are the sections devoted to ads. Here the novice becomes powerfully aware of the extent of his ignorance about the sport, for here there are ads for cockers' supplies (gaffs, cock muffs, sparkling new chrome glover spur saws, Wortham Rule Books, chick toe punches, moleskin heeling tape, gaff cleaning pads, carryall shipping cases 18½ × 16½ × 8½, aluminum leg and wing bands, conditioning books, cockers' billfolds, flat braided waxed nylon tie string, plastic coop cups, iron-on decals, leg band pliers, dubbing shears, trophies, used gaffs, leg weights, double-fold spiral leg bands, cockers' whetstones, equipment cases), nutritional supplements (alfalfa tablets, powdered whole liver, food yeast, Vitamin K, Vitamin A, sunflower seed oil, conditioning capsules, organic capsules), energy suppliers (glucose, stress capsules, maltose, dextrins, micro-activators), veterinarian supplies (Worm-X, conditioning powder, lice and scaly leg ointment, antibiotic capsules, pox vaccine, penicillin tablets, 5cc. glass syringes, needles "game fowl size," treatments for bumblefoot, infertility, and cannibalism), eggs and pullets and hens and stags of every breed imaginable, imported Staffordshire bull terrier pups, and American Pit Bull Terriers. And there are personals ("Desire working with horses, game fowl, etc. Experienced, reliable, dependable, nondrinker . . .").

You have to see it to believe it.

How cockfighting first came into the mountains is open to speculation. There is little doubt, however, that many of the early immigrants were devotees of the sport already, having practiced it in other places. And it is safe to assume that many of those who practiced here then, as now, did so in a world removed from the high-powered, highly financed, intensely well-orchestrated and supervised events that were the Kentucky Derbies of the chicken world. For most of them, in fact, it was and still is a sport practiced in a rather informal manner and setting. Stanley Hicks, for example, a favorite contact who appears in many of our books, told us, "I've fit 'em for years. I know all about fighting. We'd just raise 'em up, and then a bunch of us would meet in the woods and take roosters with us. We'd gang around there [in a circle] where the roosters couldn't get away, and then we would turn 'em down two at a time. See, you had a rooster and I had a rooster, and we would never bet. We would just see whose rooster was the best. Me and you would turn our roosters loose and if mine killed yours, you was the loser and I was the winner. We didn't use no gaffs. They was a lot of people that did, but we never did. And now the laws have got so tightened down that we just quit. I ain't fit none in fifteen years."

And Lawton Brooks, another favorite subject, said, "We used to raise them, and they liked to fight. It was bred in them. And when them old roosters seen us a-coming, they knowed just as well there was a fight up. We would just reach down there and pick them up and they was ready to go. *Wanting* to go. They would just set in your arms and crow because they knew there was a fight on hand. They was just like a bunch of dogs getting ready to go hunting. It was interesting. You'd like it!

"Anyway, we would get out and make us a round circle and set up some palings or something around about the size of this room and just throw a couple in there and let them go at it, and the best man came out. We would get out and we would make bets on the side on a chicken. Didn't have much money then, so we couldn't bet much. If you was to bet five dollars, everybody thought you was rich. Five dollars was a big bet.

"When I first commenced fighting, we couldn't get ahold of none of them old gaffs. They would just use their spurs. We would keep them spurs filed just as keen as a needle. Take a file and file them just as keen as keen can be, and he would kill him in just a few minutes. Them old devils would get to fighting and their eyes would get just as red! They would get mad. You and me ought to get us some and raise us a few!"

Some mountain people, however, have now entered the sport on a much more sophisticated—and highly funded—level, as the interview with Paul Stamey shows.

In any event, it became increasingly obvious that it was time for us to begin to gather some information on the subject. That, of course, is where Richard and Kelli and the other students entered. And they did well. What follows is a series of related topics such as breeding, conditioning, and fighting, upon which several different chicken fighters expound. These sections are followed by complete intact interviews with two of the most interesting men the students met.

And the chapter is a good beginning. We print it, however, with the cautions of one of the men in mind:

"There's not a whole lot a person can *tell* about cockfighting. It's a thing you have to learn by experience. You can sit and tell people all about cockfighting all day and they still won't know much after it's done. You've got to learn by experience about what kinds of chickens you like. Each person likes different types of chickens. Cockfighting is something that you just like to do. Once you get started in it, it's something you don't get out of real easy."

Breeds

Any discussion of the various breeds of chickens and their characteristics quickly gets confusing because, as Joe Farmer told us,
"There's as many different kinds of game chickens as they is different
kinds of dogs." The distinctive names help keep the breeds somewhat decipherable. Dennis Woods tried to explain:

"Most of the time, the different breeds of chickens are named
after people that have originated them. Like Kelso. Walter A. Kelso
developed that breed. The Blue-faced Hatch was named after a man
who wore a big blue sweater. He was called Sweater McGinnis. Lloyd
Minor originated the Minor Blues way back, no telling how long
ago. There's one type of chicken, the Aseel, that used to be raised
wild in the jungle, and it was brought over here. It's an oriental
chicken [but I'm not sure what its name comes from]."

Even with the names, however, the average person is in for confusing times. Magazines like *Grit and Steel* make heroic efforts to educate
the general reader, and their work helps. In the November 1971
issue, for example, they reprinted a "Dictionary of American Game
Strains" from a booklet, "Gamebirds," by Vasco B. Silbert (no biblio-
graphic data given). A brief sampling will give the idea:

"ARKANSAS TRAVELER: Originator, Col. Jim Rodgers of North
Carolina. Bloodlines: Arrington fowl. Description: Blue, red, grey, pea
and straight comb, red eyes, yellow legs. Shows definite relationship
to old Sumatra. The traveler in his own right has a very marked and
imperative quality to success, i.e. agility.

"ROUNDHEADS: The Roundheads originated by crossing Jap & Asil
Orientals with Straight Comb Bankava Mediterranean fowl such as
English and American Straight Combs. This began long years ago
and is currently practiced [1966]. The product is, Allen Roundheads,
Bostons, Saunders, Sheltons, Lacey's, Hulseys, Perkins, Killers, Claret
Roundheads, Negros Mayberry, Cowan, Lundy, etc. Allen made his
first Roundheads from Grist-Grady's fowl by breeding to the oriental
side around 1900. A second Allen family were an importation from
Massachusetts of Dr. Saunders Roundheads in the early 1920's.

"LACEY ROUNDHEAD hen. Originated by the late Judge Lacey
of Alabama. Smart, one stroke clippers who seldom had body contact
with opponent. Often stayed sound and unscratched to an old age.
Judge Lacey was a master breeder and like Mr. Allen believed in the
invincible. After Mr. Allen, Judge Lacey's fowl dominated the field
and for years after his death. Perhaps as important was the Judge's
influence in preventing his associates from using lesser fowl."

We asked Duncan Long to help: "They originated over in the jungles. They all was wild originally. The Spanish fowl, well, they used to hunt them and eat them. That's one of the games. Then they have the Accheets that come out of India. Originally they was all wild. That's where all of your chickens came from originally, from game chickens.

"The first chickens that came over here were the Earl of Derby's, which were red chickens with yellow low legs and white underfeathers. They finally got into the hands of William L. Morgan and he named them Morgan Whitehackles. They've been fought for years and years and they are still being fought here. They [also] had the Old Brown Reds and the Red Wheels, and the Ferris Ford Reds, and Browns.

"And they come in all colors. You've got red chickens, black chickens, white chickens, Dominecker-colored chickens, blues, all colors. Some of them are the color of a ripe pumpkin. They're beautiful. The tails and all [are] the same color. They were great chickens in their day."

Almost all the men we talked with had their own favorite breeds. Vaughn Callenback, for example, said: "I guess the best chickens that was ever bred were the Lord Derby fowl. All these good red chickens has got a lot of Derby in them. They come from England. I don't raise these though. I got interested in cockfighting from my uncle, Shorty Ritchie, who used to have some game chickens when I was a little boy. I guess I was about sixteen when I got my first games. The first pair I ever had were Clarets. I don't know how many pairs I've got right now. I use some for my brood chickens, and the ones in the yard, I just let them be setting hens. I don't breed out of all of them.

"I don't know what's the best [breed] but I like Kelsos. Kelsos are hard to raise, hard to keep, and hard to kill. I like a Kelso. They're my favorite. I've got some Kelso, Minor Blues, Hatch and Mug, and me and my buddies have got half interest in a Grey.

"There are many different breeds. New breeds are coming on all the time. Somebody will come up with a good cross, then they'll cross him with something else—like my Toppies up yonder. I call them the 'Callenback Toppies.'"

Lawton Brooks: "If I was picking a fighting chicken, I would take an Allen Roundhead. They're a plump, heavy chicken, and they've got a small head and they grow wicked spurs, and them fools won't give up or walk away or run. I mean they were ill [angry] roosters, and that old head just laid back like a crow. They've done more

PLATE 456   Duncan Long.

PLATE 457 Vaughn Callen-
back with his favorite rooster.
This one has won several fights,
and Vaughn is using him now
as a brood cock.

PLATE 458 Lawton Brooks
with Jeff Reeves.

killing for me than any other rooster I had. They was nervy little old chickens."

Clyde Gibson: "Right now, my favorite chicken is a cross of Hatch and Butcher, because in my opinion, that's about the best. A Hatch is a good fighting chicken, and you cross him and he's a whole lot better fighting chicken. A Hatch is strong, and he's not too fast and he's not too slow. He'll stay there.

"A cross between a Butcher and a Claret is a whole lot better than either breed alone. And a Kelso is a fast chicken. There are [other breeds] that might be a little faster, but that's my opinion.

"You've got to let a Nigger Roundhead mature. Then they'll fight! They're real fast, too. They fight and they're good cutters but some of them are pretty bad to run. Whenever they come down to a hard fight, they're pretty bad to run, but they'll cut you all to pieces while they're fighting. I don't know how many kinds of Roundhead they are. Let's see: there's Allen Roundhead, Nigger Roundhead, and Boston. Now Boston is a good chicken just pure, and they're good to cross-breed."

Jake Plott: "Back as far as I remember, there wasn't too many game chickens—just barnyard chickens. The first game chickens I remember were the yellow-legged W. L. Allen Roundhead chickens, which were good fighting chickens. There are still some of them around, but they're not like they were fifty years ago.

"[Some other strains popular then] were the Warhorse, the Black Henny, the Red Quail, the Morgan Whitehackle, Joe Redmond Greys, Morgan Grey, Hatch, Claret, Claburn, Black Roundhead, Wardub Brothers, and Mug.

"Now the Arkansas Traveler was a good chicken, and some of them bred out blue and [some bred out] pyle-colored. I was a little partial to the Arkansas Traveler because they wouldn't run. I've seen them cut all to hell and they will just stand there and fight as long as they can hold their heads up. If any of you boys are going to raise game chickens, you ought to get you a trio of young Arkansas Travelers. You'd like them. They're slow but they're good shufflers and good cutters. I've seen them kill many a chicken. When that Arkansas Traveler turned one loose, he was dead. They're a hard-fighting chicken.

"The Brown Red was also a mighty fine chicken, but you put that cold steel to him and lots of times he'd run. They don't have the grit that these other ones had. But I knew one Brown Red that was crossed with Arkansas Traveler, and that made a famous chicken. He was a big old blue rooster, and a boy that was raised with me down in Gum Wallow had him, and he was proud of him. They had got to fighting chickens with steel gaffs, and that rooster killed so many chickens, they named him 'Ol' John Henry.' You know, John Henry was a steel-driving man. And that old rooster, John Henry, was a good fightin' chicken.

"Another one, the best chicken ever I saw, was the Georgia Shawlneck. That was the best fightin'est chicken I ever saw. They was fast and they'd cut another chicken every time they come off the ground. There's none fight around in here anymore.

"I remember one incident that might be interesting to you. One time at a chicken fight, when times were getting better and people had more money to spend, this boy came in that I'd never seen before and I've never seen since. He drove up in an old rattletrap car with some old sacks with some little ol' pecked-up chickens in a sack. They was Georgia Shawlnecks. He didn't have no money and wasn't nobody that would fight him without he had some money. I said, 'Fight your damn chickens. I'll put some money on 'em.' He fought three of them chickens and won $350 on the three. Those three killed every chicken they fought. I give this boy half the money 'cause he was ragged and didn't seem to have any money. He only had that stripped-down rattletrap of a car. It just pleased that kid to death. Boy! Those little Georgia Shawlnecks sure did come through!

"So there's lots of different breeds. A good chicken's got a straight breastbone. You can judge him by the lines of his body, the way his wings set, how crooked or straight his legs are, how his head's formed, and how the bill comes over. A game chicken man can just tell a good one. It's easy. I've seen some game chickens come out of a flock of chickens that weren't worth a damn for nothing, and then maybe one come out of the same hatching that was a top chicken. Very few full game is topnotch. Most of them have to be crossed. That's where your breeding and experience come in."

Breeding

In breeding game chickens, some people simply throw a cock out into the yard with some hens of indeterminate origin and let nature take its course. If they get some tough young roosters out of the mating, that is all to the good. But most breeders are far more methodical.

Breeding starts with a trio—two hens and a rooster—or a pair— one hen and one rooster. The breeder knows what breeds and what generations he is mating, and he keeps the breeding pair or trio isolated in a pen in order to keep an accurate record of the results.

After mating, when the hen sets, the rooster is usually removed from the pen (some say to prevent his disturbing the nest). The eggs are then either hatched out by that hen or, in some cases, collected, identified by date and hen on the shell with a lead pencil, kept in moderate temperature with the small end down and rotated daily, and then, when there are enough, put under a different hen to be hatched out.

The birds to be mated are usually carefully selected for both their breed and their individual physical characteristics. Each breeder has his own philosophy, and each is usually free with advice. Note, for example, the following from a column on page 29 in the November 1971 *Grit and Steel,* written by Drew H. Rosenbaum:

> "This is for you boys that haven't bred many chickens. You can take it or you can leave it. In selecting brood fowl first, I have told quite a few times how I pick my brood cock in other articles. The way I select applies to both the cock and the hen to get the very best cutting qualities, and you do have to have cutting cocks and stags, to win a majority. Pick the brood cock with a lot of spring in his legs and the hen the same way. What I mean by spring in their legs is when a cock or hen is standing up have a lot of bend at the knee. They look like they're strutting. The more spring in them the better. Also pick cocks or hens that their knees set in a little and their feet set out wider than their knees. They look like they might be a little knock-kneed. If brood fowl are picked the above way you will have good cutters and you won't have to breed a lot of stags to just get a few cutters. Almost every stag that develops good will be a real cutter. Don't all you old fellows that have been breeding for a long time start a fuss with me, I'm only giving my own experience to those who want it."

The men we interviewed echoed similar concern. Dennis Woods: "You've got to have good chickens, and good chickens come from proper breeding. Pick your hens and rooster that you know will make a good cross. It takes years of experimenting. You may have one good rooster and one good hen that won't make good chickens; there are some chickens that won't cross. If you don't select your brood stock through proven trials and if you breed out of chickens that haven't been proved, you're just wasting a lot of time and money. The thing to do is to select from the best from the very beginning."

Jesse Standridge and Floyd Justice: "When getting a new breed, get one that is quick and one that is stout and can cut. If you breed

PLATE 459 Against the house, Vaughn Callenback has built large pens for his favorite chickens.

PLATE 460 Out in Vaughn's backyard, small pens each hold a breeding hen and rooster. After the hen begins to set, the brood cock is usually removed and either put with another hen or put on a tether in the yard.

PLATE 461 A breeding pair on a perch in their pen. Each pen has not only a perch the birds can fly to for exercise and to sleep on at night . . .

PLATE 462 . . . but also a nest.

these two [types of chickens] you'll come up with one of the best breeds of chickens you ever saw. Then when you fight one of these breeds of yours at the pits and he starts winning everywhere he goes, you've proven your breed. Then they start wanting to buy them. That's when the money starts coming in."

Vaughn Callenback: "I like a medium height chicken, not too tall or too short. He's got to have enough leg to reach and pull a rooster back into him. I trim the tail feathers off so another rooster can't get a bill hold on him.

"There's good and bad in all of them. You've got to watch your breeds. You've got to breed chickens to fight, not for show birds. You've got to have a rooster that's got it all—speed, power, everything. You've got to have a chicken that'll cut. If he can't cut, he can't win. He's got to know how to cut another rooster [with his gaffs] and do it regular."

A mating that occurred years ago is still looked upon approvingly by most of the men we talked to. It was the blending of North with South. Duncan Long told us about it:

"In the South they used to fight what they call shuffling cocks, and when they'd go into another chicken, they'd sound like a pheasant beating on a log or something or other. That was their wings hitting on their legs and driving the gaffs. The northern chickens were what they'd call single-stroke or riffing-stroke chickens. They were a heap stronger, and they'd stand up longer and take more cutting. So they brought them down South and crossed them into these shuffling chickens, and now they're better than they ever were."

Jesse Standridge and Floyd Justice agreed: "Back years ago, you had your northern chickens and your southern chickens. Your northern chicken was real slow, but man-o'-mighty was he stout! Then your southern chickens were quick, but they were weak. So they started crossbreeding the two and getting pretty good chickens. Then they started wanting to develop a smarter chicken, but as you know, all chickens are dumb. They did develop a smarter one to a certain extent when they developed the Roundhead. He showed more sense when he was fighting, and he still does.

"But all your chickens that were originally bred in the South were fast, like your Clarets. The only name for the chickens here in the South is 'shotgun fowl' because of their quickness. Then up North they bred these chickens that didn't fight too fast, but they had the power. I think the reason for the fast ones to be from the South is because we have better weather, and the more chickens stay outside, the faster they're gonna be. Then when they're put up because of bad weather, they get fed more and this makes them stronger. You see, up North they have longer winters than we do and this causes them to be stronger."

To be more specific about the actual process of breeding, there are several schools of thought. One advocates mating a pure hen of one breed (say an Allen Roundhead) to a rooster of the same breed to keep the results pure.

Most, however, advocate "crossing" one breed with another in an attempt to blend the best characteristics of each. As Jesse Standridge and Floyd Justice said, "Usually you come out with your crossed roosters as your 'battle chickens.' Ninety percent of the crossed are your battle roosters."

Vaughn Callenback agreed: "A crossbred rooster is a fighter. He'll whip an inbred chicken the biggest part of the time because he's more rugged and stouter. He's better for fighting."

Here's how it works. Duncan Long told us how they first crossed the northern and southern chickens:

"Those chickens that were raised—most of them came from one hen and one rooster. They single-mated them. They'd take the off-spring from that and test them in the pit to see whether they suited them or not. If they did, then they'd take six full sisters and the sisters' father or grandfather and they'd breed all those hens. That's what they call line breeding."

Clyde Gibson told us about another man who used line breeding to create his breed: "He told me he got him a good game rooster from a cross between, seems like it was a Claret and a Dominecker hen. He started from that. The first year, he had half game and half Domineckers, but he didn't fight none of them. He kept the pullets out of this Dominecker's hen and game cock. The next year he put this same game rooster back over with these pullets. Well, then he had a three-quarter there, you see. He didn't fight none of them either. He kept the pullets out of them and kept this same game rooster and put back over with them, and then he went to fighting them. I believe he said he'd won eighty percent of his fights.

"That's not considered inbreeding. That's breeding up, you see. That's called line breeding. There's a big difference in inbreeding and line breeding.

"But that big chicken give them all kinds of power. He kept breeding them on up until he got them to an eighth, and he said he was winning most of his fights. Now he told me that. I never did try it or never did see it tried."

Clyde also cautioned us about inbreeding: "You can breed a sister and brother one time, but you don't want to breed them more than that. If you do, you're inbreeding them. If you just keep inbreeding them down, they'll get to where they ain't no good. They'll be physically weak and they don't fight good. One time is all you can breed a brother and sister, and you can breed the mother to the son one time, too. I believe that's the way it is."

Jesse Standridge and Floyd Justice expanded: "To breed cocks, you use the pure lines on the side of the hen. Then you cross them. You cross your breed down if you want half of one kind and half of another. If they don't fight to suit you that way, you go back to another family and cross it down with one [of the half-breed roosters]. Then that makes it three-quarters one breed and one-quarter of the other and if they fight good like that, then you can depend on that breed again.

"Then when you buy your chickens, you have to buy them from somebody you can really trust. When you go buy some, or every time one is hatched, you write down what kind he is and mark him with a band. Then if he won't fight or something like that, you can go back and look in the book, and kill him and all the ones you bought or all the ones that were hatched at the same time because they are all usually a bad breed.

"You usually don't breed the roosters after they are about six years, but they will breed up to ten or twelve years. I believe you will find a chicken doesn't breed or develop as well when he gets on up in age. [You can either buy a new breeding rooster after the one you have gets too old or you can use one of his sons.] Sometimes you need to buy a new one to get some new blood in the breed. If you breed a stock ten or twelve years, that's when you start putting new blood in your breed. When you do this, you get a lot of your speed back and also an awful lot of your power back, too. After so many years with the same breeding rooster, the offspring start getting smaller and weaker. This new blood usually brings all this back."

Some bizarre breeding experiments have been tried, but most have been dead ends. Duncan Long gave us one example: "You can cross a game hen and a pheasant. You can have a half pheasant and a half game chicken. But the pheasants, when you fight them, they fly high and all, but when that steel hits them they won't fight anymore. They just bleed. I've seen them. They're funny-looking things."

As has been mentioned briefly, most breeders keep a careful record of the results of their work. As Clyde Gibson said: "Where you're raising [your chickens], you've got one breed in one pen and one breed in another pen. You've got them pens numbered and you know what kind of chickens you've got in each pen. Then when you go pick up them eggs out of that one pen, you set them, and you put down when you set them what kind they are. Then you write that down in that book. And you know what kind of chickens them is by that mark. You don't have to guess. You go by your number and you put them numbers in the wing band of that chicken. You can look at that number in the wing band and right there it is. Then you mark the chicks right away before they get mixed up.

"You can punch a little hole in the web of their foot. They've got three toes and there's webbing in between. And they've got two feet. There are over two hundred different marks you can choose from just on the feet alone. You might have 'double left on the left foot.' You put it down in your record book. Or you can clip their nose. They've got two places on their nostril with just a piece of loose meat there, and it don't hurt them to just clip it out, on both sides or one side. That's what someone's talking about when they say a 'double nose' or a 'single nose.' We use little bitty cuticle scissors made of surgical steel that you get at the drug store to clip the nostrils. And we use a little toe punch for their feet. Cuts a hole just like for your shoe lace. It's a little bitty hole and it never grows back up as long as the chicken lives. We'll have to write down how many punches—one or two or three—and you know what stock that chicken is."

Dennis Woods: "I've got a record of each chicken that I raise. I wing-band them and I keep records of how old they are and what day they were hatched. That way I know everything that there is to know about a chicken. I'll know his whole background when I pick him up. If somebody looks at any of my chickens, I can go right back to that book and tell him everything there is to know about them. I keep my wing-band numbers and what breeds they are. That way, I'll know if they're crosses or if they're pure, because once a chicken grows up to be a couple of years old, you tend to forget what breed they are. If you don't keep it down, you'll forget what was bred out of your best stock and what was bred out of some that weren't so good."

The record kept of the ancestry of each rooster also includes its complete fighting record. At some point, like a race horse, after winning a certain number of fights (usually six to twelve), the rooster is "retired to stud," and the cycle goes on. Vaughn Callenback, though, offers a sobering conclusion: "It's hard to get good game chickens. You'll get some pretty good chickens but they're not always good enough to bet your money on. You'll get a bunch of chickens

PLATE 463   Dennis Woods.

that'll cost you money, but when you go to a fight, a lot of times they'll quit on you. They will fight and look good and do all right but when the steel hits them, they'll run. I've lost plenty of them that way. It'll happen to you if you fool with them long enough.''

Selling

Besides fighting and winning, one of the ways a breeder can recoup his investment and make some money is by selling some of the successful results of his breeding activities. The trade magazines that serve the sport are jammed with advertisements offering chickens for sale. Clyde Gibson is one man who has sold them: "After I quit fighting them, my boy, a welder out on these contract jobs all the time, bought the pens and I fed the chickens and took care of them and we'd go as halfers on them. Whenever we fought and would win, I'd get half the money, or if we sold one, I'd get half the money. You know, you can sell a lot of them for big money. If you are into it right, you can make a pretty good living if you sell a lot of them and you ship a lot of them everywhere."

Jake Plott, the fur buyer, was also in the chicken business at one point. He told us how their business worked: "Now the man that put me in the fur business, R. J. Loudermilk, was a corker. He rode a horse. Never owned an automobile in his life. I traveled many a mile with him buying furs from trappers. We'd take some eggs, Irish potatoes, and stuff like that, and have some meat in a coffee bucket and stop at a branch way back in the mountains and cook. He was a good man.

"He had a home down in Bellview, North Carolina. See, I started in the fur business when I was twelve years old, and me and him was traveling good together when I was fourteen. Of course, I was big for my age. He told my daddy that I had it in me to be a fur man, and I feel like he was responsible for me being in the fur business.

"Loudermilk was a game chicken man too, and me and him bred up a strain of chickens we called the No-Name Blues. They were bred from a cross of Arkansas Travelers, W. L. Allen Roundheads, Georgia Shawlnecks, and Little Warhorse. It took time, you know, but we did get some fine chickens out of them. They proved it in the pit. That's the best place to prove it. I never did go for a chicken just because he was pretty. I wanted him to perform. We bred that strain of chickens up and they were *fighting* chickens! We advertised them in *Game Fowl News* and *Grit and Steel.* We shipped them to Hawaii, the Philippines, and different places. Back then, you'd ship them for a dollar, and if you got twenty-five dollars for a rooster, why that was big money. But today they bring in all kinds of prices— you know, hundreds of dollars. Good game chickens are high. We didn't ship out a *lot* of chickens. We had fun out of ours. That's what we had them for. We didn't want to go into a big dollar business. We shipped some eggs, but if any of my neighbors or friends wanted a setting of eggs I always *give* them to 'em. I never have been a money person. I've always had enough money, and I've never been tight enough to sell my neighbors eggs. When we shipped them out, the price was anywhere from four to eight dollars for a setting of about fifteen eggs. I always advised the shipping people to set them in a nice average temperature, and after they arrived I advised the customers to let them sit a day or two with the small end down [before they set them under the hen].

"It's easy to ship chickens, too. They make little crates and put them in there, just like shipping a dog or any other livestock. We'd take them to Murphy, North Carolina, and ship them by rail. They go in a baggage car. I've seen anywhere from twenty to fifty over at Murphy at the L & N Depot where they was going out.

"We were honest, and I think most of the others who advertised in those magazines were, too. You seldom ever get gypped when you order roosters out of cockfighting magazines because the people that deal and fool with game chickens are good and honest. They wouldn't gyp you. They wouldn't take a dollar out of your pocket. They're reputable people. You ain't never got to be afraid of them taking a dollar off you. They'll bet with you and win your britches if they can, but they're not dishonest people."

And sometimes, naturally, they refuse to sell their best even though they could make substantial profit. As Clyde Gibson said: "Jack turned down two thousand dollars for one of his roosters in Oklahoma after he fit him. You see, if you've got a good breed of chickens, ones you're winning with, and I come and say I'll buy some of them off of you, nine times out of ten you'll have to turn right around and fight me back with the same breed of chickens. That's the reason they won't sell them. They won't even give you an egg, unless it has been chilled in the refrigerator or a pinhole stuck in it. You see, if you sell them, that gets your breed started all over the country. If I had an awful good breed here and I let you have some of my breed, it won't be no time until I'll be a-fightin' you with the same. And someone else would come along and get some from you and it'd just keep going.

"You do want to be sure, if you're going to sell, to sell good chickens, though. You've got to sell good [chickens] to stay in business, because it'll get around if you sell sorry stuff. If you take them to a fight and you fight them, then you know they ain't no good. People will ask you, 'Where did you get them roosters?'

"You say, 'Well, I got 'em from such and such. I ordered them.'

"The next man that says anything about them will say, 'I seen them roosters fight, and they ain't no good.' The next man won't order from that man, see? You get to where you can't sell none of your chickens. You've got to send good stuff. You can get by for a couple of years, maybe, but that's it. You're through. You're ruined."

Raising

After the hens lay and nest, and the eggs hatch, the chicks often run loose around the yard with the hens, staying nearby because they are fed. The men we talked to do little more to them during this period. Sometimes they even hire others to shepherd the chicks through the first year in locations different from their own operations. Joe Farmer is an example of one who raises chicks for a cockfighter. What happens in Joe's case is that a man who is heavily

PLATE 464   A glance around
Joe Farmer's yard reveals roosters perched everywhere . . .

PLATE 465 . . . even up in his trees.

into chicken fighting will bring Joe some hand-picked brood stock, turn them loose in his yard, depend on Joe to provide some protection for them from hawks and foxes and passing automobiles, and then simply let nature take its course. Months later he comes around to collect the resulting roosters, and pays Joe a certain fee for each one.

On the day we were there, there were perhaps forty game chickens scattered about the yard and up in the hemlock trees around Joe's gunmaking shop—the results of the natural breeding between a full Hatch cock and hens that were three-quarters Lacey Roundhead and one-quarter Bruner Roundhead. We asked Joe why the man that owned them had asked Joe to raise them for him, and what kind of an arrangement the two of them had:

"I started with him about 1970, I guess. He said this was a fine location for finishing the kind of chickens he wanted. It had plenty of water, plenty of range, and it was just an ideal location to raise. And he said some of his best fighting chickens had come from up here on account of, he thought, there might be some minerals in the dirt, and plenty of water. Just an ideal location.

"The hens nest in pens. One time I had two hens that made a nest together [because they had been penned together and didn't know any better]—laid in the same nest. They had, I think it was, twenty-five eggs. Twenty-six. And they went to settin' the same day, and I thought [since] they had that many eggs, I'd just let both of 'em set. And when they hatched, in place of going separate ways, they both just stayed together and raised. Raised twenty-one. I've never heard anything like that from game chickens. They usually don't get along that good together.

"It's been my experience that the chicks come just about half roosters and half pullets. So you end up with a whole lot of chickens and about half of 'em roosters. And you raise the roosters and just eat the pullets. That's about all they'd be good for, 'cause after you get the cross you want to raise your stags from, you wouldn't want to raise from the pullets. You want to get something else for your next crop. So I raise 'em up till they're nearly a year old, and I get five dollars apiece. I figure I made maybe twenty-five dollars above the feed bill this year. So that's really not worth it. [But they don't take much care, except] just when they're first hatched. I begin to feed 'em about twice a day and take real good care of 'em then and get 'em started real good. After that, they can fend for themselves. If you don't want to feed 'em, they'll get out here and find 'em something to eat. I feed 'em some, though [to keep them from wandering off]."

"[Beyond that], the main thing is just keeping 'em separated after they get up big enough to fight. After they get up about the size of a robin, they'll take 'em a round or two to find out who's the boss. This is the roosters. And they'll fight and bloody their heads, and that'll go on maybe a day or two, and then it's over with till they get big enough to fight serious. So it's not too much to do to 'em after you get 'em past the real small stage. Except keep 'em separated. And every dog on this place is trained to break 'em up if they start to fight. They took it on themselves. I never did give 'em any real formal training. When they'd start fighting, I'd go break 'em up myself, and the dogs would watch and they just took it on theirselves to do that. Even that old big dog will break 'em up. I've not got anything around to fight now, but I'd like for you to see that. It's unusual."

When the roosters are old enough to have their combs trimmed and be isolated for special feeding and care, the owner picks them up from Joe and takes them to his farm. This usually happens when they are about nine months old. The trick is catching them:

"I used to [catch them with my dog] when I could run. He's gone now. He got run over. Him and Missy [another dog] worked together. They would run 'em down and I'd catch 'em. But now that I'm disabled and can't run, I've got—you maybe noticed—this cage out here in the yard. I catch 'em in that. Fill it full of feed and it's got a trapdoor on it. When they get in there, pull the string. They catch on [to that], but if you don't feed 'em for a day or two, it don't really matter if they *do* catch on, they're going in!"

One of the more unusual things about Joe is that he does not fight chickens himself. In fact, he claims he has never even been to a fight, saying, "I don't think I'd care to go! I enjoy raising 'em because I enjoy having 'em around. I like to hear the roosters crow. That's the main reason I got started. I don't care for the fighting part. I just enjoy the raising. And Mother likes having them around because they eat the Japanese beetles!"

Care for the year-old roosters is a different matter entirely. All the men we interviewed tie each individually by one leg to a nine-foot tether, the other end of which is attached to the rooster's own "house." Each structure is located far enough away from its neighbor that the roosters cannot reach each other and begin to fight. The arrangement is ideal for keeping the cocks in good physical shape. As Dennis Woods said:

"It don't hurt a [fighting] rooster to stay in a pen a little while, but too long in there will tell on him. Usually, to get enough exercise and to be kept in shape, he should be tied out on a tie cord so

PLATE 466   Dennis keeps his cocks in a mowed grass lot. Each has a wooden tentlike structure covered with roofing felt, and furnished with a bowl for water and a feed cup.

PLATE 467   Each cock has a leather leg band and attached tether which allows it the freedom to walk around its structure or perch on top.

he's doing stuff that's natural to him. He's walking and flying, and he's hopping up and down. It's natural for him to do stuff like that. [It's best when you can keep] a chicken out loose. Then he'll be at his peak because he gets everything he needs."

Clyde Gibson's procedure may not be typical, but it is an example of the lengths some of the owners go to to keep their roosters in top shape: "We keep our cages mobile so that we can shift them and the chickens can have green grass all summer long. I leave them sitting in one place in the yard a week. Then I'll move them out here in fresh grass the next week. Keep them on fresh grass all the time. When we had all our chickens, the field down there was just like a lawn. We kept it mowed just like this yard out here. [Each] had a nine-foot circle [he] could go in. They stayed on that green grass all summer.

"Our chickens are took care of. They have a vet. They have to have shots if you're going to ship them anywhere. They have to have a certain amount of tests to see that they are not diseased.

"We worm our chickens every two weeks to a month. Don't go over a month anyway. You just poke a tablet in their mouths. You get [the tablets] at the feed store. If they're wormy, they'll lose their color in their head and it'll look pale, white-looking. Any chicken will look that way if it is getting sick. Most of them have a real bright-red-looking color to their head [when they're healthy].

"Whenever they're molting, they get awful pale-looking, too. They lose their feathers and they're putting new feathers back in. They call them 'green feathers.' Blood comes way up in their feathers and it takes a lot of blood. You want to feed them the best of feed at that time. We feed them a lot of meats. This happens from the last of July till about November, and that molting season is when chicken fighters usually work [at other jobs]. They don't fight roosters while they're molting.

"For an illness, mostly we use a mixture of Terramycin and penicillin, or penicillin alone. We vary it, like give them one one day, and something different one or two days later.

"[When a chicken gets hurt], we mostly just confine it and watch it and see that it don't use its legs that much. We might give it penicillin. If a chicken's sick or anything, we keep him on the inside where we can watch him closely.

"When we have them penned up, the pens we keep them in are about eight foot high, four foot wide, and eight feet long. They've got roost holds or flap holds to fly up on. You've got things that you pull down over the pens to keep the cold air off of 'em in the

PLATE 468   Clyde Gibson displays tether.

PLATE 469   In Clyde's living room, a framed ad for one of the trade magazines.

PLATE 470 Medicines and supplies Clyde keeps in stock to care for his chickens.

PLATE 471 One of Clyde's pens with roost.

wintertime. They've got a blind on one side because any chicken that can see another chicken is gonna want to fight. You've got a piece of plywood four foot high. Then there is wire from there on up to the roof."

Despite all the care, still sometimes disaster strikes. Clyde Gibson continues: "The foxes get some of our chickens. One time a feller come wanting to buy a brood cock. Well, I had my brood cocks on out in the field beyond where the cocks were on them tie cords. I took him out there to show him a brood cock and I had seven brothers on tie cords there. They was just alike. You couldn't tell one from the other. You had to know them to tell them apart. He said, 'Boy, them are awful pretty roosters.'

"I said, 'Yeah.'

"He said, 'I'll give you a hundred dollars apiece for them.'

"I told him, 'I guess they're worth that but we ain't never fit [fought] any of them. We've just raised them. We ain't fit any. I might let you have some after we fight them, so we can see how they fight.' Well, a week and a half later, I didn't have a rooster. The foxes caught every one of them.

"You know that hurts, but after anything like that happens, they ain't no need to worry about it. That feller come back and he said, 'I told you you'd better let me have them roosters.' "

Combs

All the men we talked with said they trimmed their roosters' combs off well before the roosters reached their first birthday. The reason is simple. As Lawton Brooks said, "If a chicken ever gets ahold of that thing, he's got him. He can hold him by that comb and spur the devil out of him."

And its removal does not harm the rooster. As Clyde Gibson said, "That comb is just skin there a-blowing is all it is."

The timing and method varies somewhat. Dennis Woods said: "I always try to trim their combs when they're at least eight months old. If you're not going to fight them, you can wait till they're a year old. It won't make any difference because their combs ain't gonna be no bigger at one year than at eight months. It's better to trim their combs and gills at night because they don't bleed as much. They've been on the roost resting and the flow of their blood has slowed down. If they do bleed very much, you could take one of the hackle feathers (neck feathers) and clip it off with your knife and lay it on top of the cut and the bleeding will quit. I've found that they should be trimmed on the full or growing moon."

Clyde Gibson said, "We use a good sharp knife or razor blade to trim their combs off. If you cut them on the new of the moon, they bleed bad. If you cut them on the old, they do good. That goes back to these old-timers, old times. You know they went by the signs of the moon all the time, on anything they done. It don't make no difference if you trim him in the day or at night, but you don't want to get him worried, like getting him scared or roughing him up. The least you can get him worried, the better off he'll be. The easier you can be with him, the better. They don't bleed but just mighty little. Used to, you'd just pull out a neck feather and put right down over [where you trimmed off the comb]. You know, that helps seal it. Back way years ago when I was a kid growing up, they would put soot out of the chimney on 'em, sprinkle soot on 'em and that would stop [the bleeding]. Now you can cut too deep. Just cut a little thin strip. You're supposed to know just how to trim 'em."

Feed

We found wide variation in the type of feed recommended, but no variation in the amount of concern and attention given the process. For example, Vaughn Callenback: "You've got to feed fighting chickens a lot of protein. I feed mine dog food, cracked corn, oats, and laying pellets. You can overfeed one just as bad as you can have one too skinny."

Dennis Woods: "I try to get my chickens hatched off in March or April, because in the spring of the year they've got all summer to get all the bugs and grass that they really need. Grass is essential to a chicken's diet. They need something green. Those hatched off in the fall of the year take too long to mature and become good chickens. They're late coming around and they don't grow off as fast as those hatched off early. This year, I've hatched over a hundred and I guess I'm down to sixty that I've raised out.

"You've got to feed chickens the same time every day. I feed mine scratch feed, oats, wheat, laying pellets, hog finisher, rice and things like that. Sometimes I feed them table scraps, sweet milk, bread, or anything I've got that's not in their regular diet to clean them out. When they don't throw their food, you have to clean them out. You have to slop them. It's just like people taking a laxative, something to clean them out. That's what it amounts to. It's good to do that about once a month."

Duncan Long: "They feed them the best food attainable. They feed them racehorse oats; they feed them rye, barley, wheat, cracked corn, and sunflower seeds. There's nothing in the world treated better than them roosters. Then they delouse them at least once a month. Then they worm them every three months. They give them vitamins and minerals. This is some of the stuff they give them. They give them alfalfa tablets. That's to take the place of grass. A chicken eats more grass than anything else. Then they've got these capsules—stress capsules. They got the glucose. Give them cod liver powder, yeast, vitamin A and so on."

Clyde Gibson: "You can't just go out here and half-feed one today and tomorrow and on up and then when you get ready to put him up to fight, just take him on and put him in the pit. You've got to have him in good shape out here in the field. You've got to take good care of him out here in the field and keep him in good shape. First you keep water sitting in front of him all the time. Give him all the water he wants to drink. You give him milk, rabbit pellets, and scratch feed, and laying mash and calf manure. Your calf manure and rabbit pellets are pure protein. The rabbit pellets has alfalfa and a good mixture of grains in them. You don't give them but mighty little of that. I believe they claim that one pellet will do a chicken for three or four days. They get greens, cabbage leaves, and lettuce in the winter and eat grass through the summer. They get fruit occasionally—apples, oranges, a quarter to each chicken. And they get tomatoes and Irish potatoes, quartered up. Those apples and tomatoes are a good laxative. In other words, they do get the best. You take care of 'em—what they eat. In fact, you really could say they eat better than people. You feed them the very best stuff—beefsteaks. You know, just in a small piece. They are on a balanced diet, year-round. These people really do take care of their chickens. That's their pride. They think more of their chickens than they do of theirselves.

"A lot of the old-fashioned feeders say you can slop a chicken, but we don't. You know, like feeding them table scraps and bread. Lot of people say that's good for 'em. They'll live on it and get fat, but it ain't really good for 'em if you're gonna fight 'em. If it's just a chicken running around [in the yard], it's all right, but it's not all right for a chicken you care about."

Conditioning

Before a rooster is selected for a match, it is carefully examined for its alertness and readiness. Dennis Woods explains: "You can tell a good chicken by his alertness, the way he's built, the way he feels. Mostly, though, you want a chicken that's alert. If you can have a chicken twenty foot from you and he sees you throw a grain of popcorn on the ground, he's alert. A lot of times that's the way I check for alertness.

"A rooster has to be in good condition just like a boxer or a basketball player. You've never seen a fat basketball player that would do any good or a fat rooster that would do any good. If he's fat, he's strong, but he can't fight up to his ability. He should weigh around five pounds to five pounds, six ounces to fight. You want a short, stocky chicken built like a small football—little on both ends and a lot of breast. If you ain't got meat on there, you ain't got nothing.

"There are different techniques for conditioning a rooster. Every cockfighter has his own methods. The basic things are your feed and good care three hundred and sixty-five days a year. It takes year-round care for good conditioning."

Nearly all the men we talked with, in addition to keeping their roosters fit, removed those about to fight from their normal routine and put them on a special routine to build up their stamina and alertness. This regimen frequently began two weeks before the fight. Dennis agreed with this process, but offered a caution that he considered vital: "You don't do nothing to a chicken that don't come natural to him. A lot of people condition their chickens by running them sideways. I've never seen a chicken run sideways. It's not natural and you hurt a chicken's cutting ability when you do something to him that's not natural."

Others described their methods in detail. Jesse Standridge and Floyd Justice: "Training is different from conditioning. You see, training is not important because when a game chicken is hatched, he's ready to fight. All you have to do is give him a fourteen-day conditioning period and he will be ready to fight. The only thing you do is give him a series of workouts to build up his muscles, and to make him more alert.

"When you're going to fight a show of game fowls, you go out in the pens and pick out the healthiest and the strongest-looking birds you can find. Then you put these chickens up and you work them one time of the morning and one time of the evening and during this time, you keep them on a strict diet. It's just like you were training for a footrace of a mile or so. You have to eat right and get plenty of exercise to stay in the best shape you can. You do this for fourteen days and on the fourteenth day when you're gonna fight them, they're in perfect shape.

"You feed them the highest protein food you can get—the best nature can provide—like the highest quality wheat, corn, and oats. If you feed the chicken right and keep up his workouts, that chicken will be what we call 'getting sharp' on that fourteenth morning. They will notice everything that moves. They're really nervous, and ready to pit.

"And you check your chickens out during this time. You strap little rubber muffs on the ends of the spurs. The muffs are little things about three-quarters of an inch to one inch long like little boxing gloves. You train your cock against another one. You put these on both of them so they can't hurt each other. They have a little rubber band on the end to fasten them on. This way, you can pick out the best one and condition him. All you want to do is just build him up to do what he was born to do.

"During the conditioning period, you work in a building about ten by fifteen feet. You have at least eight boxes about sixteen by twenty-four inches and a table. You cover the table with something like sponge. An ideal thing for that is an old car seat. When you work these chickens, you stand back from the seat a couple of feet, throw him up in a kind of backwards position and when he comes down, he'll be working his wings real powerfully. You just keep doing that till he gets his wings built up. That's called a 'fly.' You run him by holding him up below his neck and just going across the seat real fast with him. Just as soon as you see he's breathing hard, you quit for that day. You do this about five o'clock in the morning to prevent his going too long over his feeding time. Then you do it that evening at the same time. You try your best to keep it within a twelve-hour interval. You keep practicing these flies with the rooster, increasing the number each time as he gets stronger. If he gives out at seven or ten, you stop right then and give him a real good rubdown and set him back in his box and move on to the next rooster.

"It's best to have a blind on the ones that you ain't working, because when they see the one that you're working out, they all want out to fight.

"People who have a lot of money have gone out and hired the best doctors in the world to come up with what they call a super-chicken, but I can train and condition one right here in this room that could beat it. You have to *work* with your rooster. You just can't develop one that will be the greatest without proper condition-ing. It's just like people—they all need individual care. The one best way a rich fellow can beat you is to have two or three hundred chickens, and then get somebody to work them up and pick out

the best. Then he *might* could beat you. If you've got a good blood-
line or you just love to work with them, then you can pick the winners
out, too."

Duncan Long: "They take them and build a big pen. Then they
put shucks and straw and stuff in there. Then they put them chickens
in there and let them fly up and down on it for two weeks before
they condition them. Then they start feeding them that hard stuff.
They take their feed and lay it out in the sunshine to dry it out.
Then they give them two ounces a day for two weeks and let them
fly in them pens to build their wing power up. Then they take them
and put them in three-by-three pens. They have their litter in there.
Their straw and stuff. Then they take them of the morning and
flip them [turn them over backwards] on a mattress about waist
high. They flip them about twice a day about fifty times. Then when
they get through with that they put them in a cool-off pen, which
is about six feet and is built in sections. They have this filled with
straw so the chickens can scratch for exercise. They'll leave them
there for a while and they'll put them back in those fly pens for
about an hour or two. Then they'll give them their minerals and
their other stuff. Then when it's your turn to fight, [when] you hold
them in your hand they feel corky. In other words, they feel like a
cork—you know, real light. They have a big wide breast, and if
they feel corky, they're ready to fight.

"You take them that night before you fight them and you give
them their feed. The next morning you look in his pen to see how
his droppings look. If they are hardened and have a white cap on
them, he's ready to fight.

"And during this time, they really don't seem to mind all the
handling. In one way they're the gentlest chickens there is. They
won't peck you when you're training them; you can throw them
from here to over yonder [fifteen feet] and he'll fly over there and
fight on that thing. You can just go over there and pick him up.
He don't do a thing. He'll just cluck. Maybe cut his wing down at
you and cluck. No, they are the gentlest chicken there is. They've
got more sense than any other chicken—if you want to call them
a chicken. Most of us call them birds."

Clyde Gibson: "These chickens are conditioned on much the same
basis as a boxer or anybody who trains out or learns. They are
kept in the best of condition in the yard. Then you put them up
in precondition pens from one to three weeks to precondition them.
The pens have got shucks on the floor. You feed them and they
scratch in them shucks all the time.

PLATE 472 Clyde Gibson's conditioning pens.

"Every day we clean the pens where we condition them. The shucks has to be changed with each bunch we put up to condition. You have to disinfect. In óther words, it has to be *clean!* A lot of people believe in putting down concrete and putting something like manure over it. Right now we are using just a plain dirt floor with shucks over it. Like I say, it's according to the different breeder. I prefer a dirt floor on account of they scratch down in them shucks, get down in the dirt and waller them out a hole. If you put them on a concrete floor and put shucks on that, they can't get to no dirt. All they've got is shucks in there to scratch on.

"But now in our overnight room, we have concrete floor with the green turflike stuff put over top of it. [We put] cedar wood chips in the overnight cages that they sleep in and those have to be changed regularly every week, and those roosters get put in those individual night houses every night.

"Sometimes [during this period] I just feed my chickens once a day. You watch their weight. You have a set of scales setting beside your work bench where you run them backwards and forwards and fly them, and you weigh them every night. Whenever you take them out of the pen and bring them in to work them, you set them right on them scales and see if they're gaining or losing. You want to hold them right on that same weight all the time.

"Whenever they come sharp, ready to fight, they can't hold that head still. That head's just a-popping all the time. Most people that knows what they're doing can tell by the feel of them if they're in good condition.

"If you've never fooled with them, you can make some bad mistakes. You just go out there and feed them and you wouldn't know whether or not you was feeding them right. You could give them too much feed or dry them out. They get dried up and they get so tight they can't fight at all. You've got to have them just right or they can't fight. That's the reason you've got to know how to feed them.

"Before we put them up for a pit, we always milk and bread them [mix milk and bread together] and usually that'll put that straight through them. You don't give them any water or feed the day of the fight.

"If you just drive down the road here and see all these chickens here, you'd think there wasn't nothing to [raising them]. There's a lot more work to them than it looks like. I mean, if you take care of them right."

We close this section with a bizarre twist Jake Plott added: "I didn't feed them nothing special before a fight. People used to have an idea that when you trimmed a chicken—cut his comb and gills off—you should feed it to him and *make* him eat it, but there wasn't nothing to that. I've seen many a chicken win a fight that that hadn't been done to. I didn't do it because I felt like it wasn't right to make a chicken eat part of hisself. I wouldn't do it."

Fighting

The season for actually matching the roosters against each other in the pit usually lasts from November through the winter to June. It ends with hot weather and the molting season.

The roosters are almost always at least twelve months old (or "stags") before they are fought. The older roosters, or "cocks," are in fighting shape until they are about four years old. There have been exceptions, but by the time they reach the age of four, they are generally getting stiff and losing their agility.

Stags are usually pitted against—yes, that is where the expression originated—stags, and cocks against cocks (though exceptions do occur when the owners request it), and they are matched to within two ounces of each other by weight to make the match as even as possible. (Again, exceptions occur when one owner wants to match his bird against another and their weights are substantially different, but it virtually never happens in any sort of regulation match where the birds are being fought by the rules.) Roosters that win may be fought again in a month to six weeks, but most of the men we talked with refused to fight their better roosters more than once every six months.

Unless the fight is an informal one being held between friends in some unusual location (there are rumors that a match once took place in a room in the Waldorf-Astoria), it is generally held in a pit. Pits range in style from lines drawn in a dirt floor in a shack to circular or horseshoe-shaped arenas that hold thousands of people, but the average pit is a circular area (sunk into the ground, or at floor level, or elevated to chest height) twelve to fifteen feet in diameter, surrounded by some sort of barrier that both keeps the chickens inside the fighting arena and affords the spectators who stand or sit outside it a view of the action. The only people allowed in the pit are the two handlers, who may or may not be the owners, and the referee. Most pits have a center ring and two or three smaller satellite pits, called "drag pits." Though not often used, since fights in the main ring are usually fast and conclusive, the drag pits serve as areas where injured or exhausted cocks are placed to finish after meeting in the spotlight, thus allowing a new match with fresh cocks to begin on center stage to keep the action going at top speed. These pits are placed so spectators can see them and the main pit simultaneously.

Several of the people we interviewed described the pits in more detail. Vaughn Callenback, for example, said: "The pit that you fight the chickens in is just a circular place about fifteen feet across, with a wire fence around it so the chickens can't fly out. It's usually in a big old building that's got bleachers in there just like a football stadium. There's a center ring where they fight the roosters till they get wore down. Then the handlers take them over to the drag pit, which is just a small enclosure where the hurt and disabled roosters finish their fight to decide the winner. If a rooster cuts like he ought to, he doesn't have to be taken to the drag pit. He'll win in the main pit."

Clyde Gibson described one he and some partners built, and also one his son-in-law, Jack, has visited in the Philippines, where chicken fighting is a national pastime: "We built our pit out of blocks, just

like building a house. It was a sixty by seventy [-foot building] just
like a basketball court, with bleachers in it. It had windows, just
like these here [in this house]. The pit was twenty-one feet. Just a
round circle like that barrel right there, but it was twenty-one feet
straight across that way and twenty-one feet thataway. It was wired
in so nobody could get in there but the two handlers and the referee.
The [spectators] set out here in seats around watching them. It
had a place where you cooked hamburgers, too, just like a cafe,
you know.

"It cost three dollars to get in. The ones that owned the pit [got
the money]. There'd be a lot of people come, but by time [you
paid] the expenses, you didn't make much money. You did it mostly
for a sport. Now that's what it is.

"Some pits is back in the woods and some of them ain't. They're
just back out of the way. They have nice buildings everywhere you
go. Down at Sunset, right in to the left of New Orleans, they run
theirs right in town. Right nearly in the middle of town. The law
directs you into it and the law's right in there with you, walking
around through the pit. [The law] don't do nothing to stop it.

"[There's a place] in the Philippines where the chicken fights are
held called Theresa Square Gardens. It's built out of marble, and
Jack says there is not a building in this country nowhere that's any
nicer. I've never been there. When he went to the Philippines, the
Secretary of Defense and his wife put on a meet. You've seen pictures
of Madison Square Garden in books? The Theresa Square Gardens
is a real nice place. Air-conditioned, reclining seats, glass enclosure
where the chickens are fought—you'll never see nothing like it in
the United States. The Secretary's wife put this fight Jack went to
on for charity for eyes and ears. She donated all the money and
there was plenty. She brought Jack and the guy he fights with over
there because they are a big attraction here in the United States
and she figured they'd draw a lot of money."

The fights range in type from "hack fights" to derbies to tournaments. Jesse Standridge described a hack fight as "when we just
fight one another's chickens. We just meet at somebody's barn or
out in the woods somewhere. We'll weigh them, and the ones that
match up, we'll fight them for whatever we want to bet—forty dollars,
fifty dollars, or even a hundred dollars."

Clyde Gibson described a derby: "A derby's when ever'body puts
in same number of roosters—say he's got six and I've got six
and you've got six. Every one of the roosters has got to weigh within
two ounces of each other. Most of the time you'll all call in [ahead
of time] and tell them you're gonna be there.

"[The entry fee for each person entering a derby] runs anywhere from a hundred to five hundred dollars. Some of 'em run up to a thousand. Each man puts up a hundred dollars or just ever what the entry is. Whichever one wins the most fights is the winner of the derby. Each one of us has six roosters and whichever one wins the most fights gets the money. If two people ties—say we win six straight fights apiece—we split the money. He gets half and I get half."

Jesse Standridge expanded the definition: "Everyone has to pay a fee like three hundred dollars to enter. That's considered three hundred dollars in the pot. You see, a chicken derby is like a horse derby. You take about five chickens and enter them. Then say there's fifty people who come to enter that one fight, and everybody puts up three hundred dollars. As long as all five of your roosters win, you get every penny of that. The other day this fellow from Colorado flew his chickens in on Friday, fought them on Saturday morning, and on Saturday afternoon he walked out of that pit twenty thousand dollars richer. Only one person wins the pot [and usually an accompanying trophy]. Everybody else walks home empty-handed.

"When you get to the fight, your chickens are weighed, one by one, and their weight written down on cards. You turn the cards in and they are matched with roosters weighing the same thing. Nobody knows who they're going to meet in the contest. Once they say they have the cards matched, you go and pick up your weight slips 'cause they're through with them. That's when you pay your entry fee. When you do that, it gets the derby started. They don't have any preference to how they start. They just go down the line.

"Say it's a five-cock derby and they call your number and somebody else's [whose cock weighs within one to two ounces the same as yours]. Then you fight that cock. Then they go on through the rest of the entries till it's your turn again. Say you've fought four times and have only won one fight. Then you might as well forget it because some other guy who's won three so far out of the five will win the derby whether you win the fifth fight or not.

"Take Steve here, he was thirteen years old last year and he kept wanting to fight in one of them small derbies Floyd [Justice] was talking about with a fifty-dollar entry fee. Then when he got there, there was sixty-seven other people there besides him and he went down there and won him one. There's even women at derbies every now and then. Not too many do it because when you get those gaffs on, they can be dangerous."

Sometimes the derbies take the better part of a full day. As Duncan Long said, "You go to the pit and they weigh you in about nine o'clock in the morning. Then they make the master list out, because they have about forty or forty-five entries and each entry has about six roosters—that's about 260 or 270 roosters you have there. Then they get started about twelve o'clock fighting, and it'll be over about nine o'clock that night. The one that wins the most fights gets the money, and if there is a tie they split it."

He also described tournaments: "Back yonder, they had tournaments in Florida. They had sixteen-entry tournaments, and the entry fee was a thousand dollars. They had entries from Canada, New York, Texas, Alabama, Pennsylvania, and North and South Carolina. Each man would have a 'main' and they'd weigh seventeen roosters apiece. All of them that fell within two ounces of each other would fight, and the one that wins the majority wins the 'main.' Then they had the tournaments. They had three days. They'd start maybe the four-pound, six-ounce low weight and then go to the high weight of six pounds. Then they'd fight four of the lower weights the first day. They'd fight four of the middleweights the second day. Then they'd fight four of the heavyweights the last day. You'd meet each of them once. You wouldn't meet anybody twice. Then if you won the majority of those, you won it."

No matter what the type of match, immediately before each fight the roosters are fitted with gaffs. The variety of types is immense, as a glance at any trade magazine will show. As with feed, each owner has his own preferences.

Floyd Justice and Jesse Standridge: "Before the cocks are put into the pit, gaffs are put on them. The standard length for a gaff is about two and three-quarters inches long. Of course, they get shorter each time you sharpen them. To put the gaffs on a cock, you first saw his spurs off with a hacksaw blade. Then you tape the gaff around the top, bottom, and back to make it fit definitely right. You take his toe and move it till you can see that muscle in the back of his leg move. Then when you get tape on it, you turn the gaff around and tie string around it.

"I was cut twenty-seven times in one fight with a gaff. When you get ready to go to the pit, just sterilize those gaffs. Then when you get cut, after it stops hurting it will be all right.

"The bad part about the gaff, though, is if he happened to hit a post or a board, that gaff really sticks in there. Them chickens, though, are really stout, like you won't believe! When you hold them up, you best not make one move because if you do and they're nervous, they'll be sure to get you with a spur. I've had my glasses broke, a tooth knocked out, and plenty of other things too."

PLATE 473 Floyd Justice and Jesse Standridge showed us a spur on one of their roosters before it was cut off . . .

PLATE 474 . . . and the gaff with its cuff.

Dennis Woods: "There are different kinds of gaffs but I like a bayonet or a half bayonet the best. I guess there are fifty different kinds of gaffs that people use. They can be ordered from people that make them in Oregon or Texas. A good set of gaffs can run anywhere from sixty-five dollars to a hundred. They're made out of the best tool steel there is to be made. Gaffs vary in length from an inch and one-eighth to three inches. I like to use a two and a half for almost all my roosters."

Duncan Long: "They've got a leather cuff on them that goes on the chicken's leg, and you put packing in there like a chamois skin or corn pads—you know the corn pads you use to put on your feet that's got stickum on the inside? Now, they'll cut those corn pads in little things that's a half inch wide and about two inches long, and they'll wrap it around the spur. Then they'll wrap one around the leg, one below the spur and one above the spur. Then they'll put this gaff and fit it over there where it makes it snug. Then you take a waxed thread and tie the gaffs on.

"Those gaffs sell for sixty dollars now. They are handmade—a good friend of mine over in Tennessee makes them. I've been over there and watched him make gaffs. There's the regulation. There's a jagger. There's a bayonet. There's the old hook. Then they've got what you call a full drop, comes way out, then a half drop. I don't believe there's any full drops now. They've 'bout quit using [full drops]. They use a slasher. We don't fight with them in this country. That's like using a knife, and it's too barbarous, I think."

Before the specialized gaffs available now were widespread, chicken fighters used some ingenious substitutes:

Clyde Gibson: "When I was about twelve, we'd get together [and fight our chickens] but we didn't know what steel [gaffs] was. You know what bedsprings are? We'd get steel bedsprings and we'd keep working them and make that crook around there. Then we'd sew a piece of leather around those steel pieces and crook 'em and take a file and sharpen them real sharp and make our own steel. They wouldn't break. They was solid steel. We'd put 'em on there and fight [our roosters] with them."

Jake Plott: "Before it was easy to buy gaffs in the stores, we'd get a blacksmith to make them. I remember a good set would cost somewhere from five to seven dollars, and some was even as high as fifteen dollars. They had one they called a 'twister.' I never did go for those twisters. If a chicken got [gaffed] with one, it would twist his flesh all around if he moved. I never did use 'em, and I wouldn't ever bet my money on anybody that did use them."

The rules for the fight are rigid, and though there is some variation in terminology, the actions stay the same. Three men describe briefly here what is described in more detail in the two full interviews that follow Part I.

Jesse Standridge and Floyd Justice: "When [the handlers] enter the pit, the chickens are weighed again to see if they are the right ones. Then the handlers walk out in front of the referee and he checks the gaffs to see if they are on right, 'cause you could have sharpened them to be as sharp as a razor and this would be more illegal than· the fight itself. Then he says, 'Bill your birds.' That means to hold them in your arms and let them peck at each other awhile, so they will start getting mad. Then he says, 'Get ready,' and you take your chicken to the line and put him down, but hold him with both hands. Then you take one hand off and then you let him go and that's when they start fighting.

"There's no time limit for the fight. They fight till they 'hang down.' That's when one's gaff gets hung in the other cock and the rooster is dragging him around. The referee says, 'Handle.' The first handler that gets there has to get both chickens apart. If the gaff of my chicken was in his, he would have to remove it because I could take it and do something crooked. That happens all the time. That gaff is in there at a curve and I could take it and twist it and maybe hit a wrong spot that would cause his chicken to get killed. There's nerves all over the chicken's body and if I was to hit the right one with this gaff, it could cause the chicken never to walk again. You really have to look for this because it's illegal.

"You have a thirty-second wait period. You take your chicken back to his line. The referee has a stopwatch and he gives you thirty seconds to clean your chicken up, to get blood out of his mouth or do anything you want to do to him except give him something to give him more strength. This is just like between rounds for boxers. These fights either go till the death or until one of them gives up because he just can't go on. Now if one of the roosters goes two or three rounds and gets hurt really bad and quits, then they go into a 'count.' If you can get three counts of ten seconds each, you win. If your chicken is the only one that is still pecking, you yell, 'Count,' and you do the counting, but if both of them stop, the referee gives off the three counts. Then it is a draw fight. If a guy gets mad and takes his chicken away, they can't lose, because the chicken was still fighting. As long as the roosters are still pecking, no one can lose, but when one of the two chickens stops pecking and the other one doesn't, the handler of the one whose rooster is still pecking yells, 'Count.' As soon as the count is over, the rooster who is still pecking wins. A round is as long as the roosters will fight without hanging, quitting, or dying.

"You can fight cocks as much as ten times a day, because they'll fight till they're dead. However, you usually fight them only twice a year because most owners think more of their birds than to over-fight them all the time. If you only fight him twice a year, he's gonna have time to heal in between the fights. Anyone who respects game chickens is going to give them a six-month healing period, even though he may look completely better in twenty-four hours."

Duncan Long: "They pit them ten feet apart. They draw a line ten feet apart. Then the referees say, 'Bill your birds,' and the owners hold their chickens under their arms, where the gaffs won't stick [the people]. They say, 'Face your cocks,' and the [roosters] go out there and they flutter at one another. Then they say, 'Get ready.' You set them on the score line and they say, 'Pit,' and you turn them loose. Then when they hang, when the gaffs hang each other, why you holler, 'Handle.' The handler pulls the gaff out of his own chicken. Then they wait twenty seconds. Then they say, 'Get ready,' and they go on again. Then if they both get hurt bad, the last one that pecks gets the count. They count ten, and then they say, 'Han-dle.' Then they hold the cocks twenty seconds and they'll say, 'Pit.' If the other chicken won't fight, you get ten more. Then you count ten one time more and then the third time, and if the other chicken won't peck on the count of ten more, you win the fight.

"You've got to go by the referees. They've got the full charge of the fight. You've got to go by the rules. You can't grab that chicken till they tell you to. You can't reach down and get your chicken till he tells you. If you do it twice, he'll take the fight away from you."

Clyde Gibson: "[At the start of a fight in the main pit], the roosters are placed six feet apart. There are two lines drawn, six feet apart, and a rooster is placed behind each line. The referee says, 'Space your birds.' The owners back up and space them. Then he says, 'Get them ready,' and you set [your rooster] on that line. When he says, 'Pit,' you turn them loose. They go together and whenever they get ahold [of one another], they just keep fighting, moving their feet and their wings. That's called 'shuffling.' They don't just hit one lick and quit. They grab ahold and just keep shuffling and cutting.

"Whenever they hang each other, that's called a 'hanging.' The

PLATE 475 Richard Jones attended a cockfight in an isolated, abandoned chicken house one winter afternoon, with snow on the ground outside. Sixteen people attended, some of whom walked as they were unable to get their cars across the mountain due to the snow. There was no electricity in the building. The only light came through the screened openings that ran the length of both sides of the structure. Inside a waist-high plywood barricade, the pitting lines were simply scratched in the ground. The following series of photographs was taken that afternoon. In this photograph, one of the initial pitting lines is visible in the background, and the secondary pitting lines—in this case a square with a line through it—are visible in the center.

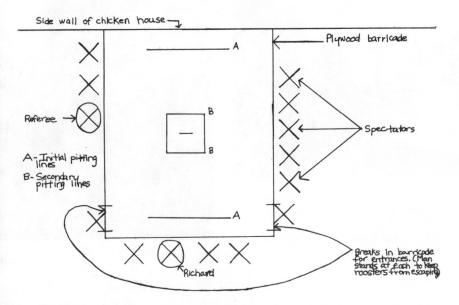

PLATE 476 A diagram of the pit where the fight Richard attended was being held.

PLATE 477 Each rooster was first weighed on the scales shown here. The sticks and tape on the platform kept the roosters from slipping.

PLATE 478 When a rooster was weighed, the owner was not allowed to touch it as he might be able to alter the reading.

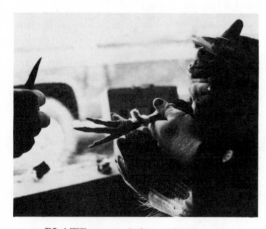

PLATE 479 When the roosters were matched by weight, the owners wrapped their birds' spurs with gauze to keep the gaffs from slipping.

PLATE 480 Then a gaff, each with its attached leather cuff, was tied to each spur with tough line tied with a special knot. The blades were cleaned with alcohol before each fight.

PLATE 481   Before each fight, each owner in turn, if he wished, allowed his rooster to walk around in the pit to become familiar with it and to arouse its sense of territory.

PLATE 482   Immediately before release, the owners, each of whom was holding his bird, approached each other, allowed the birds to peck briefly at each other, and then, holding them securely, thrust them at each other three or four times in a process called "fluffing" or "billing." When satisfied that both birds were sufficiently angry, each owner walked to his initial pitting line.

PLATE 483　When the referee said, "Toe the line," each man set his
bird on the ground, facing the other and with its toes on its pitting
line. Each man held his bird by its tail, and at the referee's command,
"Pit your birds," released it to fly toward the opponent. In the fight
pictured here and in the following photos, the two birds met in mid-
air over the center of the pit.

PLATE 484　Then they fell to the ground in a flurry of feathers in a
process called "shuffling," where one or both roosters slash repeatedly
at the other. Here the bird on the right is on the ground and the one
on the left (with the white wing feathers) is slashing at him.

PLATE 485 When the two birds hung, the referee called, "Handle your birds," and the two owners approached to untangle and retrieve them. The rule followed at this point is that if a spur of bird A is hung in bird B, the owner of bird B disengages it to prevent the owner of bird A from inflicting further damage.

PLATE 486 After a few seconds' rest, the two birds were repitted on the secondary pitting lines because the bird on the right was badly wounded. In a more formal arena, this would have taken place in a drag pit. Here, however, there were no drag pits. Had neither bird been badly wounded, they would have been repitted on the initial pitting lines.

PLATE 487   Then the bird with the white wing feathers shuffled again, and killed the wounded opponent . . .

PLATE 488   . . . and stood over the body. The man whose hand and knee are visible on the left waited to retrieve his bird until he was sure the other was dead.

PLATE 489   Later in the afternoon, the same bird with the white wing
feathers (on the left in this photo) fought and won again. He won three
fights that day.

referee tells you to 'Handle.' You don't handle until the referee
tells you to. Then the owners run and handle [their roosters] and
let them rest twenty seconds. Then he tells you to get ready and
you set them back on the line. He says, 'Pit' again.

"Well, if they get to where they can't go from the six-foot line,
they've got to come up to what's called 'beak to beak,'—two lines
twenty-four inches apart. You set them down beak to beak, twenty-
four inches apart. They fight up there close whenever they get so
weak, and whichever one pecks last is the one that wins, without
they kill one another in the first go-around.

"I've seen them fly together lots of times when the referee said,
'Pit' and both of them be dead whenever they hit the ground. Nobody
wins then.

"The referee [makes all decisions in the fight] just like in a ball
game. A running chicken can't win a fight. There's a rule book
that tells you all the rules for [how a chicken fight is conducted].
That rule book says, 'A running chicken cannot win.' The owner
wrings a chicken's neck if he runs. He's not being cruel.

"[A rooster only fights] just one fight a night, unless when they just flew together, one killed the other rooster [right away]. Then maybe later on that evening you'll match him back to another rooster."

Dope or drugs of any sort theoretically are taboo.

Duncan Long: "They used to give them strychnine, amphetamines, and steroids and all. Strychnine makes their heart beat faster and makes them fight faster, but when they get through fighting, if they win, they might shed all their feathers from all the poisons. They don't give them drugs anymore. They'll give them a little honey or some sugar in order to make them have energy just before they heel them. They don't give them drugs no more at all."

Clyde Gibson: "You can tell when a rooster's been doped up. You can tell easy that he's not hisself. Just like your drinking and [getting] drunk. Nine times out of ten you'll get him killed. All the roosters that I have seen doped has gotten killed. I've never done nothing to mine in my life."

Roosters that survive, but are hurt, are usually saved. As Floyd Justice and Jesse Standridge told us: "If a chicken gets hurt badly, you can give him veterinarian penicillin and that will help heal the wound. This also helps stop infections. Some give it to them in the wing, some in the breast, and some in the leg. You keep them in a place that is as quiet as possible, and try your best to keep them away from the wind and the cold. Sometimes when they're hurt they refuse to eat so you have to put vitamins and stuff in their drinking water 'cause they'll drink when they won't eat anything at all. Then when the vitamins get into their system, they'll start eating again, or at least usually they do. When they're hurt like this, you try to feed them a soft food like oats, because their intestines may be bruised and if so, hard grains like corn could hurt them worse than they already are."

Most say they don't seem to be able to feel the pain. Duncan Long exemplified those who said this: "Well, sure, I've had hens to get run over out in the road and break their leg. They come hopping up in the yard, and you can throw corn out or something. They're gonna eat. They don't pay no attention to it. I've set their leg and put a little stick on each side of their leg and tied them up. They'd get well. Of course, they'd be crippled a little bit. To tell you the truth, a game chicken it don't look like they can feel pain hardly. I never can beat it. They don't pay no attention if they get hurt. Maybe it's just been bred out of them. I reckon. They're just so game. See, that's the gamest thing on the face of the earth, the game rooster. The gamest thing on the face of the earth. They'll fight till they die."

The fights themselves are advertised in all the publications that serve the fans, and word of mouth adds an important dimension to the information network. Duncan Long explained: "They're all clannish. They all stick together. They know exactly where a fight's going on all over the country, all the time. What day it's going to be. They even have cards they give out with the dates on them."

The attraction, aside from the sport, is the fact that a good deal of money changes hands. Vaughn Callenback, for example, told us of one man he knew about who lost $37,000 in one fight. Jake Plott never bet that much, but he admitted, "I've never had no sense when it comes to betting on chickens, because I'll lose and take another chance. I never did gamble at cards, but I did love to bet on those chickens!"

The majority of the money is generated by the side bets that are placed between spectators who call their bets and the odds back and forth between each other during the fights, and then pay off at the end of each. Chicken fighters and their audience have a reputation for paying their debts—a reputation that every man we interviewed confirmed.

Clyde Gibson expanded: "If you're going to a chicken fight, it's just like going to a ball game. There is a whole lot more money bet on a ball game than there is on chicken fights. Like me and you going to a ball game—you pick one team and I'll pick the other. I'll say, 'I'll bet you a hundred dollars (or two hundred dollars) this team will win,' and you'll bet with me. If you lose your two hundred dollars, you're expecting it. You're expecting to win or lose, one. You don't pay it no attention.

"Nobody got mad about paying up a bet. Just like me and you a-sitting here talking. If I bet you a hundred dollars and I win it, you just hand [me the money]. Nobody don't get mad or nothing. They don't have no trouble [at the chicken fights].

"They've got a big intercom setting up there. A man is calling the fights out on a loudspeaker. [The contestants have] got a number pinned on their backs, you know, like 1, 2, 3. Say if I'm one and you're two, and I whup you, he'll announce, 'Number one wins.' Then whoever bet on number one wins the bet from the one who bet on number two. Just like I said, if you're setting way over on that side [of the ring] and you holler over here and say, 'I bet you a hundred dollars,' and I say, 'All right.' I was betting on number one and you was betting on number two. When he announces, 'Number one wins!' you'll come over here and give me my money. [The spectators] don't have any disputes or quarrels."

The fact that there is money to be made means that a part of the scene is also frequented by very wealthy fans. As Duncan Long said: "That Texas bunch is all millionaires. They fly in anywhere. They all had their own planes. Had a pilot. They'd fly into Orlando or St. Augustine. All of them would bring their roosters with them. That was in the last few years. One man died at a chicken fight in Arkansas. He also had an entry in the Kentucky Derby. Most all of the racehorse men are connected. They nearly all get game chickens. Those chickens in the big-time fights are better conditioned and they're better bred chickens. There's a lot of millionaires that fight chickens. Money always makes the best, you know. They can hire people to tend to them. The little old poor boy out here ain't got much chance fightin' against them big fellas. They hire the very best conditioners and everything.

"And the money that's bet is a sight. That's what I can't tell you about, though. After you turn that tape recorder off, I can tell you what I saw won last year. It's a sight!"

Clyde Gibson continued: "Oh, I'm a-telling you, there's people all over the United States involved [in chicken fighting]. You just don't realize how many! It's people from all walks of life. There're millionaires in it, too, not just the medium-income people. They're all organized now. There's the Georgia Game Bird Association. There's one in Oklahoma. All the states are organizing them, and they've got a president, vice-president, and so on.

"But you ought to see it in places like the Philippines and El Salvador. Over in El Salvador, Jack was in with one of these men that grow coffee. He's a doctor, but he owns the coffee plantation. He furnishes them with cars in return for Jack furnishing the chickens for fights. They bet anywhere from five thousand to a hundred thousand dollars over there on the chickens. And these rich people give five or six thousand dollars to buy a chicken.

"My son [ships his chickens] by plane, air cargo. He makes them reservations just like for himself. Our shipping crates are made out of plywood. They're nice-looking boxes. We have shipped in some cardboard boxes but we prefer the plywood because they're more stable. The chickens are usually not on the plane for any more than eight hours at the most. We feed 'em certain feed before they leave, like milk and bread or something like that to keep moisture in them, to keep them built up until they get [to their destination].

PLATE 490   Shipping crates at
Clyde Gibson's.

PLATE 491

Then the minute they get there, the person's there to receive 'em and they usually take 'em right out and feed and water them. So they're took care of. We do have to make sure the temperature's right [not extremely hot or cold] before we ship them.

"We can take chickens over to Guatemala and El Salvador, but we can't bring them back. [The customs people] won't allow you to bring them back, but most of the time we can sell them for four or five hundred, or maybe a thousand dollars. However, Jack usually keeps his. He has a friend in El Salvador where he leaves them who takes good care of them."

PLATE 492

The Law

On July 5, 1982, an article appeared in the Anderson, South Carolina, *Independent,* headlined "33 Arrested in Georgia Cockfight." The first half of the article read as follows:

From Staff and AP Reports

MARTIN, Ga.—Thirty-three people were arrested Sunday when Franklin County, Ga., sheriff's deputies raided a Fourth of July cockfight in a wooded area near this northeast Georgia town.

Roosters equipped with steel-spiked gaffs on their talons were locked in battles while spectators gathered around a waist-high wooded arena and gambled on the outcome, according to a sheriff's department spokesman.

Authorities made the raid at a site off the Freeman Road near Martin, not far from the Stephens County line.

Between 35 and 40 roosters were confiscated, Sheriff Joe Foster said. Four roosters already killed in the fighting were also found.

Deputies acting on a tip from an unnamed source raided the scene at 11:30 A.M. Sunday. Some of the participants in the illegal activity fled the area before they could be apprehended, the spokesman said.

The 23 Georgians who were arrested each posted a $1,000 appearance bond, and were released after processing from the Franklin County Jail.

The out-of-staters arrested in the raid—eight South Carolinians and two North Carolinians—were required to post a $3,000 cash bond, and they were also released, Foster said.

He said the cockfighting charge is a misdemeanor in the state of Georgia for both participants and spectators. No gambling money was confiscated, he added.

The second half of the article listed the names and complete addresses of all those who had been caught.

The sport is considered a misdemeanor in most states, the specific laws generally being found under those sections having to do with cruelty to animals. Section 2068 of the Mississippi Code of 1942, for example, reads:

Any person who shall keep or use, or in any way be connected with or interested in the management of, or shall receive money for the admission of any person to any place kept or used for the purpose of fighting any bear, dog, cock, or other creature, or of tormenting or torturing the same, and every person who shall encourage, aid, or assist therein, or who shall permit or suffer any place to be so kept or used, shall be guilty of misdemeanor; and it shall be the duty of any policeman, or any other officer of the law, country or municipal, to enter into any such place kept for such purpose, and to arrest each and every person concerned or participating therein.

The fact that spectators are gambling is also, in many cases, a contributing factor. The fact that it is against the law naturally causes some heated reaction among advocates when the subject is broached.

As Jake Plott said, "As far as I'm concerned, there's not a thing in the world wrong with it. I don't see why it ain't legal, because you turn two game roosters loose out here in the yard and they go to fighting. It's natural. But that way, they won't kill each other. They'll just beat each other's brains out, and that seems more inhumane to me. When you fight them with spurs, they don't get butchered up and left to suffer. When one gets down, he dies. He's just a dead chicken, that's all.

"But there's been a controversy over these fights. Those boys have been reported to the law. They're not outlaws. They're good boys. If they were to get caught fighting chickens, they could get fined a lot of money or could get imprisoned.

"If a man has got a cock and wants to go out there and put it in the pit and bet somebody five or a hundred dollars on it, that's his money and his cock. What it is is environmental Humane Society damned ignorance—that's what it is, pure and simple!

"And, of course, the church people don't like it either, but a lot of things go along today that the church people don't like."

Joe Farmer had a similar rationalization: "When you fight them, it's not as cruel as to just leave the chickens to go wild and kill one another slow. If they get killed in a fight, they're killed *right then.* You put two grown roosters out here in this yard and walk off and leave'em, they're gonna kill one another. It may take them till late this afternoon to do it, but there's one of them gonna die. So that looks to me like that would be more cruel than to take them and set them down and get it over with in maybe two minutes. That's what they was put on the earth for. To fight. They're gonna fight till the last of them's gone."

Or Duncan Long: "Look. The Humane Society always has a campaign against something, but they'll send a dog down to the dog pound and if you don't come to get him, they'll kill him. I don't think that's humane. Do you? It's just according to who you are, I reckon. Out there in California, they had an awful strict law about trimming a rooster, cutting his comb and gills off, you know? Then sometimes they'd get them caught. The law officers would take them and put them all in one pen. Well, they'd all kill each other. Beaked their heads plumb off. I think that's more barbarous than anything I know of. Then they wouldn't take care of them and wouldn't feed them.

"There's a lot crueler things that's done to animals than cockfighting. If you put yourself in a chicken's place, which would you rather be? A hen put in a little pen and fed high-protein feed and forced to lay? She'll lay one year and then they take her and eat her. When all the game roosters live at least two years. They don't even fight them until they're two years. Your fryer lives five or six weeks. [laughing] Hadn't you rather have a chance for your life as a chicken as to go get your head cut off?

"On top of that, game chickens have the finest life in the world. They feed them chickens two times a day, rain or shine, snow or sleet. They have a separate place to keep them. They have little teepees, made like Indian tents except longer, that they can get under when it rains. And these people love nothing more than their chickens. I had a hen nineteen years. She hadn't laid in years, but I kept her because I always liked her. You know, you love your game. The old roosters will retire [and the owners] build them a house, feed them two times a day till they die. These Rhode Island Reds, they'll live about eight or ten weeks and then somebody eats them."

Jesse Standridge and Floyd Justice repeated what almost all the men told us—that despite the existence of the laws, many law officials do not enforce them anyway, so they might as well repeal the laws and let the activity continue without the threat of harassment: "We have a pit over here that we fight in on Sundays, and as long as nobody protests, the law doesn't interfere. They said as long as there are no people complaining, that it was okay. [If the sheriff got any complaints], he would bust you if just two or three people called him. One time, all the big pits were gonna be raided—the ones in the big cities—but the law called the pit owners first."

They feel that eventually, the fact that chicken fighters are finally organizing will have the desired results: "The Humane Society was organized, but the cockfighters weren't. Then about two years ago, the cockfighters got organized and formed a nationwide movement. They took their case to Washington. They haven't gotten any laws repealed but they have blocked a lot of them. Each member that joins pays ten dollars a year and that goes to pay lobbyists in Washington."

Clyde Gibson takes a slightly different viewpoint, believing that dogfighting should be illegal since the dogs are trained to fight, but since chickens are not trained but do it naturally, chicken fighting should be left alone. The most interesting aspect of what he told us, however, concerned the time they were raided by the Georgia Bureau of Investigation—a story that pointed up, again, the haphazard way in which the laws are enforced:

"There was three young men come in to a fight in a pit me and two other boys had built. They looked like teenagers. I wouldn't have dreamed of them being the GBI [Georgia Bureau of Investigation] men. The boy at the door said, 'You can't come in here a-drinking that. We don't allow it.'

" 'Well,' these boys said, 'we'll pour it out right here.'

"He said, 'No you won't. You'll take it back where you got it and pour it out. You ain't pouring it out right here.'

"Well, nobody suspicioned nothing. They went on back out there, I guess, and drunk it. Naturally just like I said, you'll have a little drinking. If you want a bottle of beer, and you got out there and drank it, I don't think there is any harm in it. If you can come back in [the building] and set down and don't cause no trouble, I don't think there is any harm in it. Well, they came back and one of those boys borrowed enough money off the others to get in. They charged three dollars apiece at the door. They got up there and laughed and had a big time, just like all chicken fighters. They stayed all day. Late that evening, after the chicken fight was over and people was done leaving, the man at the door brought up the ticket money and I walked up there. I had been refereeing. There was a big table there and I sat down there with the other boy that owned part of the place. His wife was working in the kitchen and she hollered up there and said, 'We got a bunch of hot dogs left over. Y'all want a hot dog and a Coca-Cola?'

"I said, 'Yeah, bring me one.' And he said he wanted one too.

"Well, she came walking up with the food and this blond-headed feller came walking up behind her. I just thought he was a chicken fighter, you know. He stood there a minute and directly he said, 'Boys, I'm the GBI man.'

"I had my back kind of turned to him, you know. Boy! I turned around and I cussed him and I said, 'To hell you are.'

"He said, 'Yeah,' and he pulled his identification out. That's all he said. He just stood there. Well, a black-headed boy come walking up with another one and he said, 'You boys ain't got no guns, have you?'

"I said, 'Why, hell no. We ain't got damn guns. What do we need with guns?' Then I said, 'Do you want to search me?'

"He said, 'No, I don't want to search you.'

"Well, he went to asking who such and such a feller was. He was asking about one of the boys that refereed a couple of fights and worked in the kitchen. He owned part of the building. That boy'd went out and I thought he'd left. This man described the shirt he had on. I said, 'I don't pay no attention to what kind of shirt people wear.'

"I had caught on to what [the GBI man was wanting], but this other feller hadn't. He said, 'Why, that was Jim Stevens.' He went out and got Jim and brought him back in. [laughing] Well, then they called the other law on us—county law and all that.

"We made bond. They took us in. They just took five of us. It was a thousand-dollar property bond. Now that wasn't cash. We just signed our names. They knew we was worth that. When we went to court, it cost us three hundred and two dollars apiece and that was it. But there was politics [in that raid]. The Democratic sheriff had been letting us get by. Well, he got beat and the new Republican sheriff also said we could fight. Well, he got shot and killed and his deputy took over. We had three or four [chicken] fights after he took over, and then they raided us. So it's just up to the local sheriff. The governor or anybody will tell you that. If your local sheriff tells you you can fight, it's all right. If he don't, you can't. It's up to the local sheriff."

Conclusion

According to the cockfighters, of course, the sport in which they are engaged is one of the better activities available. For starters, the people involved are, as Duncan Long says, "some of the finest people in the world."

Clyde Gibson agrees: "Sometimes when there's sickness or a death in the family, and the family is in need of money, they have a fight and they announce that they are collecting money to help someone. That ring will be full of money. People will just wad up their money and pitch it over in the pit. There'd be three or four in there to pick it up. Those spectators would donate and help. You don't have to be a chicken fighter either. Say a person's house got burned up and a donation would be appreciated. If anybody feels like they want to donate, they'll just start giving and they'll fill the pit full [of money]."

In addition, it is considered a fine hobby, and, as Vaughn Callenback says, "A fellow's got to have a hobby."

Clayton, Ga.
Nov. 24, 1918

Dear Russ,
   Me and Col. Paris took my red cock up to Dank James and had a
fight but Dank's liked to killed mine knocked mine eye out first
lick and winded him out. I have my black one at home now. He has
changed into a dark red and shore has got the wallop and legs. He
is broad between legs and back and has a big head. I've got me a
shot gun now but haven't killed anything yet but go hunting every-
day. We all had the flu but are better. I am not able to go
opossum hunting yet. Wish you was here. We would have a fine time
hunting. My little roundhead is crowing now. I thank the world
of him and think he will make a good one.
   Donald has the flu now. The Dr. thinks your uncle will get well
now. I'm glad the war is over. Maby you can come home pretty soon.
I sure was glad to hear from you.

Your Friend,
Duncan

PLATE 493   A letter Duncan Long sent to a friend when he
was twelve years old.

Others simply enjoy the sport for its own sake. Clyde Gibson
adds, "I enjoy fighting chickens. I've made a little money at it and
I've lost money at it. You enjoy it. There's always an awful crowd
when you fight."

Or for reasons approaching the aesthetic. As Jesse Standridge
said: "If you just love the birds like I do, it's real interesting to
get into and you really enjoy it. They're just beautiful. You see,
there can be so many different colors in each one. Just like any
bird, the male is the prettiest of the species because their feathers
are brighter colors. The hen is always dull- and dingy-looking, so
she can camouflage the eggs on the nest. My main interest is the
chickens. It's just good to have them around to watch them."

We'll give Dennis Woods the last word: "Chicken fighting is a
hobby and a sport. If it's done right and you let the chickens fight
without doping them up, it is a pleasure sport. It's a challenge,
more like climbing a mountain. You do it because it's there. It's
more of a challenge to raise a good chicken than it is just to raise
something sorry that you could put off on somebody. It would tickle
me to death if I gave you a rooster and you won fights with him
and you came back and told me he was the best chicken that you'd
ever had. I'd enjoy that."

For those reasons, and more, the fighting of game roosters is
probably here to stay.

PART II: PAUL B. STAMEY, CHICKEN FIGHTER

When Dave Brewin, the blacksmith who guides Foxfire's blacksmithing program, found out that we intended to include a section about chicken fighting in Foxfire 8, *he suggested that we contact a friend of his at the John C. Campbell Folk School, Danny Logan, who knows several chicken fighters in Brasstown, North Carolina. We contacted Danny and he guided Richard Jones and me through the winding roads of Brasstown to meet Paul B. Stamey.*

When we turned up a road leading to the area where Paul lives, Danny told us that quite a bit of moonshine had been known to come out of this area. As we turned down Paul's driveway, I noticed on my left a type of barn, which showed its age by the gray boards that clung to its side. Straight ahead was a pasture that held a number of cattle. To the right was a white house.

As we waited for Paul to return from an errand, Danny pointed out an area three hundred yards across the pasture. Danny explained that this area was where Paul kept his game fowl. After about ten minutes we spotted a truck coming down the driveway. In the truck was a man who looked to be in his middle fifties. It was Paul, and he is actually sixty-four.

After Danny introduced us to him, Paul invited us in to have a seat. While we were setting up our equipment, I noticed a copy of Game Cock *magazine lying on the heater. On the wall were plaques resembling game cocks in a fighting stance.*

At the end of our interview, Paul took us down to the field where he keeps his chickens. As we walked through the field, Paul told us a small piece of information on each chicken we passed. He told us what breed each was and how well he did or would do in the ring. I dreaded the time when we had to leave Paul because he still had so much to tell. If a person had the time he could talk to Paul for hours, whether the subject was chickens or moonshine. Before we left Paul, he told us if we knew of anybody who wanted to buy some good chickens, we should give them his address. I told him I would, so I am giving it to you:

> Paul B. Stamey
> Route 1, Box 140
> Brasstown, N.C. 28902

CHET WELCH

I was raised back in them Depression days when no kind of job could be found. I was just a big old boy running around. My family and a McIntosh lived about six miles apart. He was awful busy because he had so many chickens. I went to work for him for two years. He paid me what he wanted to, which was down in the cents per day. Back then you could hire a man for a dollar a day or less.

McIntosh was kind of an ornery old guy. He didn't have no good, kind, soft words to say to you. His words were straight, plain words at all times. He wasn't a man to joke much. Sometimes he would give me heck about a rooster's water cup not being full enough or being turned sort of cockways. If he caught it, he didn't fail to straighten me out or have me correct it.

So I worked for him for two years. Then I went back home and helped my daddy cut acid wood. That's chestnut wood. McIntosh sent chickens home with me to raise for him at our house and he'd come pick them up in the fall and give me about a dollar each for them. I had a lot of his chickens in my hands before I left him. Naturally, you get to knowing more about 'em. That's what got me started into the chickens.

[And I've found that] somehow, most of the chicken people is a pretty good breed of people. I'll use that old word. If I'm at a fight and I'm setting up here by you, or over from you, and I ain't got a chicken and you ain't got a chicken in there—or even if you have—I say, "Hell, I'll bet you ten dollars," or fifty dollars or any amount. All right, we don't put up the money, but at the end of that fight you're gonna know who won and I'm gonna know who

PLATE 494   Richard Jones and
Paul B. Stamey.

won. I hunt you up and pay you if I lose, and if you lose, you'll hunt me up and pay me. If you don't, I walk over to the management and say, "I bet that man ten dollars and now he won't pay me." They'll see that he pays you. And he better not do that again or he'll be asked in a nice way to leave.

If a spectator gets to hollering during a fight—you know, making too much noise—hell, the referee will point up there at him to quieten down. If he don't, the damn management will get him. They allow no drinking or [strong] cussing because they have women, kids, and men and wives, and boys and their girlfriends, and men and their daughters. Then they have a concession stand—sandwiches, Cokes, coffee, and all that stuff. Everything has to be run in order.

It didn't used to be that way, and I believe that's why cockfighting became illegal. A few years ago, ten or twelve people would meet on Sunday where there was a level place out in the woods. All right, I'd bring four or five roosters and you'd bring four or five. It would mostly be amateurs or unexperienced people. They'd take a bunch of chickens out there and, hell, one would say, "I'm gonna take me a six-pack." See, there's no bouncers and there's no management. All right, one's going to take him a six-pack, and I'm going to take me a fifth, and so we get out there and get to drinking. It'll wind up maybe with a man fighting. Then they [disturb] some lady that lives on that road. She's one of the do-gooders in church and all. She'll say, "I saw so and so. They're fighting chickens up there. I heard my son say two men got in a fight."

Then the next thing, she'll report it to the sheriff and he's getting nothing out of it. He knows nothing about it. Hell, he raids them, catches them fighting chickens and he catches so many drunk that he has to lock them up. All right, then they say, "We can't legalize it because the sheriff just caught a bunch of drunks up there chicken fighting." They think it's just a bunch of drunks, and that's why I think it's illegal. [But even though it is still illegal, they run the fights with strict rules now.] You let things get out of order with a bunch of people and, why, hell, you'd finally wind up with man fights like in a dance or any damn thing. They are a little more tighter on a chicken fight [than a dance]. There are more rules and regulations there because they sure don't want nothing to happen for they might have to call the law in if two men kill each other or one kills the other or something. Well, right there's a bad name for the damn chicken fighters. So they just don't allow no man a-fighting. Hell, it wouldn't last a few seconds after it got started.

PLATE   495 Chet   Welch,
Danny Logan (the person who
introduced us to Mr. Stamey),
and Mr. Stamey.

The management has bouncers there, see, and they're trained what
to do. They'll have five or six there besides the management, or
they'll have extra referees, and they'll take over. I've saw it. There's
doctors there and lawyers there and more money people than you
guys would even realize. That's their sport [and they don't want it
ruined.

You'd be surprised at the big people—respectable people—that
go to fights]. I was at a fight in Toccoa, Georgia, and a man died
there. I knew him well. I knew him since I was a boy. He was an
old chicken fighter. He fought in Toccoa, Del Rio [Tennessee]—
local pits. He had a heart attack sitting right there in the seat. He
just fell over. The people that seen it brought it to the management's
attention immediately. They knew he'd had a heart attack. So they

stopped the fight and asked if they was a doctor in the building. *Two* doctors out of Atlanta run right over there! You wouldn't have thought they was a doctor sitting there. The ambulance come and they loaded the guy in the ambulance, but the report was that he died on the way to the hospital. The police that come there with the ambulance [knew there was a chicken fight going on] but they didn't say anything.

When a chicken fighter dies, there's a big memorial dinner and derby. Like some old chicken fighter that's fought a lot of chickens and been in there a lot of times dies at home or is killed in an automobile accident, they'll put on a big memorial derby in honor of that guy. They'll invite the state police, the high sheriff, the FBI. They's no police nor any law enforcement there while the chickens is fighting. They'll close the fighting for an hour at twelve o'clock for eating, and them people comes and eats, and naturally they know what's going on. They get back in their automobiles when they finish eating and visiting and talking for fifteen or twenty minutes, and then they'll leave. "Call me if there's any trouble," maybe [the police tell them that]. That's all understood.

And over at Del Rio, Tennessee, I've been going there for years. It's been run for thirty-six years and has never been raided. All right, the man that has owned and operated the pit has built a library for the town over there. He has supported with cash every church of every denomination over there in that county. And by having the chicken fights—and they hold them quite often during the season—it benefits their economy. You have to make reservations thirty days before in every motel over there, and there's a lot of motels over there. The restaurants are all full of people from Georgia, North Carolina, South Carolina, Tennessee, southern Arkansas, Ohio, and from all around in a reasonable driving distance. They'll buy gasoline, and they'll shop at night. They don't fight chickens at night over there in order to give people more recreation and time to shop around the town and look around over the Smoky Mountains. It supports the county, so a sheriff don't want to get in there and cut all the business people out.

Now a few people aren't satisfied with nothing. There's some old do-gooder woman sitting over yonder. That kind of people has got to gripe. They say it's wrong for you to drive over fifty-five miles an hour; it's wrong for you to drink beer; it's wrong for you to fight a rooster; it's wrong for you to smoke a cigarette. You know, that kind of people has got to gripe.

Let me go back and tell you how they match the chickens for a fight. That's the important thing for you to know. They send out little cards at the start of the season. Say they're going to have a derby. They send them out in advance to give you time to prepare for that particular one. These little cards tell you the amount of money it's going to cost you to enter that thing, the date, and the time you have to be there to have your roosters weighed in.

Let's use [this certain] pit for an example. I cannot see none of them people [in advance] that operates the pit, but I can have one of those cards, and I can know just what day to go, what time I have to be there if I'm gonna enter the derby, and how much money I'll have to put in the pot. All right. Now, you're supposed to get there early so you can weigh your own chickens. They'll give me a card as big as my hand, and a pencil or pen or whatever. I'll go weigh my chickens to the half ounce, but I'll usually take the half ounce to my advantage. If one weighed five pounds, two and a half ounces, I'd put down five pounds, two ounces. [Knocking a half ounce off the weight is to my advantage.] All right, I'll go down to the next one. To fight six roosters, I'd put six weights on that card. The management will put a band [with a number on it] on them roosters' legs and lock it. You've got to put that band number on that card [beside the weight] and you can't change roosters, see. You can't switch roosters no way because they've got that down in there on their books. The management takes that number, but he don't take the weight.

All right, you get every rooster weighed, and his weight is down correct. If you don't get them correct, you'll foul the whole deal up when it comes to the business part. Well, then, you put an identification mark on that card. You don't put your name. You put a crooked mark, or an "X," or a letter in the alphabet—anything you can identify that card with when you look at it again. They have a box with a lock on it sitting in there where all the spectators and chicken people can see it. You walk over and drop that card in that box. They have a time limit to have them all in there. Well, when every entry is there, three of the men that are managing the thing takes these cards all out and goes to a big table in a room by themselves. One man will say, "Here's a five-pound, two-ounce." Another man will look around over there and say, "Here's a five-pound, two-ounce." Well, them two matches. They try to match them within two or three ounces of each other. And if they can't match them that damn close, it's no match. All right, maybe you had a five-pound two-ounce, and I had one. See, we don't know,

PLATE 496

and they don't know, who's you and who's me. They just look at
that card with the mark on it. Well, they write these two matches
off. They fix that to where they can tell [that those two roosters
have been matched up]. Well, go on down here to a four-pound.
Maybe you had one and maybe I had one. Well, them two matches.

They keep marking out the ones they've matched and keep them
down on a sheet of paper, see, until everything's matched. Maybe
they'll go back and say, "God, we've run out here, but we've got
another five-pound, two-ounce. We'll have to put him with a five-
pound, three-ounce over here; and this five-pound, two-ounce we'll
put with a five-pound, one-ounce over here," [so we won't be matching a five-pound-one with a five-pound-three]. See what I mean?
We've got to redo it to get it as close as we can.

Well, when that's all said and done, they yet don't know who in
the hell's who, or nothing. So they call all the men up that's turned

in weights, you see? "Bring your money and identify your weight." Well, if I put a letter "B" on mine, I can see it and say, "That's mine there." I get it, lay the damn money down to the man. There's a man standing there special taking the money to keep the money straight. I lay the money down, and I've got my weights here. Then the next man does the same thing.

When you pick up your card, they ask you what your name is, or what entry. You can say, "I'm Pine Bluff entry," or, "I'm Paul B. Stamey entry," or something, and they write that down. Then they know when to call me out and who I'm done matched with. They don't *tell* me, but *they* know who I'm matched against. And if they told me, I couldn't do a damn thing about it anyhow because it's done and on their papers. We're done and matched, see? That's to keep it straight and no arguments and no going on and saying, "I had to fight again' you two times, and damn if you didn't have a better show of roosters than I did. Maybe if I coulda got against that weaker man over there, maybe I could've won more." See, that's to keep it straight. The little man with his weaker roosters or the newer man in the business might fight against the old pro in the damn business, or the old pros might have to be meeting each other. Hell, nobody knows. See, that's to keep arguments down and to keep it straight.

Well, then they call you out. All right, the band's still on that rooster's leg and they've got that number. You bring him out there. They'll tell you, "Go put the gaffs on your rooster. We'll give you ten minutes." Some pits will give you fifteen minutes. Lots of places, if you're not back there within the time limit, they charge you a dollar a minute for every minute you're late, and if you're too damn late they might disqualify you. That's to keep you from giving your rooster some dope or something, and to make sure you ain't out there waiting for it to take effect. You get the idea? You can't stall time awaiting.

So you go outside to where you've got your roosters up in crates, and you bring the first one in with the gaffs on him and the band still on him. All right, they check the weight right there in front of everybody. The referee, the spectators, or anybody who wants to look, can. And when we do come with our roosters, we do *have* to set them back on them scales. They've got some of the finest scales in the world. They'll get down to a damn quarter of an ounce or less. You set him up there and you take your hands off of him. You can stand there and look. If you're gonna fight against me, you can stand there and look and see just what my rooster weighs.

They check that number to see that I ain't switched [roosters]. After I've weighed in, then, they'll take a pair of shears and cut that band off the rooster. Then you set your rooster on there and I can stand there with my rooster in my hands and I can look at your rooster being weighed, and then the referee checks your band number and cuts it off and we're ready to go.

And [when you're getting ready to pit the roosters] you don't wait on no bets. We might bet when we come in to weigh our roosters, though. I can say, "How much you gonna bet me on this fight?"

You can say, "Nothing. I ain't gonna bet you a damn thing."

I'll say, "Okay." They ain't a damn thing I can do about it. Maybe I'll holler out there to the spectators, "Who wants to bet again' my rooster? I'll bet a hundred dollars on my rooster."

Maybe someone will say, "Hell, I'll bet you a hundred dollars."

I'll say, "Okay." Or maybe he'll say, "Ten dollars," and I'll just have to accept whatever he wants to bet. [If it's a derby] we're fighting for the derby money to start with, see, but we can make a side bet too. People all over the pit—the spectators—they'll say, "I'll bet on that one over there," or, "I'll bet on this one over here," and some will lay a hundred to eighty he whups this one [and they bet with each other that way]. Why, hell, you'd be surprised. Right around here, they'll bet a thousand dollars on down.

Then *during* the fight, some spectators will holler, "I'll bet so and so." You can get a lot of bets that way, too.

Okay. Then the fight starts. The referee, he's in command. He's the whole judge and jury. I've not got nothing to say and you've got nothing to say 'cause he can throw me out if I start arguing or something. You can't let that start 'cause maybe that would cause other people to start.

You've got a corner, just like a boxer. They've got a six-foot line drawed in the center of the pit. The referee will say, "Get ready." He ain't gonna hesitate. You've got to get it over. When you go to talking about way over a hundred roosters being fought that day, you've got to keep moving.

You hold your rooster and I hold mine, or we have handlers to do that for us. We turn the roosters loose six foot apart. When they go together and them gaffs hang, the referee will holler, "Handle." If my gaffs is in your rooster, I lay my hands on my rooster and keep it from hitting you, and you do the same. If my gaffs is hung in your rooster, I have no right to pull my gaffs out of your rooster because I could turn 'em. *You* pull 'em out, but I watch you so that you don't hurt my rooster's leg. The referee is bent

PLATE 497

right down over there a-looking, too. You got to pull 'em out nice, straight, and easy. You walk back to the score line and he gives you about twenty seconds to rest and get ready to go again. Then you got to let him go again when he says.

A handler is awful important. He can apply pressure and stop blood. If I'm the handler and my rooster's cut through here somewhere, I might need to put my thumb and finger on the blood vessels and press to stop that flow of blood from running up there and out that wound. I may reach down here and get a little dirt out of the pit and put on the wound to help stop some of the bleeding. I need to handle him like I was handling a little baby. Don't *finish* hurting him. He's already hurt. You just set him back there in your corner and you stay between him and the other man over there [to keep his rooster from seeing yours and trying to get away and fight]. Let him stand on his feet and try to recover hisself. He can do more for hisself than if you was helping him. You're only hurting him if you're helping him. You turn him around, then, and he's got to fight again. You keep doing that until one or the other or both roosters are dead.

I was a pretty good handler, and [my boy] Jack's an excellent handler. I would always just sit and look at that referee, and just as his lips started to work, I'd let my rooster go. Just as he said it, and not a split second late, I'd let my rooster get on his feet and get his balance to go. Hell, that'll win you a damn fight a lot of times. Lot of people fool around too long. But if you turned your rooster loose early and that other man is a good handler, he won't let his rooster go. He'll grab his'n back up. He'll try to get out of the way of your rooster. Then you've got to catch your rooster. You might do that one time. A human is subject to make an error. The referee might let you get by with it that time. I was handling a rooster up here at the Smoky Mountain Game Club one time, and an old guy there was really too old to handle roosters. He was much too feeble. Well, we pitted, and my rooster got hurt. The referee said, "Handle." We handled.

I took my rooster back over there behind the line. My rooster was spittin' blood. I set his feet on the ground and kept him in front of me to keep him from seeing that other rooster and going that way. Then the referee said, "Get ready."

Just as I went to pick my rooster up, that old guy let his rooster get loose. Well, his rooster saw my rooster from around the side. I wasn't a-lookin' at his rooster. Boy, he came around there just like a bullet. Just as I laid my hand on my rooster, he hit at my rooster and drove a gaff through my thumb. I just jumped up and there hung his rooster and the damn gaff sticking through my thumb. I let it back down on the ground to get that pressure off of it and to pull it out. I looked over there at the old guy and just smiled, you know, and was just as nice about it as I could be. He couldn't have time [in the middle of the fight] to come over there and apologize.

After my rooster whipped his, I walked out of the pit. A lot of people said he didn't let his rooster loose intentionally, and I knew he didn't. Like I said, he was a little too old to be handling, though. The damn rooster just got away and run over there and put a damn gaff through my thumb. Whew! Man, you talk about hurting. He come to me and apologized. I didn't get one bit ill [angry]. He shouldn't of done it though. He should have hanged onto his rooster. If he was that feeble, he should have known it and not been in there.

It's pretty dangerous on the handlers. I've got nicked and scratched. I've saw a lot of people get gaffs drove in their legs—come in maybe one side and out the other. One of them roosters could kill you with a gaff on. You take a three-inch gaff and you drive it in you somewhere, it's liable to do you harm. I've saw a lot of things happen in the pit.

Anyway, every time I win a fight or lose a fight, or you win or lose, it's put down on a damn big blackboard up there where everybody can see. Then it's called out over a loudspeaker. And we've won a lot of fights. We've bred good roosters, and one of ours had better fight until the last breath goes out of him, or until the last heartbeat. If he don't, his daddy is killed, his mother is killed, and everything he come out of is killed. But we don't have that problem. I'll give you an example. We were down here at a little pit below Murphy, and we were fighting a pure Hatch rooster that we had raised right here. We knew his daddy, we knew his mother, we knew his grandfather, we knew his grandmother, and we knew his brothers and sisters. Anyway, we took him down there just to fight against somebody. They was having a little old fight down there; and of all things, that damn rooster I was against flew into mine and what they call "rattled" him—hit him in the lungs—and blood just went to coming out of his mouth. He went to blowing bubbles and fighting like hell. Looked like he was gonna die. I didn't think he was gonna die that quick, and I thought they might be a chance that he'd recover over it. But I knew he'd fight another two or three pittings before he was dead. I knew he was good. He was just an outstanding damn ace in the sparring muffs. I just hollered, "I bet a hundred again' eighty that he's not whupped—that he wins." Some guy just took me. He figured he'd die. I laid the damn bucks again' a dying rooster.

The next pit, he caught the other rooster and just flattened him, just like I had figured, you know. He was powerful and strong, and when he caught him, he didn't give the other one no more chance, and [the other one] was dead. I collected my debt. The other guy wasn't gonna pay me. He said, "I don't see how in the hell you won that, but you did." By the time we got the gaffs cut off my rooster, he was dead too. I knew he was about dead when he got hit, but I thought he would last long enough to kill that other rooster. I knew he would fight. That's what we breed them to do.

Now there's different styles of fighting chickens. Just like scientific boxers, there's scientific fighters. You can breed them to fight about any way you want if you can get the right kinds of breeds and blend them bloods together. You can change their fighting style. We have studied it and we have talked it out with good chicken men. We have bought chickens for years and years. And it boils down to where we use the toughness and power.

The chickens we fight now is called Butchers. We've bred them up to what we want. The cheapest thing you can buy in the long run is your brood stuff, regardless of what it costs you. You can't take second-class and make first-class out of it—no way in the world. You've just got to start with first-class. I'll not go back and say we give a thousand dollars for the roosters and so much for the hens originally. We didn't give nothing. We got them through friendship. [We got them] from an old man in West Virginia. Occasionally he'll sell a trio of chickens. But you've got to talk about money. He don't need no money. He don't need to sell no chickens. He don't raise chickens to sell, but occasionally he will. But you're talking about money when you get chickens from him, and you're talking about not getting his best rooster. We do it the same way. Since we've had our chickens, we have never sold a trio of pure Butchers. We've sold some at a half [pure] and some at a quarter. [A man that might buy some] might breed them a couple of years and say, "I'm fighting pure chickens I got from the Stameys."

We'd say, "We doubt that very much."

But our chickens is just tough sluggers. They're not *fancy* fighters, but when they get hurt a little bit, they get madder. Then they get more vicious. They go to pushing the fight with him more. They fight straight into the rooster. They don't try to fly high, sail over and come down on him and all that stuff. In other words, we just actually breed for power and toughness. And if you don't hit our chickens in the brain, the heart, or the lungs, they's no stopping them. The more you cut them, the damn more they hit, and if they fight an hour or two hours, I guarantee you, one of our Butchers, or one of our Hatch Butchers, is not gonna hit them many more times 'cause he's exhausted, but he'll come up with the bustingest lick. It'll be one just as hard as he hit the first time, and a weak chicken or a cut-up chicken can't stand that power he's putting on him. They's a lot of men would rather have a rushing, fighting, fast, slam-banging, hitting-and-missing chicken. They like to get it over, win or lose. But a chicken that does all that damn stuff is not that good. If one of ours ever hits him, and hits him deep, it'll take that fancy stuff out of him. He's whipped.

So we breed up good chickens, and we pay careful attention to their conditioning before a fight. In the season when we're condition-

PLATE 498   The cages that the roosters are put in when they are outside.

PLATE 499   A view of some of the cages looking toward the conditioning pens on the right and the building where they check the roosters' weights and examine them.

PLATE 500 The pens that the roosters are kept in when they are being conditioned—one rooster per pen.

PLATE 501 A view from Paul Stamey's home of the area where the chickens are kept.

ing, we keep our conditioning house medicated. We've got so much light and so much heat in the wintertime, around seventy degrees. We've got fluorescent lights. We've got big four-foot by six-foot scratch pens. You put them roosters in them of a day with corn shucks about knee deep [to a person] and let them scratch and work in there [to strengthen their legs]. Sometimes throw a few grains of feed in there and the roosters sees them and digs after them. They can fly up about six foot high on the nice little perch and set up there and look out the windows and crow and groom themselves and everything. They'll set up there awhile, and they'll take a notion to fly back down and maybe get a drink of water in nice, factory-made watering cups.

At night we have special times—say six o'clock in the wintertime. We pick up one rooster at a time and we've got a workbench, got a set of scales, got his eating record, got his diet, his weight—everything—wrote down there on the tab. We work him and see that he acts good and see that he takes his work good and see that he's got his wind good like he had yesterday. If you give him fifty or sixty hard flips and flies, and if he's just exhausted before he's supposed to be, something's wrong. He's short-winded. There's something that he needs. If he acts good and everything, it's wrote down. His weight is checked. If he has lost an ounce or two, you'd better go to looking. Write that down.

Next morning when you get him out, work him, weigh him, go through the same procedure; and if he's lost an ounce or two, something's wrong maybe inside his stomach, or he ain't taking that hard work too good. He just ain't up to par.

So you go through the whole bunch that way, day in and day out. Their food is rotated in accordance to their weight and all that. They get so much good beef cooked, so much lettuce—it's high in protein—and so much good cracked corn, washed and scalded.

You get your chickens in lots of different ways. I got some chickens in the state of Oregon from a man. To him, it looked like I was a good handler. And he had come originally from over here about Waynesville. He went to the state of Oregon when he was a real young man, and he took some chickens that his daddy had give him. They was called a Boston Roundhead chicken. He seemed to be a good breeder because when he bred something, they was still coming uniform and looking good and they could fight.

He walked up to me—someone had told him I was from back

here in North Carolina—and he introduced himself. He was a pretty sensible-talking fellow. He said, "I'm fighting a man with a ten-thousand-dollar main right here at this pit next week," which was on a Saturday. He said, "I'd like to hire you to handle my chickens in that main."

I said, "Man, I can't afford to do that. Maybe I'm not that good of a handler." A main—that's just two men, you see. And my God, there's maybe hundreds of people there betting each way, and, damn, they're looking at you. You might try to cheat or hurt the other man's chicken in them handles or something. They've got money involved, and I didn't want to get involved. He just kept on talking to me, you see. He said, "If you like the chickens that I've got good enough, after the main you come down to my place. I'll be there and you can pick you out a rooster and a hen of anything I've got." He said, "And I'll give you a hundred dollars." Of course, that was back several years ago when a hundred dollars was a hundred dollars. Said, "I'll give you a hundred dollars to handle for me next Saturday, and if we win"—see, he was putting a little pressure on me—"I'll give you two hundred dollars." I finally wound up to agree, you know, so we fought the main and won by winning the majority of our fights. I believe we won seven out of eleven, which was good.

I went down to his place and I walked out there. I'd never saw so many beautiful roosters. They was all awful dark red. I kind of like a solid color, and they was awful dark red. They had a pretty stance. They stood pretty and looked good. He cared for them good. Water and feed and proteins.

Most other people would have took one of them roosters that had fought in the main but hadn't got hurt too bad, see, and would have said, "I want this one." But being me, when a man offers to give me something, I don't want to say, "Well, give me the best thing you've got." So I didn't even name one of the roosters that had fought and showed so good and everything. We went out there, and they were beautiful roosters. Roosters two years old and eighteen months old there that hadn't been fought, and some that had been fought. [He would explain] "This one won a good fight, and that one won two good fights," you know. We was going from pen to pen. "That one hasn't been fought." So we came to a year-old rooster. That's called a stag. I looked at that thing and he looked like he was going to make a fine brood cock. It was his stance. He was the right-length legged, too. He wasn't too short-legged. He wasn't too long. He looked medium, and he stood upright good.

He kind of leaned back and his eyes shined, and he was noticeable. You could walk on that side of the fence and you'd take one step and you could see him turn his head and his eyes look at you. You could step a step the other way and he was watching every little move.

So I said, "I'd like to have that one right there if it's all right with you, and if you haven't got it picked for no special reason." I'd done went over them nice young eighteen-month roosters, and I was not a-wanting to make the man think I was just a damn bum or ripoff or something.

Then I went out there to another pen and he had twelve hens in this pen. He said, "Now you pick either one you want." Well, they was all so near alike and them all fixing to mingle. He said, "I'll hold the door. You get in there and pick you one out." He said, "They are all the same thing. No difference." Same bloodlines, you know.

I said "Okay." So he opened the door. I stepped inside. I grabbed the first son-of-a-gun I could grab, and I brought them two back here and bred the hen and rooster together. He had told me before I left that they wasn't brothers and sisters but they was related closely. Then I bred them, like I said, for a number of years. They cut so good when they flew into a chicken and they didn't miss it. They sure hit it with the gaffs. We kept them for quite a few years and done good with them. Of course, we crossed them to give them a little more power, but we saw finally they was second-best to what we had, and why have second-best when it takes just as much to take care of them and raise them. So we kind of let them go. Sold them locally.

[But sometimes you can get fine chickens that way. Sometimes you buy them from another breeder. Sometimes you swap. Then some people even buy them through advertisements. You really have to be careful there, though. I'll tell you a story about that. One time I advertised some chickens I had.] They were Brown Reds—dark chickens that were fast, high-flying, fluttering chickens which you could win with. They were good old fighting chickens. Through my advertisement, I sent a man in Texas a trio of them. Three or four years later, he came out advertising them Brown Reds and how much he'd won with them. A man right over here had been over here and he'd saw my Brown Reds. He knew I had them, but it seemed like instead of buying something locally from me here, if he could get it from Texas or somewhere it would be worth more. Well, he ordered a trio from Texas from that man.

PLATE 502 This chicken fought in a fight where knives were used instead of gaffs. He lost a leg and went on to win the fight. He is presently being used as a brood cock.

He was proud—and he used pride, you know. He got them out of the train depot when they come in and he had them up there at his house. He come down here and he said, "I want you to come over and look at my Brown Reds I got from Texas."

I said, "Okay," and he told me who he got them from, so I kind of backed off. I didn't know what to say. I'd sent the man the damn chickens to start with. This neighbor thought they [were originally from Texas] when they come right off this place right here to start with. He didn't know whether to believe me or not.

I said, "Just wait a minute. Let me see if I can find those letters and show you just what he paid for the chickens and everything."

I come to the house here and got it and took it out there and he read it. It kind of knocked him down. At that time, him being a neighbor, he could have come down here and I would have sold him a trio of the same things, and probably a little better rooster, for fifty dollars, but he paid $150 because they come from Texas. He could have come down here and gave his neighbor fifty dollars for the same thing!

[Even when you're as careful as you can be about the breeding and selection and all, though, you just never know how they're going to do until you get them in a pit.] I went from here to Boxwood, Virginia—you've probably heard them talk about fighting a big event each year at Boxwood. Jack and I and a bunch of us from western North Carolina went up there. There was people with chickens there from every state in the United States, nearly. They were fighting a big and little derby. It took eight cocks to enter the big derby. In the little derby, it took only four and about half the money to enter. That was for people who had took extra roosters in case one got sick or one got culled out. You could put them in the little derby and they might win.

Well, this doggone little boy, he must have known something about game chickens. I don't know who he was or where he was from, but he was about sixteen years old. He must have had some money. He kept running around there with them chicken men saying, "You got an extra rooster you'll sell? I want to enter the little derby."

My God, he bought four that they had culled out. You know, these culls—you'd sell him the sorriest you thought you had 'cause you wouldn't want to sell your best. So they sold him four, and he bought them.

We went back the next morning. The sun was bright. It was up in the spring of the year. Naturally, we'd go before the fights started and mill around on the grounds and talk. I heard a lot of people mentioning the boy and how he'd do that day with them roosters he bought. [laughing] That morning, the event started. I was setting on the front row in a reserved seat right up front looking at everything. Sure enough, he met a man from Birmingham, Alabama. That man had a Grey cock. Beautiful. They wasn't a feather out of place. Them eyes just a-glistening, you know, and that rooster just a-moving in that high spirit ready to go. He had a man handling his. He wouldn't handle it hisself. See, he was getting old. The little boy there, he had a little old long-necked-looking rooster, you know, that looked kinda shaggy. Couldn't get no bets. Spectators just kept their mouths kindly shut 'cause, hell, ain't nobody gonna bet against

that Alabama rooster. Every man there knew those roosters and
the man who owned them.

I was sitting there—just had pity. They turned them roosters loose.
They both buckled hard off the ground, and that man's rooster
fell back, both legs knocked out from under him. He hit him in a
nerve in the back somewhere there. Paralyzed both legs. There he
lay. Why, he couldn't get up, sit up, he couldn't go or nothing.
There stood that little boy's rooster. Damn old man came up out
of his seat hollering over there to his handler to do something—
to get him back on his feet. They got the handler to handle, but
the handler couldn't bring him back. [They pitted again] and that
boy's rooster just fought harder 'cause he didn't have nothing to
fight, so he took advantage of that man's rooster and killed him
on out.

That just put him out of the derby. One fight would put you
out in a four-cock derby. Somebody would win four or maybe somebody would tie you. He just shook his head and he never would
discuss the thing. Everyone that was there knew that it was just a
perfect accident.

After a while, they called the boy out again. He had a pretty
good fight. It didn't go that easy, but he won it. He went on to
win four fights with four roosters that he bought right on the
grounds. The whole derby worked out to where there wasn't a man
tied, and by God that boy won $22,000 off them old culled-out
roosters that he bought. He was sixteen years old. Wasn't even
out of school. That was the happiest little boy you ever seen. He
was jumping up and down and he was talking to everyone whether
he knowed you or not. I bet he went back to a lot of fights and
bought roosters [there], and I bet he never won again 'cause you
can't do that and really win [consistently], you know. But he won
that time, and I've heard his name a hundred times down through
the years, but I've forgot it.

You can really win some money, though, once you get in that
big-time situation. Some of them are millionaires. One time I took
eight roosters in my car to Philadelphia. They was having a chicken
fight and they wanted me to bring some up there if I could and
fight. I had corresponded with a man up there that I had sold a
chicken to. He said I was welcome to come and put my chickens
up at his place for three or four days ahead of time, before the
fight. That was to give them rest from the trip.

The building that the pit was in was a brick building with shrubbery
and walkways. It made me have the idea we had to walk around
back.

PLATE 503

He introduced me to a lot of world-famous chicken fighters. There was a few of them there that I had heard about and read about like Billy Ruble, who won the world's championship in Orlando, Florida, three years in a row. He was a boy in a small town in Ohio. He was interested in game chickens by his thought and in his mind. I don't know how he got it there. Anyhow, there was a man by the name of Percy Flowers in Winston-Salem, North Carolina. He was awful good at fighting game chickens. I heard this told. Billy Ruble ran away from home and hitchhiked to Winston-Salem. He had seen these books and heard about Percy Flowers. Ruble walked in there and told him who he was and said, "I want a job cleaning chicken pens and helping you with your game chickens."

Percy looked at him and said, "Son, you're not out of school."

He said, "No, I lack two more years." The boy had no experience, but anyway, Percy took a liking to the boy. Percy said, "I'll have

to call your folks and all that and explain all this deal to them."
So they did. Percy told them, "I want to keep the boy and give
him a job. I'll put him right to school to finish if he's willing to
stay after he sees what he's got to do."

They agreed to it. He finished school and he worked [with Percy's]
game chickens. Percy Flowers would make mains with some people
in Canada so they went to Canada and fought quite a few mains.
He had his own personal plane and pilot. That's how he got to
Canada and back and forth. Percy Flowers was beating them people
up there. He was winning more mains than he was losing. He was
[already] in the money. He was what you call a millionaire, but he
was making another million fighting them chickens. He was beating
them people, but they kept right on making mains with him trying
to beat him. That's human nature.

Billy Ruble finally learned everything Percy Flowers knew about
game chickens. He knew just what he fed them, when he fed them,
how much, and how he conditioned them and all that stuff. After
Billy got over twenty, he wanted to leave and go back home. Percy
Flowers told him, "Go out there with me and we'll pick you out
two trios of chickens. You know how I breed them and how I select
my brood stuff. You know everything I know. You take them to
Ohio with you and see what you can do."

He took them to Ohio and he bred them. Then he won the Orlando
tournament three years in a row. People all over the world go down
there. When they have that [tournament], you can't get a damn
motel within five hundred miles of that place. Now Ruble sells roosters and he shows a few. Not many of them showing. Most are in
battle. Them game roosters put him a millionaire, too.

But people fight them things all over the world. In Guatemala,
they fight what you call "short slashers." Instead of fighting with
round gaffs, they fight with slashers. They are an inch and a quarter
long and they cut anywhere you touch them. They're sharp as razors
on either side, and the tip is as sharp as a needle. A fight don't
last very long with them.

We knew that the money was over in the Latin American countries
with the big game fighters. But us being poor mountain people, it
was hard for us to break through and have enough money to back
ourselves. We knew we had the chickens—or thought we did—but
we hadn't tried them over in Guatemala, and they hadn't saw the
breed that we had. So we advertised, and we got a sale or two
over there, and we sent—not the special cocks we had, but we sent
good chickens. The man we sent them to kinda liked them. He

PLATE 504 Danny Logan, Paul Stamey, and Chet Welch.

owned two big coffee plantations and one cotton mill and some motels. We corresponded with him through mail, and he said he would back us with money if we would bring an entry of chickens over there. He would pay the expenses out of Atlanta. We had to get the chickens to Atlanta. He would have paid it from here if he would have known it. He just thought you could get on a plane from here.

He said, "I'll give you two hundred dollars for the roosters and I'll give you twenty percent of the winnings if we win. I'll do the betting of the money." The man who paid our expenses would only pay for one person. He didn't get down to them words, but we knew what he was talking about. He was expecting one person. So Jack took these roosters that were crossed. They had a little more speed. That's what we usually do in our Butcher chickens, and like some boxers, you better not try to crowd them too much. Better stay back a little because they will slug you.

He took an entry of these chickens—us a-wondering if they'd be all right or if they'd just all get killed. He entered them in a pretty good derby, and the man tried to bet four thousand dollars on each fight to give us enough money on the percentage of the winnings. He wanted to make it worth our while. He said he didn't care how much he paid for a rooster as long as it was a good one.

Well, when our chickens would get cut, that made them madder, and them Butchers would climb them digging just as hard as they could dig. Jack said they would just cut them roosters literally all to pieces, and they'd hit the ground. That was the first time them people at that pit had saw anything like that. They was used to high-flying, rough slam-bang with them slashers. They thought you had to fight quick or you'd get killed. You would, lots of times. But they wasn't killing them old Butchers. They're so damn tough, cutting a leg off wouldn't stop them.

Them game chicken people there got to walking around Jack saying, "Man, what kind of chickens *is* them? I'd like to buy some of them. They don't fight but they win." These old Butchers were in good shape. They didn't parade around. They would just take their time. And they'd win.

[Now, one thing you really want to watch out about if you get into this business is getting sweet on one of your roosters. The minute you think he can't be beat is when it'll happen.]

I met a rooster one time over at an old barn. A bunch of them boys that live off Slow Creek had won eight or ten fights [with this rooster]. He was one of them awful rushing fighting speedy roosters. His name was Buckshot.

I picked out a rooster to whup that rooster. I *went* to *win*. I knew the fight was coming up. I went out there in the field and got a cock. I wanted to pick one out a little faster [than Buckshot]. I wanted to show them boys a little more fun. I knew the other rooster's weight. I had scales here, too, and I found one the same weight.

I took him over there. They fought roosters nearly all day. It came down to about getting toward the end of the fighting and they went to going around hollering "Who's got a five-two they'll match?" He weighed five pounds, two ounces. I never will forget it. They wouldn't say what price or nothing [they'd fight for]. Nobody had one close to that. I said, "Hell, I got a five-two."

Well, this guy said, "Will you match him?"

I said, "Yeah, I'll match him." I said, "How much you want to fight for?" I said, "Hell, you fellows just make up a hell of a pot and I'll cover it."

"All right," he said. All of his friends went in about twenty-five dollars apiece, and some spectators come up and said, "I want ten dollars on old Buckshot." They had saw him fight, you see.

So this guy said, "We've got a pretty good pot made up over here." They had two hundred and thirty dollars made up. They was really just gonna take me for a damn ride.

A friend of mine walked over to me and said, "Paul, do you know what you're again'?"

I said, "Yes, I do. Old Buckshot."

I walked back over and I said, "Let me show you guys what my rooster weighs."

They wadn't even gonna weigh it. They didn't think that much about it. So I set him up on the scales there and he weighed five pounds three ounces with gaffs on. Then they weighed theirs and they weighed the same thing.

When we pitted the roosters, old Buckshot came across that pit a-flying, and just about the time he started to leave the ground, mine had just a split second done left the ground and hit him right up in about the neck here somewheres. He was over him that much, them feet just a-rolling, you know.

We handled them. I looked around. I'm bad to tease, and I said, "Boys, old Buckshot gòt hurt."

They said, "Yeah, but you just wait a minute." They didn't know he was hurt that bad.

I said, "He'll never come across that pit like he crossed it the first time."

So when the time was up for us to handle them, we pitted them back. Buckshot come. He was a-coming straight but he wasn't a-coming fast. My rooster caught him again 'fore he got off the ground and cut him good and deep with both gaffs. He kinda shook him, you know, with both gaffs? I was a little slow about handling. I knowed I was in deep.

The third pitting, mine caught Buckshot and he just didn't let up on him, and there laid Buckshot. That was the sickest bunch of people. I couldn't believe it. There stood my rooster. Didn't have a damn gaff in him. He was just like brand new.

Now that is getting sweet on a rooster. I know not to get sweet on a rooster. He might meet his match.

My oldest boy Jack and I went to a little chicken pit over here another time just to kinda watch them. We thought we'd just take a couple of roosters. We took them right out of the pen. They had no conditioning. We could afford [to lose] them.

We took them over there to hack them. That's you and I just getting together and making up a fight and betting. They were two little old Butchers. They was small. Weighed about four pounds, fifteen ounces, or something like that. They was in derby weight.

This pit was just across the line over there. This feller and his brother from over here at Helen and some of them boys over there had a rooster. It was a Brown Red crossed rooster. It was extremely fast. They had brought him over there three times and fought him.

He'd kill a rooster in the first pitting and he'd just rush into a rooster. I'd say he was a good-cutting rooster and he fought with style. He'd get right on a damn rooster and win. So they got awful sweet on that rooster.

But anyway, we didn't do it on purpose or nothing like that. We would match the two little old Butchers for ten dollars apiece. You know, just fight them and let it go—win or lose.

The way it worked out, they couldn't get nobody to match that rooster. They was trying to get so-and-so weight to match it. We set there in silence. Finally we said, "Damn, we've got one that'll match him. We'll match him for any amount of money you want to. Ten or fifteen dollars or all the money we've got. This feller wanted a hundred, his brother wanted a hundred, and the guy with them wanted a hundred. So I was thinking, "We're gonna whup that rooster. He's not all that good. We'll knock that fight out of him and surprise him." I actually thought that.

So we matched them for the three hundred dollars. We had just one little old Butcher out of the pen right over there. He had never fought. Of course, we knew his fighting style even though he'd never been hit a lick in his life. We let Clyde [Gibson's] boy Bobby handle him. Bobby was a pretty fair little old handler. When they pitted, their rooster rushed across there and caught our Butcher. He put one gaff right down the side of his neck plumb to the hub there, and the other gaff over on the other side flashed there a little bit. One of them went deep. I saw it. I was sitting there, you see. You get used to it. You can tell. Lord, that hurts. That didn't kill us, but that hurt. I was scared it might make him wobble a little bit, but that just stirred him up and made him that much madder.

When we got to handle, Bobby took the little old Butcher back over there and set him down and he just raised up his head and kind of cackled a little cackle or two and looked at the people. Like I said, he wasn't conditioned. He wasn't used to noise.

He kind of cackled and Bobby picked him up, and when the referee said, "Pit them," boy, the other rooster shot across there and when he did, he caught that Butcher in his wing plumb out in the end of his wing which wouldn't hurt him at all. And we got another handle.

That Butcher was really getting mad. The third pitting, the other rooster come across there running extremely fast. When he came off the ground, that Butcher came up with him and laid a gaff under each wing there. I really couldn't see how deep they was, but I knowed they was deep because a Butcher puts them in deep. They handled—took the other rooster back over to the fence—and I was sitting by some people there. I said, "That rooster will never come across that pit like he did. That's a whupped rooster."

Guy sitting beside me said, "Would you bet ten dollars?"

I said, "Well, Lord, yes. I'll bet you just whatever you want to bet."

And the guy bet me ten dollars. I didn't care about betting him ten dollars, but he bet me ten dollars.

So when they pitted again, Brown Red came across that pit weaving slowly. That Butcher just stood there and waited on him. He got over there and, why, that Butcher caught him and shook him. Got him with a gaff under each wing. That's a dangerous place to hit a rooster—under the wing or down the back. That Butcher just set there and shook him, you know, before they could get to handle. That other rooster just spread his wings out there and went to dying right then. By the time they handled, that rooster was dead and three hundred dollars gone. That dern Butcher was just standing there. He could have fought a dern hour or two hours, whatever.

Now that was getting sweet on a rooster. The boys couldn't afford three hundred dollars. They had it to bet, but what I mean, they couldn't afford it. Really, they needed that at home for groceries or something more than they did on the rooster.

We got the other one matched, I believe, for thirty or forty dollars, and he showed a better fight than the other one because he took off a little better. But Brown Red had just run into something he couldn't kill. He could hit, but he couldn't kill, see? Then when he got hit back hard and deep enough, he was out. He just couldn't take it. They wadn't no way he could take it.

Let me tell you one last thing—don't bet more than you can afford.

PART III: REX DUVALL, CHICKEN FIGHTER

Rex is the kind of man who doesn't like to be around too many people, and so he lives back in the hills on a gravel road in a small wood-frame house. The house is surrounded by big poplars, and behind it are Rex's beehives, his garden and lettuce patch, his dogs, and the spring that runs water into his house. A small barn is used for storage for his lawnmower, tiller, and parts for his hives.

Rex also has a log cabin back in the woods where he can go deer hunting and things that he likes to do. There is also a huge river where he likes to go fishing. Rex says it has only frozen over two times in his life.

My mother and Rex are good friends, and Rex and Wig and Mama were talking about Foxfire *articles, and Rex mentioned that he knew a few people to interview. One of them was Aunt Ethel, and I interviewed her for* Foxfire 6 *[page 311].*

Since Rex used to fight chickens, and we were collecting information about cockfighting, I decided to interview him too, and this is what he told us.

RONNIE WELCH

The best cross I ever had was a Claret and a Allen Roundhead. A Claret was a kind of a yellowish-reddish, but a Roundhead is a real red chicken. Beautiful. They stand up *tall.* And I crossed them.

The first thing in chicken fighting is, you gotta get a breed of chickens that you know is a proven breed. You can't just start with anything. Be *sure* you get this point over. You gotta be right when you start. It's like raising bear dogs. You don't raise any kind of dog for a bear dog. I used to have dogs and used to hunt. You have to get 'em out of [stock] that you *know* will fight a bear. You could put in for three or four years and never have a winner with game chickens, see?

You just wouldn't *never* just go and get you a trio and bring 'em home and start raising chickens 'cause you got too much [unknown]. You gotta know *definitely* that they'll take the steel. That they won't run. Other words, they'll die first, see what I mean? I've had some game cocks that got killed and I've checked their breast, and I've found as high as eight places where they've took the steel. They took it and come back fighting.

Then, every guy you'd see, he'd say, "Well, why don't you take some of mine up there? They're good stock." And you can't *do* that. You gotta stick with what you started with, see? Other words, you know you've got something that's all right, and so you stay with it just like anything else, see what I mean? You might go to a fight and if you got some good chickens, if you win—say three or four of yours win out of six—why, some guy'll try to con you out of 'em. He'll try to get some eggs, he'll try to get him a stag, or he'll say, "I'd like to bring a hen up there and let you put that cock over her," or something like that, and you don't go for that, see. You just work by yourself, see, because that's the way it is.

I started with a trio I got in Fort Scott, Kansas. We went to a big derby up there and they'd been fighting a couple of days, and they had a *sled load* of dead game cocks piled in the corner when I got there. The guy that I got mine from, he was in this derby at

PLATE 505 Rex Duvall on the front porch of his house with two of his dogs.

Fort Scott, and so I liked the way his chickens done. And so I talked to him. I asked him if he'd sell me a trio, and so I wound up when he left following him about seventy or eighty miles. And when we got there, he told me to pick 'em out myself. I had a buddy named Bill I worked with, and so me and Bill went around and picked us out the game cock first, and we got the two pullets to suit us, and he furnished us a crate and we loaded 'em up and left. And I brought 'em to Arkansas and I started raising chickens. It was two years after that till I ever had a chicken.

Then I went through the long ordeal of putting 'em in pens, and getting the eggs and then getting the chickens. And the first thing you done before you got 'em off the nest, you made sure that they wadn't lousy, they didn't have any mites. Other words, when they hatched out, they was clean.

And you don't inbreed 'em. If you inbreed a game chicken, their tails is crooked. Now their tails is supposed to be like a Chinese pheasant's and hang straight out. If you start inbreeding 'em, their tails'll turn around to one side or the other, and I can tell 'em that quick [snaps fingers]. Don't ever inbreed 'em.

Then say you got to the point where you had to make a different cross or something with another chicken. You just gotta go hunt a good proven cock. It don't matter what you have to pay for him, you know, within bounds of reason. Then you might take him and cross him over some of the pullets that you had, but we really wasn't concerned about the damn pullets 'cause half of them we used to kill anyway.

But, now, if you got a strain of chickens that was really going and was *right,* then you was particular with your pullets. You'd wind up and put her in a pen and you'd put one game cock over her, and then when he mated her, she'd start laying and you'd get him out and she'd lay every egg. She'll take care of her eggs and hatch 'em out. And when she hatches 'em, you gotta get her out of the pen and put her in a scratch pen somewheres.

Then, you went through the ordeal of growing 'em up. You can't grow 'em too fast. You feed 'em a lot of scratch feed which is cracked corn, and it's got oats. Different companies put in different stuff, but it's got wheat, cane seed, and all kinds of junk in it. And we used to have long pens built out of wire. And then when they got grown up, they kindly begin to get cocky. The only time we ever let our chickens run loose was when maybe a hen had ten or twelve and we turned her out. But the rest of them was never out after they got up stags. We always picked 'em up and put 'em in scratch pens.

And then you trimmed 'em. And the way we used to trim 'em, we used to bore a hole through a piece of plywood or some kind of a piece of board, and you put his head through there. And in trimming 'em, now they've got a real tall comb, and you'd leave not quite three-quarters of an inch—maybe a little over a half inch. And you leave that for protection 'cause if you cut him real close to his skull he ain't got any protection when a chicken pecks him. And so you leave that good half inch on top of his head. And you cut these little gills out from right in under here. If you don't, another chicken can start to get a bill hold. In other words, you've seen fellows fight? They'll try to get somebody by the shirt, you know, to hold him with one hand and beat the hell out of him with the other? That's the same way a chicken does. But if he can't get ahold of his gills and if he can't get him by the bill, he'll usually get some feathers on his neck [which won't hurt anything because] he'll pull the feathers out, see? Now if he could just reach and get him and hold him, he'd be a sitting duck 'cause he'd just start that steel spinning and he'd have him cut all to pieces in just a minute, see?

So you've got to cut its comb down and take these gills out. And I kept a cup of sugar when I was trimming 'em and I throwed sugar on there, see, to clot the blood. And then when you trimmed a bunch of 'em, you couldn't put 'em all together 'cause they'd all start fighting.

So you go ahead and grow him and watch him and keep him watered, and then when he goes to gettin' up, say two pound and a half, why, you start talking about *fighting*. Now they'll be real wild. All right, you take one out of the pen and the main thing, you blow on his head with your breath, see, and that tames him down quicker than anything. Every time you touch him, you blow on the head. Then he gets used to you handling him. It gives him confidence. He knows you're not gonna hurt him, see? 'Cause he gets used to it and he likes it. And then you stroke his hackle [around his neck]. Lots of times when you pet 'em, they'll push their hackles up and look real bad? And you stroke him and it gives him confidence when you do that. When you blow on his head, he knows that you're not gonna hurt him, see? Other words, after a while he says, "Well, this guy's pretty good. He's pretty nice."

And course when you're working 'em, you might have you a little can of whole kernel corn. You might let him peck a few grains of it, and that gives him confidence.

And then I used to let him peck another chicken on the head. Like I had another'n in a cage somewhere, you know. I'd let him peck that chicken, but I didn't want another chicken to peck *him*, see, *really hit* him in the head. And you can spar 'em out, but you don't let 'em really *peck* each other all that much. Little gloves is what we used to put on 'em. We'd let 'em hit to see if they was gonna break high, break low, or how they was gonna break.

Now you're ready to do your conditioning. There's a lot of different ways that we used to get 'em in condition to go to a fight. I had some rubber blankets I used to bounce mine on. Anything that'll make him use his wings and use his feet is fine. These rubber blankets I used, I used to cut holes through 'em [at the edges] and pull 'em real tight, see? Then I attached a thing under the bottom where you could bounce it—where you could jerk it and make him use those wings.

And I never did do this, but a lot of fellows used to get up a little old slow-rolling motor. They used to put like a bank plumb around it [like a treadmill] and they used to walk 'em on that. It run towards the chicken and it turns right out from under him, and makes him keep walking all the time.

And then we had weights we put on their legs. We used to put them around their legs and make 'em wear those. After he wears those weights for a while, he starts developing good strong legs. Then you take the weights off, and then you put him in one little individual pen, real small, and you got a little old watering cup when he's got to stick his head outside to drink. And you keep working 'em. When you're getting 'em ready, you want their craw to disappear. When they go to really getting in condition, they haven't got any craw. A week before you fight him, you feed him like canned corn—whole kernel corn—and hamburger meat, see. Something that will go through him quick. You don't want nothing to stay in his craw. When you're conditioning your chicken, everything has to go through it real quick. Hell, if a chicken gets its craw full of scratch feed, it might stay in there a couple of days before it's ever digested, see? When you pit your chicken in the ring, you [don't want to even] *feel* their damn craw. All the craw it [will have] is way down in this fork right here on the breast. Rest of it's just a place where the craw ought to be. If you had one up here that had a crawful of corn and a chicken hit him with the steel good in there, why that would be it.

All right, you're getting ready for the big day. You're still working your chickens. Then, every morning, first thing a rooster does when it comes off the roost, it automatically gets a drink of water. We always fought of a night, so we wouldn't give 'em any water that morning, see. They didn't have nothing. We fed 'em the night before. And so then we took one orange to the fights with us—just a regular orange.

And by that time, he's got a little spur about an inch long on each leg, and you don't dare cut those off till you get to where you're gonna fight. If you do, it'll get sore. We use a little coping saw to cut the end of that off to heel him, and the steel went right on it. They don't bleed when you cut that off, but if you saw that spur off that chicken too fast, you make it hot. You have to be careful or it'll get sore, and you don't *know* it's sore, but it is. We didn't never trim ours till we started to [put them in the ring]. And if it was a dull saw, we just didn't use it. One guy held him and you done it real slow, and it didn't hurt him. Now especially in an old cock, you can look up on its spurs and you can tell where the quick is 'cause it's a different color. And you'd *never* go up in the quick part of it. And you don't want to leave much of a knob out there either, for him to tangle up on. Now that spur grows back out eventually, and you might have to cut it again sometime after six or seven months. But say you had that one cock and he won you five fights. If I had one that won five fights, I wouldn't never fight him anymore. I'd want to put him over some pullets when he got a little older.

But when you cut that spur off the first time, that's his first fight. All right, you got to the fight, and then you got weighed in. They had all kinda pens there with numbers on 'em and you drawed a number. You didn't know who you was gonna fight till you got there. Ever' which guy's weight compared closest with your weight was the guy that you fought. And they all fight the same damn rules that's been laid down for years, see. It's a *standard procedure*. When they go there, they know what to expect.

And the referee weighed 'em, too. They had three or four guys that didn't do anything but weigh 'em and tag your pens. And when you went up there to get your chicken, you looked at the chart and you knew exactly what size chicken you was gonna fight.

And then you got to the fight and some guy'd come around eventually and say, "You're up next." So you went in there real quick and you took the coping saw and you sawed his spur off and you heeled your chicken.

After you heeled him, you didn't put him back in the pen. You held him a certain way. I can't show you without a chicken, but you cross their legs so you don't put his legs in no bind. You hold him and make him comfortable. All right, he's ready.

Then they say, "Well, you're up next." You take that orange and you make a little hole in it, and you take that chicken's bill and you push it all the way down to the bottom of that orange. He just gets enough of that juice to make him really go nuts, 'cause he's hungry for water, see? When we stuck his bill down through that orange and pulled it straight back out, he was ready to kill *anything*.

And you never dared to give 'em any water while you was fighting. That was out. You didn't never ask for no water because you might pour some water in his throat or something and he might fly out of the pit. You just stick his bill all the way down in a good juicy orange about three minutes before you set him in the pit, and that's all he had all that day.

Now the pit itself is usually owned by some guy that's got the nerve. He might set up a pit in a barn or in a building. [And he'd get a cut of the money.] We had to pay a cover charge when we went in. If you was fighting, you didn't pay a cover charge. But

PLATE 506

like me and Ronnie went, whenever we went through, we had to pay a cover charge to get in.

Now say you wound up with ten guys fighting. That'd be sixty chickens that was gonna fight in it since each man fights six. So all the guys got together and they decided what they was gonna fight for. Say they was ten of 'em. If they was gonna fight for fifty, seventy-five dollars, all that money went in a pot. Then the winner took all. If two guys tied, they'd split. But usually one guy took it all. Say you went in there and won five of your fights, you'd place first, see, so you'd take the whole pot. Simple as that.

And then they bet all the time on the side. Everytime a guy came out with a chicken in his hand, when he was pecking 'im on the head he'd pay so much or you'd give him even money. You might say, "I'll take eight to five" or "I'll take even money." Or, "I'll bet twenty my chicken wins." Or whatever. And then a lot of times when they get cut, if he's a good handler, he knows what is going on, and he looks at the other chicken real quick, see, and then he might give odds. He might say, "Well, I'm going to give ten to five," and so paying starts going up, you know.

The pit we used to fight in was a round pit, with two ways in there. It's got a opening on this side, opening on the other side. It's got a dirt floor, and it's just kinda soft dirt. We'd take a little old garden broom or rake and get in there after every fight and level it up and get the feathers out. And then some had 'em built real neat. They was fixed real nice with little old bleachers all the way around the pit. I did go to one one time where it was [rimmed] out of gunny sacks, but most of 'em are real neat.

And one thing I didn't mention. You can't have it real hot in there. You can't ever let your chicken get hot. You have to watch that close. I've been to places and walked in and I knew it was too hot as quick as I walked in there 'cause I could feel the heat. Naturally, everybody's trying to keep warm, but that's one thing you gotta be real particular about 'cause that chicken will get hot in there after about the second pittin' and he'll start opening his mouth and you know it's too hot. Then you make them cut the gas down or cut it out or something. You just tell 'em you ain't gonna fight unless they do. He might not show it the first time you pit him, and he might act real cool, but when you get him back, he'll be tryin' to get some air.

So now we're ready for the fight. You walked in there with your chicken. You was holding him. And so then when the referee said, "Peck 'em on the heads," you walked straight up and let 'em peck each other. You had to let your chicken and his chicken peck.

Then you backed up and got ready, and he said, "Pit your birds."
So then you turned yours loose here and he turned his loose there,
so they come together. Sometimes they got up in the air and fought
and sometimes they fought on the ground. I've seen 'em pit two
damn chickens and they'd hit that high up in the air, like two whirl-
winds, and feathers a-flyin', and the next time you pit 'em, they
might hit right on the ground. You don't know how they're gonna
do. I like to see 'em fly up in the air 'cause he's up there cuttin'
and he's using his wings and he's using his feet. You just ain't got
no idea till you *really* see what it's like and see two chickens that's
in tip top condition. So I like to see 'em come up in the air. Then
you don't worry about nothing. So they might fight twenty seconds
before one of 'em'll hang, or they might fight twenty-five seconds
and one of 'em'll be dead. A lot of chickens throw the steel a different way, and if they hang, why, they're more or less helpless, so
they say, "Handle your birds." Then you go in and get your bird
back and that's the end of that round. You estimate the damage
real quick and see what you're like and by then you'll pretty well
know if you're gonna win this fight or if you're gonna lose it.

So if they hung the steel anywhere—if one hung the other—they
say, "Handle 'em!" and you gotta go right there and get your bird.
And way I used to get mine to keep from gettin' cut with the steel
[I seen one guy get a steel all the way through his hand], I used
to get him high up on the tail and drag him back with my left
hand and get his feet with my right so I wouldn't get cut with the
steel. I used to reach and get mine with my left hand. Not on the
tip of his tail, Ronnie, but back where you couldn't pull no feathers,
see. And then while I was pulling him back, I used to reach and
get him and get his legs crossed, and then I could manage it.

Now if you got hit in the chest—in that chicken's breast—he was
all right usually. He can take the steel time and time and again in
his breast. But if he got hit in the head, or if he got hit under his
wings or in his wings, he was usually in big trouble. If you got a
leg broke, that was it. And some of 'em used to nerve-blind each
other. Maybe one of 'em would get hit in the head and he would
go blind and he'd be fighting and him blind, but he'd still fight.
He'd strike at anything that moved, just like a copperhead. Every
noise it heard, it'd strike.

And so then you got your chicken back and real quick you looked
at the damage and you had to see what you was up against. Sometimes a clot of blood would hit in their throats and they'd start
rattling and you had to try to make him throw the rattle before
you pitted him the next time. He'll sling his head sideways and

throw a clot of blood out of there, see, but then he's ready to go back.

I've seen guys put a whole chicken's head in their mouth, see. Now that don't make sense to you, but they'd have such a rattle in their throat that they couldn't sling it up, and he'd try to help him get that loose 'cause he had his money riding on it. So, if he put his head in his mouth, he would suck real hard and try to loosen that up. Then he'd turn it loose and then the chicken would make a rattle and sling it out. But that's *blood*. When he is taking the steel, if he gets hit under the wings he'll get a rattle. He'll start bleeding. I've seen 'em fighting with the blood pouring out their mouth and them a-slinging it out and still fighting.

And one trick I've seen—you'll see it too if you go to a lot of fights—they will blow that chicken in his vent, you know, if he's about dead or about cut down or something. They'll blow him back there to try to help him get a little air and get him cooled off.

The referee went by a stopwatch. You got so much time to look at your bird and when he said, "Pit your birds," you had to be ready. So if you pitted 'em that time and you got cut down or he got cut down bad, and they hung again, he'd say, "Handle your birds," and you had to handle your bird and get him back and see what you could do for him again.

Then if you was cut bad, they'd draw a line in the center and they'd say, "Pit 'em on the short line." When he says that, he'll draw a line through the center and you gotta pit 'em right real close to each other, see. That's when they're cut all to hell and one of 'ems fixin' to go. That's the final climax.

So, you don't take one out. In other words, nobody can't pick a chicken up and take it out of the pit before it's dead. If you had him cut down, and he was fixing to die or if you was fixing to die, you pitted him anyway. And the last one that pecks is the one that wins the fight. If the winner is hurt real bad, I kill him.

And the referees don't make any bad calls. Not like a basketball game or not like the football game the other day when the guy called a bad call. When a referee in a chicken fight makes a call, it is the definite official right call.

But *that* is the object of the game. When you go to a chicken fight, and when you pit your cock, you pit it to kill somebody else's cock! And if your chicken quits in the ring and starts to try to running, you just kill it right then. The referee usually carries a little old short stick, so you might reach over and get his stick and knock its head off 'cause you don't want to take it back home if it runs, see?

But that's rare. You know what I've saw? I've saw chickens that was broke down that would still peck and try to fight. A game cock is the *gamest thing on this earth!* There is some records in Arkansas where a game hen was out with her chickens and a hawk dived in and she killed that hawk. She met that hawk in aerial combat to protect her chickens. Now you find me something that game over the country, you know what I mean?

A dog couldn't even get near them. You could take a hen with a gang of little chickens and she would jump on the biggest damn dog in the country and she'd ride him all the way from his tail to the tip of his nose.

When they're small, you use a short steel. But then as they got heavier, you had to use heavier steel. And so an old chicken was called a "shake." If he weighed over five pound and a half, he was a shake. And that's what *really* made a dirty fight. We used to fight a lot of them.

Other words, if a guy's fighting a six-cock derby, he might bring along a couple of shakes with him and before it got going, he might say, "Well, I'll fight somebody five-and-a-half-pound shakes." And so they would go ahead. Maybe have half a dozen fights or a dozen fights before the derby actually started. And course we used to bet on 'em, see. And we used to always try to get odds every time. You'd jump out in the ring and say, "I'll take ten to five," or "I'll take eight to five." That's the name of the game. [And they wouldn't mind risking them.] Maybe they bought 'em, or maybe somebody'd take one to someone and say, "I want you to work this chicken and take him to the fight. He's done this and he's done that." So you wind up with those proven birds in there. And *then* that was *really* a rough fight 'cause them was old, smart chickens that had took the steel, see, and they knowed what it was all about. And with two weighing five and a half pounds apiece, you wouldn't know which bird to bet on 'cause it was just a half a dozen of one to six of the other. Either one of them could get cut down and killed like that. I've seen 'em just make one pitting and meet in the air and one of 'em'd just fall down dead. That fast. If one really took the steel in the head—if it hit his brain or anything—just like that [snaps fingers] it was over.

Now I've watched real smart chickens in a fight that's took the steel like them old shakes. They've had the steel stuck to 'em before. And they *learn.* You may not believe this, but they know when you buckle that steel on 'em what they're up against. And I have seen

PLATE 507 Rex keeps bees at his farm, and he works them without protection. The white spot off the end of his nose is one of them in flight.

'em miss the chicken. He'd vary around him or something and make moves. And then I've seen 'em *taking* the steel, you know, and they knowed they was getting hurt, see. You might not think that, but they do. They know that. But they never get fight-shy. If he lives to get out of that ring and he's whipped that chicken, and you get him well and you get him healed up, and he gets all the soreness out of him, he gets cocky again and he'll go and do the same thing over and *over*. If he wins and you get him out and he gets toughened up again, he'll come back.

And a good thing we used to do—like, you went to a fight and got your chicken hit in the leg or got him stove up? A good thing to do is throw him in that scratch pen with shucks. You just bed him down in there and throw some scratch feed in there and let him scratch for his feed. In other words, he starts using his feet and gets built back up again.

But he's got to be conditioned to fight. I had one and I could not do anything with him, and I'd trimmed him. And these kids lived a little piece from me and they had some banties. So I took him up there and they kept him about eighteen months, and he started killing their banty roosters. He was mean. And they sent me word to come get him, because they couldn't do anything with him. So this man at Conway, Arkansas, I let him have this one chicken, and he killed four cocks. And I come home one weekend and went down there and he was gonna fight him again. And so I felt of him myself and I told him, I says, "This cock ain't ready to fight."

And he says, "Yeah, he don't need no training or no conditioning."

And I says, "You'll see."

So that was the night he got him killed, see? He didn't condition him. Takes a *solid week*. You have to go out early in the morning and get him and bounce him and throw him and make him use his wings and make him do everything. You just got to get him as hard as nails.

Now the men that fight chickens, they're just good people. Chicken fighters are good people. They're like bear hunters. Bear hunters are a strain of good people. And if you're an old front-line chicken fighter, you're respected. When you walk in there with them carrying cases in your hand . . .

And usually if a guy's got some *good* winnin' chickens, everybody knows it. Like Wes Hunt. This one man killed two marshals, and he was tough. Lived at Clinton, Arkansas. He was a Tennessee boy originally and he done time down in Arkansas for seven or eight years and come back out, and the only thing he ever fooled with

was white liquor and chickens. Bootlegged. And when Wes Hunt
come into the ring with a chicken, everybody *respected* that. But by
the same token, at the same time, everybody was trying to breed
up something and have a better chicken to whip Wes Hunt. But
before he set his chicken down, if he said, "Well, I'm payin' ten
to five on my chicken," people really thought and listened when
he spoke. You know what I mean? I saw him about five years ago.
He was a real black-headed guy. And I've seen his eyes shine like
a Indian. He'd be looking at that chicken real quick, you know,
when he was handling his chicken, tryin' to figure the odds—tryin'
to figure what kind of a chance he had. And I've seen them eyes
just *shining.* And when he spoke, people listened.

Course, they'll be somebody call you, I don't care what you're
doing, because this other guy, he feels good himself. He'll breed
him up something and he'll go in there with some whirlwind to
cut you down. I don't care how good you are, somebody'll cut you
down sometime or another.

In this country right here, people are not really chicken fighters
now. They used to be. [I know a man here] who's been in some
whing-dings of a shootout where they pulled their pistols when men
was mean and they'd kill you at the drop of a hat. They'd go to
hell if they was right. He's played poker so much by kerosene light
till his eyes are real red.

And you *never*—that's one of the unpardonable sins—try to welch
at a chicken fight. If you lose, if you don't go *straight* and pay off—
Nobody ain't gonna come and *tell* you, "Hey, gimme my money."
But if me and you're at a fight and you jump up and you say, "I'll
take ten to five, if I hold up my hand that I'm gonna take [that
bet] and then lose, I go straight and pay you when it's over. You
don't never go around and ask the guy, "Gimme your money."

Now the law's against it. I never got raided at a place, but a lot
of the boys has got raided and they paid a fine. They damn sure
paid a fine for it. A big one. They took 'em into court and their
goal was to pay out of it and not get drug through big court and
not get no publicity and not get no pictures made. So they probably
get drug before some JP [justice of the peace] and he sums it all
up to see what the take is gonna be and what he can get off 'em
and says, "Well, I'm gonna charge you boys so much apiece and
let you go," and so then they go back to fighting chickens. They
fight chickens *everywhere.* You can study the history and it goes *way*
back.

It's a fascinating sport. If you go to a fight, you'll understand
all this and you remember what I told you.

"LET ME TELL YOU ABOUT THIS MULE"

We first heard about "Po' Boy" Jenkins from a former Foxfire student, Claude Rickman. Claude, who was helping his brother build a house outside Athens, Georgia, met Mr. Jenkins there, and the two of them became friends.

Mr. Jenkins's roots go deep in Madison County. His great-great-grandfather White was born in Virginia in 1787 and came to Madison County when he was a young man. He and his wife are buried in the White cemetery on the Rogers Mill Road, along with Mr. Jenkins's great-grandmother and great-grandfather White, his grandmother and grandfather White, and two brothers and two sisters. Recently he had the cemetery cleaned off: "The White cemetery hadn't been cleaned off in twenty-five or thirty years—maybe forty. I don't know how long. Last summer I got me a man and went up there and showed him what I wanted done, and I said, 'Now, I'm going to pay you three dollars an hour, and you just keep your own time.' He used to work for me here in the mule barn. And he cleaned it up—cost me about $130. And then when I got it cleaned off, I got this herbicide and sprinkled it on it to kill all the vegetation. And so I'm right proud of it.

"Now when I was a young man, I could have got with my great-uncles and have found out who all was buried there. There are some graves up there that I don't even know who they are."

His grandfather Jenkins moved to Madison County from Hart County in 1875, and he and his wife are buried in the Union Church cemetery in Danielsville, along with Mr. Jenkins's wife, three brothers, one sister, and his mother and father who settled near Danielsville above Booger Hill in 1888.

Two of his sisters once taught school in Rabun County. One, Ruby Jenkins, started teaching here in 1925, and the other, Mrs. Grady Gower, started out here in 1935.

Mr. Jenkins went to college at the University of Georgia for one year in pre-med, but, as he says, "We got to dissecting those frogs

PLATE 508 "Po' Boy" Jenkins with Foxfire student Johnny Scruggs.

and snakes and things and I got sick to my stomach and quit! I went over there in the fall of '26. I had a brother that graduated from the law school there."

When we asked him to tell us some more about himself, he continued: "I was raised on the farm. My daddy kept about eight or ten mules there in the lot at the house at all times. Five miles up here. Where [Claude's] brother is building a house, that's my daddy's estate. He had 640 acres of land there. When my mother died, my bachelor brother got it, and when he died in '66, I was in bad health so I couldn't buy it. I was afraid I wasn't going to live. And two of my other brothers were in bad shape. Since then, three of my brothers have died. I've got one of my brothers living and he's ninety years old. And I've got one sister living. She's seventy-seven.

I'll be seventy-two tomorrow. There were thirteen of us born. Four of them died before I was born. Died small. I lost my wife five years ago the sixteenth of January, and I don't have any children. Nobody but just me and 'Po' Boy.' That name came from back in the livestock days. I bought twenty-six steers from a fellow in Franklin County, and I carried them down to Atlanta and put them in the auction and put them all in the ring at one time and knocked them off at twenty-five and a half cents. I jumped up, commenced whooping and hollering and cussing and raising sand, and I said, 'I don't mind you stealing my steers, but don't steal my truck! I want to bring a load next week!'

"An old farmer up in the stand hollered, 'Po' boy, po' boy!' And it started from that.

"Then when I went on the road selling semi trailers and truck bodies, the first trailer I sold was to Cliff Ragsdale on the stockyard, and he told that tale on me, and that got started in the trucking business. And then I just finally put 'Po' Boy' on my cards. I sold semi truck bodies and trailers fifteen years after the mule business was over. I had a farm out here. I moved out there on it and I couldn't do any good with it, and I went on the road.

"Then I got sick, and I got over it, and I stayed on the road then until '69 and I quit. I had a brother running that country store over yonder, and he died. I bought it and went to running the store. And they robbed me twice and I give it away. The last time they got me, took $700 away from me. Blindfolded me, carried me over there in the woods and turned me a'loose. Sure did. Had a snub-nosed pistol. Had it in my face, and had a hole in the barrel looked like as big as your finger. You couldn't afford to argue! I drove up there in my station wagon that morning just a little before daylight. He come around the corner of the building—had a pillowcase on his head and an eyehole cut in it, and that snub-nosed pistol. Come around in a trot. And I give it away and *quit*."

The house he lives in is a beautiful two-story white house overlooking the town square and the courthouse in Danielsville. There is a statue of Crawford W. Long in the square. He told us about his home: "When this house was built, there wasn't any automobiles here, and they built everything around the square. I bought this house in 1963. Me and my wife moved here, and I had to have some work done on the downstairs, and so we moved in here in February of 1963 and we moved upstairs. Well, when they got the work done downstairs, my wife didn't want to move down there. She said, 'I'd rather live up here.' [So I rented the downstairs] and

I've been up here now fifteen years. It's a good house. Sturdy. I don't like the location. It's an old-timey house. But I'm here by myself. And if I get where I can't drive my car and go places, if I have to have a loaf of bread, I can walk over yonder to the store and get it. And then the bus comes through here, and I'm right here close. I've got a telephone there at the head of my bed. If I need anything at night, I can just call Civil Defense and they'll be here in two or three minutes.

"I think I'm pretty well fixed, the shape I'm in. Now if I was a younger man, hell, I wouldn't live here. But I'm situated, and nobody but me, and seventy-two years old. And I can't work. I weigh 275 pounds. I have a slight case of diabetes. And I've had a little pain in my heart once or twice. Doctor said walk more. I joined the Spa Health Club over at Athens. I go three times a week when I am at home and ride the bicycle, pull weights with my hands, push weights with my feet, and then go in the rock sauna at about 108 degrees, the steam room at about 110 degrees, the whirlpool bath at about 108 degrees, and then I swim in the large pool. I work hard for a man my age and weight."

Mr. Jenkins would probably still be trading mules if the business hadn't ended in this part of the country.

"What brought it on, actually, was these big plants—Westinghouse, General Time, Reliance, DuPont—all them big plants. And these young people [that] used to work a mule, they quit and went to Athens and went to work. They'd go out there and work forty hours a week—work eight hours a day and they got sixteen hours a day to loaf and raise hell and run around on Saturday and Sunday. And when they worked on the farm, it took most of their time—about from sunup to sundown, six days a week."

Though the business is ended now for the most part, we're fortunate that men like "Po' Boy" Jenkins are still around to tell us what it was like when it was one of the most active businesses around.

Interview and photographs by Wesley Dockins with help from Alan Mashburn, Clay Smith, and Johnny Scruggs.

I started in the mule business in 1930, and my last was in 1950. The mule business actually quit in '50 or '51. After the mule business was over, these people got to buying them and shipping them and making dog food out of them, and I was about to get into that once. I went home that night and studied about those mules and rolled and tumbled and couldn't sleep. Finally I called the man and told him to forget it. I wasn't going to buy those mules and butcher them. I'd made a living off of them that many years, and I wasn't going to buy them and butcher them and feed them to dogs. But they kept doing it until the mule supply ran out.

[In the thirties, the farmers depended on mules] one hundred percent. They was so damn poor they couldn't buy a tractor. Had to buy a *mule* on credit. They didn't work many horses. They wasn't but very few horses *in* this country. A horse couldn't stand this heat. And then a mule's small foot didn't tear your crop down— your cotton—like a horse. See, they grew cotton and corn in this country. They'd buy a mule on credit in the spring of the year and then buy fertilizer and rations on the credit, and sell their cotton in the fall of the year and pay out. Some of them paid out and some of them didn't. Some of them had a little money left [over]. And a few of them had enough money to run their own businesses. The ones that stuck me the worst was the boys that went to World War II and come out and got in the farming program. The Government backed them up for farming—give 'em a hundred dollars a month to go to school one or two evenings a week, you know, and teach 'em *how* to farm. And they was going to pay you by the month. And them boys [were] harem-scarem and they wouldn't pay nothing. They stuck me. The Government would help them when they come out of the service, you know, but I got stuck.

When the Government really bought the mules was the rehabilitation program [the Agricultural Adjustment Act, during the Depression]. That started back in '34, and in '35 I guess I sold a hundred mules to Farm Security. They had four men here in this county supervising farmers, and I'd sell those mules to 'em. The [farmers] would be down and out, you know, and the Government would loan 'em five or six hundred dollars to make a crop with. And they'd have a woman home economist to go around and make a list and buy 'em cooking utensils—pressure cookers—and this and that and the other. Furnish 'em garden seed and fertilizer. Buy 'em a mule and a few farming tools. And some of 'em made good and some of 'em—the Government lost it.

I know a few of 'em that got on that program and made first-class citizens, and then I knew some of 'em that wasn't any good. But overall it was good. The intention of it was *fine*. But it was the most abused of any program I nearly ever knew. All Government programs are abused. You know that. I hate to say it, but a big percent of the people think that when they beat the Government

PLATE 509 Johnny Scruggs, Clay Smith, and Wesley Dockins interviewing "Po' Boy" on the second-floor porch of his home.

out of some money, that's all right. "Let 'em lose it. We'll stick 'em." And I know a few people that was on Farm Security that bragged about how much they beat the Government out of. But then I know another fellow right up the road here about a mile out of town—they bought him a farm and he went out and went to work and made cotton and paid for it in three or four years. Paid it all back. Says, "I didn't owe nobody a nickel."

Now there's not but one breed of mule and that's a cross between a horse and a jackass. You breed a stud horse to a jenny and you'll get a mule. You breed a jackass to a mare and you'll get a mule. And the mule is blank [infertile]. Now there's been one or two in the history that had a colt. Here several years ago, there was a Negro in Mississippi that had a gray mule that had a colt. All I

know about it is what I saw in the paper. You're old enough to
read the paper. You could have seen it. And the man that let him
have the mule which had the colt, he went out and tried to trade
him out of it and the Negro wouldn't let him have it. And then
some zoo bought the mule with the colt. Paid him a good price
and put her in the zoo 'cause it's very, very unusual.

Now, a stud mule, he'll go to a mare mule. He'll go to a mare
just the same as any, but he can't do no business. He's a hybrid.
A mule is a hybrid animal. But once in a while—very, very seldom—
they're prolific. Not often.

I used to keep a jack. What I would do, these farmers would
have the mare and they'd bring her in and I'd stand the jack to
'em and charge them twenty-five dollars. I'd charge 'em ten dollars
when I stood the jack to them and fifteen when the colt come and
was all right. It didn't make no difference to me what kind of a
mare it was. Just whatever kind of mare the man wanted to breed.
If he had a good brood mare, it wasn't none of my business. See,
I just kept the jack there more or less to accommodate the people.
I didn't breed him hardly enough to make any money. To tell you
the truth, I did not want one. I just kept him to accommodate my
customers. Now I'm gonna tell you something you're gonna want
to cut out, I think. I kept the jack down there in the shed at the
mule barn, and a man could bring a mare up there to breed her
and he'd get to braying and before we could get the mare unhitched
and the harness off and put her in the stand there and let the jack
to her, the barn'd be full of men come down to *see* it!

Why do most breeders use a jack instead of a stud and a jenny?

You get a better mule from a jack and a mare. A jenny is a mother
and she's small and she don't bring as big a colt as the mare. Now,
you do get some difference from different mares. Used to be, the
buggy horse was shipped in here from Tennessee and Kentucky. I
reckon you'd call them American Standard bred. Well, now you
breed a jack to her and you'll get a mule with real slick hair and
it'll be trim. It wouldn't be broad and blocky like one bred to a
Belgian mare or a Percheron mare. And then you breed a little
old sorry jack to a Shetland pony and that's where you get these
two- and three-hundred-pound mules. And why they want 'em is
just to play with. They're no good for nothing. Now these boys
from Tennessee had this little pair of mules that weighed four hundred and sixty pounds that I saw the other day. And all they'd do
with 'em was just go from one show to another and pull with 'em.

Are there any differences in coloration?

Yes. Breed those spotted Shetland ponies and get a spotted colt. I *have* seen a spotted jack. You don't see many of them. Most of them are black or gray or red sorrel. But now the jacks they're keeping, I'd say ninety-eight percent of them are red sorrel.

Now I went to the Tennessee State Fair two years ago this fall, and I guess they was two hundred mules and colts there, and they wasn't but two black mules in the bunch. Every one of them red sorrel but two, and those two belonged to Loretta Lynn.

What do you look for when you're buying a mule?

Look the mule over. Son, buying mules is something you can't get out of a book. Now you can learn the age out of a book up to five year old. You know how to tell the age of a young mule, don't you? I'll tell you. When he sheds the two front teeth, he's a three-year-old. Now sometimes it'll vary. Sometimes he'll shed them teeth three months before he's three, or might be three months after he's three. They'll vary a little. But then the next year he'll shed the next two, and that's a four-year-old. He's just got six front teeth, bottom and top, when he's young. And when he sheds those last two teeth in the front, he's a five-year-old. And then you just watch it from there on and judge how old he is by how the teeth develop. And those tushes here between the jaw teeth and the front teeth? All right, now a horse mule *will* have tushes but a mare mule *won't.* Oh, I've seen exceptions. I've seen one or two mare mules in my life with a very *small* tush, but now listen, they ain't no one rule in the world will run for judging a horse's age. I can sell you two four-year-old mules today and you can take them home and work them six years and they'll be the same age. That's just something you have to spend your money and get in the game and learn yourself. Can't nobody teach it to you.

But then you've got to look over that mule. He's got to have good eyes, and see that they ain't no knots—no swelled joints—on his legs. See that he's smooth. Rub your hands over his ears and see that he ain't foolish about his ears, and so forth. And see that his wind's good. When they sell a mule in the market, they'll guarantee him to be sound. When they say a mule's sound, that means good eyes, good wind, not lame, and no kicker. Sometimes you'll get hold of a mule and put him to a single-plow stock and he'll kick loose. I've owned a lot of them. Every trick I've ever heard of, I guess I've owned it.

You can test his wind by just looking at him. He'll come in that auction and they'll be cracking the whip over him and the mule'll get excited, and if he's got bad wind, why, he'll show it in the way he gets his breath—the way his nostrils open up. They puff. It's something happens in their lungs and in the skiffing between their lungs and their insides. And they open up in their flank when they get their breath.

Now there's another one they call a bull mule that's hurt in the throat and there's no cure for it. If you fracture that windpipe, and then you run him maybe for a hundred yards—or maybe before he makes it a hundred yards—he will roar just like a bull. And he ain't worth fifteen cents.

And then there's one they call a choker. That's a growth on the end of the windpipe. Now, you can operate on them. A veterinary can operate on them and cure 'em and they'll go ahead and work. But a bull mule ain't no good for nothing except cheat somebody with. A bellesed mule *will* work a little, but they can't do a day's work.

And you can't spot them right off. You just get suspicious. Whenever a fellow goes to trade you a mule, you're suspicious [anyway]. Have a boy with you and let him lead him out yonder and crack the whip behind him and let him jump and get a little excited and a bull mule will go to roaring.

But I always run from those kind. When I got in the stockyard to buy a mule, I tried to buy a mule I thought was sound. If he wasn't, I'd always take him back, except you lose transportation on him from Atlanta down here and back up there and feed two or three days. You lose ten or fifteen dollars on one if you get your [original] money back. But that's better'n losing it *all.*

What about mule diseases?

Worst one, I guess, is bellyache. They give 'em too much corn, or they won't water 'em regular and then let 'em drink too much water. Now there's where the Government made a mistake. [They'd take men that weren't experienced farmers and put them on the program.] I sold one fellow a mule up here, and he didn't even have a stable to put that mule in, and we had a winter about like we've got now, and that mule stood tied out there to a peach tree all the winter; and time come to go to work and the mule was dog poor and looked worse than everything and wasn't able to work. Course, now I blame the supervisor with that.

What I done to cure bellyache, I kept a potent medicine that had a lot of paregoric and alcohol in it, and I'd drench 'em with that and ease 'em. Sometime I'd call a veterinary for one. But it takes bigger'n a co-cola bottle to drench a mule, son. Takes a quart bottle. And then if you get him over the bellyache, then the best thing to do is pour a quart of raw linseed oil in him and in about two days work him out good and get all that trash out of him. It'll take twenty-four to forty-eight hours for a quart of raw linseed oil to go through him. If you give a mule *cooked* linseed oil, it'll kill him. But that raw linseed oil'll work him out.

Will a mule eat too much and make himself sick?

Some of 'em will and some of 'em won't. Now you can open the crib door and let 'em eat all the corn they want, and some mules, when they get enough, they'll quit. A horse will come nearer eating too much than a mule. And then, mules are just like men. You might eat a bunch of collard greens and it wouldn't hurt you at all; and then this boy eat a bunch of collard greens and might give him a stomachache. Mules are the same way. Some feed'll agree with one mule and won't agree with another.

What about lampers [lampas], when their gums swell up?

That's a bunch of tommyrot. They ain't no such thing. A mule's gums'll get sore and swell up, but when y'get to where he don't bite off corn good, well, there's where your good horse master comes in. Have some oats and a hammer mill and run some oats through the hammer mill. Mix in some corn. Give 'em a little ground feed. When you go to working a mule hard in the spring, some people pour the corn to 'em and they quit eating. Well, now, my idea always, when you put a mule to sure enough hard work in the spring all of a sudden [after he's] been standing up all the winter—why, mix his feed. Give him oats one day and corn the next. Don't just feed him one thing. Give him all the good hay he'll eat. Give him plenty of salt to lick. Let him drink plenty of water. You rotate his feed with oats and corn and plenty of good hay and the mule'll come nearer standing up. Just like giving you ham and biscuit. You want some beans and some cornbread and some field peas and cabbage and turnip greens. Well, it's just as essential to rotate a mule's feed as it is yours.

Regardless of what you say, most boys like you like fried chicken. You give you fried chicken three times a day and it wouldn't be long till you'd say, "I wish I'd never *seen* a damn fried chicken!" Same way with a mule.

PLATE 510   A poster on the wall of "Po' Boy's" home. The poster's caption reads: "I ain't doin' quite as well as I expected but then I never really expected I would."

What are some other ailments and remedies?

Bleeding 'em. All right. There's a certain kind of blind staggers that a mule will get. They call it botulism, but I call it blind staggers. And I never did do it, but I had another man to do it. He'd cord that mule's neck and find that jugular vein and have what they call a flim. It'd be about the size of half a nickel on a handle just like a pocketknife, and had that little half-nickel just as sharp as could be. He'd put that against the jugular vein in that mule's neck and take a stick and hit it and cut in there and the blood would speen out. And he'd bleed that mule anywhere from three quarts to a gallon and a half. Bleed it till the blood changed its color. Then he'd pull the cord and it would quit bleeding. Then he'd take a pin and stick through that gash and get some hair out of his tail and wrap around that pin and then next day pull that pin out and the mule would get well.

And then there was another kind of blind staggers they'd get. I don't know. There's different kinds of it. There's another kind, though, that the mule will go wild. And they ain't no cure *for* him.

But the blind staggers, they tell me, is a kind of high blood pressure. When you bleed these mules, sometimes it'll help one in the spring of the year just to bleed him. I had a neighbor here one time—her sister was up at Lavonia and was real sick, and they wanted some blood for her, and this neighbor's wife wasn't in too good a health, but she gave a pint of blood. Well, when she got home, her husband didn't like it. Said, "You had no business giving blood. You're not able."

I said [to her husband], "Dillard, she's just like a mule." I said, "Bleed her and it may help her." Well, that woman had the finest health for about the next twelve months that she'd had in ten years, and I believe bleeding helped her.

Have you ever filed a mule's teeth?

I don't know *how* to file one's teeth, but I've seen those Irishmen do it. Stand there all day long in the stockyard. They had an electric outfit just like a dentist. They put a long stick in [the mule's] mouth as big as my arm and pull it way up in there and have a rope tied to one end and put the rope over his head and they would run that stick up just as high as they could and tie it, and then they'd tie his head over the fence. Well, there wasn't nothing he could do, and he couldn't bite 'em. And they'd take that drill and they'd put cups in his lower front teeth—take a file and knock off his upper teeth and make them shorter. Then they'd have a buffer there on that machine and dress the teeth and make 'em white just like a dentist cleaning *your* teeth. There wasn't many farmers that could tell one that'd had his mouth fixed. There wasn't but very, very few knew anything about the age of a mule after he got a full mouth.

Were the mules shod?

Farriers were around, but if you just kept the mule in the field, he didn't need shoeing much. Way back yonder when I was a boy, everybody done their hauling with wagons and drove the mule to the buggy, and they had to keep them shod. I have been to the blacksmith shop and taken five or six or eight, ten mules for my daddy and be gone nearly all day to the blacksmith shop getting them shod. Back then, they'd furnish the shoes and shoe a mule all around for a dollar. Now, if they was to shoe a mule—put four shoes on him—they'd charge at least twenty.

They had mule shoes up yonder at Columbia the other day. A man was selling them for souvenirs—antiques—and he was getting a dollar apiece for them secondhand shoes. You know a mule shoe is more narrow. You can take a horseshoe and make it fit a mule foot all right, but it's hard to take a mule shoe and circle it and make it fit a horse's foot.

How hard can you work a mule?

Well, if you can take a fellow who's got any sense and knows how to take care of a mule and he's got a decent mule, he can plow him from sunup to sundown six days a week. But sometime, you know, you get hold of a fellow who'll ride his plow, or he'll walk along and let his plow handle go up and down and he'll plow a mule down. It takes a fellow to be trained to *work* a mule. And back then, the little boys was trained from the time they was old enough to know anything until they was big enough to plow, and all of 'em wanted to plow before they was big enough. They thought it was something else when they got to plowing, you know. Yeah, they was all wanting to go out and go to plowing before they was big enough *to* plow.

Is a mule better if he has a big neck and shoulders?

I guess he pulls better when he weighs muscle. And then some mules are just like a man. You can take two hundred-and-fifty-pound men and put them out there and one of them can pick up more pounds on the ground and pitch it on his shoulders than the other one, and they weigh exactly the same thing. One of them can run a hundred yards quicker than the other one. It's the same way with mules. You take two mules weigh a thousand pounds apiece, and one of 'em'll outpull the other one. One of 'em'll outrun the other one.

How old do mules live to be?

I traded with one of my neighbors up here, and he told me she was thirty-nine years old. I carried her up to Lavonia and traded her for a horse colt. Brought the horse colt back here and swapped it for a Jersey heifer with a young calf, and sold the Jersey heifer for sixty dollars. I give ten dollars for the mule. I allowed ten dollars for a mule thirty-nine years old, and made a pretty good profit. You don't make fifty dollars on all the mules you sell.

But that's about as old a mule as I could swear to. But I know that was right on that particular mule. Way back yonder, now, when they drove 'em to the buggy and done all the wagon work, they'd live to about twenty years old. But then when the tractor came in to help fix the crop, and then they got to hauling the fertilizer from town on a truck, and haul the cotton to town on a truck and quit driving the mule back and forth to town to the wagon, and got a few paved roads, why then the mule went to living longer. But on this mule that was thirty-nine years old—that old man that had him, he worked the fire out of that mule. He was a hard worker. He worked that mule every day. But he looked after the trough. He looked after her to see that she had water, and he kept salt so that she could lick salt when she wanted it. And in the spring of the year, he'd give her a medicated brick so she'd shed off and so forth. He looked after his stock.

Did you ever raise mules from colts?

No, I'd buy them from the stockyard. Bought a few from Tennessee. I bought most of them down in Atlanta. At one time they had the biggest mule market in the world. I bought the mules at Union Stockyard there, and then I'd bring 'em back here. I'd go up there and buy a truckload and bring 'em back here and sell 'em and go back and get another truckload. During the mule season, I'd be on the Atlanta market practically every Monday. See, they had two auctions there. Ragsdale, Lawhorn and Weil Commission Company; and Patterson Commission Company. They'd have it two days a week—Monday and Tuesday. And so one week Ragsdale, Lawhorn and Weil would sell in the morning. Start at about ten o'clock and run till about one. And then they'd start ringing their bell down the street and then that bunch would quit and all the crowd would go down to Patterson's auction. Then the next week, Patterson would have the auction in the morning and Ragsdale in the afternoon. And then there was the National Stockyard Commission Company.

I guess they sold five or six thousand mules a year. It was all private sale. And then there was Hudson and Couch, and different ones there in private sales in the wholesale business.

They'd have the mules back in the yard. They'd have a barnful of mules—about fifteen or twenty to the pen. They'd have *acres* of mules—used to. All the stockyards're torn down now. Ain't no stockyard down there. And say a man from Kansas City would ship in two load of mules—have fifty to fifty-two mules. Most of the time he'd get up and stand by the side of the auctioneers and sell 'em. Then another fellow would come in there from St. Louis, one come in from Illinois, one from Texas. Might be one or two shippers there from Kentucky [or] Tennessee. They'd ship them in and those commission houses would auction them off just like a cattle sale. They would charge so much commission according to what they brought. And then they'd have twenty-five cents a head on 'em for insurance and fifty cents a head on 'em for yardage and then a commission. I don't remember just exactly how much for commission. About two and a half on a decent mule plus fifty cents yardage and twenty-five cents insurance.

I'd buy and sell and swap. Fellow come in there and have one mule he wanted to trade for a pair. I'd take in his mule and charge him the difference. Some fellow come in there with a mule fifteen year old and want a four-year-old mule, and I'd swap with him and charge him the difference. I done more swapping, I guess, than selling. I'd take hogs, cattle. I traded one mule one time for a Model A Ford.

I sold 'em over about four or five or six counties around here. I went up to Clayton [Georgia] one spring in '39. Carried some horses up there—some saddle horses. And that same year, then, I camped in Bill Shore's barn there in Baldwin and we sold mules all around the lower end of Habersham and up into Banks County one spring. Carried them on a truck. Ford or Chevrolet truck. Have a twelve-foot body and pack seven mules in it. Seven would pack a twelve-foot body. That's all you could get in there. Big mules, you couldn't get but six. But I mostly shipped little mules that would weigh nine hundred to a thousand pounds. That's what they wanted to plow cotton. Some of them would buy a smaller mule—small as seven hundred and fifty pounds. A few people around here worked thirteen-hundred-pound mules. They plowed cotton and corn. Take a mule and work ten or fifteen acres of cotton and five or six acres of corn. When crop season came in the spring of the year, a lot of them had mule work every day that the weather was suitable.

PLATE 511

They'd work the garden with them [too]. But since you can remember, they haven't worked the field with old mules. They do all that now with tractors.

When I first started in it, you could buy a choice pair of mules for $400. And then in '31 and '32 they got cheaper. And then in '33 they picked up a little, and '34, then, that's when the Government bought so many mules to put out here. Then they jumped up right sharply. Right now they're the highest I've ever seen 'em. I was in Columbia, Tennessee, the other day and I met a fellow that specializes in jacks and jennys, and he told me that he sold a fellow in Texas a jack last year for $5,000, and then he wanted a jenny, and he sold him a jenny for $3,000. And they went to Texas. They were just good animals. You know, a jack and jenny's just like a mule—there's different classes of 'em. This fellow wanted this good jack, and he wanted to take him to Texas to breed the mare, and this was an extra good jack—big jack—and he was prolific.

The main thing they're doing with these mules now is putting them in shows and so forth. Now, last year in Glasgow, Kentucky, there was a man there from California who bought sixteen of these red sorrel mules—tremendously high price. And I said, "What are you going to do with those mules when you get them to California?"

And he said, "We're gonna put 'em in a zoo." And says, "In the summertime, we will have straw rides, and in the wintertime, have sleigh rides. Put 'em out for people to look at." And he said, "If I can get some of 'em trained, I'll put a team of 'em in the Rose Bowl parade on television here this year." And this six-mule team come up—red sorrel mules—all of 'em just alike, and they were pretty, and whoever the commentator was on the television for that show made the remark that that was the only mules that had ever been in the Rose Bowl parade. And I guess—I wouldn't swear it—but I think I saw those mules sell in Glasgow, Kentucky.

They had a mule day at Chatsworth last fall, and I went over there and watched 'em pull. Crippled fellow from Missouri judged the show. They had some good mules there. They had a little pair of mules that weighed four hundred and sixty pounds—both of 'em. And they pulled 1,700 pounds ten feet on a ground sled. But when they put on fifty more pounds they couldn't make it. You put on whatever weight you want to each time. They got the weights there. They got 'em marked, what they are. And see, the way they do it, they'll have a string tied to a nail in the back of the ground sled. Then they drive a nail in the ground right under there and tie the other end of the string to that. That string is ten feet long, so when they tighten that string, that's the ten-foot pull. The one that pulls the most weight gets the blue ribbon. See, these mules pull according to the weight of the mule. They got a set of scales there and they weigh the mules and they pull 'em according to the weight of the team.

What age do you look for in a mule?

Well, I loved to buy mules from four and five and six years old. That's the age I liked to buy. Sometimes I'd buy a colt mule—two-year-old. I had a friend that lived out the road here. I sold him a pair of mules at two years old. Charged him $325. They was nice colts. He took them and worked 'em four years, and they was six years old. And I gave him $550 for them back. He made $225 profit and worked 'em four years.

But I [didn't deal with younger mules because] I didn't want to break them. I wanted to *sell* 'em. I wasn't interested in breaking no mules. I was interested in selling 'em and making a living—getting a profit on 'em just like a man in a grocery store trying to sell you a can of beans. He's got to have a profit on it if he stays in business.

And if the mule traders had been as *crooked* as the public accused them of being, they'd be dangerous men to turn loose in the public. They wasn't near as crooked as people accused them of being. You hear all those tricks. Ain't nothing to it. The best thing to do if you get 'hold of one that ain't no 'count—and the way I would do it if some farmer come here and put one off on me and it wasn't any 'count—call him in there and tell him what you got. I'd say, "Now you take it and whatever you get out of it, take out your commission and gimme what is left." I didn't want to fool with 'em.

Just look for something that you'd *like*, and if *you* like it, you can sell it. If you get one you don't like it's going to be sort of hard for you to sell. And then if you buy a little off-grade mule, you get the price down and you think you might attract somebody on that price, then make a little profit on him. See, all I cared for was to make a profit on that mule. I wanted to leave my customers satisfied and make a profit. I wasn't like a gypsy. Those Irish gypsies, they'd come through here and they'd cheat the—excuse my horse-trading language—they'd cheat the hell out of a farmer and let him have a kicker or bad-eyed or winded, and the next day here'd come another one back out of the same bunch and tell the farmer what he had and get him all tore up and swap another trick, and first thing you know, the farmer was out of a mule and the gypsy would be gone. But see, I was here permanent. If I let a man have a mule and anything the matter with it, they'd come back and I had to make it good.

And I'll say this to you. A man who was reasonable and fair-minded, if you sold him a mule and the mule wouldn't work, he'd come back and you could adjust with him. But a fellow that didn't know anything about a mule—not nothing—he'd come to the barn to buy a mule, and he'd come expecting to get cheated, and then somebody come along and tell him some trick about the mule and not a word of truth in it, he'd come back dissatisfied. Then he's hard to satisfy. That horse-trading game, it's a game that's in a market all by itself.

Did you get bad mules at a sale very often?

Well, not too often, no. I remember one time I bought a pair of mules private there in Atlanta. They was shipped in there out

of Tennessee. They was a pretty pair of mules. They'd have weighed
a thousand, a thousand and twenty-five apiece. And a man come
over and wanted to buy *one* of 'em. Well, it was a mare mule and
a horse mule. I wanted him to buy the mare mule 'cause I thought
it'd suit him the best. Well, he bought the horse mule 'cause it
was twenty-five dollars cheaper. And the mare mule was as pretty
as you ever saw and had a white star on her face which was a little
unusual for a mule. Well, I sold that mare mule in Oglethorpe
County, and the man hitched it to the plow stock and she got loose.
He wrote me a letter and told me the mule kicked, and I went
down there and let him have another mule. Brought the mule back
and I didn't believe it'd kick. So we got her out back of the barn
and hitched her to the plow stock and you never saw a mule kick
so in your life till she kicked loose. So I carried her back to Atlanta
and got my money back for her from the man I bought her from.

When a man is caught with a bad mule, what is done?

Well, all horse traders have got a trick in them and if they had
a kicker or something, they would go to the auction and sell him
and keep their mouth shut hoping that person that bought him
would trade him off and not say nothing about it. But if the man
come back, they would have to take him up [make it good].

Did you ever pass on any bad mules?

I've swapped off lots of them, but I'd always take them up. But
I'll tell you one time I didn't. I sold my brother a four-year-old
mule that would have weighed about a thousand pounds, and he
worked him about three years and that mule got something the
matter with his back. When he was going off from you, it looked
like he was sore in the rear end. Turn around and come back trotting
to you and it looked like he was sore in the front. And you could
drive him up here and throw a bundle of fodder down at his feet
and it would take him two or three minutes to get his head down
to the ground to eat that fodder. Then you could let him be grazing
in the pasture and you run up behind him and pat your britches
at him and run him off and he would go fifty yards before he would
get his head up on the level. And I had this mule on the truck in
Bowman, Georgia, one time. A fellow looked at him, saw it was a
young mule, saw it was a good-sized mule, and said, "What'll you
take for this old horse mule?"

I says, "Let me tell you about this mule."

He says, "Don't tell me nothing. I wouldn't believe nothing no horse trader ever said about a mule," and says, "I'm my own judge." They laughed at me. There was a big crowd, and they laughed big.

And I walked up and put my arm around his shoulder and said, "Neighbor, I've been hunting you for three years. I want somebody won't believe nothing I say." I said, "I'm going to sell you that mule for a hundred and fifty dollars."

He said, "I'm going to give a hundred and twenty-five, and that's it."

I said, "Well, just pay me. I'm going to sell him to you."

He said, "My money is in a post office in Royston." Says, "Take him out here to my brother-in-law's, George Colbert," and says, "I'll be back there in a few minutes." Says, "I'll pay you."

"All right." So I just waited there at Bowman till he got back, and I chased him out there and he says, "Now I want to hitch this mule."

So we backed up to the plowed ground. I had a drop gate on the truck. I could load him or unload on the level, but I put that mule off in the plowed ground. And I hitched that mule to the plow stock and he plowed perfect.

He said, "Let's hitch him to the one-horse wagon."

I said, "Now if he runs away, it's your wagon and my mule."

He says, "All right."

I said, "Pull the wagon out here in the plowed ground." He pulled the wagon out and I kept the mule in the soft dirt, hitched him to the wagon, drove him around the field, come back and backed the wagon under the shelter.

He said, "Take him out and put him in that stable." So we took him out, put him in the stable, never drove him out of a walk. We didn't let him get his head up nor down. I put him in the stable and he paid me.

Two or three days later he come back and says, "You put a trick mule off on me."

I says, "I know it."

He says, "You knew it was a trick."

I says, "Yes, sir," I said. "You told me in front of a dozen people you wouldn't believe nothing I said." I said, "Now I told you the mule was yours, and he's still yours." I'd of sold him the mule for fifty dollars and told him the truth about it.

I remember another time a fellow over in Oglethorpe come over here and picked out a mule and this mule was a little sore. But she was a good work mule. Put her on the plowed ground and she'd just work good as any mule, but on the hard ground, she was sore.

Well, I went over there. Put her on the truck, carried her over [to his farm] and hitched her up to the plow stock for him, and he liked the way she worked. He brought out an old mule there that was wind-broken. She was bellesed. But he'd been wetting the feed and thought he had her shut down, and [that] I was young and I wouldn't know it.

Well, sir, I give him that mule for his bellesed mule, a milk cow and a good bull calf, and fifty dollars. So two or three days, *he* come back. He was in a good humor. He says, "Sonny boy!" He said, "Did you know that mule you let me have was sore?"

I said, "Yes, sir."

He said, "You didn't tell me nothing about it."

I said, "Well, you didn't tell me about the old mule I got from you being wind-broken."

He laughed, said, "Well, I guess we're about even, then."

I said, "Well, I'm satisfied." And so I traded him another mule for it just as pleasant as could be.

When was the biggest trading time?

Well, court week used to be a big day here. I remember one court week here that I netted eleven hundred dollars buying and selling mules. And when I wound up, I lost every nickel of it. I went broke selling mules on the credit in 1950. The bottom fell out of 'em. You'd sell a mule in the spring of the year for two or two and a quarter, and that fall he wouldn't bring but forty or fifty. They'd turn the mule back on me [without paying for it]. Some of them, I just let 'em keep 'em. I just lost what I'd made.

Was mule trading a good way to make a living?

It was *good* years ago, but it's not worth anything now. You can't make a living at it in this country now. You couldn't pay a feed bill for the stock, much less feed yourself. That's all I've done. I'd trade livestock, I'd buy and sell mules and horses, and buy cattle. And bought a few hogs in the deal. I enjoyed it. Made a good living at it. I enjoyed it. Lots of people got rich at it. I never did get rich. I was right well-to-do one time. Lost it all and I went broke. [I was sorry to see mule trading go out.] That's all I knew how to do. Started trading when I was twenty-four years old and stayed in it about twenty-five years.

Are mules smart?

Well, yes, sir. A horse, I reckon, might be a little smarter than a mule. But now up yonder in Tennessee the other day, a fellow

PLATE 512 Johnny, "Po' Boy," and Clay walking across the
courthouse square in Danielsville, toward "Po' Boy's" home in
background.

had a little pair of red sorrel mules [that would] weigh about nine
hundred pounds. He didn't put 'em on the auction block. He was
trying to sell 'em for $1,400. He could talk to them mules there
hooked to the wagon: make 'em turn to the right. Talk to 'em,
they'd back up. Talk to 'em, they'd start off. Just make 'em do whatever he wanted 'em to do, and he'd never touch the line.

And some know "gee" and "haw." "Gee's" to the right; "haw's"
to the left. But there you come again. Some men can work a mule
forty years and never teach him "gee" and "haw." Another'll teach
him "gee" and "haw" in a half a day.

Some of 'em are [stubborn] and some of 'em aren't. A mule is
not any more stubborn than that man you hear talking about him.
He's just as stubborn as the mule. Some people think it's smart
[clever] to run a mule down. Back when I was in the mule business,
a lot of people thought it was smart to say something ugly about
a mule. But when you make your living off them, you *love* that mule,
and you don't appreciate people coming up and talking about him
like that.

And they're just like these old men. Some of these mules are mean and some of them are obedient. These old men are the same way. I believe the mule's better-natured, though, than the men. I believe men are meaner than mules.

And when people say mules are unpredictable, that's just people who don't know anything about a mule that go to talking like that. They're not any more unpredictable than a horse. I'd rather risk a mule as to being a safe work animal than a horse.

INDEX OF PEOPLE

Students at Rabun County High School who produced this book are also engaged in numerous other similar educational activities concerning their culture and the Appalachian Mountains as part of the Foxfire program. For a free brochure about the Foxfire program, please write:

The Foxfire Fund, Inc.
P.O. Box B
Rabun Gap, GA 30568